THE POLITICS OF ITALIAN NATIONAL IDENTITY

THE POLITICS
of
ITALIAN NATIONAL IDENTITY
A Multidisciplinary Perspective

Edited by

GINO BEDANI

and

BRUCE HADDOCK

UNIVERSITY OF WALES PRESS
CARDIFF
2000

© The Contributors, 2000

British Library Cataloguing-in-Publication Data.
A catalogue record for this book is available from the British Library.

ISBN 0-7083-1622-0

Typeset by Action Publishing Technology, Gloucester
Printed in Great Britain by Dinefwr Press, Llandybïe

Contents

Notes on contributors   vii

Introduction   1
Bruce Haddock and Gino Bedani

1   *State, nation and Risorgimento*   11
Bruce Haddock

2   *A patriotic disaster: the Messina–Reggio Calabria
earthquake of 1908*   50
John Dickie

3   *The things that make Sicily Sicily: considerations on
Sicilian identity*   72
Joseph Farrell

4   *Language and Italian national identity*   98
Howard Moss

5   Il bel paese: *art, beauty and the cult of appearance*   124
Stephen Gundle

6   *The mass media and the question of a national
community in Italy*   142
David Forgacs

7   *Italian national identity and Fascism: aliens, allogenes and
assimilation on Italy's north-eastern border*   163
Glenda Sluga

8   *Making better Italians: issues of national identity in the
Italian Social Republic and the Resistance*   191
Jonathan Dunnage

9   *The Christian Democrats and national identity*   214
Gino Bedani

Contents

10 *The Italian Communists and Italian national identity: the question of difference* 239
    Patrick McCarthy

11 *Challenging the nation-state: the Northern League between localism and globalism* 259
    Anna Cento Bull

12 *Concluding reflections: Italy, Europe and multiform identities* 277
    Bruce Haddock and Gino Bedani

    Index 286

Notes on Contributors

Gino Bedani is Professor of Italian at the University of Wales Swansea.

Anna Cento Bull is Professor of Italian at the University of Bath.

John Dickie is Senior Lecturer in Italian at University College London.

Jonathan Dunnage is Lecturer in Italian at the University of Wales Swansea.

Joseph Farrrell is Senior Lecturer in Italian at the University of Strathclyde.

David Forgacs is Professor of Italian at University College London.

Stephen Gundle is Senior Lecturer in Italian at Royal Holloway College, London.

Bruce Haddock is Reader in Politics at the University of Wales Swansea.

Patrick McCarthy is Professor of Politics at the Johns Hopkins University in Bologna.

Howard Moss is Lecturer in Italian at the University of Wales Swansea.

Glenda Sluga is Senior Lecturer in History and Deputy Director of the Research Institute for Humanities and Social Sciences at the University of Sydney.

Introduction

BRUCE HADDOCK AND GINO BEDANI

Our concern in this volume is both to fill a gap in the academic literature and to contribute to the reappraisal of Italian political and cultural identity which has followed in the wake of the upheaval in Italian politics after 1992. Scholarly discussions of nationalism and the idea of the nation have tended to fragment – historians intent upon debunking various myths that have served as validating principles for the Italian state, political theorists and scientists focusing largely on institutional devices for facilitating constructive opposition, literary critics restricting their attention to texts (even if they are intent upon rejecting the idea of an autonomous text).[1] We propose to bring these various academic disciplines together by focusing on the Italian tradition as a 'national text', open to multiple (and deeply contrasting) interpretations, but constituting a discursive framework which links groups and subcultures that may well have incompatible goals and values.

We take seriously the theoretical claim that national identity is a discursive construction rather than a 'natural' fact, though discourses themselves are far from arbitrary in their impact. By focusing on moments in the development of modern Italy when conceptions of the nation were most sharply divided or problematical, we aim to highlight the contested cultural boundaries which legitimize different conceptions of the Italian nation and state.

We begin (paradoxically) with the French Revolution. Here was an event of European significance which imposed conceptions of popular sovereignty and national identity on all states. For while the rhetoric of the 'rights of man' may well have been universal, the realization of these rights in political form presupposed (something like) national states. States were generally treated as if they were far more than units of convenience, but it was unclear at the time (and remains unclear to this day) precisely how their parameters should be fixed.[2] What might seem like a purely theoretical question

1

became urgent after 1796, as French armies made dramatic incursions into Italy, opening up possibilities which had previously been foreclosed. It was not simply a question of borrowing from France or accepting French tutelage; rather that French rhetoric and propaganda had far-reaching implications for Italy as a political form. From a national perspective, French (or any other) administration and control could not be a lasting arrangement. But the status quo ante had become equally problematic, in terms of both administrative efficiency and principles of legitimacy. The peninsula was thus propelled towards intense debate after 1815 on the political implications of Italian national identity, extending beyond constitutional and legal questions to more fundamental assumptions about the character of Italian language, literature and culture.

Thus, as Haddock's opening contribution shows, the Risorgimento, which has always been regarded as a defining 'event' politically, must be seen in broader cultural context. The debate between 'romantics' and 'classicists' in the pages of *Il Conciliatore* and the *Antologia*, ostensibly about literary judgement, was also an attempt to shape a national tradition. And while it would be wrong to see, say, Manzoni's *I promessi sposi* or De Sanctis's *Storia della letteratura italiana* as narrowly political texts, by the same token it would be misleading to neglect the wider cultural assumptions which informed the more directly programmatic writings of the 'high' Risorgimento. The contrasting attempts of Mazzini and Gioberti, for example, to mobilize 'national' constituencies are unintelligible outside a context of assumptions about an actual or emerging culture. Even technical legal and constitutional discussions of the prospective form for an Italian state invoke deeper assumptions about the appropriate institutional framework for cultures and economies responding in different ways to the demands of modernization. As more recent work (by Putnam and others) has shown, judgements about technical efficiency cannot properly be made in disregard of a complex cultural inheritance.[3] The original case for a federal Italy (made by Cattaneo and others) was based upon a very specific reading of Italian history, highlighting the polycentric character of Italian society.[4] This was a literature which triumphant unitarists were keen to forget in 1861, though it has returned to haunt successive establishments at times of political crisis.[5] The point to stress here, of course, is that political crises cannot be conceived in narrow terms. Our concern in this volume is precisely to examine discussions of cultural foundations which surface in troubled times. Haddock's contribution deals with the complexity of these cultural issues leading into the founding moment of the Italian nation-state.

Interpretation of the Risorgimento has thus once again become a major theme in political debate in Italy. The debates and arguments between unitarists and federalists in the build-up to unification failed to yield a theoretical consensus, though the demands of political organization meant that a settlement had to be imposed. It still remains an open question whether a highly centralized system of administration was an appropriate option for Italy. It can even be argued that the entrenched divide between north and south was exacerbated by the process of unification.[6] At the very least, it is clear that the politics of élite accommodation served to obscure and render ambiguous the objectives which had been at the heart of the Risorgimento as a 'national' movement.

Far from settling sensitive political and constitutional issues, experience of the unitary state actually generated intractable dilemmas of its own. The form of the state might have been regarded as sacrosanct, but its efficacy and legitimacy were challenged on other grounds. In D'Azeglio's memorable phrase, 'l'Italia è fatta, restano a fare gli italiani.' But precisely how Italians might be 'made' was obscure to contemporaries. What is certain is that early efforts by liberal governments to build a national culture had unfortunate results. One of the first fruits of unification was virtual civil war in the south (1861–5), where traditional problems of brigandage were magnified by the machinations of the Church, Bourbon loyalists and a disbanded Bourbon army. The reality of central administration and control was clearly a disappointment to citizens who expected political unification to usher in a period of economic and cultural renewal. A distinction was soon drawn between 'legal' Italy (modern, responsive and humane, matching the best achievements elsewhere in Europe) and 'real' Italy (locked in an intricate complex of clientele relationships which perpetuated the personal dependence of the poor upon the rich). We can in fact trace back to this period the beginnings of the systematic collusion between the state and the Mafia (in its various guises) which has been a persistent feature of modern Italian political life. Both the Church and the Mafia flourished outside the formal legal framework of public institutions; but (in their different ways) they had roots in Italian society which the liberal state could not match.

Italian political identity has thus always been problematic. Dickie and Farrell focus on aspects of the vexed relation of national identity to the south. Both authors draw on a variety of perspectives and disciplines in order to gauge the extent of cultural integration at the periphery. Dickie's examination of the official and public response to the Messina earthquake of 1908, one of the worst natural disasters in Italian history, highlights the role of the royal family (especially through Queen Elena's widely reported involvement in providing immediate help for victims) in transforming a regional calamity into a *national* tragedy. His use of personal testimonies, official reports and newspaper accounts illustrates how a concept of 'nationhood' was both constructed and extended. Farrell focuses on literary sources, especially the historical novel, in order to chart shifting attempts to relate a distinctive Sicilian identity to a wider national identity. In culture, Sicily has remained distinct, with a tradition of writing which is self-consciously autonomous. This has, if anything, been reinforced in recent years, with writers such as D'Arrigo, Consolo and Silvana Grassi making use of Sicilian dialect in their fiction. The growth of the Northern League since the late 1980s has forced Sicilians to re-examine their place in the Italian state. Farrell explores the roots of a complex 'identity in difference'.

In many ways the new Kingdom of Italy was forced to confront the problems of unity which had been implicit in the Italian literary and linguistic traditions. Touched only partially by the romanticist revolution, Italian culture in the new era struggled to create linguistic and literary forms adequate to the times. Italian literature had to become very specifically a literature for modern Italians before it could contribute in its own way to the nation's new role in the world, a task defined in De Sanctis' monumental *Storia*.[7]

On the surface the task of unification appeared to be easier, or at least more clearly delineated, on the linguistic level with the adoption of the literary language, based on fourteenth-century Florentine, as the language of the whole peninsula. But alongside the debates of academics on the unity of the language, and the measures adopted by educationalists to produce school texts checked by Tuscans, and by publishers to commission dictionaries of the Italian language, the daily reality of the highly regionalized mentalities profoundly embedded in their dialects continued to reflect a diversity that was implicitly denied at the level of the unitary state. As Moss illustrates, the 'language question' is in many ways inseparable from the 'national question' in Italian history. At the time of unification, the literary language was accessible to only a small section of the population. The implications of this state of affairs go to the root of national identity. The split still exists in Italian society between the reasonably unified 'national' language and the dialects that vary from region to region.

In his contribution to this volume, Gundle shows that from the very beginning of unification Italians have shared a conception of their homeland as the home of beautiful landscapes, things, places and people. Used from the very beginning by patriots as a method of singling out one of the nation's unique artistic and cultural missions, this particular sensibility has undergone a series of transformations, being employed politically, socially and economically in the process. This development has lasted till the present day.

National communities can be both circumscribed and decentred by what Forgacs calls flows of communication. His discussion of the role of the mass media in constructing identities questions deeprooted assumptions about the way in which the strong sense of local belonging in Italy is presumed to have inhibited the creation of a sense of nationhood. He also challenges traditional views about the debilitating effects of illiteracy, and offers a reinterpretation of Gramsci's ideas concerning the lack of a 'national-popular' culture in Italy. The issue of the media's role in creating national cohesion or erosion of boundaries is shown to be highly complex and articulated, and increasingly problematic in an age of globalization.

There have, however, been explicit attempts in Italian history to project unitary trajectories. One such venture followed the triumph of Fascism in 1921, and its exposure of the shortcomings of the Italian liberal state. What was presented in Fascist rhetoric as a revolutionary beginning was actually an abdication of responsibility by a political and cultural élite which felt itself to be powerless in the face of the traumas of modernization. The liberal élite, having failed to create anything resembling a deeply rooted national culture, was overwhelmed by demands forced to the top of the political agenda by mass movements which refused to accept the limited terms of public debate in liberal Italy. Socialism, political Catholicism and nationalism were each conceived as threats to the liberal state. The usual tactic of half-hearted accommodation proved inadequate as crises precipitated by war and economic dislocation deepened. But it was by no means clear in 1921 what endorsement of Fascism might have amounted to. In rhetorical terms, we see a brash attempt to reinterpret Italian history and culture in support of new conceptions of both nation and state. The language of 'construction' was self-consciously adopted, though the constraints which had shackled the liberal regime were still very much in place. The obsessive nature of the search for a 'national' culture illustrates nothing so much as the ambiguous, deeply variegated, and sometimes incompatible assumptions which had contributed to the diversity of Italian culture throughout the modern period. In effect, Italians were asked to suspend all forms of scepticism and endorse the new Fascist reading of their culture. In the event, the costs to their various ways of life proved to be too high to endure. Sluga shows how attempts to create cultural homogeneity in some of Italy's borderlands illustrate aptly both the priorities of the regime and its limited impact on the embedded cultures of the peninsula. She demostrates how the existence of multi-language communities in the Trieste area sharpened the imperative that Fascist authorities felt to define Italian identity in opposition to specified 'others'. In the event, following the crisis of the regime in 1943, Trieste remained a 'hybrid' city, despite the sustained programme of social engineering it had been subjected to.

Dunnage takes up the question of national identity in the period which followed immediately upon the collapse of Fascism and the war of national liberation. Italy was literally divided by war, as Mussolini and Hitler sought to establish the new Republic of Salò in the north while the allies continued their advance from the south. Dunnage examines competing concepts of the nation on both sides of the civil war, as the partisans attempted to defeat and delegitimize a last-ditch effort to revive the Fascist regime. This highly contentious material has assumed new significance in the wake of the rise of Alleanza Nazionale, which has created its own ideological niche by challenging the national representative basis of the resistance movement.

The establishment of the Republic in 1948 marked the beginning of a much more subtle commitment to national consolidation. McCarthy and Bedani examine the two largest political forces in the post-war history of the nation. They both show how the post-war Republic sought initially to forge a sense of nationhood around the notion of anti-Fascism. Yet Italian Communism and Christian Democracy remained deeply ambiguous in relation to the Italian state. McCarthy highlights the distinctive contribution of the Partito Comunista Italiano (PCI) in the delicate discussions leading to the drafting of the constitution. Indeed the PCI identified itself with positive traits in Italian identity, standing for high standards of efficiency and public honesty in the face of widespread corruption, while accepting the need to collaborate with Catholics in times of national crisis. McCarthy notes, nevertheless, that the PCI's projection of its 'Italianness' could never be unconditional, nor could it ever quite shed the negative image which party political machines acquired as the republic developed.

The Democrazia Christiana (DC) will always symbolize the janus-faced nature of the republic most effectively. As Bedani argues, despite its negative reputation for corruption and clientelism, the DC has had a positive role in developing a sense of nationhood. It provided long periods of stability, allowing democracy to develop in the country, and it was the first party to have a truly representative function in all parts of the peninsula. The DC, most distinctively, appealing to anti-statist notions of national solidarity, managed to create a bridge between the state and civil society which was to prove much more effective as a means of popular involvement and control than the cumbersome apparatus of public institutions created by the Fascists. The studied avoidance of 'high' political language, however, should not obscure the cultural foundation of what has been a surprisingly stable polity. Political scientists have tended to focus on the role of patronage and clientele relationships, rather than the more elusive conceptions of legitimacy which underpinned the state. DC practice in government may indeed have encouraged such a narrow concern. But it was not merely patronage which enabled the state to survive the *anni di piombo*. In the final analysis, as mass-based popular parties, both the PCI and the DC provided large sectors of the population with their first experiences of collective belonging beyond their deeply rooted regional identities.

What finally brought the republic to the verge of implosion was systematic breach of the tacit rules of self-restraint which the political élite had exercised down to the 1980s. A 'lax' political culture could turn a blind eye to informal arrangements which fostered social solidarity. At some obscure point (1985?), however, irregularity became both too costly and too shocking, triggering a reappraisal of principles of solidarity. The Lega Nord challenged the murky understandings which had linked the Roman élite, northern business, and the Mezzogiorno. Cento Bull examines claims made by the movement for the independence of the northern area it calls 'Padania'. Although the area has never formed a single polity or shared a common language apart from Italian, it has nevertheless succeeded in gaining considerable support in many parts of the north, and has increasingly imposed itself on central government as a serious threat. Cento Bull focuses on one of the least-studied of the ambitions of the Lega, reducing what it sees as the intrusive and counter-productive role of central government in economic life. This development is set in the wider context of globalization and the possibilities which have opened up for 'peripheral' regions to play major roles beyond the conventional parameters of nation-states.

Developments in Europe and the wider world have clearly had a huge impact on Italian politics and culture (see the concluding article, Bedani and Haddock). The end of the Cold War forced a fundamental overhaul of the theory and practice of opposition; and pressure for European integration obliged the state to count the cost of redistribution and to justify economic policy in a much more transparent fashion. Issues that had scarcely been discussed since 1948 suddenly became explosive, including the form of the state itself. All European states have had to come to terms with forces which have reinforced both supranational institutions and the regional and local dimensions of politics, leaving the old élites in capital cities with a plethora of issues to manage, while deploying significantly reduced options. This represents both a challenge and an opportunity for Italy. It remains to be seen whether the cultural flexibility of Italy's regions will contrive an effective institutional response.

What we seek to do in these chapters is to set contemporary political soul-searching in the widest context, focusing on self-understandings within Italian culture which are neglected in the ordinary business of daily life. Our hope is that our collaborative (and multidisciplinary) efforts will set in clearer relief the larger picture which is barely visible from the perspective of more specialized concerns.

Notes
1   The relevant literature is immense and growing exponentially. See, for example, John Hutchinson and Anthony D. Smith, eds., *Nationalism* (Oxford, Oxford University Press, 1994); John Hutchinson, *Modern*

Nationalism (London, Fontana, 1994); Walker Connor, *Ethno-nationalism: The Quest for Understanding* (Princeton, Princeton University Press, 1994); Ernest Gellner, *Nations and Nationalism* (Oxford, Blackwell, 1983); Peter Alter, *Nationalism* (London, Edward Arnold, 1989); Benedict Anderson, *Imagined Communities: Reflections on the Origin and Spread of Nationalism* (London, Verso, 1991); Liah Greenfeld, *Nationalism: Five Roads to Modernity* (Cambridge, MA, Harvard University Press, 1992); Sukumar Periwal, ed., *Notions of Nationalism* (Budapest, Central European University Press, 1995); Stuart Woolf, ed., *Nationalism in Europe, 1815 to the Present* (London, Routledge, 1996); David Miller, *On Nationality* (Oxford, Oxford University Press, 1995); Margaret Canovan, *Nationhood and Political Theory* (Cheltenham, Edward Elgar, 1996); E. J. Hobsbawm, *Nations and Nationality since 1780: Programme, Myth, Reality* (Cambridge, Cambridge University Press, 1990); Anthony D. Smith, *Nations and Nationalism in a Global Era* (Cambridge, Polity Press, 1995); Geoffrey Cubitt, ed., *Imagining Nations* (Manchester, Manchester University Press, 1998); Giuseppe Galasso, *Italia. Una nazione difficile* (Florence, Le Monnier, 1994); R. Cartocci, *Fra Lega e Chiesa: l'Italia in cerca di integrazione* (Bologna, Il Mulino, 1994); G. E. Rusconi, *Se cessiamo di essere una nazione. Tra etnodemocrazie regionali e cittadinanza europea* (Bologna, Il Mulino, 1993); M. L. Salvadori, *Storia d'Italia e crisi di regime. Alle radici della politica italiana* (Bologna, Il Mulino, 1994); John Dickie, 'Imagined Italies', in David Forgacs and Robert Lumley, eds., *Italian Cultural Studies: An Introduction* (Oxford, Oxford University Press, 1996); R. D. Putnam et al., *Making Democracy Work: Civic Traditions in Modern Italy* (Princeton, Princeton University Press, 1993); E. Galli della Loggia, *L'identità italiana* (Bologna, Il Mulino, 1998); and Stefan Berger, Mark Donovan and Kevin Passmore, eds., *Writing National Histories: Western Europe since 1800* (London, Routledge, 1999).

2   See David Held, *Political Theory and the Modern State* (Cambridge, Polity Press, 1989); David Held et al., eds., *States and Societies* (Oxford, Martin Robertson, 1983); Andrew Vincent, *Theories of the State* (Oxford, Blackwell, 1987); and John Hoffman, *Beyond the State* (Cambridge, Polity Press, 1995).

3   See Putnam et al., *Making Democracy Work*.

4   See Carlo Cattaneo, *Stati uniti d'Italia. Il federalismo, le leghe*, edited by Daniele Vimercati (Milan, SugarCo, 1991).

5   See Walter Maturi, *Interpretazioni del Risorgimento* (Turin, Einaudi, 1962).

6   See S. Jacini, *Sulle condizioni della cosa pubblica in Italia dopo il '66. Lettere agli elettori di Ferni* (Florence, Giuseppe Civelli, 1870); L. Franchetti, *Condizioni economiche ed amministrative delle provincie napoletane*, ed. Antonio Jannazzo (Bari, Laterza, 1985); S. Sonnino, *I contadini in Sicilia* (Florence, Vallecchi, 1925); and L. Franchetti and S. Sonnino, *Sicilia nel 1876* (Florence, Barbera, 1877).

7   See Francesco De Sanctis, 'Storia della letteratura italiana', in his
    Opere, edited by Niccolò Gallo (Milan and Naples, Riccardo Ricciardi,
    1961).

1

State, nation and Risorgimento

BRUCE HADDOCK

Interpretations of the Risorgimento have always been sensitive to the
shifting fortunes of Italy's political culture. It should not surprise us,
then, that the political crisis which shook Italy's ruling establishment
in the early 1990s should be associated with an agonizing reappraisal
of the significance of the Risorgimento for the Italian state. This has
led some commentators to declare that the Risorgimento had been a
'mistake'.[1] Historians have been more circumspect, focusing instead
on currents within the Risorgimento that had been neglected in
various celebrations of the different guises that the national tradition
had assumed. Federalist writers, in particular, have recently gained
a prominence which can hardly have been matched since the heady
days of 1848, when federalist arguments were still dominating
discussions of the prospective form of an Italian state. Cattaneo has
been the focus of most attention. He has been described as the 'most
coherent and lucid figure' in the history of 'Italian federalism',
whose federal theory offered 'a solution to the problem of the
Risorgimento'.[2] Indeed Cattaneo's terms of reference have dominated attempts to fashion a federal solution to Italy's intractable
institutional difficulties.[3] What is more surprising is that the roots of
federalist thinking should not have been traced further back into the
early history of the Risorgimento. Serious attempts to respond to the
foundational issues raised by the federalists have still tended to
endorse the unitary position, focusing on the conventional distinction
between radicals and moderates rather than the starker contrast
between unitarists and federalists.[4] Yet it was not clear before 1830
precisely what a 'moderate' position might amount to. What later
became a dominant current had barely been articulated before the
seminal contributions of Gioberti, Balbo and D'Azeglio in the
1840s.[5] To use the mature form of the moderate position as an inter-
pretative key to the earlier debate is seriously to distort the original
form of the argument. It also creates the quite false impression that

11

the federalist thinking of the 1840s came somehow unannounced, without roots or antecedents in the Italian tradition.

My concern in this chapter is to trace the tangled arguments which led to the emergence of (something like) a set of coherent (though contrasting) conceptions of the state and nation in the *Risorgimento*. The context, of course, is complicated by the entrenched political and cultural divisions inherited from the *ancien régime*, coupled with the ambiguous legacy of French administration and control in the revolutionary and Napoleonic years. What is certain is that the settlement of 1815 was far from a restoration of the *ancien régime* in practice, despite the ambition of certain monarchs to treat the revolutionary period as an irritating interregnum.

The European context

At the level of political ideas, Italian intellectuals found themselves confronted by two failed models. The *anciens régimes* (the plural is essential in the Italian context) had proved ineffective both as vehicles for administration and as foci of political allegiance.[6] The various French-dominated alternatives, though they had enabled administrative and legal structures to be modernized, had involved the systematic subordination of Italian to French interests. Whatever view intellectuals might have of revolutionary principles (the 'rights of man') they could hardly ignore the neglect of popular sovereignty. The rhetoric of mobilization (a 'nation at arms') clearly lost something of its effectiveness when foreign interests were principally at issue. The situation in 1815 was thus fraught with difficulties. Italy was left weak and divided, with a dawning awareness of a contested (but shared) cultural identity which had yet to assume a settled political shape. And given the role of Austria in the politics of the peninsula, open expression of political ideas was difficult and sometimes dangerous.

Yet politically articulate Italians could at least look back to the Napoleonic period to see the rudiments of a modern state established in their country. The French invasion of 1796 had redrawn the map of Italy, leading to the adoption of new principles of political organization and administration.[7] Very many intellectuals, far from resenting the imposition of foreign forms of rule, welcomed the opportunity to sweep away the remnants of the *ancien régime*.

Whether or not republican principles were endorsed, there was a widespread feeling that the new scheme of things offered possibilities for modernization which would have been foreclosed under previous regimes. Political participation on a wider scale, the expectation of a career open to talents, and the dismantling of aristocratic and ecclesiastical privilege were prospects which fired the enthusiasm of the small class of intellectuals.

The legacy of the revolutionary years was, however, deeply ambiguous. While Italian reformist intellectuals might treat French expansion as a means of breaking decisively with the *ancien régime*, it soon became clear that France was intent upon exploiting Italian territories for diplomatic and economic advantage. A policy which had begun under the Directory was merely extended as Napoleon's imperial plans became more ambitious.[8] To be sure, specific Italian territories might be able to establish a degree of autonomy in confined spheres. Francesco Melzi, for example, vice-president of the so-called Italian Republic which succeeded the Cisalpine Republic in 1802, managed to proceed with a programme of administrative and legal reforms, very much in the tradition of the Lombard Enlightenment, though he constantly met opposition from Napoleon in his abortive attempts to establish the foundations of a genuinely autonomous northern Italian state.[9] And in Naples, Joachim Murat, who succeeded Joseph Bonaparte to the throne of the Kingdom of Naples in 1808, was sufficiently ambitious to ensure that he became a focus for specifically Neapolitan interests.[10] But all Italian territories, no matter how constituted, operated in a national and international context dominated by France.

Intellectuals were thus faced with an acute dilemma. The automatic identification of French policy with the ideals of 1789 clearly could not be sustained. Nor, indeed, could it be claimed that French power had helped to promote Italian economic interests. The extent of French manipulation of the Italian economies was obvious, especially to the emerging business classes in the north. In terms of the day-to-day balance sheet, it was easy to present an account of French policy as exploitative in the narrow economic sense and detrimental to the wider indigenous development of Italian economic life. All this was grist to the ideological mill of the various groups which had supported the *ancien régime*, ranging from the old aristocracy to lowly clerics. The Italian 'patriots' who had welcomed the French with open arms could be portrayed as betrayers of the Italian people, of Italian culture and of the emerging Italian nation.[11]

These were sensitive charges which forced upon intellectuals a reappraisal not simply of their political attitudes, but also of their larger assumptions about Italian history and culture. They could clearly not endorse attempts to restore the edifice of the *ancien régime*. Despite the setbacks and disappointments of the years of French dominance, genuine progress had been made in certain spheres. Legal changes, in particular in relation to private property, had unleashed social and economic forces which would prove impossible to shackle. There could be no wholesale reimposition of complex feudal arrangements. Even the most fiercely reactionary of the restored regimes after 1815, such as Piedmont and Naples, had to accept that very many of the legal and administrative innovations introduced by the French were essential to the functioning of states in the circumstances of post-revolutionary Europe. Intellectuals had thus to tread a tortuous path, disentangling the lasting achievements of French rule from the detail of French policy. What had changed decisively was the unquestioned assumption that the way to progress and prosperity lay in imitation of France and all things French.

Ambivalence towards France is illustrated perfectly in the career of Vincenzo Cuoco (1770–1823). Cuoco was a product of the juridical culture which had been so strong in southern Italy throughout the eighteenth century. He had always shown an interest in the reform movement but had consistently raised his voice in favour of moderation. He rejected, in particular, the utopianism of Jacobin assumptions about politics; and in the heady constitutional debates leading up to the declaration of a republic at Naples in 1799, he argued consistently that a constitution based on the principle that each representative should speak for the nation as a whole would lead to neglect of the particular and practical problems which any set of political arrangements had necessarily to face. Cuoco favoured, instead, a system of representation based on municipalities that reflected in a concrete fashion the particular needs of the various communities.

The plans of reformers, however, could make little headway in southern Italy against entrenched feudal and clerical interests. The reform movement became more radical as its proposals for practical improvement were disregarded. Towards the end of the century, Jacobinism became the predominant political influence among the intellectuals. As the French revolutionary armies advanced down the Italian peninsula after 1796, so the situation in various Italian states seemed ripe for revolution. In the practical tumult of 1799, Cuoco put his theoretical qualms on one side and joined forces with the revolutionaries.

The revolution turned out to be a dismal failure. A Parthenopean Republic was briefly declared in the name of the people. But the people themselves were either uninterested or hostile and were easily manipulated by established interests. Following the withdrawal of French troops, the republic was easily crushed by the Sanfedisti led by Cardinal Ruffo. Cuoco was lucky to escape with his life in the ensuing repression. Exiled in Milan, he sought to set the personal and national disaster of 1799 in wider perspective.

The first fruit of Cuoco's exile was a sustained historical critique of the rationalism that had informed the ideas of the 'patriots' of 1799. His *Saggio storico sulla rivoluzione napoletana del 1799* (1801) attributed the failure of the revolution to a forced attempt to solve the specific problems of southern Italy by imposing ideas and patterns of conduct that had developed in France in 1789.[12] What might be appropriate for the unique conditions that prevailed in France, Cuoco argued, would not necessarily be suitable in the circumstances of another country. France had a long tradition of rationalism in philosophy and centralization in administration. A predilection for resorting to abstract ideas could, however, have the most disastrous consequences. There would be a natural tendency, on any given occasion, to ignore those features of a situation which could not be specified in a general theory. In the last resort (as the French Revolution had shown) authority exercised in the name of abstract theory was capricious and brutal. Cuoco regarded such rationalism as entirely foreign to Italian traditions. He saw Jacobinism as a specifically French ideology that had been grafted on to an Italian situation which could not properly assimilate ideas of that sort. The theoretical inspiration for his own work had come from Machiavelli and Vico. And he held that solutions to Italian problems might more readily be found if native patterns of thought were exploited.

Cuoco's *Saggio storico* shares many features in common with works written in reaction to the French Revolution and its excesses. He had himself absorbed the ideas of Burke and de Maistre and thoroughly endorsed their arguments against rationalism. What distinguishes his thought, however, is a continuing commitment to economic modernization and legal reform. He was not an apologist for the *ancien régime*. Indeed his analysis of the shortcomings of feudalism remains one of the most incisive contemporary accounts that have come down to us.[13]

The specific thrust of Cuoco's *Saggio storico* was largely negative. Yet he was clear that a positive strategy for Italy could be gleaned from the experience of abortive revolution. Between 1803 and 1806 Cuoco immersed himself in political journalism, coming into direct (almost daily) contact with his politically active contemporaries. He was the founder and first editor of the influential *Giornale Italiano* (1804–6). The political purpose of the journal was clear. Cuoco announced in the first edition that it was not simply 'a matter of conserving the public spirit but of creating it'.[14] The point was to lift the minds of the Italians, to mould the inhabitants of provinces into citizens of a state. To this end, he directed the journal to the principal achievements of Italians in the history of philosophy, literature and politics. There would be articles on different aspects of modern European thought and their significance for Italian culture, together with studies and reviews of current developments in the worlds of politics, economics, the arts and education – all designed to foster awareness of the central problems facing Italy.

In many of Cuoco's specific articles the themes which had emerged in the *Saggio storico* would be generalized and used as a key to interpret recent events in Italian political history. His range of topics extends from detailed studies of individual writers (notably Machiavelli, Vico and Pestalozzi), through a general characterization of the Italian political tradition, to analyses of principal developments in Europe (the impact of the French Revolution and Napoleon).[15] The tone is more didactic than the *Saggio storico* but the message remains the same. If Italy were ever to revivify her political culture, it would be in terms of the resources of her own tradition.

Nor was Cuoco's exploration of a distinctively Italian tradition restricted to journalism. In the same fertile period in which he was immersed in the *Giornale Italiano*, he produced a philosophical romance, *Platone in Italia* (1804–6), which sought, through a series of mythical dialogues, to unearth a specifically Italian contribution to the western philosophical tradition at its inception.[16]

Cuoco's fortune changed abruptly in 1806 with the reassertion of French hegemony in Naples. From 1806 until the Bourbon restoration

16

of 1815, Cuoco assumed a range of important administrative functions. Nominated as adviser to the Court of Appeal in 1806, he was in 1807 made president of a commission charged with the reorganization of the legal system in the Kingdom of Naples. In 1809 he was asked by Murat to draw up a plan for the modernization of the educational system. This project was to be his most important work of these years, not only as an illustration of his lifelong concern to strike a balance between continuity and change but as a statement which, through De Sanctis and Gentile, was to have a lasting influence on the theory and practice of education in Italy.[17] Further important administrative responsibilities were to follow, culminating in his appointment as director general of the Treasury in 1812.

Despite reservations about the wisdom of imitating French thought and practice, Cuoco was thus prepared to exploit the possibilities offered in Napoleonic Italy for reform and development. It was only French dominance that had enabled him to become a public figure in Milan and Naples. Yet he was aware that France had exploited Italian territories and distorted the 'natural' evolution of Italian public life.

What could not be doubted, however, was that political debate in Italy had been stimulated by experience of French rule. While deploring Italy's subordinate status, moderate reformers such as Cuoco could nevertheless welcome attempts to consolidate some of the achievements of the revolutionary years. The social conservatism of the Napoleonic regime thus accorded well with basic tenets of their own political thinking, looking to modernization rather than popular involvement in government. Yet foreign influence and administration, no matter how efficient, could not be regarded as an end in itself. Italy's weak and fragmented condition might well require a period of external rule; but this was no more than an interlude which would enable indigenous political forces to regroup, orientating themselves around national rather than provincial concerns. In due course a distinctively national political tradition would emerge in Italy which would demand an end to foreign control of whatever kind.

Prospects for change

Radical revolutionaries found the Napoleonic years even more difficult. Filippo Buonarroti (1761–1837), for example, whose

commitment to Robespierre's policy and practice remained un-
shaken, could not but find himself in difficulties once Robespierre
had fallen from power. He consistently argued against the betrayal
of the revolution in France and was imprisoned after the failure of
the Conspiracy of Equals in 1796.[18] Where moderate Italian liberals, in common with a broad spectrum of European opinion, sought
to take the lessons of revolutionary failure on board, Buonarroti
persisted in his commitment to a unitary state, rigidly centralized
and directed by a dedicated élite, as the only means towards an egalitarian republic. What is striking about Buonarroti is precisely how
little he had adapted his views. A conception of the state which had
been common to most revolutionaries before 1799 had by 1815 come
to require especial justification.

In *Riflessi sul governo federativo applicato all'Italia* (1831), for
example, Buonarroti sought to rebut the suggestion that the Italian
revolutionary movement should seek an alternative to the unitary
model of the Jacobins.[19] He argued that a federal republic in Italy
would only perpetuate the power of established regional élites, effectively blocking the wider transformation of society which he deemed
essential, while the natural clash of interests between federated or
confederated regions would weaken Italy in her dealings with
foreign powers, enabling neighbours to exploit splits within the
Italian polity for their own ends. A successful revolutionary movement, instead, should devote all its energies to the destruction of the
status quo. An egalitarian regime based upon 'simplicity of customs'
should be inaugurated.[20] But this could only be achieved if a level
of violence were employed against the rich which was 'incompatible' with conventional 'constitutional forms'.[21] A committed élite
had to assume the direction of the revolution; and this would not be
obtained through popular elections. In short, there was no alternative to a tightly organized central authority.

Nothing in the *Riflessi sul governo federativo* should be regarded as
original. The objections raised against federalism were conventional,
looking back to the Girondin reaction of 1793;[22] and unitary principles were advocated in terms which could have come from Saint-Just
or Robespierre. But it is significant that, at a crucial juncture, as revolutionaries throughout Europe faced the tantalizing possibilities which
had arisen in 1830, unitary principles should be defended in essentially negative style. The old confidence of the Jacobins had gone.
Both the methods and objectives of the revolutionary movement were

being bitterly contested, yielding incompatible conceptions of the state and political organization.

Throughout the turbulent Napoleonic years, attitudes to the state hinged very much upon attitudes to France. It was only to be expected that the early Italian 'Jacobins' would defend the political form favoured by their French mentors. Moderate reformers, too, could justify their preference for the unitary state in terms of earlier experiments in enlightened absolutist rule. Indeed in the early 1790s opposition to the unitary model came exclusively from vested interests whose positions had been shaken by revolutionary upheavals. The classic example in Italy is Galeani Napione's plan for an anti-revolutionary confederation of Italian principalities. The idea was taken up by Vittorio Amedeo III of Savoy in 1791 but came to nothing, encountering opposition from both the other Italian states and the wider anti-revolutionary powers.[23]

The more orthodox position in 'enlightened' circles was that defended by Melchiorre Gioia in his *Quale dei governi liberi meglio convenga all'Italia* (1798).[24] Gioia's ideal was the free and independent republic, based upon equality before the law and a solid phalanx of property owners. Above all, for Gioia, the state should be unitary in form. He saw the federal alternative as both weak in relation to foreign powers and vulnerable to internecine quarrels between constituent groups. Gioia broadly endorsed the French constitution of 1795. But this was before the full impact of French rule on Italian political life could properly be weighed in the balance.

The first response of Italian 'Jacobins' to the reactionary waves which undermined their positions in 1799 was not to abandon the unitary model altogether but to seek a genuine revolution in Italy. In an anonymous pamphlet of 1799, *Aperçus sur les causes qui ont dégradé l'esprit public en Italie et sur les moyens de le relever*, the failure of popular support to rally to the cause of the 'patriots' is specifically attributed to the exploitative policies adopted by the French. What had occurred in Italy was not an 'Italian revolution' but a 'French revolution in Italy'. National sentiment would respond to a national convention; but the sight of Italy weak and divided, left a prey to economic exploitation by a foreign power, would leave the people indifferent or hostile.[25]

These and similar complaints made little impression upon the leaders of the Directory, fearing as they did a fresh wave of radical enthusiasm. With Napoleon's accession to power on 18 Brumaire, all hopes of an extension of revolution in Italy could be set aside. Far-reaching legal and administrative changes could continue, with long-term implications of which men could be but dimly aware; but proposals for a free and autonomous unitary republic in the peninsula could no longer be seriously entertained.

A division which was to assume larger significance in the later history of the Risorgimento becomes evident in the Napoleonic period. On the one hand we have moderate reformers – Cuoco at Naples, Melzi and even the more committed Jacobin Gioia at Milan – backing Napoleonic administrations in order to advance social and economic modernization; on the other hand radicals sought instead to undermine the status quo in Italy through the organization of secret political societies. The objectives of the different sects varied widely, and in the Napoleonic period they cannot be said to have been effective. But they at least enabled activists to maintain contact with one another in a situation which would otherwise have left them isolated. In northern Italy, for example, Buonarroti, who was released from prison in 1806, was able to use the Adelfi as a means of orchestrating revolutionary activities on an international scale, while in southern Italy the Carboneria, which emerged as a focus for opposition to Murat in 1807, enabled small groups to project their endeavours in a wider national context. It was the fall of the Napoleonic empire, however, which gave the sects a more central political role, leaving them for a time as the only channel for political opposition.

The revolutionary and Napoleonic years had turned Italy upside down. Not only had the ideals of 1789 excited expectations which were unlikely to be satisfied in any polity; but the economic and legal order established by Napoleon had significantly boosted the interests of new entrepreneurial and professional groups. Powerful interests had clearly suffered. With the defeat of France, it was only to be expected that the old order would reassert itself. Much of the upheaval of these hectic years would, of course, prove to be irreversible. Few informed observers believed that the complex economic, administrative and legal arrangements of the *ancien régime* could be resurrected. Yet efforts could still be made to limit the political and social impact of the recent innovations. In 1815 the great powers, with Austria at their head, were concerned to restore the political divisions of Europe as nearly as possible to their pre-revolutionary condition. In accommodating past changes, the powers showed themselves to be in some measure flexible and pragmatic. With regard to the future, however, they were adamant. Austria, in particular, had learnt from experience of revolutionary turmoil that a local uprising could constitute a threat to the peace and stability of Europe as a whole and with it the security of her empire. What this meant, in effect, was that the settlement of 1815 was to be treated as a definitive solution to Europe's political problems. Attempts to placate liberal or nationalist pressures by piecemeal political or constitutional reforms would be precluded. Not the least of the paradoxes of these difficult years is that in treating local political issues as international problems, the powers had exaggerated their significance and contributed to the generation of the revolutionary pressures they had been so anxious to avoid.

The impact of the restoration on the politics of the Italian peninsula was decisive, though the reactions of the reconstituted states varied greatly. All the states paid lip-service to the ideology of 'throne and altar' which characterized the restoration; but only in Modena and Piedmont were determined efforts made to return to the status quo ante. In Piedmont, in particular, where Joseph de Maistre held high office, the restoration was seen as a literal reaction – clerical influence was encouraged, Napoleonic legislation overturned, personnel 'tainted' by association with the French shunned in public appointments. In practice, however, the demands of running a complex state were such that experienced administrators could not be ignored. Elsewhere the quest for administrative efficiency was seen as a higher priority than the maintenance of ideological purity. In Austrian-controlled Lombardy and Venetia, for example, the Napoleonic administrative structure was amended only in detail. The Austrian legal system was, in any case, modern and humane, a product, like the Napoleonic regime, of the cult of enlightened despotism. The transition from the one system to the other presented no great problems of adjustment.[26] Austrian influence in the rest of the peninsula also went some way towards moderating reactionary enthusiasms. It was pressure from Austria, Russia and Britain that led to the dismissal of Canosa at Naples as minister of police in 1816, thus obviating the threat of a reaction on the scale of 1799; and in the Grand Duchy of Tuscany, where Austrian influence was indirect, the Leopoldine tradition of benign administration was continued.[27]

The position with regard to political discussion displayed the more sinister side of restoration policy. The scope for public debate, whether in books, journals or through associations, was drastically reduced. Republican and Jacobin ideas and activities, which had been treated with considerable suspicion in the Napoleonic period, were everywhere suppressed. But moderates, too, found their political aspirations and expectations rudely interrupted. Hopes for the modernization of Italy had, for the moment, to be set aside, while any suggestion that Italy should, in the longer term, strive towards independence was regarded as unrealistic and dangerously utopian.

Restrictions on the style of political opposition varied from place to place. Milan remained the most vibrant intellectual centre. Austrian administration, though geared to the economic exploitation of Lombardy, was efficient and, in limited respects, progressive. The provision of elementary education, indeed, bears comparison with any contemporary European centre, yielding levels of basic literacy that would be of crucial importance in the turmoil of 1848. Yet there were limits to Austria's concern for the well-being of her subject territories. A flourishing Lombard economy, in particular, was seen as a vital prop to precarious imperial finances. The Austrians were always anxious, however, to ensure that indigenous economic development in Lombardy did not threaten economic interests closer to home. Most important of all, they were adamant that the potent combination of education and economic development should not issue in demands for political autonomy. Secret Austrian instructions to the director general of police at Venice make the point clearly. In addition to the usual business of 'unmasking conspiracies, plots, plans, undertakings and enterprises which tend to endanger' the imperial interest, the police are specifically instructed to keep 'a watch over the influence on public opinion of gazettes, newspapers, pamphlets, books or pictures of any sort, but especially if they are of a political nature'.[28] The problem for the Austrian authorities, of course, was that it was by no means easy to draw a clear line between political and literary, economic or technical matters.

The dilemma for Austria is best illustrated in the brief history of the celebrated journal *Il Conciliatore* (1818–19). The journal was the brain-child of the liberal aristocrats Luigi Porro-Lambertenghi and Federico Confalonieri, and became a forum for intellectuals concerned with the economic and cultural regeneration of Italy. It was specifically launched as an alternative to the official *Biblioteca Italiana,* which the Austrians had conceived as a means of creating a cultural climate sympathetic to Austrian rule. *Il Conciliatore,* however, was not cast in a narrow literary mould. The controlling group viewed cultural renewal in the broadest sense, embracing science, technology and commerce in addition to literature, history and philosophy. In a programmatic introduction, the editors specifically repudiated the old-fashioned journals which would be the special preserve of a narrow clique – vehicles of a 'minute erudition' which might better be described as 'pedantry'. The guiding principle of their own journal would be public utility ('general utility must without doubt be the principal aim of whoever wants to dedicate his thought to the service of the public'); and it was obvious from the outset that the distinction between 'public utility' and more narrowly political objectives was extraordinarily difficult to sustain.[29]

The scope of the journal made it difficult for the authorities to pin down its specific political thrust. Articles might range from technical discussions of the best sources of power for the modern factory, through treatments of educational theory and practice, to sensitive questions of economic policy.[30] But it was in the literary and historical fields that the journal made its most decisive impact. Literary establishments throughout Europe were dividing on the relative merits of 'romanticism' and 'classicism'. Everywhere the drift of the avant-garde was towards 'romanticism', in clear reaction to the cultural and political hegemony which France had enjoyed in the seventeenth and eighteenth centuries. *Il Conciliatore* came down decisively in favour of 'romanticism'. Yet whereas in Germany, France and England 'romanticism' was generally associated with conservative or reactionary political views, looking back to the 'organic' social systems of pre-revolutionary Europe as models of harmony, in Italy positions were reversed. 'Romantics' championed a literature adapted to the changing needs and customs of communities, while 'classicists' continued to parade tired and archaic literary forms which reflected the ethos of other times and cultures.[31] The political implications of these positions seem clear in retrospect. Italian literature would reflect an emerging national culture only if it were rid of foreign censorship and control. The contributors to *Il Conciliatore* were not themselves arguing for immediate political independence in 1818; but they had made it difficult for Italian intellectuals to see Austrian control as anything other than a temporary (though perhaps necessary) expedient.

It was in the reappraisal of the significance of the medieval period that Italian 'romantics' marked most clearly their distance from the commonplace assumptions of the wider European romantic movement. Where in other cultures the vogue for things medieval could so easily degenerate into a vapid nostalgia for an idealized past, in Italy the imprint of medieval life and attitudes was everywhere evident. Pietro Borsieri, reviewing the Italian translation of Müller's *Prospetto generale della storia politica dell'Europa nel Medio Evo*, argued that modern Italian culture owed much more to the medieval than to the classical Roman period.[32] He saw the emergence of small city-based republics in the thirteenth century as the key to the expansion of wealth and population in Italy, providing 'the impetus for the great revolutions of subsequent centuries'.[33] All that had been wanting in Italy was good government. Venice and Florence, for example, were able to survive the far-reaching political changes in Europe because of the strength of their commercial networks.[34]

But it was not simply a question of tracing the roots of modern institutions and attitudes. Inspiration could be drawn from Italian medieval history for a future prospect better attuned to the reality of Italian society and culture. Sismondi's *Storia delle repubbliche italiane del Medio Evo*, also reviewed by Borsieri in *Il Conciliatore* on its appearance in Italian translation in 1818, became a crucial source for theorists who wanted to preserve the best of Italian municipal culture.[35] In a wide-ranging discussion, Borsieri contrasted the sort of moral instruction which ancient historians had drawn from their narratives with the complex picture of overlapping functions and practices which emerges in historical work on the medieval period. In administrative, political and economic terms, Borsieri saw modern Italy as the specific product of the post-Roman era. He vigorously endorsed Sismondi's contention that 'government is the first cause of the character of a people', informing the 'virtues and vices of nations, their energy and laxity, talents, wisdom and ignorance'.[36] Rejecting the fashionable deterministic accounts which derived a culture's peculiar attributes from climate, Borsieri redirected attention to those dimensions of human experience which ingenuity and initiative could mould. Sismondi's analysis of the greatness and decline of the Italian republics thus had clear implications for policy and practice in modern times.

Theorists suspicious of the centralist thrust of so many of the political proposals spawned in the French revolutionary period could build an alternative case upon medieval foundations. Carlo Cattaneo, for example, who embraced the link between liberty, science and progress as enthusiastically as anyone, traced the roots of his own political vision in the variegated civic cultures which flourished in Italy after the fall of Rome. In a later phase of the debate, Cattaneo argued that the basically decentralized character of Italian society was a source of strength rather than weakness, ensuring that institutions remained accessible to people in their day-to-day dealings with authorities. Municipalism, the *bête noire* of so many nationalists, became in Cattaneo's treatment both a guarantor of political freedoms and an expression of Italian identity.[37] The point to stress, though, is that the revival of interest in things local and particular could itself be progressive, heralding a rather different future for Italy from that envisaged in the years of French hegemony.

What medievalism offered in the political sphere was a significantly enhanced range of options which might be entertained for a putative Italian state. The seeds of what was to become the neo-Guelph movement in the 1840s can be traced back to a reappraisal of the medieval Catholic tradition. Alessandro Manzoni, for example, in *Osservazioni sulla morale cattolica* (1819), sought to dispel the negative impression of both Italy and the Church in Sismondi's *Storia delle repubbliche italiane del Medio Evo*.[38] Sismondi's contention was that Italy had endured a virtual religious despotism, stultifying the spirit and initiative of her people while at the same time fostering widespread neglect of religious observances and moral duties. In short, in common with Protestant orthodoxy, he attributed Italy's so-called 'decadence' in the post-Renaissance period to Catholic doctrine and practice. Manzoni's response was twofold. On historical grounds he argued that Italy's religious institutions and practices were by no means unique. If the Church were to be regarded as the source of Italy's decline, then the whole of the Catholic world should manifest the same symptoms. Explanation had thus to be sought elsewhere if Italy's plight was distinctive. On philosophical grounds, too, Manzoni found Sismondi's position wanting. The assault on the moral influence of the Church depended upon a crude and uncritical utilitarianism. But instead of accepting that interest was the basis of morality, Manzoni turned the argument around to suggest that the good men do in particular spheres depends upon a wider foundation of faith such as that furnished by the Church.[39] Whether or not his argument against Sismondi is finally defensible is beyond my present point. What Manzoni had done, however, was to demonstrate how the Catholic tradition could be invoked in an essentially forward-looking debate.

Nor was the revival of political Catholicism restricted to a general defence of the Catholic tradition. Foscolo, for example, turned back to the contentious figure of Gregory VII, so often regarded as the advocate of theological despotism, as a staunch defender of spiritual authority and independence.[40] The political lesson soon became clear to his contemporaries. The authority and jurisdiction enjoyed by the papacy in Gregory's day could not be resurrected. But something of that authority remained; and in the meantime the Papacy had become a specifically national institution. Defence of the traditional authority of the Church thus served a more narrowly national purpose, reinforcing a distinctive international status for an Italian institution. As the Risorgimento gathered momentum, so a rereading of both spiritual and secular traditions figured more largely in furthering the national cause. With the publication of Gioberti's *Del primato morale e civile degli italiani* in 1843, political Catholicism would have acquired its own national manifesto.[41]

Radicals, too, were beginning to look beyond the French unitary state in their proposals. Federalism, which in the revolutionary period had been largely associated with conservatism or reaction, was adopted by many democrats anxious not to repeat earlier Jacobin errors. Francesco Salfi specifically stressed the risk of oscillating between despotism and anarchy, with the French Revolution and its aftermath cited as a standing lesson.[42] He highlighted the basic divisions between the existing Italian states as a fact of political life. Any solution to the Italian conundrum, in his view, had to accommodate political, economic and cultural diversity, without exposing Italy to exploitation by foreign powers. What was needed, essentially, was a form of territorial representation which secured the state from both external interference and domination by any of the constituent units. A federal constitution fitted the bill, modelled largely on the German confederation established in 1815.[43]

Luigi Angeloni also saw a federal republic as the best defence of political freedom. He argued that no political solution could ignore the reality of a complex balance of powers within and between states. What he sought was a minimal programme which would secure Italian independence with the least possible upset to the national and international status quo. Inequality between individuals and regions was inevitable. The task of politics was simply to ensure that interests were pursued through 'laws of association'.[44] Adopting an essentially utilitarian perspective, Angeloni could argue that the pursuit of interest was maximized through free civil association. Such association, however, depended crucially upon consensus. And consensus in a new political community would not be forthcoming if established interests were sacrificed. A federal republic, in the Italian context, could secure political identity without undermining the divergent interests of autonomous communities. The federal experiment had proved to be a conspicuous success in the United States of America.[45] The same success for a republic might be anticipated in Italy. Natural disparities within the peninsula restricted the range of political forms which could plausibly be adopted. Only a federal constitution could guarantee both the autonomy of constituent states and national independence.

Arguments for a federal Italy could not, however, be openly canvassed. Salfi and Angeloni, like so many activists after 1815, were both living in exile.[46] Their contributions could help to keep the debate about Italy's future alive, though without any real expectation of influencing the course of events. Political debate within Italy had, for the most part, to be conducted either in clandestine fashion or through indirect channels. It remained the preserve of a tiny élite, largely divorced from the daily concerns of the wider population.

The position in Austrian-controlled Lombardy and Venetia should be seen in perspective. The cultural climate in Milan, in particular, remained much more congenial to general intellectual discussion than Turin or Modena, Naples or Rome. *Il Conciliatore*, however, had sailed too close to the political wind for the comfort of the Austrian authorities. Skirmishing with the censor came to an inglorious end with the closure of the journal in October 1819. Other, more technical, journals continued to flourish, such as the *Annali universali di statistica*, and after 1839 Cattaneo's *Politecnico*, which would have an incalculable influence on a generation of reformers.[47] The Austrians, indeed, may well have been slow in their failure to recognize the political implications of detailed studies of society and economy. They had always been prepared to tolerate discussion of the reform of industry and society. When it came to arguments

27

defending a necessary link between economic progress and the extension of political liberties, however, they felt a stand had to be taken. To campaign even for the limited constitutional guarantees advanced by Benjamin Constant and his circle in France was regarded as a revolutionary threat to the status quo. The choice for committed activists was thus between exile and the political underworld.

Florence was the only other intellectual centre to approach Milan in vitality. Censorship in the Grand Duchy of Tuscany was known to be the most relaxed in Italy. In the 1820s, especially after the forced exodus of intellectuals from various quarters of Italy following the failure of the revolutionary upheavals of 1821, Florence became something of a national cultural centre. The principal figure in this development was the remarkable entrepreneur and publisher, Gian Pietro Vieusseux. In 1821 he established a journal, the *Antologia*, devoted, like *Il Conciliatore*, to intellectual and cultural renewal in Italy. What might have been simply one of a number of reformist initiatives became, in the special circumstances which prevailed in Florence, a journal of genuinely national scope. Contributors ranged from major figures such as Romagnosi, Leopardi and Foscolo, through leaders of the Florentine intellectual establishment, to emerging men such as Mazzini and Cattaneo, striving to make an impact in the cultural and political world.

The *Antologia* was thus eclectic in scope, offering itself as a vehicle for progressive ideas of whatever provenance. The practical application of ideas and theories was a dominant concern, with especial emphasis on economic and educational policy. But literary and philosophical matters were not neglected. What distinguished the *Antologia*, however, was its commitment to the treatment of even local Tuscan issues in a wider national context. A group of intellectuals had begun to emerge, not only better informed about the variety of cultural and economic circumstances to be found in Italy, but also aware of their responsibilities as a class to create an informed public as a necessary condition for the establishment of responsible government.[48]

It should be clear, then, that contributors to the *Antologia* felt able to address political issues directly. Specific articles would seek to elicit changes in government policy, arguing for reform of the *mezzadria* system of landholding, or issuing warnings against the dire consequences of unbridled industrialization.[49] Preoccupation with public policy had long been a feature of the reformist tradition established in the Grand Duchy in the eighteenth century. But the political argument had been taken several steps further. Gino Capponi, for example, very much Vieusseux's right-hand man at the *Antologia*, was an open advocate of constitutional reform. His position, though modest enough, guaranteeing the interests of the landowning classes, could appear threatening to the Austrians, obsessed as they were with reform and revolution on a European scale. Francesco Forti could attack the abstract ideologues of the French Revolution in a style which actually made a case for moderate constitutional reform.[50] He could also stress the crucial role of municipalities in an alternative vision of political reform, focusing on decentralization and wider involvement rather than radical solutions imposed by an enlightened bureaucracy.[51] In an important review he also looked at a confederal alternative to the standard unitary state as a means of securing political liberty.[52]

Vieusseux himself also favoured a confederation of Italian states, involving common economic and foreign ministries, a common currency and the removal of all internal tariff barriers. In a proposal which had some affinity with Gioberti's better-known argument, Vieusseux envisaged a confederal political form which stopped short of full independence from Austria, involving a diet convened for three months of the year at Rome under the auspices of the pope.[53] It was unthinkable that such arguments could have been mooted in territories directly controlled by Austria. Austrian influence, however, was never far away. The 1830 revolutions sharpened the clash of interests between governments and governed throughout Europe. Opinion-leading journals found themselves forced into the adoption of positions which they might have been able to avoid in more settled times. Radical arguments with the most far-reaching practical implications could find favour even with the moderates of the *Antologia*. The response of governments in general, and Austria in particular, was predictable. Fearing a snowballing of political demands, the Austrians brought pressure to bear upon the Grand Duchy to shackle the *Antologia*. Publication was suspended in 1833.

Organized political opposition was thus forced to operate underground. Secret political sects had proliferated throughout Italy since Napoleonic days. All that changed with the restoration was the principal target for operations. It was clear in the north that little would be achieved while Austrian occupation and control persisted. But putting an end to foreign rule was no more than a first step on a long road that led to a variety of (often incompatible) political destinations. In Piedmont, for example, where sects had managed to infiltrate the army and sections of the nobility, demands in the 1821 revolution focused principally upon the establishment of a constitution. Other conspirators would have more ambitious goals. Filippo Buonarroti's group, the Sublimi Maestri Perfetti, formed in 1818 following the fusion of the Adelfi and the Filadelfi, was intent upon the creation of a radically egalitarian republic. Not all members of the organization, however, would be aware of the long-term political goals of Buonarroti and his close associates. Recruits would be inducted into different levels of the sect. Lower-ranking members would generally have their attention focused on immediate political goals – the need for a constitutional regime in northern Italy – while overall direction and strategy would be the concern of the tiny élite gathered around Buonarroti at the apex of the organization.

The Carbonari were rather more loosely organized. Like the Sublimi Maestri Perfetti, they held to the most elaborate ritual in the conduct of their affairs. The need for absolute secrecy meant that ideological objectives could not be openly canvassed. The many Carbonarist groups, indeed, would often find themselves pursuing rather different political goals. All would be committed to the creation of a secular, constitutionally based regime, though opinions differed on the kind of constitution deemed to be most desirable. Moderates tended to favour the French charter of 1814, while more democratically inclined groups supported the Spanish constitution of 1812. Central co-ordination was much less evident than in the groups which fell within Buonarroti's sphere of influence. Just how far they constituted a threat to established governments is a much-disputed question. Metternich himself seems to have formed a rather exaggerated view of their effectiveness. The initial success of the revolutions in Turin and Naples in 1820–1 is indicative of their capacity to act if occasion arose, though it is equally clear that their lack of strength in depth left them vulnerable to resolute counter-measures.[54] The point to stress here, however, is that political opposition of any kind in Italy had been forced to assume a conspiratorial and revolutionary form. Indeed the failure of the authorities in the various Italian states to establish a *modus vivendi* with their moderate opponents would ultimately prove to be their undoing.

Between revolution and reaction

The situation in 1830 was hardly propitious for a national movement of any kind. Any groups arguing for the eventual emergence of an Italian state, even in the most theoretical terms, were liable to find themselves harassed or suppressed by the authorities. The conditions in which political campaigns had to be conducted meant that little could be done to persuade wavering or neutral opinion. Not only were political activists an isolated minority; but political information and know-how were restricted even in wider literate circles. Political initiative in the Napoleonic and restoration periods had largely come from disenchanted members of the liberal aristocracy. Small groups of friends and trusted associates acting in concert, however, could hardly sustain a campaign likely to threaten resolute governments. They would find themselves isolated from their peers, yet with little chance of establishing solid connections with broader social groups. Nor, indeed, were liberal aristocrats anxious to generate a mass following. Liberals throughout Europe were still haunted by the example of the French Revolution, where the lofty principles of 1789 had degenerated into the bloodletting of the Terror of 1793. Cuoco's analysis of the problems which bedevilled the Neapolitan Revolution of 1799 was still relevant in 1830. He had seen how a dedicated and sophisticated minority had forged so far ahead of the solid majority that they were vulnerable to élite-led but mass-based counter-measures. Little had changed by 1830. Certainly the Napoleonic period had given the liberal aristocracy wider administrative and political experience. But they remained isolated in relation to society at large. In the prevailing political conditions, little could be done to create an alternative consensus.

Part of the problem, in Italy as elsewhere in Europe, was that political consciousness was still dominated by the French Revolution. Both revolutionaries and reactionaries would interpret their experience in the broadest possible terms, seeing connections between events which might often have been occasioned by local and particular circumstances. The impact of ideologies, in particular, was often exaggerated. Defenders of the status quo were fearful that limited concessions might fire the enthusiasm of rising generations and classes for wholesale political transformation. What this meant in practice was that even the most cautious liberal reformers could be portrayed as threats to the established order. The terms of ideological discourse had thus served to narrow the middle ground of politics alarmingly. They had also excited what might best be described as a collective political paranoia. A riot in Palermo, for example, had only to be matched by disturbances on the Paris streets for establishments throughout Europe to take fright. Upheavals in Paris in both 1830 and 1848 sent shock waves through the Continent, lending a larger significance to disturbances that might otherwise simply have fizzled out. Modern historians, of course, are often inclined to take a rather different view of such events, stressing political adjustment to structural changes in society and economy. What concerns us here, however, is the ideological perspective which informed the decisions of political actors. And it is clear that ideological polarization was a principal factor in rendering difficult situations explosive.

Liberals, for their part, tended to view events from two quite distinct points of view. They could happily embrace technological and economic progress, accepting, in the longer term, that demands for limited constitutional reform would ultimately lead to more far-reaching political changes. Cavour, for example, who was always anxious lest the fine line dividing political reform from social revolution be crossed, nevertheless acknowledged that nothing could stop the inexorable advance of liberalism and nationalism. In the short term, however, liberals took a clear stand. Democracy was to be opposed, precisely because it would release uncontrollable social pressures. It was one thing to accept that the political tide might be running in a particular direction; and quite another to assist in immediately undermining the foundations of a way of life. To be sure, conservative liberals of Cavour's ilk were unduly pessimistic when they surveyed their political options. Liberalism was to prove itself a far more flexible and enduring plant than its advocates dared hope in the 1830s. But the ideological atmosphere was such that few could see liberal constitutionalism as a political creed that would tame the wilder beasts of revolution and reaction.

Prospects for radical change in Italy were thus severely limited in 1830. In the ideological sphere, in particular, the multitude of seething discontents had yet to coalesce into a political programme. Nor could it be expected that a consensus would readily be achieved. Not only were the various regions of Italy deeply divided in terms of language and culture; but the pattern of economic development was uneven, leading to vast discrepancies of wealth and clashes of interest. The array of political proposals advanced in the Risorgimento can clearly in part be explained as expressions of the diversity of social and economic conditions in the peninsula. Our concern here, however, is more specific. The crucial question, raised at the time but unanswered to this day, is whether or not the essentially polycentric nature of Italian culture is to be regarded as a strength or weakness. Certainly very many patriots saw municipalism as a principal obstacle to the emergence of an Italian state. But there is another side to the story. Devolved political institutions can be valued both as a reflection of Italian conditions and as a bulwark against tyranny, ensuring that institutions and procedures remain familiar and responsive to people's interests. The debate between unitarists and federalists during the Risorgimento must be seen in this context. What we see in the period from 1796 to 1830 is the establishment of terms of reference which were to dominate later (more familiar) discussions. Fundamental issues were raised about the nature of the state and the identity of the Italian nation. And though it would be futile to contend that either one side or the other had the better of the argument, it remains the case that the political outcome would have a decisive impact upon subsequent Italian development for better or worse.

Political prospects were transformed as more and more groups came to see the achievement of an Italian state as a necessary condition for the advancement of their particular interests. This development, to be sure, was not without its own difficulties. As national passion reached a peak in 1860, expectations were pitched so high that the actual state established in 1861 could not fail to be a disappointment. Without the initial ideological momentum, however, little could have been achieved.

Giuseppe Mazzini (1805–72) emerged as a dominant figure in the ideological ferment of the 1830s. He set the idea of the unitary state at the heart of his nationalist propaganda. His distinctive contribution to political thought and revolutionary strategy was a response to the lessons that might be learnt from the failed uprisings of 1830–1, in which local groups had operated in isolation and secrecy, often fearing popular involvement quite as much as Austrian intervention. It became clear to him that a politics of constitutional contrivance, designed principally to secure sectional interests, would not tap the latent energy and enthusiasm of broader groups within Italian society striving to fashion a public role for themselves.

Mazzini had been inducted into the life of political activism and subversion in 1827 through the Carbonarist movement, but he quickly became disillusioned with the secrecy, ritual and failure to articulate clear ideological objectives. Looking back on his career in his *Note autobiografiche* (1861), he claimed that from the outset he was 'surprised and suspicious that the oath of allegiance contained but a formula of obedience and not a word on ends'. His initiator had given not the slightest hint about the kind of state that the Carboneria sought to attain, whether 'federalism or unity' should be the goal, a 'republic or a monarchy'. To Mazzini it seemed that the commitment was to 'war against the government, and nothing else'.[55]

A more broadly based revolutionary strategy was thus a crucial desideratum for Mazzini. To this end, while exiled in Marseilles in 1831, he directed all his energy to the creation of a new movement, La Giovine Italia (Young Italy), which would serve as the focus for the drive towards an Italian state. La Giovine Italia combined the dual aims of educating the people politically and organizing popular insurrections. Its mission was to foster a distinctive role for the Italian national movement in an age in which the national principle had effectively undermined the legitimacy of outmoded political forms. Italy would be a free, independent and unitary republic, enabling Italians to live together in a spirit of harmony and co-operation. But the status which beckoned would be achieved only if Italians themselves were able to seize the initiative and fashion a new political identity through their own efforts.[56]

Mazzini's practical achievements were limited. The insurrections he inspired in the 1830s were dismal failures which antagonized moderate and sceptical groups whose support was indispensable if entrenched ruling interests were to be effectively challenged. Yet Mazzini nevertheless became something of a *bête noire* in the perceptions of the authorities. Though the insurrections he encouraged might look pathetic in retrospect, they could not be disregarded. Governments had been momentarily overturned in Turin and Naples in 1820–1. And no government could be sure that a local spark would not ignite a wider conflagration. More important, though, Mazzini had forced Italian activists to think in terms of national political categories. Traditional loyalties to city or region had begun to seem anachronistic in the brave new world he evoked. For Mazzini it was simply an article of faith that a people's sense of national identity (formed through the medium of language, indigenous cultural traditions, etc.) should be reflected in their political institutions.

Mazzini was far from creating an ideological consensus. Even in radical circles, there was widespread disquiet about his identification of an Italian nation-state as the key to the regeneration of wider aspects of life. Carlo Cattaneo (1801–69), for example, editor of the influential Milanese journal *Il Politecnico* (1839–44), was unhappy with the mystical strain in Mazzini's thinking. Political reform was valued by Cattaneo as a means towards concrete improvements in society and the economy. He had made a name for himself as an economist, arguing vigorously for a general extension of free trade areas. When the issue of possible enlargement of the German *Zollverein* was being discussed, Cattaneo pressed for Lombard involvement, despite the reservations of nationalists. In the pages of *Il Politecnico* Cattaneo consistently championed the cause of modernization, in transport, industry, administration and the law. In his view, the lot of the ordinary Italian would be improved by applying the latest scientific ideas in these various spheres rather than by ambitious political reconstruction. Indeed, for Cattaneo, preoccupation with the national issue was something of a distraction, diverting attention away from the urgent task of raising the general educational level of the Italian people. Cattaneo would later play his part in the national movement; but before 1848 he was so far distant from nationalists such as Mazzini that he could vest his principal hopes for political change in the reform of the Habsburg Empire along federal lines.[57]

Stress on the limitations of a purely political solution to the Italian question was a recurring theme in radical writings in the 1840s. Giuseppe Ferrari (1811–76), a friend and close associate of Cattaneo, worked in France in the decade following 1838 and was exposed, through Proudhon, to the discussions of contemporary socialists. Where Mazzini focused on the special mission of the Italian people in the European political scene, charting a direction for other peoples to follow in their drive towards statehood, Ferrari highlighted, instead, the degeneration of Italian culture since the Renaissance. He argued that high Italian culture, in particular, had become stale and derivative, with leading ideas originating in the more vibrant cultures beyond the Alps. In politics her weakness was manifest. Since the French Revolution, political opinion in Italy had been dominated by French issues. Mazzini had certainly tried to arouse the Italian masses to work for their political salvation. But, writing in 1844, Ferrari was all too aware of the limitations of his approach. Ideological zeal alone would not create a successful revolution. The people needed to be persuaded that their real needs would be served in the scheme of things that revolution ushered in. It was not simply a case of responding to the cause of the nation but which national cause to respond to.[58]

The 'nation' was clearly far from a straightforward or self-evident entity. Scepticism about precisely this question led moderates to seek minimum terms of political accommodation between the constituent states of the peninsula compatible with independence from foreign rule, rather than an 'ideal' unitary polity. The position is most famously exemplified in Vincenzo Gioberti's *Del primato morale e civile degli italiani* (1843). A leading (though heterodox) liberal Catholic, Gioberti sought to exploit both regional diversity and cultural unity in a papal-led confederacy. He had no faith in the Mazzinian formula of popular insurrections supported by ideological propaganda. Nor could he envisage institutional unity emerging from Italy's disparate regional polities. Instead he sought to use the spiritual authority of the Papacy as a means of brokering the rivalries of the separate states. He was aware that military resources would have to come from somewhere. He anticipated a special role for Piedmont ('the warrior province'), with her independent status and proven record in recent European diplomacy.[59] Indeed his confederacy of equal partners begins to look on closer inspection like an axis built around Rome and Piedmont, the former 'the privileged seat of Christian wisdom', the latter 'the principal base of Italian military strength'.[60] Gioberti avoided discussion of constitutional or practical details. His concern was to strike a balance between constitutional prerogatives and *de facto* power, specifically in order to make the prospect of an Italian confederation as attractive as possible to the powers most likely to make it a success.

His tactic, at least in the short term, was strikingly successful. But what his more discerning readers focused upon was not so much the role of the Papacy as that of Piedmont. Cesare Balbo (1789–1853) and Massimo D'Azeglio (1798–1866) argued both that constitutional change was essential, but that ill-considered popular enthusiasms could very well blow the whole process off course.[61] They felt that unthinking defence of the status quo would drive the mainstream of informed opinion into the camp of the Mazzinians. If that were to occur there would be an inevitable drift away from the principle of constitutional monarchy towards popular democracy, with all the dangers that that involved for moderate liberal values. No one could be sanguine about the outcome of such a development after the experience of France in 1793. From this perspective, it was felt that the political initiative should be left in the hands of the Piedmontese élite. Piedmont was the only Italian state with independent political options; she was accordingly best placed to foster the national movement without sacrificing the principle of constitutional monarchy to popular enthusiasms.

The position of the moderates was thus complex. Though by upbringing and culture they might readily be identified as monarchists, they nevertheless had profound reservations about monarchical rule. They were opposed to autocracy in all its forms, whether exercised by the Austrians, the Church or the Bourbons. Even Piedmont was far from satisfying their constitutional requirements before 1848. As opponents of the settlement imposed on Italy in 1815, they could respond with guarded enthusiasm to the national movement. But they were reluctant to force the pace of political change for fear of upsetting the social status quo. Between the established order on the one side and the Mazzinians on the other, they had to tread carefully. In the early 1840s they had, essentially, been responding to what they saw as the misplaced initiative of the Mazzinians. In the ferment of 1848, however, they found themselves thrust to the centre of the political stage.

1848

The detailed story of these tangled events cannot be told here.[62] A concatenation of uprisings throughout Italy and beyond led to precisely the kind of revolutionary situation that the Mazzinians had hoped for and the moderates privately feared. Disturbances in most of the urban centres, ranging from Milan, Turin and Genoa in the north, through Parma, Modena, Naples and Palermo, though they might have been sparked off by a variety of local issues, assumed a weightier aspect in relation to the wider national movement. Hastily drawn constitutions were conceded in the early months of 1848 but, as would happen so often in Europe's revolutionary crises, the pace of change gathered a momentum of its own. Initial uneasy alliances between ruling families and moderates were soon outflanked by more radical popular demands. But this was a route moderates were deeply reluctant to take. As proposals became more radical, so the commitment of many to the national movement would waver, leading influential activists to put commitments to family and class interest before abstract ideals. In these circumstances, the princes could bide their time. The 'democrats' of 1848 simply lacked the material resources and popular support that the assumption of responsibility for government and administration presupposed. As the revolutionary tide receded throughout Europe in 1849, so the various ruling families could respond to the efforts of the Austrians to restore the status quo.

In the immediate aftermath of the failure of the nationalist revolutions, nothing seemed to have been achieved. All that had survived from the early months of 1848 was a constitution for Piedmont, restrictive in its provisions, leaving ample powers of political initiative in the hands of the king. Yet certain lessons had been learnt. Insurrection as a tactic had been shown to be almost wholly worthless without extensive co-ordination of policies across a wide range of political fronts. Nor could kings or popes be trusted to pursue nationalist goals if these clashed with established dynastic interests.

What we see after 1848 is a new tone of realism. Where discussion of Italy's future had so often been couched in abstract or utopian terms, it was now felt that attention should be focused on more immediate concerns. After all, little was to be gained from endless consideration of the ideal form of an Italian state, whether unitary or federal, republican or monarchical, if the deep divisions which such discussions revealed were to weaken the conduct of a national campaign. The revolutions in different parts of Italy had foundered in the face of intractable practical problems. The regions of Italy simply had divergent economic and cultural interests, as did the liberal aristocracy, the professional and entrepreneurial classes, the artisans and the peasants.

New regimes in Milan, Rome, Venice, Naples and Palermo had proved to be evanescent. Talk had been of Italy, but regional and class rivalries reasserted themselves. Hostility to Austria or the Papacy or the Bourbons quickly gave place to more traditional resentments: Palermo against Naples, Milan against Turin, the north against the south. But if disappointments were acute, the inference to be drawn seemed clear. Rhetoric and pious expectations would never overcome the profound divisions between the various subcultures within Italy, nor would theorists succeed in fashioning a common programme without widespread support. What was lacking was a focus of political power that could manipulate propaganda in order to achieve practical objectives. Mazzini, to his credit, had long argued that ideological disagreements would have to be set aside in the national cause, and had vigorously endorsed Carlo Alberto of Piedmont's leadership in the war against Austria. But in 1849 it seemed that Piedmont had betrayed Italy. And no other Italian state had sufficient independence to assume her mantle.

Recriminations, especially among the radicals, were intense. Among the first to offer an analysis of the failure of revolution was Cattaneo. His *L'insurrezione di Milano nel 1848*, written while in exile in Switzerland, has remained a classic to this day.[63] He had always been a reluctant revolutionary, and the events of 1848-9 generally confirmed his earlier reservations about precipitate action. What should have been a revolution in the name of liberty was transformed, for both the patricians of Milan and the Mazzinians, into the pursuit of independence for its own sake. Yet without liberty, the sacrifices incurred in political struggle would be futile. The interests of the Italian people would only be advanced, in Cattaneo's view, if the achievement of independence from foreign rule brought domestic liberty in its train. Piedmontese domination of the peninsula was certainly not an attractive proposition to him. Above all, however, Cattaneo stressed the need to acquire detailed knowledge of a host of economic and political questions. Nothing could be expected from the masses until their level of civic and scientific awareness had been raised to a higher plane. The task ahead was thus essentially educational.

Cattaneo remained critical of Mazzini throughout the 1850s. He could accept neither the value of Mazzini's insurrectionary methods, nor his final goal of a unitary state. Political unity on Mazzinian terms would only constitute a thin veneer over a variegated mosaic of distinct cultures and economies. Italy certainly had an identity when considered in relation to foreign powers, but only a federal state would properly reflect the reality of her domestic conditions.

Mazzini came under pressure, too, from radicals influenced by socialist ideas. Ferrari, in *Filosofia della rivoluzione* (1851), stressed the inadequacy of purely political solutions to the effective unification of Italy.[64] In his view the French Revolution had made giant strides forward, but it had stopped short of eradicating the foundations of the *ancien régime*. What was required before a new order could be established was a determined assault on religion and property as the crucial props of a hierarchical society. Mazzini's preoccupation with the nation simply glossed over the larger social, cultural and economic implications of revolution. Yet without fundamental structural changes, political innovation would be merely cosmetic.

The 1848 revolutions had been vitiated, according to Ferrari, by a failure to develop radical social programmes which would be attuned to the needs of the masses. Mazzini himself had always tried to avoid confronting social questions directly for fear of fostering class divisions within the national movement. For Ferrari, however, it was only by attending to the social needs of ordinary people that a defensible polity would ever be established.

Nor was Ferrari happy with the political form favoured by Mazzini. In *La federazione repubblicana* (1851) he argued that a unitary state could be imposed upon Italy's diverse traditions only at immense political cost.[65] A federal republic, on the other hand, would be responsive to the needs of the people, without undermining a deeper Italian identity. Most important of all, however, Ferrari could see little chance of a radical revolution succeeding in Italy without parallel revolutionary upheavals occurring elsewhere in Europe. And, no matter how painful it might be to Italian national pride, revolutionary initiative on such a scale could only come from France.

Among the radicals, then, the post-mortem on 1848 exacerbated differences of view which had always been evident. Groups were split on the most fundamental questions. Cattaneo and Ferrari were sharply critical of Mazzini's conception of both the nation and the state; Mazzini despised the materialism of radical and socialist positions; Cattaneo could not accept Ferrari's arguments on redistribution of wealth; and there was no settled view on the vexed question of the relation of the Italian revolution to the European balance of power.

Problems among the moderates were more practical and more pressing. Piedmont, the focus of moderate aspirations in the 1840s, had proved herself to be wanting. Yet her constitution and independence still singled her out as the one state that could lend political, economic and military weight to the national cause. Much needed to happen, however, before Piedmont would feel able to launch further initiatives. In the first place, the precarious gains of 1848 were under threat. King Victor Emmanuel and the clerical right were intent upon emasculating the Piedmontese parliament. That constitutional government survived in Piedmont owed a great deal to the skill and tact of D'Azeglio, prime minister from 1849 to 1852. Here was a man of impeccable nationalist (albeit moderate) credentials, who nevertheless enjoyed the confidence of the king. He was able to support the king in his stand against the democrats without compromising the principle of constitutional monarchy too far. But at the same time he could push the king further than he wanted to go, isolating the clerical right with the passage of the Siccardi Laws (1850) which ended a variety of ecclesiastical privileges and irreversibly shifted the balance between state and Church.[66]

D'Azeglio lacked the temperament and technical expertise to tackle Piedmont's deeper problems. That role fell to Cavour, who from 1852 until his death in 1861 was to dominate the politics of Piedmont and Italy. The details of his remarkable career are familiar and cannot be dealt with here.[67] The point to stress is that throughout his career he sought to negotiate a fine line between the monarchic right and the Mazzinian left. He recognized that modernization on a large scale was a precarious undertaking. He had to negotiate the twin perils of revolution and reaction at home, while ensuring that his policies were sufficiently well received abroad to enable him to maximize his diplomatic options at times of crisis. Under his premiership, Piedmont began to look like a modern state, but at the price of massive indebtedness.

Piedmont and the national movement

Cavour's ambitions for Italy in the early 1850s were limited. He set himself the task of advancing the immediate Piedmontese interest. Yet he also recognized that public opinion in Turin was much more cosmopolitan and volatile than had been the case before 1848. Heady expectations could erupt again. And if they did, Cavour was clear in his mind that he would swim with the political tide. Taking a wider European view, he could see liberal and nationalist ideas becoming dominant everywhere. His main concern throughout the 1850s was to ensure that moderate reformism was not swamped by the 'wilder' ambitions of democrats and socialists.

Cavour was led to embrace unification of the whole peninsula only when he became convinced that it might otherwise be secured on terms which might threaten his vision of a liberal capitalist future. He channelled domestic opinion effectively, especially after the formation of the Italian National Society in 1857. The group, led by Pallavicino, Manin and La Farina, served as a bridge between Cavour and the wider nationalist movement. It had one article of faith: that the unification of Italy would only be possible under Piedmont's banner. Branches extending throughout northern and central Italy enabled a new cohesion to be brought to the national campaign. The society was never simply Cavour's instrument, but it certainly performed a crucial role in fomenting popular demonstrations and insurrections in favour of Piedmont in 1859–60.[68]

Cavour had thus prepared his position assiduously. Yet he still had to wait upon events. He played a gambler's hand diplomatically in 1859, seeking to trigger war with Austria without undermining support for Italy in France and Britain. Domestically, too, he could never be sure that radical opinion was effectively under his control or marginalized. At the very last Garibaldi's expedition to Sicily risked precipitating a much more 'democratic' solution to the Italian question than Cavour was prepared to accept. His handling of this particular crisis is deeply revealing. Initially he tried any number of unscrupulous stratagems to undermine Garibaldi's position. When it seemed likely that Garibaldi's triumphant march would continue, Cavour raised the stakes. He was prepared to risk civil war in order to prevent Garibaldi from reaching Rome. He sought diplomatic pretexts for Piedmontese intervention, but his real object was to stop Garibaldi in his tracks.[69]

Once the Piedmontese army, with Victor Emmanuel at its head, had been brought into play, it was inevitable that Garibaldi would concede. He had always acted in the name of the king. Having devoted his life to the cause of Italian unity, he would not, at the last, risk sacrificing everything by waging a ruinous and unwinnable civil war. He was aware that much that he had striven for would be hopelessly caricatured by Cavour and the Piedmontese politicians. But the political battle had already been lost. The Piedmontese parliament had opted for annexation of the south after a series of popular plebiscites. All that remained for Garibaldi was to offer the kingdom he had liberated to Victor Emmanuel.

Unification and its consequences

The state established in 1861 is always seen as the culmination of a series of developments stretching back to the first stirrings of nationalist sentiment in the late eighteenth century. Yet from the very outset it was regarded as a hollow achievement. For Garibaldi, in particular, it was a deep disappointment that a final military effort was not made to bring the whole peninsula under Italian control. Rome and Venice remained in the hands of the Papacy and Austria respectively. And they did not become a part of the Italian state until the balance of European power had shifted again. Nor was Italian military or diplomatic initiative crucial in the completion of the state. Prussian expansion obliged Austria to accept the cession of Venice to Italy in 1866, while the Franco-Prussian war of 1870 forced the withdrawal of French troops from Rome, leaving Italian troops free to take an almost defenceless city. It remained a source of deep shame to later nationalists that Italians had played such a minor role in the last stages of unification. Indeed some of the more strident groups, including the early Fascists, contended that the process had never been completed, arguing for a renewed drive to bring all Italian speakers under the Italian flag.

Disillusion with the state went deeper than the question of frontiers. The various nationalist theorists had always seen political unification as the first phase in a larger process of economic, social and cultural renewal. Yet the preoccupation with the state by no means reflects a national political consensus. Groups which could agree on little else had grown accustomed to regarding the emergence of an Italian state as the key to peace and prosperity in the peninsula. The deep divisions which had been evident in the immediate aftermath of the failures of 1848–9, however, still persisted. Arguments still raged, especially in radical circles, about whether an Italian state should be unitary or federal in form, republican or monarchical in constitution. In the event, such cohesion as existed in demands for unification in the hectic years after 1857 reflected an acceptance that constitutional issues should be treated as secondary to the freeing of Italy from foreign rule rather than a genuine political consensus.

This, in itself, represented a significant political victory for Cavour and the Piedmontese moderates. Piedmont had been presented as the state most likely to translate nationalist aspirations into political reality; but unification on these terms amounted to the acceptance of a Piedmontese state writ large, with the wider benefits which (it had always been assumed) would follow in the wake of political independence postponed for consideration in an indefinite future.

What unification amounted to, then, was a conservative (or, in Gramsci's term, 'passive') revolution, designed to accomplish far-reaching political changes while preserving the social status quo.[70] In the prevailing national and international contexts, it may well have been all that could have been achieved. But it left united Italy with a host of dilemmas that the liberal regime was never to resolve satisfactorily. Unification had been the work of a narrow political élite that was deeply suspicious of popular social movements. Radicals could thus feel, with some justification, that Cavour had robbed them of their revolution.

Liberal leaders in united Italy persisted in regarding the democrats of 1848 as a potentially revolutionary threat. Yet they were faced with problems enough at the other end of the political spectrum. Unification had been achieved in the face of fierce opposition from the Church. Not only had Pius IX argued against liberalism and nationalism on doctrinal grounds, he also could not accept the loss of his temporal powers. Problems were exacerbated after 1870 when Rome was finally added to the Italian state. Pius refused to recognize the state. He withdrew to the Vatican, urging Catholics not to involve themselves actively in political life. But the impact of this injunction on the liberal élite was slight. Most of the leading figures were either anticlerical or indifferent to the Church, and even those with religious sympathies (such as Ricasoli and Minghetti) recognized the need for far-reaching reform of the Church. In the longer term, however, serious damage was done to the reception of the state in the country at large. The Church had always remained closer to the ordinary people than had the political élite. Its active hostility to the state (formally ended only in 1929) effectively prevented the emergence of a broad-based conservative party which might have given the regime much-needed stability. Instead political life was conducted on the narrowest of foundations, with leaders feeling themselves unable to respond positively to threats from left or right.

In retrospect it looks clear that the unification of the state involved the imposition of political terms by a narrow élite on a collection of widely diverse cultures and economies. Successive leaders in the early decades, in fact, recognized the fragility of the regime. But instead of seeking to bridge the gulf between the political élite and the wider society, policy and practice served further to isolate the political class.[71] The most urgent task facing the leaders of the new state had always been the creation of a genuine national political culture. Among moderates, D'Azeglio had early recognized that a unified state which failed to reflect the sentiments of the people would be a worthless thing. Yet his was a voice in the wilderness. The conventional wisdom was that a vulnerable state would have to be resolute in its suppression of civil unrest. This authoritarian attitude, however, deepened the afflictions of the regime. In the longer term, with the emergence of ideological movements not amenable to parliamentary control, it was to prove its undoing.

Notes

1   See Gianfranco Miglio, 'Le leghe regionali: il mito della nazione', in his *Il nerbo e le briglie del potere* (Milan, Il Sole 24 Ore, 1988), 303–6; Gianfranco Miglio, 'Toward a federal Italy', *Telos*, 90 (1991–2), 19–42; and Gianfranco Miglio, 'The cultural roots of the federalist revolution', *Telos*, 97 (1993), 33–9.

2   Gianfranco Morra, *Breve storia del pensiero federalista* (Milan, Mondadori, 1993), 65, 71.

3   See Zeffiro Ciuffoletti, *Federalismo e regionalismo: da Cattaneo alla Lega* (Bari, Laterza, 1994).

4   See Giuseppe Galasso, *Italia, nazione difficile. Contributo alla storia politica e culturale dell'Italia unita* (Florence, Le Monnier, 1994).

5   See Vincenzo Gioberti, *Del primato morale e civile degli italiani* (Brussels, Meline-Cans, 1843, 2 vols.); Cesare Balbo, *Delle speranze d'Italia*, ed. Luigi Taroni (Milan, Edizioni Alfa, 1944); and Massimo D'Azeglio, *Degli ultimi casi di Romagna* (Lugano, Tipografia della Svizzera Italiana, 1846).

6   See Alfonso Scirocco, *L'Italia del Risorgimento* (Bologna, Il Mulino, 1990), 29–105.

7   See Renzo de Felice, *Il triennio giacobino in Italia (1796–1799)* (Rome, Bonacci, 1990); and Eluggero Pii, *Il confronto politico in Italia nel decennio 1789–1799* (Florence, Centro Editoriale Toscano, 1992).

8   See Stuart Woolf, *Napoleon's Integration of Europe* (London, Routledge, 1991).

9   See Giorgio Candeloro, *Storia dell'Italia moderna* (Milan, Feltrinelli, 1956–86, 11 vols.), I, 296–311; and Stuart Woolf, *A History of Italy, 1700–1860: The Social Constraints of Political Change* (London,

Methuen, 1979), 197–205.

[10] See Candeloro, *Storia dell'Italia moderna*, I, 326–39; and Woolf, *A History of Italy*, 213–18.

[11] The terms 'patriot' and 'Jacobin' were applied almost indiscriminately to anyone who had been active in the reform or revolutionary movements. Though generally identified with the French cause before 1799, 'patriots' or 'Jacobins' did not share a common ideology or constitute a disciplined political organization. It should certainly not be supposed that they necessarily endorsed the political or philosophical views of the French *Jacobins*.

[12] See Vincenzo Cuoco, *Saggio storico sulla rivoluzione napoletana del 1799*, edited by Fausto Nicolini (Bari, Laterza, 1929). For discussion see Fulvio Tessitore, *Lo storicismo di Vincenzo Cuoco* (Naples, Morano, 1965); Fulvio Tessitore, 'Vincenzo Cuoco tra illuminismo e storicismo', in his *Storicismo e pensiero politico* (Milan and Naples, Riccardo Ricciardi, 1974), 3–40; Fulvio Tessitore, 'Vincenzo Cuoco e le origini del liberalismo moderato', in Giovanni Cherubini et al., eds., *L'Italia giacobina e napoleonica* (Milan, Teti, 1985), 329–69; Benedetto Croce, *Storia del regno di Napoli* (Bari, Laterza, 1965, sixth edition), 217–40; and for Cuoco's place in the wider context of historical thought, B. A. Haddock, *An Introduction to Historical Thought* (London, Edward Arnold, 1980), 90–105.

[13] See Cuoco, *Saggio storico*, 121–7.

[14] Vincenzo Cuoco, *Scritti vari*, edited by N. Cortese and F. Nicolini (Bari, Laterza, 1924, 2 vols.), I, 4.

[15] See ibid., I, 45–52, 78–80, 103–8, 109–11, 125–9, 134–44.

[16] See Vincenzo Cuoco, *Platone in Italia*, edited by Fausto Nicolini (Bari, Laterza, 1924, 2 vols.).

[17] See Cuoco, *Scritti vari*, II, 3–122.

[18] See Buonarroti's own account of the conspiracy and its justification in Filippo Buonarroti, *Conspiration pour l'égalité dite de Babeuf*, edited by Gastone Manacorda (Turin, Einaudi, 1982). For wider discussion see A. Saitta, *Filippo Buonarroti. Contributo alla storia della sua vita e del suo pensiero* (Rome, Edizioni di Storia e Letteratura, 1950–1, 2 vols.).

[19] See Filippo Buonarroti, 'Riflessi sul governo federativo applicato all'Italia', in Franco Della Peruta, ed., *Giuseppe Mazzini e i democratici* (Milan and Naples, Riccardo Ricciardi, 1969), 188–94.

[20] Ibid., 193.

[21] Ibid.

[22] See ibid., 190.

[23] See Candeloro, *Storia dell'Italia moderna*, I, 94.

[24] See Melchiorre Gioia, *Quale dei governi liberi meglio convenga all'Italia*, edited by Carlo Morandi (Bologna, Zanichelli, 1947). The French model is also endorsed in Matteo Angelo Galdi, *Necessità di stabilire una repubblica in Italia*, edited by Valentino Cecchetti (Rome, Salerno, 1994), where the international context is stressed.

[25] See Candeloro, *Storia dell'Italia moderna*, I, 281.

[26] See Carlo Ghisalberti, *Unità nazionale e unificazione giuridica in Italia*

(Bari, Laterza, 1979), 212-15.
27 See Luigi Ambrosoli, 'La restaurazione e gli stati italiani', in Giovanni Cherubini et al., eds., *Il movimento nazionale e il 1848* (Milan, Teti, 1986), 13-44; Candeloro, *Storia dell'Italia moderna*, II, 7-73; and Woolf, *A History of Italy*, 229-46.
28 See Denis Mack Smith, ed., *The Making of Italy, 1796-1870* (London, Macmillan, 1968), 35.
29 V. Branca, ed., *Il Conciliatore, foglio scientifico-letterario* (Florence, Le Monnier, 1948-54, 3 vols.), I, 4, 6. For discussion see K. R. Greenfield, *Economics and Liberalism in the Risorgimento: A Study of Nationalism in Lombardy, 1814-1848* (Baltimore, Johns Hopkins University Press, 1965, revised edition), 150-7; and Candeloro, *Storia dell'Italia moderna*, II, 31-40.
30 See, for example, Branca, ed., *Il Conciliatore, foglio scientifico-letterario*, I, 238-43, 284-9, 374-5; II, 37-41, 46-9, 426-34, 460-9, 726-31; III, 71-5, 207-11, 249-59, 268-73, 347-9, 370-8.
31 See ibid., I, 359-63, 376-85, 391-405, 406-7, 421-5, 441-6.
32 See ibid., III, 3-10, 340-7, 448-57.
33 Ibid., III, 343.
34 See ibid., III, 347.
35 See J. C. L. Simonde de Sismondi, *Storia delle repubbliche italiane del Medio Evo* (Capolago, Tipografia Elvetica, 1817-18, 16 vols.); and the review by P. Borsieri in Branca, ed., *Il Conciliatore, foglio scientifico-letterario*, vol. I, 223-34.
36 Ibid., 233.
37 See, in particular, Carlo Cattaneo, 'La città considerata come principio ideale delle istorie italiane', in Ernest Sestan, ed., *Opere di Giandomenico Romagnosi, Carlo Cattaneo, Giuseppe Ferrari* (Milan and Naples, Riccardo Ricciardi, 1957), 997-1040.
38 See Alessandro Manzoni, 'Osservazioni sulla morale cattolica', in Giuseppe Lesca, ed., *Tutte le opere di Alessandro Manzoni* (Florence, Barbera, 1928), 93-225.
39 See ibid., 105-22.
40 See Ugo Foscolo, 'Dello scopo di Gregorio VII', in *Edizione nazionale delle opere di Ugo Foscolo*, vol. VII, edited by Emilio Santini (Florence, Le Monnier, 1933), 381-401.
41 See Vincenzo Gioberti, *Del primato morale e civile degli italiani* (Capolago, Tipografia Elvetica, 1844, second edition); and for discussion Bruce Haddock, 'Political union without social revolution: Vincenzo Gioberti's *Primato*', *Historical Journal*, 41 (1998), 705-23.
42 See Francesco Salfi, *L'Italie au dix-neuvième siècle* (Paris, Dufart, 1821), 13.
43 See ibid., 108-18 and 150.
44 See Luigi Angeloni, 'Della forza nelle cose politiche', in Franco della Peruta, ed., *Giuseppe Mazzini e i democratici*, 34.
45 See ibid., 33.
46 See Candeloro, *Storia dell'Italia moderna*, II, 147-55.

47   See Greenfield, *Economics and Liberalism in the Risorgimento*, 158–98.
48   See Raffaele Ciampini, *Gian Pietro Vieusseux. I suoi viaggi, i suoi giornali, i suoi amici* (Turin, Einaudi, 1953), 182–229.
49   See *Antologia*, 7 (1822), 72–84; and *Antologia*, 10 (1823), B51–79 and C111–36.
50   See Francesco Forti, review of Lazzaro Papi, *Commentarii della Rivoluzione Francese dalla morte di Luigi XVI sino al ristauramento de' Borboni sul trono di Francia, Antologia* 41 (1831), B88–112.
51   See Francesco Forti, 'Dell'utile riordinamento delle storie municipali', *Antologia*, 45 (1832), A77–89.
52   See Francesco Forti, review of F. Kortum, *Dell'origine delle confederazioni libere, Antologia* 45 (1832), B132–3.
53   See G. P. Vieusseux, *Frammenti sull'Italia nel 1822, e progetto di confederazione* (Florence, Tipografia Galileiana, 1848).
54   See J. M. Roberts, *The Mythology of the Secret Societies* (London, Secker & Warburg, 1972); Woolf, *A History of Italy*, 252–5; and Harry Hearder, *Italy in the Age of the Risorgimento* (London, Longman, 1983), 176–8.
55   Giuseppe Mazzini, *Note autobiografiche*, edited by Mario Menghini (Florence, Le Monnier, 1943), 14. For full discussion of biography see Denis Mack Smith, *Mazzini* (New Haven, Yale University Press, 1994); Luigi Ambrosoli, *Giuseppe Mazzini. Una vita per l'unità d'Italia* (Rome, Piero Lacaita Editore, 1993); and Pietro Barbieri, *Vita e identità di Giuseppe Mazzini* (Milan, Editrice Italia Letteraria, 1984).
56   See Giuseppe Mazzini, 'Manifesto della *Giovine Italia*' and 'Istruzione generale per gli affratellati nella *Giovine Italia*', in his *Scritti editi ed inediti*, edited by L. Rava et al. (98 vols., Imola, Galeati, 1906–40), vol. II. For discussion see Bruce Haddock, 'State and nation in Mazzini's political thought', *History of Political Thought*, 20 (1999), 313–36.
57   See Carlo Cattaneo, *Carlo Cattaneo, 'Il Politecnico', 1839–44*, edited by L. Ambrosoli (Turin, Bollati Boringhieri, 1989, 2 vols.); and for discussion N. Bobbio, *Una filosofia militante. Studi su Carlo Cattaneo* (Turin, Einaudi, 1971); G. Armani, *Carlo Cattaneo. Il padre del federalismo italiano* (Milan, Garzanti, 1997); Clara M. Lovett, *Carlo Cattaneo and the Politics of the Risorgimento* (The Hague, Martinus Nijhoff, 1972); Martin Thom, 'City, region and nation: Carlo Cattaneo and the making of Italy', *Citizenship Studies*, 3 (1999), 187–201; and Martin Thom, 'Unity and confederation in the Italian Risorgimento: the case of Carlo Cattaneo', in Stefan Berger, Mark Donovan and Kevin Passmore, eds., *Writing National Histories: Western Europe since 1800* (London, Routledge, 1999), 69–81.
58   See Giuseppe Ferrari, 'La révolution et les réformes en Italie', *Revue des Deux Mondes*, 16 November 1844, 573–614 and 1 January 1845, 150–94. For discussion see Clara M. Lovett, *Giuseppe Ferrari and the Italian Revolution* (Chapel Hill, University of North Carolina Press, 1979).
59   Gioberti, *Del primato morale e civile degli italiani*, I, 165.

60 Ibid., 177.
61 See note 5 above.
62 For analysis from various perspectives see Giovanni Cherubini et al., eds., *Il movimento nazionale e il 1848* (Milan, Teti, 1986).
63 See Carlo Cattaneo, 'L'insurrezione di Milano nel 1848' and 'Considerazioni sulle cose d'Italia nel 1848', in his *Il 1848 in Italia. Scritti 1848–51*, edited by Delia Castelnuovo Frigessi (Turin, Einaudi, 1972).
64 See Giuseppe Ferrari, *Filosofia della rivoluzione* (Capolago, Tipografia Elvetica, 1851).
65 See Giuseppe Ferrari, *La federazione repubblicana* (Capolago, Tipografia Elvetica, 1851).
66 See R. Marshall, *Massimo d'Azeglio: An Artist in Politics* (London, Oxford University Press, 1966).
67 See Denis Mack Smith, *Cavour* (London, Weidenfeld & Nicolson, 1985); Rosario Romeo, *Vita di Cavour* (Bari, Laterza, 1990); and Rosario Romeo, *Cavour e il suo tempo* (Bari, Laterza, 1969–84, 3 vols.).
68 See Raymond Grew, *A Sterner Plan for Italian Unity: The Italian National Society in the Risorgimento* (Princeton, Princeton University Press, 1963).
69 For detailed discussion see Denis Mack Smith, *Cavour and Garibaldi 1860: A Study in Political Conflict* (Cambridge, Cambridge University Press, 1954); and Denis Mack Smith, *Victor Emmanuel, Cavour and the Risorgimento* (Oxford, Oxford University Press, 1971).
70 See Antonio Gramsci, *Il Risorgimento* (Turin, Einaudi, 1949).
71 The problem is most dramatically evident in relation to the 'southern question'. See Lucy Riall, *Sicily and the Unification of Italy: Liberal Policy and Local Power, 1859–1866* (Oxford, Oxford University Press, 1998).

2

A patriotic disaster: the Messina–Reggio Calabria earthquake of 1908

JOHN DICKIE

Introduction

On 28 December 1908, at just after 5.20 a.m., an extremely violent earthquake, with its epicentre in the middle of the Straits of Messina, struck the coastal cities of Reggio Calabria and Messina, and the villages and towns around them. The fact that the majority of the population were indoors maximized its lethal effect. The architectural lessons of the quakes since 1783 had not been heeded: many buildings were built of fragile materials, upper storeys had been added on without reinforcement to those below, and many structures had been weakened by the quakes of 1905 and 1907.

Thirty to forty seconds of violent tremors were followed, some ten minutes later, by a tsunami comprising at least three waves which reached a height of between two and three metres above sea level in the port of Messina. The destructive force of these waves can be judged from the fact that they broke down the gate of the dry dock and pulled the vessel out from the basin; the ship was then wrecked nearby. At Pellaro on the Calabrian coast the sea destroyed the town and moved an iron bridge over thirty metres.[1] Although there were no major fires in the aftermath of the quake in Reggio, fire immediately broke out in five areas of Messina.[2] Giuseppe Mercalli calculated that 98 per cent of the buildings in the city were destroyed or so badly damaged that they had to be demolished.

To this day, no one knows beyond a very approximate measure how many victims there were. The Messina municipal archive was completely destroyed. The census information which is the only basis for many calculations dates from 1901.[3] During the days following, the figure of 200,000 victims was often cited. In his detailed report to the Italian Geographical Society, based on research carried out in January and February 1909, Mario Baratta gave an estimate of 50,000 deaths, whilst making it clear that he thought that his figure was, in all likelihood, an underestimate. Modern historians tend to plump for figures between 80,000 and 100,000. Even the lowest of all these numbers is enough to make the 1908 earthquake equal with the worst natural disaster of all time in the Italian peninsula (equal, that is, with the 1693 Sicilian quake). Some estimates make it one of the four or five worst disasters in the world in the twentieth century.[4]

What the disaster did produce was a movement of patriotic sympathy and solidarity on a scale unprecedented in Italy. Volunteers from across the country journeyed southwards to help with the rescue and rebuilding efforts. Others sheltered refugees and orphans. The king and queen joined in the effort. Special issues of newspapers and magazines disappeared from the kiosks as quickly as they arrived. As the *Corriere della Sera* commented on 2 January 1909,

> newspapers are never more at one with what is ardent and vital in the people's soul, than in moments like this. . . . And it is not the damage that we are examining, but ourselves, the hundred variations of our anguish from hour to hour, from bulletin to bulletin, from one conjecture to the next . . .[5]

Civic committees were set up across the country to gather and direct funds and other contributions. Existing bodies within civil society – rifle, automobile and cycling clubs, mutual aid societies, congregations, choral societies, groups of workers, apprentices and school children – organized benefit events and collections.[6] First-hand accounts by those involved in the rescue effort tell how it transcended bitter political divisions between Catholics and Socialists.[7]

These aid efforts were thought of overwhelmingly in patriotic, rather than, say, humanitarian terms. For example, the near-coincidence of the catastrophe with the fiftieth anniversary of the events of 1859 was not lost on public opinion. Milan council gave the funds set aside to celebrate the anniversary to the victims. In Rome, a 'plebiscite of pain' was held on 3 January 1909: citizens deposited their offerings in tricolour-wrapped 'ballot boxes' and signed registers of condolence. The event was repeated in Milan a few days later. For some contemporaries the movement of patriotic solidarity with the stricken zones was unprecedented, and proof that an Italian nation had been made.

Given the extent of the destruction and the huge number of deaths caused by the earthquake, tidal waves and fires, it is hardly surprising that contemporary witnesses and commentators frequently compared the events of 1908–9 to a war. The corpse-strewn city of Messina was frequently likened to a battlefield:

> On the sea, amongst the ships offering help, and on land amid the stench, the wailing and the ruins, one has the impression of being on a battlefield after an incalculable defeat. It would be no less a disaster if Italy had lost half its army in war.[8]

The fact that the army was the major instrument with which the state responded to the emergency reinforced the parallel. Such comparisons had particular meanings in the tense international climate of the time. The earthquake was a convincing picture of the *kind* of war that the Italians were expecting in Europe, involving the destruction of civilian buildings and lives on a huge scale through massive artillery bombardment. Memories of the Russo-Japanese war of 1904–5 were fresh: interviewed for *La Stampa* late on the evening of 2 January 1909, Giolitti compared the task of clearing the ruined city of Messina to the aftermath of Mukden. Luigi Barzini's immensely popular exclusive reports from China in the *Corriere della Sera* had interpreted this first great industrial war as a test of national character in which the Japanese underdog had won out through the self-abnegating courage of its officers and men. Accordingly, the catastrophe of 1908 was widely viewed as a test of individual mettle and national unity.

My research is at too early a stage to make any ambitious claims about the patriotic disaster's longer-term significance. (It is, for example, worth testing the hypothesis that the public reaction constituted something like a dress rehearsal for the First World War.) Here my interest is in the Messina–Reggio Calabria earthquake as an opportunity for an experiment in the historical study of national identity. I will use some of the material thrown up by the catastrophe to develop arguments I have outlined elsewhere for a particular understanding of national identity.[9] 'National identity' – Italian or otherwise – is most fruitfully understood to refer to the forms of individual and collective selfhood that are constructed as an integral moment of social relationships. What is national about these identities is that they are created as meanings are given to a range of ambiguous, politically contested and socially prized terms such as 'nation', 'identity' and 'Italy'. Of course these meanings are socially real in the sense that they shape how social actors influence and are influenced by the world around them.

Part one of my article uses some very simple examples to set out this model of national identity in greater detail. But this illustration of a method is also conceived of as a polemic against two tendencies in historical work on Italian national identity. The first – glibly metahistorical – involves reifying national identity by thinking of it as the abiding, typical features of a society that are left over when change and conflict are subtracted. The second – fixated on 'lacks', 'delays', 'failures' and 'divisions' – involves conceiving of 'nation' as an ideal of social homogeneity towards which societies are supposed to move or from which they are deemed to deviate.

Although not a single scholarly article has ever been devoted to the widespread patriotic reaction to the earthquake of 1908, it is one of the two aspects of the disaster which are always recorded in general histories of Giolittian Italy (the other being the delays, inefficiencies, political battles and spoils-taking which characterized the reconstruction). In part, the lack of interest in Italy's first great national movement of solidarity derives from what Piero Bevilacqua has termed a 'denial' of earthquakes as a topic of historical analysis.[10] For all its subsequent social components, an earthquake has no social trigger. This discontinuous nature does not square easily with the mindset of a historiography on the lookout for chains of human cause and effect or for social phenomena that are typical rather than exceptional. Moreover, as Augusto Placanica has suggested, the almost universal association of the earthquake with dramatic transformation, with an overturning of the state of things, and the almost equally widespread failure of those expectations to bear fruit in the aftermath of real disasters have contributed to the relative inconspicuousness of earthquakes in the corpus of history writing on Italy.[11]

It is always a speculative exercise trying to explain why something has *not* been studied, but it seems likely that we also owe the historiographical neglect of the patriotic efforts of 1908–9 to the limitations of prevalent ways of thinking about nations and national identity. The public response to the disaster seems only too easy to contextualize and explain away. Existing secondary accounts argue, plausibly enough, that the patriotic response to the earthquake

highlights the developments during the Giolittian era in the nationalization and politicization of the masses. In line with a more
interventionist approach to social issues generally, it was during the
first decade of the twentieth century that the state first took it upon
itself to step in on a massive scale after natural disasters. On such
occasions, the Giolittian state was putting itself up for examination
before an increasingly large, literate and politicized public opinion.
The disaster also focused patriotic attention on what were thought of
as weaknesses and imbalances in the fabric of the nation, notably the
increasing divisions between north and south following the season of
rapid growth in the industrial triangle.

The way the government managed the disaster area by imposing
martial law has also been read (not entirely justifiably in my view)
as yet another example of the liberal state's authoritarian face, and
of the mutual hostility between citizen and state.[12] The struggle to
augment and control the resources allocated for reconstruction
throws up other characteristic features of Italian society: the clientelistic basis of power at a local level, and the uneasy distribution of
power between centre and periphery.[13] It would also be easy to
argue that the patriotic solidarity expressed in the weeks following
the catastrophe was superficial and transitory: the real and irreconcilable antagonisms between Italy's political cultures re-emerged
quickly enough in the vicious dispute over the upbringing of the
many earthquake orphans, for example. The Catholic daily *Corriere
d'Italia* – just to give a flavour of the way the debate was conducted
– accused the government of complicity in the 'moral prostitution'
of orphans to Waldensian 'heretics'.[14]

It may seem, in short, that the earthquake only tells us what we
already know about Giolittian Italy. It would not be difficult to set
the catastrophe of 1908 in context and use it as a particularly
dramatic example of some of the canonical issues in early twentieth-
century Italian history. There has been a recent trend to re-describe
issues of this kind – diverse political cultures, the economic imbal-
ance between north and south, the clientelistic brokerage of money
and power, mistrust between 'legal Italy' and 'real Italy' – in terms
of 'nation-building' or 'national identity', whether in relation to the
Giolittian period or the whole of post-unification history. My own
view is that, as they are conventionally used, these terms do very
little to clarify the issues. Not only is there notoriously little agreement over what they actually mean, they also have an inbuilt bias

towards a judgemental, dualistic view of the world. It is for this reason that my article is *not* a study of the national or regional 'identity' of southern society, or indeed of the southern problem seen as a structural weakness in 'national identity'.

Historians' curiosity about the events of 1908–9 has perhaps also been blunted by the assumption that such widespread sympathy with one's fellow nationals is merely a natural response, as exceptional in its apolitical unanimity as the earthquake itself is in its violence. The outburst of patriotic sympathy seems an ephemeral product of deeper changes which should be the real focus of the historian's attention. It is impossible to describe a phenomenon like nationalism without resorting to the vocabulary of sensibility: pride, love, shame, nostalgia, fear. Yet in this instance as in others historians seem not just to be reluctant to study feelings, but also sceptical about the very possibility of understanding them outside of the frame of reference provided by a naturalistic psychology.

To understand the events of 1908–9, we need a greater sensitivity to the symbolic and anthropological problems that underlie the emotional reaction to the catastrophe. An understanding of national identity along the lines I have suggested can help make such episodes as the patriotic aftermath of the earthquake newly available for historical study. Whether or not it had longer-term effects, the response to the disaster was a far more complex process than an outpouring of collective grief and sympathy. If we are to understand national belonging, we need to shed our habit of thinking that politics happens when emotion ends and rational calculation begins.

To these ends, in the next part of my article, I outline a way of understanding the cultural consequences of disaster as a symbolic crisis. In the last part I carry out a study of one localized aspect of the patriotic response to the earthquake-related symbolic crisis of 1908–9. The many images of the nation which were generated in the earthquake's aftermath are both responses to and symptoms of that crisis.

Some aspects of patriotic emotion

Nationalism can be thought of as a loose set of languages that modern societies use to think about a whole range of social and anthropological problems such as political legitimacy, solidarity, conflict, time, death and outsiders. On this reading, a national identity does *not* comprise a putative underlying culture, mentality or memory gradually sedimented out from contingent events (such as great calamities). Instead identities are an integral part of the way those contingent events are lived out socially, and then remembered in changing and contradictory ways. Nationalist discourses, like many other languages, are used to manage events, and to construct often conflicting identities around them.

A simple example from the time of the catastrophe – so simple and so typical of disaster response in modern societies that its significance is easy to overlook – is the fact that on all sides the Messina–Reggio earthquake was seen as a disaster affecting the *nation*. More than the dead and their families, or the regions concerned, it was the nation that was the victim. This view was common to many sides of Giolittian Italy's divided political domain. Socialist Filippo Turati can refer on 1 January to 'the tremendous loss that has struck the *patria*'.[15] Another Socialist, Claudio Treves, expresses the same thing in bodily terms: 'the body of the *patria* has been mutilated; it has lost two of its provinces.'[16]

Such tropes have several effects that make them more than just a convenient short-hand denotation of common emotions. Firstly, they have a gently coercive force. What if one's primary reaction to the disaster were anger, indifference or morbid fascination? On one level, public assertions like 'the nation is in mourning' try to make such feelings illegitimate, unpatriotic. (On another level, these statements may amount to concessions to collective piety that buy the right for less legitimate emotions to be indulged.)

Secondly, Turati's and Treves's platitudes make grief a public matter. When one makes the claim that grief is shared, it is often a way of acquiring the kind of stake in that grief which is necessary to orchestrate the emotion, to make political use of it.

Thirdly, these statements beg the question of what *patria* is used to mean. Doubtless Turati's and Treves's nation was a very different beast from the country imagined by conservatives or Catholics. The two Socialists are making a bid to be included in the political mainstream, and at the same time to shift the mainstream their way.

Each of these effects is implicitly boundary-creating. Each instantly defines an imagined community, an identity for those who, for example, share a sense of the right way to express grief, subscribe to the right implied meanings of *patria*, and agree on the right political programme. Thus there is not one national identity in Italy, but a theoretically limitless multiplicity of them. They are generated as an integral moment of a social activity like reacting to a major disaster. Of course no identity of this kind can be created outside the power relationships in a social context. But then neither could any of the great social collectivities such as classes and parties exist without a massive and continuous discursive labour of identity construction.

Patriotic utterances use the language of the *general* interest to define the boundaries of a *particular* social identity. Therein lies a great deal of their political force. Nationalist discourse (I use the term synonymously with patriotism) also inscribes those boundaries in a normative sensibility, a prescribed pattern of emotion. The frontiers of a given patriotic identity can be *felt*. For this reason there is no way of deciding *a priori* on the particular mixture of Machiavellian political intention, learned political *fiuto* and 'genuine' emotion which lies behind statements like those by Turati and Treves. Patriotic emotions have their own system of calculation, their own language. Like other feelings, patriotism is inseparable from ways of talking about emotion, from customs and norms that govern the appropriate forms of expression for those feelings. The concept of nation is at home as part of the interpersonal dimension of grief, and in the politics of the public pronouncement.

The anthropology of catastrophe

Great earthquakes present society with great symbolic challenges. They are, to use Ernesto De Martino's terms, metaphors of a 'permanent cultural risk'.[17] Disastrous earthquakes concretize a fear of anomie; that fear is one of the motors of culture itself, it is inseparable from it.

Although, in percentage terms, the death toll in some of the Calabrian villages was the worst, Messina was the largest and most densely populated area to be destroyed on 28 December 1908: some two-thirds of all the victims died in the city. Its ruined streets became the dominant image of the effects of the disaster. Railway and telegraph communications were destroyed. Newspaper readers were presented with terrifying scenes: thousands of dead bodies were scattered over and under the rubble; semi-naked survivors fought over scraps of food; looters roamed the ruins.

The urban aftermath of the 1908 earthquake was seen as a return to a state of nature. It was a scene where instincts had won out over reason: 'Nature's cruelty has unleashed the base instincts of the human beast' (Giuseppe Piazza).[18] There had been a sudden and headlong fall into barbarism: 'The survivors? . . . They are human creatures who have gone back through the centuries, moved far away in space' (Goffredo Bellonci).[19] The disaster was a flattener of social hierarchies: 'a catastrophe that brought the mighty level with the humble, just as it made palaces level with hovels' (Luigi Ambrosini).[20] 'The social fabric, like the houses, disintegrates under the impact of the earthquake' (Leonida Bissolati);[21] it was 'the absolute end of every human relationship: property, kinship, citizenship, the end of everything' (Paolo Scarfoglio).[22] Individual psychology had capsized, crumpled or shattered: 'The overpowering nervous shock has blown and broken people's nerves just as an overstrong electrical current blows and breaks the carbon wires in electric lamps' (Paolo Scarfoglio).[23] Messina was a hell on earth, or 'the vision of the Apocalypse . . . become a reality before our eyes' (Vittorio Emanuele Orlando).[24] The social order was not just changed or threatened, but inverted: 'normality is death. There is a complete overturning of values: life is nothing any more' (Luigi Barzini).[25] 'Down there, man is not the man of our anthropology' (Claudio Treves).[26]

These motifs are versions of the stock human response to disaster. More than just symptoms of a crisis, they are in part also the first stage in the reconstruction process. By representing the earthquake as a spectacle at the symbolic antipodes of normality (rather than being merely a transformation of reality like others), these negative pictures helped fix a simple, positive image of the kind of situation that people's thoughts and actions should be directed towards re-establishing. Catastrophes release society's useful nightmares.

Apocalyptic representations of this kind also limit options and create boundaries around a space of social consensus: one is either working towards the collective good, or one is an agent of destruction. By invoking the seemingly pre-political metaphors of social order, earthquakes call into question the sources of political legitimacy.

In addition, in the aftermath of the 1908 disaster, a whole series of concerns which are normally the province of ritual, custom and kinship set in a private, familial or local context – such as death, grief, odour, food, parenting, cleanliness, shame and the sacred – were suddenly set loose in the public arena. The earthquake put into doubt the boundaries between what is public or political and what is not.

Through the press, these images of a generalized symbolic crisis in the disaster area were projected across the national domain, they became a national problem. The earthquake seemed to show the real nature of a people, or of people in general: 'in these moments of extreme crisis, in the space of a few hours a people shows all the good and all the evil that it has within it: cruelty, greed, selfishness, devotion and heroism come out into the open' (Luigi Barzini).[27] The disaster area became highly semiotically charged: every scene became a symbol, every anecdote the encapsulation of a wider truth, every person a personification; the earthquake became the most important source of potential clues on the state of the nation as a whole.

A blue dress and cap: Queen Elena in Messina

The royals visit the disaster area

At 1.30 p.m. on 29 December 1908, with newspaper headlines speaking of thousands of victims in the earthquake zone, of fires, and of a complete breakdown in law and order in Messina, the king and queen, accompanied by the justice minister, Vittorio Emanuele Orlando, set off southwards in a special train from Rome. At 9 the next morning, the royal couple arrived in Messina by ship from Naples. At about the same time, the first special correspondents sent by the Italian press also arrived. The king toured the ruins both in Messina and in Reggio. He telegraphed his impressions to the government, and received petitions from survivors. His bouts of weeping were widely reported. The ruins were considered too dangerous for Victor Emmanuel's Montenegran wife Elena to visit. Instead, she moved between the various ships gathering in the shattered harbour of the Sicilian port. On 31 December, she spent time on a battleship named after her which was being used as a hospital. Dressed in a modest dark blue dress and matching cap, she undertook nursing tasks. The royals returned to Rome on 3 January, the same day as the issuing of a royal decree which appointed Lieutenant

General Mazza as plenipotentiary in the disaster area and established martial law.

The Savoyard royal family was of course not new to this kind of public role during disasters. King Umberto's visits to Ischia after the earthquake of July 1883, and even more his efforts during the Neapolitan cholera epidemic of the following year, had helped establish disaster response as one of the central public functions of the royal family in post-unification Italy. As a young prince, Victor Emmanuel is reported to have given his savings to the victims of the Ischia earthquake. The monarchy had for a long time also been conceived of as an appropriate hegemonic instrument in the 'less developed' polity of the south: the House of Savoy sought to step into the shoes of the Bourbons and appeal to the 'impressionability' of the southern masses.

What is striking about the royal reaction to the 1908 catastrophe is the extraordinary success of Queen Elena's visit. Her nursing the injured on board the *Regina Elena* became the most widespread patriotic image of the earthquake's aftermath. By comparison, the figure of the king seems almost marginal. One can sense a certain doubt, in the innumerable newspaper and magazine accounts in which the actions of the royal couple are juxtaposed, about what the king was actually supposed to be doing in the earthquake zone. The image of him as dynamically co-ordinating the rescue effort sat uneasily with his tears. Still today, the only monument commemorating the 1908 disaster in Messina is Antonio Berti's statue of Queen Elena, inaugurated in 1960 following a newspaper subscription.

'Umili preghiere'

The popular impact of the figure of Queen Elena in the earthquake's aftermath is beyond doubt, as is the extent to which the state lent its efforts to exploiting the queen's hold on the popular imagination. Amongst the papers of the Central Committee set up by Giolitti to co-ordinate the relief effort are hundreds and hundreds of telegrams requesting help which were received by the royal family's private telegraph office following a return visit to the stricken areas of Calabria in early May 1909.[28] These messages make relentlessly repetitive reading: in the passage from dialect into Italian, and from Italian into the untranslatable, staccato formulae of the telegram, one loses all but glimpses of the real social and psychological texture of life in the disaster's aftermath, and of the survival strategies adopted: 'sofferenze inaudite', 'giacente lastrico', 'languente miseria', 'umile preghiera'.

The vast majority of these petitions are addressed to the queen, and a smaller, but still substantial majority – very roughly 85 per cent – are from women. Their telegrams speak of childbirth amidst the ruins and of hungry children. But almost as insistently, they invoke the loss of sewing machines, and even more, of bedlinen as emblems of 'squallida miseria': bedlinen was of course the most common form of dowry, the price of a daughter's access to the marriage market, and the only property married women possessed. These messages give very little idea of the image of the queen which the earthquake survivors had created: they are inevitably limited to codified appeals to her 'august heart'.

The handling of these telegrams required a considerable administrative effort. They were transcribed by the staff of the royal telegraph office and forwarded to the Central Relief Committee, who forwarded them to the prefect, who in turn asked the *carabinieri* on the ground for individual, face-to-face confirmation of the claims made: their observations were recorded in a log. Sums of around 100–200 lire were then distributed to the people – a clear majority of those presenting petitions – who proved to be in genuine hardship.

What the state was doing amounts to sanctioning a 'charismatic', personalized form of mediation between the people and the state through the figure of the queen. Clearly part of the function of this personalized channel was to compensate, both materially and ideologically, for the failings of the rescue and rebuilding effort. (The first violent disturbances involving survivors still without shelter were reported within a month of the earthquake in Delianova, Calabria.) Nevertheless, these telegrams remain as cryptic as they are moving. They illustrate once again the difficulties of getting a grasp on the quality of popular patriotism in the absence of a sufficient bulk of textual evidence.

Ermine and bandages
The queen's actions also struck a chord amongst patriotic public opinion. Pictures of the queen on board the *Regina Elena*, and even of her tending the wounded amidst the ruins of Messina – which, of course, she had not done – were published in all the major illustrated

magazines. On 5 January 1909, the pro-government Roman news-paper *La Tribuna* published an interview with the navy minister, Vice Admiral Carlo Mirabello. Mirabello was a man under consid-erable pressure. In the immediate aftermath of the earthquake, the formidable Sicilian parliamentarian Napoleone Colajanni had made it his task to call Mirabello to account for delays in the navy's response to the catastrophe. Mirabello responded to Colajanni's crit-icisms, and went on to issue particular praise for the queen's work as a nurse. He tells the story – destined to become one of the most famous anecdotes of the catastrophe's aftermath – of the queen's being knocked over and slightly injured by a hysterical patient who had attempted to flee the ship following an aftershock. According to *La Tribuna*'s interviewer, Tullio Giordana, Mirabello could not finish the story, overcome as he was by emotion.

> The minister falls silent . . . Once again, around his ship, he sees the marvellous city in ruins; he can still hear the groans of the injured as they wail and wail, ceaselessly. Still before his eyes he can see the queen's mouth red with blood – the queen's body too bears the same wound that has lacerated Italy.[29]

The political purposes of this little cameo are evident enough: they are part of an attempt to make criticism of the government seem unpatriotic and tasteless at a time of national mourning. But even if the incident is cannily presented – and even, indeed, if the admiral's moment of overpowering emotion is entirely invented – the inter-view nonetheless gives us a sense of the symbolic power of this particular image of Queen Elena, of the lump in the country's collec-tive throat that the incident seems to have provoked. I want to devote some space to attempting to unravel the various strands that go to explain the success that Queen Elena's actions had in giving shape to the patriotic reaction to the disaster to the extent that – as here – the queen's body becomes a metaphor for the nation as a whole.

As the symbolic importance of the queen-as-nurse developed in the days following the earthquake, so the tale of her exploits grew in the telling. According to a brief report in *La Tribuna* on 1 January, the king's consort had spent about four hours on board the *Regina Elena* the previous day. In a dispatch sent to Giolitti on the night of 31 December, Orlando described her as having personally tended to 'more than a hundred' injured survivors.[30] In an interview published in the *Corriere della Sera* on 4 January, Orlando claimed that she had bandaged more than 200 people.[31] On 10 January, the *Domenica del Corriere* accompanied its illustrations of the royals at the scene of the catastrophe with the claim that she had swathed nearly 300 survivors.

Almost without exception, newspaper reports and subsequent eulogistic re-evocations of the queen's role have as their central theme the humility of her actions and particularly of her dress. The *Corriere della Sera* reported her as being 'dressed like a worker' or as wearing 'a very poor dress, like a woman of the people'. On his return to Rome, Orlando spoke to Tullio Giordana of how the queen had held a patient's legs during an operation. The interviewee is again most moved when he tells of the queen's work as a nurse, and again stresses that this work has involved her renouncing some of the habitual symbols of her status: 'those aching legs, soiled with blood, resting on shoulders used to being covered with ermine'.[32]

Through Orlando's comments after his return to Rome we can also trace the formation of a myth of the queen's anonymity during her time on board the *Regina Elena*. As Orlando remarked, 'She was not known, and did not wish to make herself known as the queen, and so many women thought she was an ordinary nurse.'[33] This is a theme which is re-evoked repeatedly in the subsequent days and weeks. For example, on 24 January, Treves's *Illustrazione Popolare* published a poem, 'Il gran cuore' ('The great heart') by Luisa Pirani Barozzi, which describes the scenes on board the hospital ship and reports the actions of an unidentified female figure who shows an all-encompassing sympathy for the suffering of the victims. The last two stanzas run as follows:

> E i mesti tra loro chiesero:
> – Chi è mai questa Donna divina? –
> Qualcuno sapea, ma a quei miseri
> Non disse: – *La nostra Regina!* –
>
> E allor tra i fanciulli e le vergini,
> Tra i vecchi dall'anima affranta,
> S'alzò come un inno di gloria:
> – Fratelli, fratelli, è una Santa –[34]

(And the sad ones there asked, / 'Who could this divine Lady be?' / Someone knew the answer, but did not tell / those poor folk, '*Our Queen*!'

And so, from the boys and maidens, / from the disheartened old men, / there arose, like a hymn of glory, / 'Brothers, brothers, she is a Saint'.)

Immediately following her return to Rome, the queen and the press put the symbolic capital accumulated on board the *Regina Elena* to work. The queen turned the throne room in the Quirinale into a sewing workshop where local seamstresses, ladies-in-waiting and the queen's own daughters mingled as they made clothes for the survivors. According again to the *Corriere della Sera*'s report, 'the queen immediately sought to make all social distance between her person and those women of the people disappear.'[35] The scenes in the throne room were again widely shown in the illustrated magazines.

Both of these tales – emphasizing alternately the queen's anonymity and her humility – borrow something from the traditional fables of monarchs passing unnoticed amongst their people (fables which are in turn related to popular Christian stories of Jesus in disguise). Such tales stage a relegitimation of royal authority. The naturalness of the monarch's exalted station is reasserted following a temporary suspension of the hierarchical distance between the crown and the people. The *humility* of the queen's actions as represented in the press can be seen as a lay, patriotic version of the penitential strategies adopted over many centuries by rulers whose religiously sanctioned authority had come into question following a divinely inspired calamity. The scenario of the queen's *anonymity* is also part of a well-known mechanism of pathos. The people who are the objects of the queen's gesture, and putatively the objects of the public's patriotic sympathy, are ignorant of the gesture's real meaning and the sympathy's source. The onlooker, like Mirabello or Orlando, or the reader of the many reports on the queen's actions, is thus invited to supply the missing meaning, the missing sentimental content, and to emote in the place of the survivors. These sentiments – in part vicarious – are stronger because of the imaginative work which goes into them.

The Messina–Reggio earthquake, like many disasters before it, puts into circulation some powerful metaphors of chaos, and particularly of the upsetting or levelling of social hierarchies. The image of the queen – simultaneously lowly and elevated, secret and widely proclaimed – serves to incorporate those threatening metaphors into something more like a traditional narrative, and a powerful, if familiar, scenario of pathos.

The regal eternal feminine

The anthropological crisis provoked by the Messina disaster also had multiple gendered dimensions to which the celebration of the queen's role as a nurse can in part be seen as a response. The nakedness or inadequate clothing of many of the survivors in the stricken cities offered itself to onlookers as an image of the failure of the most basic signals of personal propriety and gender identity. As Arnaldo Cipolla commented in the *Corriere della Sera*, 'Many men of a certain social position [di condizione civile] dressed in women's clothes are the most dreadful image of torment.'[36] The tearing open of domestic interiors, profoundly associated with femininity, lent itself to the language of desecration. As Giovanni Cena said of the houses open to the street in Santa Caterina near Reggio: 'It is the brutal violation of domestic intimacy.'[37]

At other times the female presence in the ruined towns and villages was more disturbingly ghostly. Of all the corpses on display, it was those of attractive young women, and particularly rich, attractive young women, which exercised the greatest horrified fascination over journalists, all of whom were men. A morbid interest is evident from many of their accounts. From Reggio, Oddino Morgari writes in *Avanti!* of being shown the body of one wealthy girl:

> She was an extremely lovely girl, engaged to I don't remember who. She was suffocated in the bed where she lay face up. The spotless sheet in which she is wound does not prevent one observing the purity and elegance of her shape. The only things that appear from under that shroud are a braid of ebony hair and a wax-coloured hand. And now she is there, laid out on a plank in the middle of a street, with the drizzle falling on her, almost naked before the eyes of all, at the foot of the ruins of her proud house.[38]

Morgari's account displays tensions: it stresses the innocence of the unfortunate young woman ('spotless sheet'; 'purity . . . of her shape') while *both* lamenting her availability to the public gaze *and* indulging in a certain voyeurism. Like that of a prostitute, this young woman's body occupies the space of the street rather than the home; it can be looked at without the danger of embarrassment. No longer the vehicle for the transmission of a patrimony, she is mocked by her wealth. It seems that, in the minds of the correspondents roaming in the ruins, the earthquake brings about the worst possible outcome of that moment of transition in kinship relations which is embodied by nubile women. The naked body of a young woman, its 'innocence' that is the most carefully guarded sexual property of men, is destroyed and exposed for the visual possession of all.

The widespread public grief after the disaster seemed to bring with it a danger that the 'feminine' nature of the Italian national character might find unchecked expression in hysteria and confusion. This was, after all, a historical moment when the homology between individual, gendered psychological traits and those of whole peoples was part of the everyday coinage of political discourse. Hence Francesco Gaeta's concerns in *La Tribuna*:

> Italians are a holiday people. More than too many other nations, Italy finds moments of great happiness, and immeasurable calamities useful. Such moments are manifested in passion and display that allow an indefinite suspension of what the virile Anglo-Saxon race has called 'the day's work'![39]

The parallels constantly drawn between the disaster and a war also put the 'masculinity' of national behaviour into the balance.

The national response to the tragedy was also represented as properly *maternal*. An example is the following passage by Giuseppe Piazza, from a report dated 2 January:

> Can Italy get the measure of the immense misfortune that has struck it? Does it know that there is no tragedy of past centuries that can be compared to the one unfolding here today? And so why then have all of Italy's mothers not squeezed all the milk from their breast to restore the thousands and thousands of children that I have seen being pulled out, exhausted, from the rubble? Why have all the women of Italy not yet woven an immense shroud in which to gather and compose the broken limbs of the two stricken provinces? Oh . . . official Italy has come, and is doing its best.[40]

The enormity of the disaster is here imagined and measured from a maternal point of view which in itself implies a criticism of the state's less than warm-hearted handling of events.

In a context of anthropological crisis, where motherhood, like so many other basic features of social existence, seemed to be in doubt, it was also generalized: its importance grew to the point where everyone seemed to have to contribute to it. (This was particularly strongly felt in the case of the many hundreds of orphans produced by the disaster: parenting became a highly controversial public issue.)

It is of course also true that the earthquake came at the end of a decade which saw feminism emerge into public debate for the first time. Women's intervention in the relief effort took various forms, and had various political slants. The charitative efforts of upper-class women gave an opportunity for social hierarchies to be restated, for wealth and benevolence to be linked. Yet the records of some of the civic relief committees reflect the way traditional gender roles were mimicked in response to the tragedy. These booklets radiate civic pride; they are a kind of flattering group self-portrait of the urban élites of the day. Of the ninety pillars of the community whose names are listed as making up the Comitato Provinciale Bergamasco pro Calabria e Sicilia, for example, none are women.[41] The symbolic centrality of femininity and motherhood in the emergency did not find a correspondingly prominent real role for women in the relief effort.

Nevertheless, Ada Negri and other members of the Unione Femminile sought to use the disaster to lever women away from their unhealthy interest in crimes of passion and into a more public role. Negri herself published two prominent articles in the *Corriere della Sera* in which, using the semi-sexualized language of melodramatic self-sacrifice, she urged women to leave their families behind and lose themselves in the pursuit of the patriotic common weal. The only woman on the Milanese relief committee was from the Unione Femminile.

The earthquake's aftermath did in fact see one very small step forward in women's legal position in society. For the first time article 1743 of the civil code was suspended and women were allowed to take part in an activity in the public domain without their husband's permission: the activity in question being the care and supervision of orphans. Some members of the legal establishment expressed concern at the precedent. It is worth speculating whether Queen Elena's prominence as *both* a public *and* a maternal figure helped create a climate in which such a concession could be made. Indeed, the queen had an absolutely central role in this amplification of the theme of motherhood and femininity around the earthquake's aftermath. She was titular head of the body set up to look after the welfare of earthquake orphans, a body that also bore her name. With reference to the orphans, Goffredo Bellonci refers to her as 'Italy's most complete mother'.[42] For Antonio Scarfoglio she is 'the regal eternal feminine'.[43] The two sides of the queen-as-nurse image – humility and femininity – were combined in the frequent descriptions of her as a 'sister of charity'.

Queen Elena's image as nurse and mother had predominantly conservative meanings: the reinforcement of a traditional role of self-abnegating motherhood at a time when established images of femininity, like many other socially important images, seemed temporarily to have come loose after the earthquake.

Conclusions

The wave of patriotism which followed the disaster was undoubtedly far from entirely spontaneous or politically innocent: that much is evident from the way the state capitalized on the success of Queen Elena's visits, for example. But the patriotic aftermath also needs to be understood as a way of articulating and reacting to the fears of symbolic contamination or collapse that the disaster engendered. For example, images of the nation were often organized around the hunt for common enemies and scapegoats (looters, stock market speculators and bureaucrats were the most frequently evoked culprits in the early days of 1909). The story of Queen Elena's nursing exploits was only one of a vast number of narratives competing to respond to the political and symbolic demands of the situation by creating distinct scenarios in which versions of the nation could be constructed. To discover precisely what factors determined that one story should win out over another would require a comparative study that is beyond the scope of this chapter. Nevertheless, it would seem that several influences would need to be taken into account, from the political and economic power behind the medium in which a given story was presented, to the skill of the journalist in manipulating narrative conventions. The sheer number of stories in circulation, and the symbolic flux created by the catastrophe, would suggest that it would be reductive to view any one of these factors as predominant.

In the aftermath of the great earthquake, political decisions, and even decisions about how to administer the relief effort, could not be made independently of the need to manage a crisis of legitimacy, and of the boundaries between what we could call the 'anthropological' and 'political' domains. In that situation, nationalism's capacity to endow simple events and symbols with the kind of meanings normally associated with ritual came to the fore. The idea of the nation, variously understood, helped to conceptualize the crisis and smooth the passage back to a normality that it also helped to define.

Notes

1   Gaetano Cingari, *Storia della Calabria dall'Unità a oggi* (Rome–Bari, Laterza, 1982), 165. I should like to thank the Leverhulme Trust for their support for this research.

2   These details of the destruction are taken from: Mario Baratta, *La catastrofe sismica calabro messinese (28 dicembre 1908). Relazione alla Società Geografica Italiana* (Rome, Società Geografica Italiana, 1910).

3   On the gaps in the records in Messina, see O. De Fiore, *Demografia di Messina dal 1909 al 1931* (Messina, D'Amico, 1932).

4   See, for example, the comparative tables in Romano Solbiati and Alberto Marcellini, *Terremoto e società* (Milan, Garzanti, 1983), 275–83, which give a figure of 90,000 deaths for the Messina–Reggio disaster. The book is also a handy introduction to many aspects, scientific and historical, of the study of earthquakes.

5   Renato Simoni, 'Seguitando', *Corriere della Sera*, 2 January 1909.

6   See, for example, the lists of contributions published regularly in the *Eco di Bergamo*.

7   See, for example, Enzo D'Agostino, 'I terremoti del primo Novecento nell'ex circondario di Gerace', *Rivista storica calabrese*, 1–2 (1993), 31–46 which tells of an expedition to bring help to Reggio organized by two priests from nearby Gioiosa Jonica. The article reproduces the account by one of them, Pasquale Sansotta.

8   Antonio Scarfoglio, 'Nel dedalo delle rovine', *Il Mattino*, 2–3 January 1909.

9   John Dickie, 'Imagined Italies', in David Forgacs and Robert Lumley, eds., *Italian Cultural Studies: An Introduction* (Oxford, Oxford University Press, 1996), 19–33.

10 Piero Bevilacqua, 'Catastrofi, continuità, rotture nella storia del Mezzogiorno', *Laboratorio politico*, 5–6 (1981), 177–219.

11 Augusto Placanica, 'Le conseguenze socioeconomiche dei forti terremoti: miti di capovolgimento e consolidamenti reali', *Rivista storica italiana*, 3 (1995), 831–9.

12 See Romano Canosa, 'Terremoto e potere', *Sapere* (August–September 1981), 74–85.

13 Giuseppe Barone, 'Sull'uso capitalistico del terremoto: blocco urbano e

ricostruzione edilizia a Messina durante il fascismo', *Storia Urbana*, 19 (1982), 47–104.

14 See the newspaper's comment on the article by Giuseppe Toniolo, 'Per la tutela morale degli orfani', *Corriere d'Italia*, 29 January 1909.

15 Filippo Turati, 'Lutto di patria, lutto di famiglia, forse!', *Critica Sociale*, 1 January 1909, 11–12.

16 Claudio Treves, 'La sorpresa', *Il Tempo*, 7 January 1909.

17 Ernesto De Martino, *La fine del mondo. Contributo all'analisi delle apocalissi culturali*, edited by Clara Gallini (Turin, Einaudi, 1977).

18 'La terra dei morti', *La Tribuna*, 2 January 1909.

19 Goffredo Bellonci, 'Dal golfo della disperazione', *Giornale d'Italia*, 7 January 1909.

20 Luigi Ambrosini, 'Verso il Mezzogiorno', *Il Marzocco*, 10 January 1909.

21 Leonida Bissolati, 'Un'altra rivelazione', *Avanti!*, 8 January 1909.

22 Paolo Scarfoglio, 'Racconti dei superstiti', *Il Mattino*, 7–8 January 1909.

23 Ibid.

24 The minister of justice, Orlando, interviewed on his return from the disaster area where he had been with the king and queen, in 'Le impressioni di due ministri', *Corriere della Sera*, 4 January 1909.

25 Luigi Barzini, 'I fenomeni della rinascita fra le rovine', *Corriere della Sera*, 21 January 1909.

26 Claudio Treves, 'Laggiù a bordo della Lombardia', *Il Tempo*, 6 January 1909

27 Luigi Barzini, 'Visione di Messina distrutta', *Corriere della Sera*, 14 January 1909.

28 Archivio Centrale dello Stato. Ministero dell'Interno. Comitato Centrale di Soccorso pei Danneggiati dal Terremoto della Calabria e Sicilia del 28 dicembre 1908. Buste 75–7.

29 Tullio Giordana, 'L'on. Mirabello nelle acque di Messina', *La Tribuna*, 5 January 1909.

30 'Ciò che narra l'on. Orlando', *La Tribuna*, 2 January 1909.

31 'Le impressioni di due ministri', *Corriere della Sera*, 4 January 1909.

32 'La regina dello Stretto risorgerà', interview with Orlando by Tullio Giordana, *La Tribuna*, 5 January 1909.

33 'Le impressioni di due ministri', *Corriere della Sera*, 4 January 1909.

34 *Illustrazione Popolare*, 24 January 1909.

35 'Al Quirinale', *Corriere della Sera*, 6 January 1909.

36 Arnaldo Cipolla, 'I vinti', *Corriere della Sera*, 3 January 1909 (dated Messina, 2 January 1909), 69.

37 Giovanni Cena, 'Lungo le rive della morte', *Nuova Antologia*, 16 January 1909, reproduced in Francesco Mercadante, ed., *Il terremoto di*

Messina. *Corrispondenze, testimonianze e polemiche giornalistiche* (Rome, Ateneo, 1962), 76–93 (84).

38   Oddino Morgari, 'Fra gli orrori della città distrutta', *Avanti!*, 9 January 1909.

39   Francesco Gaeta, 'Ritorniamo alla vita', *La Tribuna*, 10 January 1909.

40   Giuseppe Piazza, 'Dai luoghi dell'immane ecatombe', *La Tribuna*, 5 January 1909.

41   *Bergamo e provincia per i fratelli di Calabria e Sicilia* (Bergamo, Mariani, 1909).

42   Goffredo Bellonci, 'Nella tragica immobilità della morte il faro splenderà ancora', *Giornale d'Italia*, 8 January 1909.

43   Antonio Scarfoglio, 'Nel dedalo delle rovine', *Il Mattino*, 2–3 January 1909.

3

The things that make Sicily Sicily: considerations on Sicilian identity

JOSEPH FARRELL

'No, no – 'tis no laughing matter; little by little,whatever your wishes shall be, you will destroy and undermine, until nothing of what makes Scotland Scotland shall remain.' And so saying, he turned round to conceal his agitation – but not until Mr Jeffrey saw tears running down his cheek.

J. G. Lockhart: Life of Sir Walter Scott

Giovanni Gentile, Idealist philosopher and later minister for education under Fascism, chose 1916 as the year which marked the closure of an epoch in Sicilian history, perhaps even of Sicilian history *tout court,* and as the year of a fundamental, irreversible shift in Sicilian identity *vis-à-vis* mainland Italy. The title of his pamphlet, *Il tramonto della cultura siciliana*[1] (The Twilight of Sicilian Culture), could not have been more explicit. The choice of year was determined not by what was occurring on the battlefields of Flanders or Gorizia, but by events on the island. As he explained,

> Between 19 March and 10 April, with the death in Palermo of Salvatore Salomone-Marino, Gioacchino Di Marzo and Giuseppe Pitrè, there vanished a trio of the most highly regarded and representative writers of Sicilian culture of the nineteenth century. A whole literary and spiritual world, once lively and overflowing with life, looked set to end with them, and to end forever. (p. ix)

The judgement that the three folklorists had been the foremost Sicilian writers in a century which had produced Verga, Capuana, De Roberto and had seen the early productions of Pirandello must now seem odd, but Gentile was concerned not with the overall quality of the writing, but with its Sicilianness. Although Sicilian by

72

birth, Gentile was an Italian nationalist and unqualified supporter of unification, and from that perspective he welcomed the suppression of divergences inside Italy and the total incorporation of the Sicilian tradition into a wider Italian culture. The loss of Giuseppe Pitrè affected him personally, for Pitrè had been his mentor and master, but did not influence his political judgement. In the introduction, he set out in uncompromising terms the purpose of the pamphlet, which had originally appeared as a series of articles in Benedetto Croce's *Critica*:

> I proposed to set out the rationale of that form of native, wholly Sicilian, culture which had continued to flourish even after unification, but which by the end of the century was being stripped of its regional character. So much so that today in Palermo, and in the rest of the region, an Italian and national culture will be found, while a Sicilian culture is to be sought only in books written in earlier times. (p. 4)

While his ultimate aim was to advance 'a historical judgement on a period of Sicilian history and of the modern history of Italy', he found it necessary to ward off misunderstanding by repeating that this period 'can be considered definitively closed' (p. x). A purely Sicilian culture was to be consigned to the embalmers, leaving the way clear for a new, integrated national culture.

His assessment of Sicilian culture was not generous. The analysis, dictated by his own nationalistic standpoint, required him to downplay even past achievements or worth, and to distort into self-absorbed parochialism that obsession with selfhood which many later commentators noted as characteristic of all Sicilian artistic output:

> Sicilian culture, even if wanting in content and in tenacity of tradition, did not, however, lack a well-defined character of its own: and it was scarcely possible that there would not be traces of that geographical and historical isolation, which caused it to be totally closed in on itself, like a nation of itself, until the eve of Garibaldi's landing. Indeed it could be said that if no Italian, once he had left his own region, was after 1860 less regionalist than the Sicilian, none had shown such a proud regional spirit before that era, and even later if he remained tied to his own land. (pp. 4–5)

The benighted narrowness imposed by geography could now be damned to oblivion. The sense of Sicilianness had been, for Gentile, extinguished, with one exception which was, for a man of his Hegelian background, of no importance. 'Today a Sicilian culture is no longer distinguishable (except among the lowest strata of society, which have no great historical importance), because there is no longer any Sicilian soul to be counterposed to the general Italian spirit' (p. 28). This one exception Gentile specifically allowed later irked Leonardo Sciascia who, in a note of trenchant criticism, reversed the judgement on what constituted dusk and what dawn. Writing on Pirandello and Sicily, he agreed, with less reserve than Gentile, that from around 1916 Sicilian culture had become part of a wider culture, although he identified that culture as European. Nevertheless, this transition had occurred without the culture 'alienating itself from its deep and specific character' (pp. 1075–6). Sciascia also believed that the culture became European, not in spite of, but precisely on account of, those wholly Sicilian elements which the 'lowest strata', held in contempt by Gentile, had kept in existence. Sciascia's thesis, influenced by Gramsci, was that Pirandellismo was an elaboration not of German philosophy but of Sicilian popular culture. Through Pirandello, that culture entered and influenced European thought.[2]

The skirmish between Gentile and Sciascia over Pitrè can be seen today as the first instalment of a continuing debate over Sicilian identity inside Italy, and as setting the parameters for such discussions in the future. After unification, Sicily's cultural boundaries could not have the crispness of its geographical borders. Sicily's identity was after 1860 to be based on a meeting with a civilisation beyond it, whether that civilisation be French, Spanish or Italian. Pitrè had examined Sicilian culture and identity in itself, but in the new order such debates had to take account of a relationship, whether with the emerging, still frail Italian identity, as Gentile wished, or with wider, still unformed European identity, as Sciascia hoped. Pitrè had not taken account of the fact that a sense of self is invariably intertwined with the selfhood of others, making it inevitable that any act of interpretation of identity will involve what a person or a cultural unit is not, as much as what it is. Sciascia, although more closely in conformity with Pitrè than was Gentile, saw Sicilian culture as requiring differential, comparative definition but also saw it as a still living entity and, as such, capable of evolution in a new context, and of enriching the cultures of Europe.

For Gentile, the narrative of Sicily's independent self-image, and self-interpretation, had to be given a closure. His creed was what Sergio Romano has categorized as the 'Risorgimento ideology', by which he meant that complex of convictions and ambitions held, either out of altruism or out of self-interest, by those functionaries of the state whose aim was not to make Italy but to make the Italians.[3] Since Gentile's aim was to ensure the full assimilation of Sicily into the Italian state, he saw, with perfect logic, a specifically Sicilian culture as an obstacle and so was constrained to accord Pitrè only the respect given to the manufacturers of gas-mantles in the age of electricity. The autonomy of Sicily and things Sicilian belonged to prehistory; the crucial assertion in Gentile's pamphlet was that 'there was no longer any Sicilian soul to be counterposed to the general Italian spirit'. The dialectic between 'Sicilian soul' and 'Italian spirit' is, post-1916 or post-1860, the heart of the matter in any consideration of identity. The cultivation of the 'Sicilian soul', like that of any autonomous or national spirit, is a project which requires a shared community past and a future, or which allows for the reinvention of the past and the invention of the future; Gentile wished to leave Sicilians freedom to reinvent the past, but to deny them the right to invent an autonomous future. His statement represents a watershed in Sicilian literary and cultural history, of equal importance in that history to the landing in Marsala in political history. It marks the transition from nation to region, leaving Sciascia to advance the same kind of demand which his Sicilian predecessors had put to the Piedmontese after 1860, for cultural federalism now, for political federalism then.

Since the status of Sicily as a region of Italy is not in doubt today, when challenges to Italian unity come from the north, the importance of this intellectual shift can be easily underestimated, but in its own terms it was revolutionary. Gentile was right to see in Pitrè's work a danger, none the less real for being unintended, to the unitary impulse of 'Risorgimento ideology'. Pitrè may have believed that he was engaged on an exercise of nostalgia, akin to Walter Scott's collection of Border ballads after the Union of Scotland and England, but the task he had set himself involved the construction for Sicily of that 'social-imaginary' dimension which is the precondition for the existence of a nation, or any social-political unit,[4] and which the Italian people so evidently and paradoxically lacked. 'Of the three characteristics', writes Sergio Romano, 'which distinguish a nation in the liberal and romantic ideology of the nineteenth century – language, history and faith – Italy had only the third' (p. 68). Ideally, all three would combine to create the overarching consciousness which gives a community its culture, or 'mythistorical energy',[5] and while Italy lacked two elements, Sicily had all three.

Pitrè, an adherent of the nineteenth-century liberal and romantic ideology Romano identified, was not an isolated figure in Europe, but was one of that band of folklorists, willed into existence by the thought of Johann Gottfried von Herder (1744–1803), who believed that the essence of a people's being was preserved in the beliefs, folktales, myths, customs, legends of the *Volk*. Herder, as Isaiah Berlin has written, was not concerned with political nationalism as such, but his central belief was that the essential prerequisite for shared community existence was a common culture.[6] It is beyond discussion that his ideas had their greatest impact among peoples which were not yet states and which were without any of the institutions which embodied sovereignty, but where an oral or folk culture, often in a language not spoken by the ruling élite, had been preserved among the peasantry or the subaltern, uneducated classes. The distinction between cultural and political nationalism, although tenaciously adhered to by Herder, was difficult to maintain in practice. All over Europe, intellectual, bourgeois minorities dedicated themselves to the search in the vernacular culture for the roots of separate selfhood, and whether involved in the 'invention of tradition', in Eric Hobsbawm's phrase, or in the 'imagining of a community', to adopt Benedict Anderson's terminology, these researchers were in fact laying the bases of the post-romantic nationalisms which emerged in Europe. The Finnish Literature Society, founded in 1831, which led to the publication of the codification by Elias Lonnrot of the *Kalevala,* the national epic, became nation-builders whatever their initial intentions had been, while in the case of the Gaelic League in Ireland, established in 1893, it was often the same people who were involved both in establishing vernacular culture and in the process of nation-building.[7] 'The development of Irish nationalism was strongly influenced by the transference of these forms (i.e. folk-tale, myth and saga) into the narrative of nationality',[8] writes Roy Foster, and similar statements could be made about Greece, Romania, Estonia and Catalonia.

The anomaly of Pitrè's operation (no term will be more frequently employed regarding Sicily than 'anomaly') was that it was bereft of all nationalistic aspirations, but he himself shared the philosophical preconceptions and cultural objectives of his fellow researchers elsewhere, and like them made no distinction between oral and written history as sources. In his introduction to the four volumes which make up his most important work of ethnography, Pitrè writes that while his aim had been to make Sicily known 'from a new and unexplored point of view,' his principal target audience had been fellow scholars and folklorists in other nations: 'It is', he wrote, 'those dedicated to folklore and ethnography that I address with these superstitious customs, in which old generations live and breathe . . .'[9] He was fully, even proudly, aware of the unrepeatable specificity of the culture he was describing and analysing. He devoted special study to the language, favoured topos of the Herderians, in his *Grammatica del dialetto e delle parlate siciliane* (1875), and in his principal work, *Usi e costumi, credenze e pregiudizi del popolo siciliano*, employed the shamanic word *popolo* at a time when terms people, nation, state were not clearly defined or differentiated. The volumes which made up the *Usi* were published in a series entitled Biblioteca delle tradizioni popolari siciliane. Pitrè's fieldwork concerned Sicily alone, but his interests in that area were encyclopaedic. He assiduously collected popular song and children's fairy tales, examined the legends of Orlando and King Arthur in the form these tales had been handed down in Sicily, and in which they had furnished the material for puppet theatre, provided accounts of the activities of storytellers but also analysed customs relating to birth, marriage and funeral rites. His work provides a systematically compiled compendium of Sicilian life and culture, gathered in the course of his work as a doctor in Palermo, but enriched by travelling, as Elias Lonnrot had done in Finnish-Russian Karelia, to towns and villages all over Sicily. Pitrè was more than a dilettante, and was anxious to establish his scientific credentials in his introductory *Avvertenza* to his work by listing all the towns he had visited and the people whose testimony he had taken. His impulse was to preserve ancient customs and beliefs he feared were threatened by new ways. Pitrè was the purest of followers of Herder, and belonged to the liberal bourgeoisie which saw in the Risorgimento and unification with Italy the only possibility for the future of Sicily. Nothing had been further from Pitrè's mind than the prospect of laying the foundation for a revived Sicilian *Staatsnation*, but his political realism cloaked a romantic (Sicilian) nationalism. Certainly this would have unfortunate consequences, and would lead Pitrè to offer the most outrageous apologia for the Mafia,[10] and later to involve himself with the Pro Sicilia committee for the defence of the Mafia politician Raffaele Palizzolo when he was convicted of the murder of the banker Emanuele Notarbartolo. In both occasions, he saw the honour of Sicily impugned, and entertained no other consideration than the need to offer a defence against 'continental' detractors.

Giovanni Gentile's interpretation of Pitrè amounts to a neutering of it. He had to make Pitrè's researches compatible with the strengthening of an Italian identity, and to ward off the possibility of its being established as some anti-Risorgimento force. 'Separatism', writes Isaia Sales, one of the more forceful and clear-sighted of the new *meridionalisti*, 'has always been a typical objective of some sectors of the southern bourgeoisie, one which has been present in Italian history until it exploded with the Sicilian separatist movement in the immediate post-war period.'[11] Don Luigi Sturzo, founder of the Partito Popolare, the first Catholic party in post-unification politics, noted the strength of 'legitimist' feeling in whole areas of Sicily, principally those linked to the Church.[12] Gentile ensured that any political equivocation was deleted. His refrain was that Sicily was now and forever more a region, so that Pitrè had been, Gentile underlined, operating in a regional, not national or nationalist, context, and that his work had no implications for the future. 'Erudizione regionale' was the title he gave a chapter on learned reviews which had circulated in Sicily. Gentile required special delicacy in his treatment of the Sicilian language, or dialect, since this, together with religion and community, was one of the elements inextricably interwoven into Herder's concept of a self-sufficient culture. Language was not only the medium of self-knowledge but the indispensable matter for the construction of those relationships which underlie community. It provides a link with the past, but also provides the means by which a culture can be projected into the future and can perpetuate itself. Some of the other scholars whom Gentile discusses, most notably the novelist and critic Vincenzo Di Giovanni (a friend of Verga, who told the novelist that *I Malavoglia* should have been written in Sicilian dialect) and the historian Michele Amari were, much more than Pitrè, convinced of the status of Sicilian not as dialect but as language. 'The origins of the language . . . were for me', wrote Di Giovanni, 'an object of patriotic affection.' Di Giovanni added that he could not conceive of an Italy which did not recognize that it was a mosaic of regions, and which gave a place of honour to Sicily, with its history, traditions, customs and speech. This was too much for Gentile, whose aim was integration and homologization. 'Italians yes, but first Sicilians', was Gentile's accurate but disapproving verdict on such notions. He accused these writers of having failed to 'ponder whether this sense of the particular, justified in its original impulse, was not exaggerated in its tendency to obscure the awareness of common nationality, in which it ought to sink deeply its own roots' (pp. 84–5). 'Antiquam exquirite matrem', he quoted as Di Giovanni's motto, and provided those enquiries remained rooted in the past, he had no objection. Without its own language, equipped with a culture which Gentile presented as impoverished and threadbare, Sicily was left with an identity and selfhood which may have been strong but which were singularly ill-defined. Gentile would not tolerate even a hybrid nationality.

There was another possibility which Gentile was incapable of preventing, or even of foreseeing, that is, the emergence of a Sicilian cultural nationalism bereft of political implications. The most comprehensive definition of 'cultural nationalism' was provided by Tzvetan Todorov: 'cultural nationalism (that is, attachment to one's own culture) is a path towards universalism, by deepening the specificity of the particular within which one dwells.'[13] Sicilians have, long after 1916, continued to dwell in that specificity, and mainland Italians have had little problem in accepting that identity. In the plebiscite held by Garibaldi in 1860, some 99.5 per cent of the island's population voted in favour of integration with Italy, and the separatist movement in the immediate post-Second World War period was the creation of a gallimaufry of unscrupulous aristocrats and opportunistic mafiosi (is there any other sort?), given strength by Salvatore Giuliano's ragamuffin army of bandits. It lacked popular support, and the separatist party had disappeared by 1951.[14] Sicilian politicians in the Sicilian Regional Assembly, whose first elections were held in 1947, found Sicilianness a useful card to play in negotiations with Rome: it could be employed to extract additional funds for problems which concerned a region with an identity of its own, but could not be played too hard by a region which had no aspirations to alter regional status.

An identity is by its nature an inheritance from history, but not one which is immobilized in that history. Sciascia's concept of

Sicilian identity was dynamic, allowing him to see, where Gentile saw only threat and danger, an opening on to a hybrid identity: Sciascia was alert to the possibility of Sicilians viewing themselves as Sicilian-Italians, or even Sicilian-Europeans, whose keynotes would become part of a chorus which swelled beyond the confines of the island. Sicily as a cultural, if not ethnic, minority had an unrepeatable identity, but one which was separate from politics and which was fluid, contradictory, problematic. The dilemmas associated with analysis of Sicilian identity can now be viewed as being of the same order as those universal problems concerning de-individualization, depersonalization and de-identification which had been first given masterly expression by Robert Musil, as regards Austria at the point of disintegration of empire, in his *Man without Qualities*. Austria was emerging from transnational statehood, while Sicily was losing individual statehood to merge with a larger entity. In a Sicilian context, this theme of collective cultural erasure and individual depersonalization or, more concretely, the sense of the precariousness of Sicily's identity and fear for its survival, received its definitive treatment in Antonio Pizzuto's enigmatic novel, *Signorina Rosina*. The Rosina of the title is dying at the opening of the novel, and is buried in a cemetery far from her native village. She lingers on as a memory of loss, rather as Gentile would have all Sicilian culture linger, but her selfhood and identity can no longer be precisely located. As Robert Dombroski put it, 'it [the novel] thematizes the disappearance of Sicily as essence and origin . . . Pizzuto's Sicily, like Signorina Rosina, is gone, and with it the sense of human community . . .'[15]

From the perspective of the mainland, Sicily assumed a split personality. It can appear that writers in Italy refashioned their own Kingdom of the two Sicilies, or attributed to the one island two clashing images of identity, one an image crafted in sunlight and the other at blackest midnight. Nothing has contributed more to establishing the identity of Sicily inside and outside Italy than the presence in Sicily of the Mafia, the most violent of all organized crime syndicates. Originally this midnight image was of a land infested by brigands and bandits, of bandits of a type known to the traveller Patrick Brydone in the eighteenth century, and given picturesque prominence by Alexandre Dumas with his novel, *Pasquale Bruno*. The most recent representative of this type was, in history, Salvatore Giuliano, and, in fiction, the same character as he appeared in Mario Puzo's blockbuster, *The Sicilian*.[16] Hollywood produced several other examples of this stereotype, but Italian and Sicilian playwrights had already done so in the nineteenth century. As a negative stereotype of the Sicilian, the bandit quickly gave way to the mafioso. Whatever its derivation, and the matter has given rise to endless disputes, the first time any derivative of the term 'Mafia' appeared in print was in 1863 with the performance of Giuseppe Rizzotto's play, *I mafiusi di la Vicaria*. The word gained immediate currency as mainland Italians read of the influence of this body over life in the island.

The early reports from civil servants dispatched to Sicily and the south report their alarmed reactions to the power of crime over many sectors of life. The criminologist Cesare Lombroso, in *L'uomo delinquente,* offered overtly racist explanations of the retarded development and the prevalence of crime in Sicily. The Italian Parliament felt obliged to respond to public concern. The Bonfadini report was commissioned by Parliament in 1875, but was overshadowed by the unofficial but immensely insightful work of Leopoldo Franchetti and Sidney Sonnino, *Condizioni sociali e amministrative della Sicilia (*1877). If to this are added the *Lettere meridionali* (1875) by Pasquale Villari, and perhaps the works of Napoleone Colajanni, *La delinquenza della Sicilia e le sue cause* (1885), as well as the later, highly influential *Nel regno della mafia* (1900), the groundwork for study of the Southern Question and for what would come to be called *meridionalismo* is complete. Behind the denunciation of exploitation of the peasantry, the exposé of the backwardness of agricultural operations, the analyis of corruption in police and politics, the proposals for state intervention and, most famously, the analysis of the conditions which produced the Mafia, lay a paradoxical combination of both the unitarian Risorgimento ideology and of an awareness that two distinct socio-economic systems and two distinct cultures had been brought together inside the one state. It could be remarked that Giovanni Gentile, in his interpretation of Pitrè, can be termed a cultural *meridionalista*, in that his aim was the integration of a culture he presented as impoverished with a national culture which was more advanced. In this he was in step with the founding fathers of political and economic *meridionalismo*, who were deeply imbued with Risorgimento ideals and with the forging of a genuinely national identity. For Franchetti and Sonnino, the exposure of inequalıty represented a demand for remedial action, not an acceptance of the innate inferiority of the poor. They were aware that integration was not complete and could be regarded as finished business only when some form of economic parity had been established throughout the peninsula. None of the early *meridionalisti* had any intention of setting north against south, or of contributing to an image of a corrupt south as a cancer in an otherwise healthy state. 'One of the unquestioned points and one of the most important results of liberal reformism, which will then be accepted by all the authentic strands of *meridionalismo* and will give to the *meridionalista* battle its highest meaning, is precisely the unitary, national vision of the problem', writes Rosario Villari.[17]

These works, sober in their analysis of the conditions of Sicily as were Franchetti and Sonnino, or impassioned in their polemics against the government as was Colajanni, were capable of varying interpretations, and gave rise to the most diverse intellectual systems, not all of which were in keeping with the intentions of the authors. In the first place, it produced *meridionalismo*, a complex of attitudes and beliefs united by the protest against the fact that by any social index employed, the south was poorer and more backward than the north.[18] The Cassa per il Mezzogiorno, established after the Second World War, was, whatever its eventual inadequacy, the most concrete of political expressions of this dissatisfaction with inequality. On the other hand, the increased awareness of conditions in the Mezzogiorno, especially in Sicily, produced in certain sections in the north the irritation the prosperous always feel towards the poor, and a self-justifying perception of Sicilians as self-serving, dishonest, potentially violent parasites, unwilling to undertake honest labour and preferring instead to live on state benefits. This image of the inferior southerner persisted and was one of the factors behind the rise in the 1980s of the Lega Lombarda and the other Northern Leagues.[19] This state of mind finds definitive statement in the splenetic books and articles of the journalist, Giorgio Bocca.[20] Neither Bocca nor Bossi invented this image of the southerner, which is as old as Italian unity. Its roots can be traced not only to a misinterpretation of the enlightened reports, but also to the impact on public opinion of the Notarbartolo case. The importance of this *cause célèbre* for the formation of a mainland Italian view of Sicily can hardly be overstated.

In 1893, Emanuele Notarbartolo, ex-director of the Bank of Sicily, was murdered on a train bound for Palermo.[21] After some years of inactivity, the authorities were obliged by the weight of public opinion to charge Raffaele Palizzolo, Member of Parliament and known Mafia boss, but after a series of sensational trials held in Milan, Bologna and Florence, Palizzolo was finally acquitted in 1904. The event was greeted in Sicily with celebrations, but the effect in the rest of Italy was to reinforce an already emerging Sicily/Mafia equation. In 1900, at the completion of the Milan trial, the writer Alfredo Oriani wrote in *Il Giorno* an article entitled 'The sewer', in which he referred to Sicily as 'a cancer at the foot of Italy'.[22] Don Luigi Sturzo gave a speech in Bologna shortly after the closure of the trial there in which he spoke of his dismay at the identity attributed to his native place, Sicily, in Italy as a whole.

> To penetrate the heart of our southern problem is for many, for very many, like penetrating unexplored territory, where geographers have no more competence than those of the man who scrawled on the Vatican map of Africa *Hic sunt leones;* similarly for many Italians, the geography of Italy goes down as far as Rome, and the rest is marked with the words *Hic sunt meridionales.*[23]

For subsequent generations, this identification of Sicily as the criminal island would be reinforced by subsequent Mafia outrages, including the killing of left-wing opponents of land reform in the 1950s, the massacre of Ciaculli in 1963, the Mafia wars of the 1970s and 1980s, the accumulation of 'excellent corpses' from Pietro Scaglione in 1971 to Giovanni Falcone and Pietro Borsellino in 1993.

The Sicilian response to what they perceived as a calumny perpetrated on them by the Italian nation emerged in outline form in the furious reaction to the Franchetti–Sonnino report. Pitrè rejected the interpretation of the Mafia as criminal body contained in the work, and composed a paean of praise to the Mafia code, even including dark suggestions that the honoured society had been unknown until the arrival of Garibaldi and the northerners.[24] Luigi Capuana wrote in indignation the pamphlet *La Sicilia e il brigantaggio*,[25] which contained passionate passages on the splendours of the 'Island of the sun', passages marred only by evident bad faith. Capuana excoriated 'two disinterested young men' who had hurled themselves on the island, and went on to wonder why Mafia crime was more worthy of note than comparable activities in other cities of Italy and Europe.

These pages were the first manifestation of an inchoate, defensive and occasionally dishonest outlook – it never attained the systematic coherence of an ideology – later known as *sicilianismo*. The most discordant definitions of the phenomenon have been advanced. For S. F. Romano, it was essentially 'a vague state of mind involving solidarity against foreign governments, occupations and interventions, a complex and confused outlook which ended up incorporating into itself certain elements of the Mafia spirit', while Nando Dalla Chiesa emphasized the element of solidarity against outsiders, but also the sense of 'mass victimism' which underlay it. In his most trenchant criticism of the phenomenon, he defined *sicilianismo* as the 'ideological bulwark of the Mafia', although he also included in the definition, and viewed as deserving criticism, the belief in the 'sociological theorization of the exceptionality of Sicilian civilization in the European and Italian historical context'.[26] There is a tone of lofty exasperation in that last comment which owes nothing to 'sociological theorization', and suggests that Dalla Chiesa had as little sympathy with cultural nationalism as Gentile. *Sicilianismo* is the underside of Sicilian identity, the inevitable, if also inevitably inward, reaction of small peoples to injustices they see perpetrated by large powers with whom they are constrained by geography or geopolitics to live cheek by jowl. For decades, some, but never all, mainland Italians and Sicilians have glowered at each other across the Straits of Messina, the first motivated either by well-meaning *meridionalismo* or, alternatively, by mean-minded pseudo-racism, and being met from the Messina side by shafts of protective *sicilianismo*.

Meridionalismo embodied both the 'Risorgimento ideology' and social-democratic objectives of redistribution of wealth, and perhaps for that reason has been recently the object of sustained attack. The most obvious aggressive front has been *leghismo*, the code of Northern Leagues, who are out to unmake the Italy of the Risorgimento. In the new Europe of the Treaty of Maastricht, the Leagues deny political, cultural and national kinship with Sicily and the south, and complain of the expenditure of Lombard taxes for the benefit of the disadvantaged parts of Italy. In their own dream dimension, they see themselves as aligned with the nations north of the Alps. The *leghisti* have found unlikely bedfellows in the neo-Orientalists, who try to apply Edward Said's[27] invaluable insights into the western, neo-imperialist deformation of oriental culture to

Italian visions of Sicily. This viewpoint underlies *Italy's 'Southern Question': Orientalism in One Country*, where the inverted commas are a polemical weapon, indicating that the southern question was not a political-economic reality, did not involve social poverty or the pestilence which was the Mafia, but was all a consequence of a distorted northern perspective on a culture which was alien to them and beyond their understanding. Jane Schneider, who has written movingly and tellingly elsewhere on the impact of the Mafia on Sicilian life, goes so far as to attack Sicilian intellectuals who denounce the conditions they see in Sicily for 'complicity',[28] presumably with denigrators of the island. The candid forthrightness of Sciascia, Consolo or, presumably, Verga and the young Pirandello in exposing conditions of life becomes not a reason for praise but for blame. Attacks on Franchetti and Sonnino are repeated in terms which recall Capuana and Pitrè in the nineteenth century.

The observer cannot fail to note the gulf, which is not 'orientalist', between the domestic image of Sicily's identity as cultivated, or agonized over, by Sicilian writers, and that purveyed from the perspective of continental Italy. For the majority of Sicilian writers and thinkers, Sicily became one of those small communities, some of which were stateless nations, dotted around the periphery of Europe, each convinced of possessing an identity and consciousness which differentiated them from other peoples, but unable to be dogmatic about the nature of that differentiation. Their distinctiveness lay in the dialectical relationship with other peoples since, as the Catalan writer Salvador Giner has expressed it, 'tota identitat és relacional' (every identity is a function of a relationship).[29] The open question was whether, in cultural matters, the defining relationship, the other element of Sicily's hybrid identity, would be with mainland Italy or with Europe. While that question remained, and remains, unresolvable, identity, consciousness, selfhood, the meaning and interpretation of Sicilianness became the prime concern of the Sicilian writer. Bufalino put the matter crisply: 'I do not know if it is so in other places, but Sicily – whether the cause be an excess or deficiency of identity – has done nothing other than investigate herself and debate, somewhat touchily, about herself.'[30] Such scratching at wounds, such swings between, in Bufalino's words, 'viewing herself as the mathematical navel of the universe . . . and flopping into a rancorous stupor' are common symptoms of the insecurity of small nations and of the national anti-syzygy which is a consequence of it. Bufalino would have found counterparts for his dilemma among the intelligentsia of Barcelona, Edinburgh, Prague or Helsinki. Sciascia himself was often ambiguous about his identity as a writer. It has been noted that there is a gradual diminution of Sicilian linguistic elements in his output, even if Salvatore Sgroi believed that Sciascia deceived himself on this point,[31] but the crux of the matter is that Sciascia was, like the Neapolitan playwright Eduardo de Filippo, simultaneously a propagandist and apologist for his native place and chary of being identified too closely with vernacular elements lest this be taken as a lessening of his wider interests and appeal. 'I am an Italian writer who concerns himself with Sicily', was the formula he once used.[32]

It is at this point that it becomes necessary to insist on a distinction between cultural images and anthropological or historical inquiries, a distinction rendered almost nugatory by those strands of postmodernist thinking which have been responsible for the 'transformation of reality into images, and the fragmentation of time into a series of perpetual presents',[33] in Frederic Jameson's trenchant phrase. The notion of a 'perpetual present' is wholly inapplicable to Sicily, where the past is a force which conditions the present, or where, in Pirandello's words in his historical novel *The Old and the Young*, children grow up among monuments.[34] However, the images, not the anthropology or the sociology are our prime concern here, since it is they which are responsible for determining the nature of that mental reality which is culture, and which is intrinsic to any perception of identity. Since Benedict Anderson published his immensely influential study, *Imagined Communities*, the dimension of the imaginary, or the social-imaginary in Gourgouris's gloss, has dominated inquiries of a national or regional identity. It has been common ground among all Sicilian writers, whatever political ideology they espouse and however 'Italian' their sentiments are, that there exists a 'social-imaginary' specific to Sicily, independent of Italian culture.

Antonio Di Grado gave his investigation of the literary identity of Sicily as developed by the island's writers over the past century the ingenious title *L'isola di carta* (The Paper Island).[35] Plainly mental reality must be to some extent an assemblage of idiosyncrasies, inherited prejudices, aspirations and local rodomontade as much as of rational analysis and intuition, but inquiry into it will help establish the fragmented images by which Sicily establishes its own identity. These images are not a closed code, but impact on reality. Virtually every Sicilian writer or artist has added his flourish to the vast fresco which has overhung Sicilian life. Among painters, Renato Guttuso once said that even when he painted an apple, Sicily was present, and his contemporary, Santo Marino, wrote that his every canvas was a contribution to the synthesis between despair and aspiration which he believed was the overriding characteristic of Sicilian civilization. Not even Gentile could resist giving a judgement on what had been, in his view, the dominant traits of the culture whose demise he was marking. He noted an antithesis between a 'spiritual Risorgimento', which in mainland Italy in the nineteenth century, had taken the form of 'romanticism in literature and Idealism or spiritualism in philosophy', and the 'materialist tendencies' which were rooted in Sicilian life. This materialism was not the attachment to 'la roba' which was the passion and tragedy of Mastro don Gesualdo and of others among Verga's characters, and which was analysed by Sebastiano Aglianò[36] in his study of Sicilian life, but a philosophical materialism rooted in Enlightenment thought, and particularly in the theories of David Hume. David Hume, it will be recalled, was the philosopher most revered by Marianna Ucria, the heroine of Dacia Maraini's eponymous historical novel set in eighteenth-century Palermo.[37] The isolation from, and rejection of, the new European 'spiritualist impulses' of European thought – which in fact through Dilthey and Georg Simmel had an impact on Pirandello during his time in Bonn – account for what Gentile considers to be the relative failure of Verga. Although Gentile does not regard *verismo* exclusively as a product of Sicilian culture (p. 4), it satisfied, too easily for his tastes, the expectations of Sicilian writers, and meant that Verga, Capuana and De Roberto were destined to remain within an island framework, and show themselves incapable of fulfilling either their own potential or their own needs in a new national culture. Pirandello is not mentioned by Gentile. The island had always been 'cut off, because of the sea and the paucity of commerce, from every relation with the rest of the world' (p. 5).

The geographical position of Sicily was viewed as an essential formative element by others who took a different view of its impermeable uniqueness. 'An island not island enough', wrote Giuseppe Antonio Borgese, novelist, critic and anti-Fascist exile, in 1933.[38] 'In this contradiction is contained the historical theme, the vital substance of Sicily', he added. It is an arresting, deftly phrased paradox. The island was too large to be ignored but too small to dominate, had too rich a culture to be suppressed but not sufficiently rich to be autonomous. Glossing Borgese, it could be added that geography gave Sicily the potential for being either an island in the centre of the Mediterranean, or an offshore island of Italy. To settle for the condition of offshore island has implications for identity, for both the islanders and the mainlanders, since it involves asserting a sense of self, but one tempered by an acknowledgement of dependency. Sicily demonstrated for Borgese the characteristics of incomplete hybridity, but he went on to draw attention to a different kind of hybridity, or mongrelism, which was internal to the island. No tradition is unitary, no culture is monotone, no identity is singular, but Borgese was the first to make of the historical mosaic of peoples and cultures inhabiting Sicily a cause for celebration. Borgese believed that the mixture of cultures and peoples in the island had added to the complexity or, to adopt the terminology of later ethnographers, the pluralism which characterized Sicilian culture. He wrote:

> The vision of modern life has not cancelled the general impression of complexity which we have: the mixture of types and races left over from the days when the island was a conquered land and the most varied peoples met and merged there; from this have derived the most characteristic environmental and folkloristic aspects. (p. 23)

The notion of Sicily as site of heteronomy, home of successive, differentiated civilizations or mosaic of simultaneously existing centres of creativity or of units of cultural energy which were to exert an influence on each other, either mutually self-absorbing or self-repelling, was a bracing one. In an overtly racist form, it was suggested by some early writers that the Mafia, which developed in the provinces of Palermo, Trapani and Agrigento in the west of the island, was in some unstated way a deformed, mutant descendant of the Arab colonization of Sicily,[39] but this racism has passed.

No notion is more frequently encountered than that of an island culture segmented by its own historical past. The most common division is into two, although Gesualdo Bufalino, a man of some expansiveness of vision, located more than one hundred Sicilies, all competing for critical attention.[40] Variations of this notion can be found in writers as diverse as Bufalino himself, Vitaliano Brancati, Leonardo Sciascia, Vincenzo Consolo and Tomasi di Lampedusa. *Il gattopardo* is, among other things, an extended meditation on Sicily and Sicilianness, however annoying the ideas contained in the dialogues have been to other Sicilians. The *locus classicus* of discussion on the impact of history is the monologue of the Prince of Salina to the Piedmontese envoy, Chevalley. Lampedusa is frequently charged with fatalism, immobilism or essentialism, as holding an inchoate belief that there existed some mystical, eternal Sicily, unchanging from age to age, the nature of whose inhabitants was determined by climate or factors outside history. There is an undeniable truth in the charge, but it coexists with another Lampedusa who spoke, disconsolately, of the weight of history,

> of the long, long hegemony of rulers who were not of our religion, and who did not speak our language . . . For at least twenty-five centuries we have been carrying on our backs the weight of magnificent, foreign civilizations, all from outside, none born among us, none in which we have set the tone.[41]

It is disconcerting to find the aristocratic Tomasi, whose protagonist feigned to forget the name of Karl Marx, writing in tones which would have been familiar to Frantz Fanon, but his views on the effects of colonialism on the formation of a subaltern mentality are not dissimilar to those of the guru of anti-colonialism. The experience of inhabiting an island ruled by outsiders, however benevolent, and dominated by institutions which are not those legitimized by the consent of the native peoples has produced the famous distrust with which Sicilians are accustomed to viewing all institutions and all people in government.

Brancati, and later Sciascia, took a geographical divide as a metaphor for a cultural differentiation, but suggested that that divide itself corresponded to marks left by the island's geopolitics and history. In a riot of aesthetic enthusiasm and verbal exuberance, the youthful Brancati, himself from Pachino in the extreme south-east of the island, wrote of Sicily as a mingling of Europe and Africa, and as representing something which was intellectually superior to both; in 1938, he modified this view to a slightly more sober pageant of Sicilian history with processions entering from opposite sides.

From this side [Palermo], there entered the Arabs, sophistication, subtleties, the ego and non-ego, melancholy and mosaics. The subtleties and the melancholy ended up in part in Agrigento, in the head of Luigi Pirandello, in part in Castelvetrano, in the head of Giovanni Gentile. From the eastern gate, entered the Phoenicians, the Greeks, poetry, music, trade, deceit, clowning and comedy: Stesichorus, Bellini, Di San Giuliano, De Felice, Rapisardi, Verga, Martoglio.[42]

Sciascia wrote in similar vein when identifying differences of mindset and belief between Verga and Pirandello. The clash of psychology between the characters was a consequence of collective psychology, itself the result of 'a geographical divide, between Catania and Agrigento, between the Val Demone where the Arabs did not succeed in penetrating with any certainty, and the Val di Mazara, where over centuries they were secure in their domination'.[43] In Catania, home of Verga, the ancient (Greek) distinction between comedy and tragedy still held, while in Arab Agrigento the distinction between the two had been enfeebled by endless interplay, producing the fusion which Pirandello was to term *Umorismo*, from which he forged a new vision and even a new theatre.

Vincenzo Consolo weaves the rich historical and cultural diversity of Sicily into his fiction. In *Retablo*, the traveller Fabrizio Clerici makes his way through eighteenth-century Sicily, stopping as guest of a Soldan at a castle which is Arab, while en route for the Greek temple at Selinunte, but diverts to a Norman church and later to Trapani and the island of Mozia, where he spends time rooting among Phoenician ruins uncovered by the Siculo-English botanist and ornithologist, Giuseppe (Pip) Whitaker. What makes Consolo stand out is the inspiration he finds in the linguistic variety of Sicilian speech patterns, which are for him history crystallized. The language of his novels is not the pastiche of invented words which James Joyce or Carlo Emilio Gadda revelled in, but a musical poetry of terms culled indifferently from a standard, Tuscanized vocabulary and from vernacular dialects used only in Sicilian centres. This style of writing coincides with postmodern preferences, but has different roots and agendas. The poetic diction represents an attempt to reinstate the novel among art forms and to snatch it away from the consciously colloquial media-speak in vogue elsewhere in Italy, while the unselfconscious use of dialect terms represents a convergence of an aesthetic and a political protest against the concentration of power and, more concretely, against the demeaning of Sicilian identity. Consolo restores to Sicilian speech a dignity denied by inhabitants of capitals. Centres of power impose not only codes of conduct and (mal)distribution of wealth, but also remove dignity from the speech and cultures of the periphery. By employing common speech in novels which are works of high art, Consolo is seeking a basis for the restoration of esteem to a people which had been marginalized. The distinction between dialect art, which could be patronized and ignored, and high art is undermined by Consolo. *Pace* Gentile, Sicilian culture is restored to actuality. Language has remained a no man's land over which grenades have been tossed. Not all writers made the same linguistic choice as Consolo. Bufalino was Sicilian by his choice of material, but he wrote only in standard Italian, a choice which explained in part the disputes between the two men. The detective writer, Andrea Camilleri, sets his novels in Sicily and writes in Italian with some Sicilian words as embellishment, but they are given a Tuscanized form, far removed from the robust dialect form of Consolo's writing.

Consolo was dismissed by some critics on his first appearance as a 'a writer out of time', but he sees the present through the past. For him, as for others, history is the indispensable reference point for any interpretation of Sicily. It would be stretching semantics and credulity to suggest that these quintessentially writerly debates are empirical, ethnographical case studies, but neither are they the products of free imagination restrained only by the limits of verbal inventiveness. Identity belongs to the dimension of the 'imagined', but that does not make it less real. In the identity of any small, marginal community, be it Catalonia, Ireland, Finland or Sicily, which is the object of history, history itself is a living force and a determinant of self-image to an extent which is unthinkable in the major powers which are the subjects of history. Some topics, episodes or incidents become the very matter of that identity, while others are shut out; some interpretations of these memories are sanctified and justify a particular view of selfhood, or a particular view of neighbouring peoples. In Italy as in Spain, Arab history had long been, and remained even after the publication in 1834 of Michele Amari's classic *Storia dei Musulmanni di Sicilia*, a taboo topic, a source of ignominy for a Catholic people, but Brancati and Sciascia, like Garcia Lorca in Andalusia, rescued that epoch from historical neglect and presented it as decisive for the creation of one of the mindsets which together constituted Sicilian consciousness and culture. That action is of greater importance than the actual content of their speculation, and retains its value even for those who reject as fanciful the view of history they propose.

It is the primacy of history which goes some way to explaining the domination of the historical novel in Sicilian literature. There is a need in Sicilians to explain to themselves the historical forces which have shaped the island and to come to terms with a history which they view, unanimously, as tormented and afflicted by the most backward forces which foreigners, or malign powers in their own society, could unleash on them. 'Even Verga and Pirandello', wrote Vincenzo Consolo, 'paid their dues to history', before adding, in his own idiosyncratic spin to the theme of the divided island, 'the historical aspect is more marked in the west of the island.' Elsewhere, he made a distinction between horizontal and vertical writers, where the first included Lawrence and Hemingway, the nomads of world literature, who could find their subjects in any country to which they travelled. On the other hand, he wrote,

> the vertical writers are us, the Neapolitans, the South Americans, all marked by conditions of life too strong for us not to root our writing in them. The greater the social unhappiness of a country, the more its writers are 'vertical', because of a need to explain its pain, and to understand why.[44]

The 'social pain' is a consequence of decisions taken at certain, well-defined historical turning-points, and these decisive moments, principally 1860 and the aftermath of Garibaldi's landing, and 1943 and the consequences of the Liberation, have been the subject of obsessive reworking by novelists. These are the points when Sicilian identity and its relations with Italian identity were shaped. The Risorgimento in Sicily was the subject of such diverse works as De Roberto's *The Viceroys*, Lampedusa's *The Leopard*, Pirandello's *The Old and the Young*, Sciascia's *The Forty-Eight* and Consolo's *The Smile of the Unknown Mariner*, while the Liberation has featured in a range of works which would include Consolo's *April's Wound*, Sciascia's *Candido* or Enzo Lauretta's *Sicilian Vacation*.

For all Gentile's efforts, it is plain that a distinctive Sicilian identity and culture survived unification, but in a national context that identity became increasingly subject to anxious questioning.

Straightforward ignorance, sometimes masked as romantic attachment, has often been a factor in the dealings of the north with Sicily
and the Mezzogiorno as a whole. Denis Mack Smith writes that
'Cavour confessed to knowing far more about England than
Southern Italy – he once told Parliament that he thought Sicilians
spoke Arabic'.[45] Referring to the often well-intentioned bafflement
of Piedmontese civil servants during the Risorgimento, the same
historian wrote: 'Northern officials found Sicily hard to understand.'
While the incomprehension was mutual, that of the northerners was
of greater import, because with unification power moved decisively
to the north. Mack Smith acidly suggests that one of the reasons for
the misunderstandings in general, and specifically for the belief that
in the nineteenth century 'Sicily was one of the most fertile countries in Europe' was that 'Cavour and his associates knew the island
not at first hand but by report and by reading ancient history or
modern poetry'. [46]

Patrick Brydone, the first of the travellers to extend the Grand
Tour beyond Naples, wrote an enormously influential book which
was translated into many languages and was carried by Goethe on
his tour of the island. For Brydone, Sicily was the 'land of myth'.
As a quintessential product of the Scottish Enlightenment, he found
it easier to respect the ancient gods and cults than modern saints and
religious practices. Hélène Tuzet, who examined with magisterial
authority the intuitions and the blindness of the travellers in Sicily,
declared that Brydone was the perfect exemplar of the *homo novus*
of the eighteenth century, and that as such 'il ne respecte rien'.[47] He
was, however, an acute observer of contemporary reality and could
have corrected the later beliefs of the Piedmontese when he drew
attention to 'the great fertility of the island, were it peopled and in
industrious hands'.[48] The inheritance of antiquity hung long about
the island, making it as much an area of the European imagination
as a location on a map or a site of political dispute. Paul-Louis
Courier, Napoleonic soldier and pamphleteer, was becalmed in
Calabria with the French army, waiting in vain for a wind which
would transport them across the Straits of Messina. Although later
Leonardo Sciascia, and the historian Francesco Renda, would lament
that the French failed to arrive and bring with them the winds of
change and the ideology of the French Revolution, Courier's
personal regret was that he would never see 'the fatherland of
Proserpina and understand why the devil had taken his wife in that

land'.[49] John Henry Newman, later Cardinal Newman, but then still a clergyman of the Church of England and on the point of launching the Oxford Movement, made the only extended trip abroad of his life in Sicily, to which he came as the theological traveller. While Sicily filled him with 'inexpressible rapture', he viewed the island as the acme of classical civilization, but for him that also meant civilization without Christ or grace, 'the most noble record of stone over high hopes and aims, pride, sin and disappointment'.[50] This inherited excitement, which placed Sicily in a dimension of the imagination rather than of physical reality, affected even Giuseppe Cesare Abba, one of Garibaldi's expeditionary party, whose *Noterelle* established for succeeding generations the heroic image of the invasion.

> Sicily! Sicily! Something hazy appeared on the blue between sea and sky, but it was the holy island! On the left we have the Egadi islands, in the distance, facing us is Monte Erice, covered in clouds. A Sicilian who was with me on the bridge told me of the adventures of Eryx, son of Venus, killed by Hercules on these peaks. The ancients were kind, but my friend is much more so in finding time to talk about mythology![51]

Perhaps the difficulty is that too much mythology has been spoken about Sicily. On 13 April 1787, in the diary which was the basis of his *Italian Journey*, Goethe wrote that 'without Sicily, Italy leaves no clear and lasting impression; this place is the key to everything'. The key has in the past opened on to too many blind alleys. The identity of Sicily was once constructed, in every European culture, of an amalgam of myth, legend, Renaissance epic, georgic, pastoral or bucolic poetry, imprecise recollections of Thucydides, and, more recently, of a few garish newspaper cuttings and Hollywood films. Elsewhere, this was a harmless enough indulgence in *salon* Arcadianism, but in Sicily itself the risk was that these sentiments or fantasies could become the basis of policy. The identity of Sicily is still as elusive as the golden honeycomb Daedalus concealed in some undiscovered spot on the island.

Notes

1 Giovanni Gentile, *Il tramonto della cultura siciliana,* second edition (Florence, Sansoni, 1985).

2 Leonardo Sciascia, *Pirandello e la Sicilia,* in *Opere 1984–1989,* edited by Claude Ambroise (Milan, Bompiani, 1991).

3   Sergio Romano, *Storia d'Italia dal Risorgimento ai nostri giorni* (Milan, Longanesi, 1998), 382.

4   Benedict Anderson, *Imagined Communities* (London, Verso, 1991).

5   This term was coined by Stathis Gourgouris in his study of the evolution of Greek consciousness, *Dream Nation: Enlightenment, Colonization and the Institution of Modern Greece* (Stanford, Stanford University Press, 1996), 11.

6   On Johann Herder, see *Herder on Social and Political Culture,* edited by F. M. Barnard (Cambridge, Cambridge University Press, 1969), and Isaiah Berlin, *Vico and Herder* (London, Hogarth Press, 1976). There are now many works on the development of modern nationalism, and on the connections between culture and nationhood, all of which have some discussion of Herder's role. In addition to Benedict Anderson's seminal work, the following may be cited: Ernest Gellner, *Nations and Nationalism* (Oxford, Oxford University Press, 1983); E. J. Hobsbawm, *Nations and Nationality since 1780* (Cambridge, Cambridge University Press, 1990).

7   Declan Kiberd, *Inventing Ireland* (London, Jonathan Cape, 1995), 3

8   Roy Foster, 'Storylines: narratives and nationality in nineteenth-century Ireland', in Geoffrey Cubitt, ed., *Imagining Nations* (Manchester, University of Manchester Press, 1998), 40.

9   Giuseppe Pitrè, *Usi e costumi, credenze e pregiudizi del popolo siciliano*, 4 vols., 1870-1913; second edition, edited by Diego Carpitella (Palermo, SCRL, 1978), ix.

10 Pitrè, *Usi e costumi*, II, 287-302.

11 Isaia Sales, *Leghisti e sudisti* (Bari, Laterza, 1993), 9.

12 Luigi Sturzo, *La battaglia meridionalista* (Bari, Laterza, 1945).

13 Tzvetan Todorov, *On Human Diversity: Nationalism, Racism and Exoticism in French Thought* (Cambridge, MA, Harvard University Press, 1993), 172.

14 Denis Mack Smith, *A History of Sicily: Modern Sicily after 1713* (London, Chatto & Windus, 1968), 529.

15 Antonio Pizzuto, *Signorina Rosina* (Milan, Lerici, 1959); Robert Dombroski, 'Re-writing Sicily: postmodern perspectives', in Jane Schneider, ed., *Italy's 'Southern Question'* (Oxford, Berg, 1998), 264.

16 Mario Puzo, *The Sicilian* (London, Bantam Press, 1985).

17 Rosario Villari, *Il Sud nella storia d'Italia* (Bari, Laterza, 1978), 132.

18 There is a vast literature on this subject, including Piero Bevilacqua, *Breve storia dell'Italia meridionale* (Milan, Donzelli, 1993); Francesco Barbagallo, *Mezzogiorno e questione meridionale (1860-1980)* (Naples, Guida, 1980).

19 Umberto Bossi, *Il vento dal Nord* (Milan, Sperling & Kupfler, 1991).

20 Giorgio Bocca, *La disUNITÀ d'Italia* (Milan, Garzanti, 1990), and

L'inferno, (Milan, Mondadori, 1992).

21 Rosario Poma, *Onorevole alzatevi!* (Florence, Edizioni Scorpione, 1976); Salvatore Lupo, *Storia della Mafia* (Milan, Donzelli, 1993), 67–105; Giulio Speroni, *Il delitto Notarbartolo* (Milan, Rusconi, 1993).

22 Quoted by Massimo Onofri, *Tutti a cena da don Mariano* (Milan, Bompiani, 1995), 102.

23 Sturzo, *La battaglia meridionalista,* 46.

24 Pitrè, *Usi e costumi,* II, 287–93.

25 Luigi Capuana, *La Sicilia e il brigantaggio* (Rome, Stabilimento Tipografico Italiano, 1892).

26 S. F. Romano, *Storia della Mafia* (Milan, Mondadori, 1966), 91–2; Nando Dalla Chiesa, *Il potere mafioso* (Milan, Mazzotta, 1976), 169.

27 Edward W. Said, *Orientalism* (London, Routledge and Kegan Paul, 1978).

28 Jane Schneider, ed., *Italy's 'Southern Question': Orientalism in One Country* (Oxford, Berg, 1998).

29 Salvador Giner, 'L'esdevenir de la identitat nacional', introduction to Joan M. Pujals, *Les noves fronteres de Catalunya* (Barcelona, Columna Assaig, 1998), xi.

30 Gesualdo Bufalino, *Saldi d'autunno* (Milan, Bompiani, 1990), 7.

31 Salvatore Sgroi, *Per la lingua di Pirandello e Sciascia* (Caltanissetta–Rome, S. Sciascia, 1990).

32 Interview with present author at Racalmuto, 1985.

33 Frederic Jameson, 'Postmodernism and the consumer society', in *The Cultural Turn: Selected Writings on the Postmodern, 1983–1998* (London, Verso, 1998), 20.

34 Luigi Pirandello, *I vecchi e i giovani,* in *Tutti i romanzi,* edited by Manlio Lo Vecchio-Musti (Milan, Mondadori, 1969).

35 Antonio Di Grado, *L'isola di carta* (Syracuse, Ediprint, 1984).

36 Sebastiano Aglianò, *Questa Sicilia,* new edition (Milan, Mondadori, 1994).

37 Dacia Maraini, *La lunga vita di Marianna Ucria* (Milan, Rizzoli, 1990).

38 G. A. Borgese, introduction to *Sicilia* (Milan, Touring Club Italiano, 1933), 7.

39 See the views of the unnamed speaker in Gaia Servadio, *Mafioso* (London, Secker & Warburg, 1976), 222.

40 Gesualdo Bufalino and Nunzio Zago, eds., *Cento Sicilie* (Milan, Bompiani, 1992).

41 Tomasi di Lampedusa, *Il gattopardo* (Milan, Feltrinelli, 1960), 209.

42 Quoted by Leonardo Sciascia, introduction to Vitaliano Brancati, *Opere 1932–46* (Milan, Bompiani, 1987), viii.

43 Sciascia, *Pirandello e la Sicilia*, 1052–3.

44 Vincenzo Consolo, in *Grazia,* 30 October 1988 and *Europeo,* 31

October 1987, 123.

45 Denis Mack Smith, *Cavour* (London, Weidenfeld & Nicolson, 1985), 216.

46 Mack Smith, *Modern Sicily after 1713*, 453–4.

47 Hélène Tuzet, *La Sicile au XVIII siècle vue par les voyageurs étrangers* (Strasbourg, Heitz, 1955).

48 Patrick Brydone, *A Tour through Sicily and Malta*, third edition (Dublin, United Company of Booksellers, 1735), 33.

49 Paul-Louis Courier, *Lettres de France et d'Italie*, quoted in Sciascia, *Opere*, I, 487.

50 John Henry Newman, 'My illness in Sicily', in *Autobiographical Writings*, edited by Henry Tristam (London, Sheed and Ward, 1956), 119–20.

51 G. C. Abba, *Da Quarto a Volturno. Noterelle di uno dei mille*, new edition (Milan, Mondadori, 1980), 38–9.

4

Language and Italian national identity

HOWARD MOSS

In late 1991 a proposed law on language went through the lower house of the Italian Parliament. Approval by the upper house, the Senate, was expected in a short space of time. The legislation provided for use in education, broadcasting and administration of thirteen 'minority languages' (Albanian, Catalan, Franco-Provençal, French, Friulan, German, Greek, Ladin, Occitan, Romany, Sardinian, Serbo-Croat, Slovenian) used in various different parts of Italy. But its prospect caused such a furore among cultural and intellectual commentators that the politicians had second thoughts. This was easier for them as, hard on this controversy, there followed the dissolution of Parliament amid the 'Tangentopoli' scandals, and attention became focused on more compelling issues. The new administration that came to power placed the legislation on a high shelf where it lay for almost a decade.

The interesting thing about this law, aside from the option of linguistic autonomy to minorities that it had been designed to grant, was the vociferous opposition to it and, in particular, the sources of that opposition. Historical experience might lead us to expect that such legislation would be the ideological preserve of the political and cultural left, and that opposition to it would come from the traditional forces of nationalist reaction, the right. Here, after all, was a reform that could be interpreted as tending to undermine national unity in its granting to 'foreign' tongues a status equal to that of the national language. Such expectations were not fulfilled: the right's reaction was muted, while the left fought out among itself a furious ideological battle for and against. Eventually the opponents, arguing that such reforms would have 'perverse effects' on national unity, won the day.[1] Yet the divisions and ambiguities do, on close inspection, echo the ideologically untidy and often unpredictable reactions of Italian intellectuals all along the political spectrum to matters of language ever since Italy became a nation almost a century and a half ago.

A unified state without a unified language

Perhaps it is not surprising that language has aroused strong emotions among the Italian political and intellectual classes. After all the Italian state began its life in 1861 without a common language among the mass of its people, and with the crucial need therefore of a national tongue to articulate and forge the national consciousness which did not exist but would need to be spread. In a country where the language that most people knew was one of the many and often vastly diverse dialects of their locality or region, another language through which all citizens of the newly founded nation could freely and spontaneously communicate with one another could only present itself as a matter of urgent priority.

This is not to say that the Italian language, or at least a language known as 'Italian', did not exist before the unification of Italy or was not known by people throughout the Italian peninsula and on the islands. The problem was that this language was not known by *many* people; it was known in fact by only a small sprinkling. Its use was exclusive to the small élite who were literate and therefore had access to the written tradition of Italian composition which had, ever since the fourteenth century, used as its medium the language of the great Florentine writers of that century, Dante, Petrarch and Boccaccio. The prestige of those writers and of Florence itself at this early stage of historical development had led to that city's language being codified as the accepted form for written usage in Italy, even though everywhere in Italy the spoken languages were diverse and ever evolving. Even Florentine itself, in its spoken usage, diverged from its early form as time went by. So, over a number of centuries, Italian existed as a language for use predominantly in writing, its only use in speech being on formal or ceremonial occasions or as a somewhat unsatisfactory lingua franca for the educated from different parts of Italy whose different spoken languages, their dialects, would otherwise have been a serious barrier to mutual intelligibility. Tuscans, too, even though their language had undergone evolution since the fourteenth century, were often thought of as speaking Italian, as their language remained close enough to the written language to be identified with it. Rome, furthermore, because of its cosmopolitan tradition as home to the Papacy, had over several centuries tended to absorb Tuscan linguistic norms and forms.

However, even if all these categories are added together – the literate of all Italy and the populations of Tuscany and Rome – research has indicated that the proportion of people who could be said to know 'Italian' at the time of unification could not have been more than 12 per cent and may have been as low as 2.5 per cent.[2] What the new national Italian government was facing therefore was a situation in which, out of a population of 35 million, at least 31 million did not have a common language. It was a situation that needed to change, and change it did. The way it changed over the decades to come was that the mainly written form of expression, based on the fourteenth-century Florentine idiom and already known as Italian, gradually spread to the spoken domain to become eventually the language of the whole nation for both spoken and written purposes, so that today, less than 150 years after unification, it is known and used on a daily basis by the overwhelming majority of Italian citizens.

Language as the 'ideal sign of the nation': which language for Italy?

How was this gradual spread effected, and how in turn did it affect the local and regional languages which have historically been the means of expression of most inhabitants of Italy? Above all, for the purposes of this discussion, how closely bound up has all this been with questions of national consciousness and an identity that could be called Italian? In Italy the language came a long time before the nation, but to what extent can the Italian language be said to have been, as one commentator has put it, 'the ideal sign of the nation itself'?[3]

As Italy moved painfully slowly along the road to political unity in the first half of the nineteenth century, in some quarters the question of linguistic unity was already being raised. This was not the linguistic unity in the written language which, as we have seen, Italy already had and which had already been established beyond recall by the end of the sixteenth century on the basis of an acceptance of fourteenth-century Florentine usage. Nor did it have much to do with the matters of linguistic unity which had been discussed in the eighteenth and nineteenth centuries and which largely concerned the acceptance or otherwise of Spanish and French terminology in the written tongue. The subject now was unity in the spoken language. This was the new twist in Italy's long-running *questione della lingua* (language question), which was brought about largely through the influence of the nineteenth-century poet and novelist, Alessandro Manzoni.

The new resonance that Manzoni gave to the language question arose from the frustration he experienced as a young man in not being able to communicate adequately with other Italians in parts of Italy other than his native Milan. The interest in language matters this provoked in him caused him very quickly to turn the *questione della lingua* on its head. No longer was the central issue to be the nature and specific forms of the written language but rather the kind of Italian which was to be used for everyday spoken purposes and on which would then depend written usage. Manzoni wrote extensively on this topic throughout his long lifetime and much has been written by others on what he wrote. Yet his themes and preoccupations are fairly simple to explain. After discarding certain theories and experiments of his earlier years, by the 1840s he had come to focus sharply on the idea that Italian as a spoken language, and consequently in its written form too, should be represented by educated contemporary Florentine, a language that was not his own.[4] This idea arose from two sources: firstly from his perception of the enormous gap that existed between most people's spoken language (dialect) and Italian (fourteenth-century Florentine); secondly from an espousal of *uso* (usage) as a guiding concept in determining what the spoken language should be. The term 'usage' occurs frequently in Manzoni's writings on language and by it he means the best of living contemporary usage. This, in Manzoni's opinion, is not to be found in the archaic written practice dependent on fourteenth-century Florentine but in the kind of spoken language which he sees as coming from educated speakers of nineteenth-century Florentine. Though Manzoni's choice of Florentine as the best tongue for the spoken language essentially reflects a personal preference (conditioned in its turn no doubt by the geographical provenance of the language that had historically been known as Italian), the important thing at this stage was that a figure with considerable resonance was saying that a unified spoken language was necessary for Italy. This is a line to which he held tenaciously up to unification and beyond, when his increased prestige and influence on government gave rise to a many-sided debate which involved a number of eminent protagonists, including of course Manzoni himself.

Manzoni, in wishing to see contemporary Florentine established as the national language of the newly established state, suggested such strategies as the publication of dictionaries of Tuscan, the sending of Tuscan primary school teachers to schools throughout Italy, Tuscan teachers giving instruction to teachers from other regions, and free visits to Tuscany for the most able schoolchildren. Such proposals were contained in Manzoni's report to the Italian government in 1868.[5] This was followed in 1871 by the publication of the first part of the dictionary of Tuscan usage which Manzoni had recommended and which the government of the time had agreed to, the *Novo vocabolario della lingua italiana secondo l'uso di Firenze*.[6] Among figures to react to Manzoni's scheme was the language scholar Graziadio Isaia Ascoli who, in the introduction to the first issue of his journal, *Archivio glottologico italiano*, argued strongly against Manzoni's ideas.[7] In his argument and in many other writings on language, Ascoli shows himself to be the first linguistic commentator in Italy to bring to the study of Italy's language question what might be called a modern historical dimension. Ascoli's view was that it was unnecessary, and indeed impossible, to start from scratch in spreading a national language. In fact Italy already had one: fourteenth-century Florentine. Though it was only thinly spread over the population and was largely used for written purposes, it did exist and, as such, it would be – it would have to be – the language, both spoken and written, of the newly united nation. As it spread to the masses through the agency of social forces, it would evolve, as languages always do under such influence, but it would begin with its basis in the forms Italian had known for centuries. As for contemporary Florentine, while it had retained a fairly close resemblance to the fourteenth-century language, it was nevertheless a municipal dialect. Manzoni's choice of it as the national language was unhistorical and arbitrary and any attempt to impose it artificially on Italy to the detriment of the already existing Italian language would be doomed to failure. At the same time Ascoli did not deny – on the contrary he confirmed – the importance of 'usage', but he insisted that the usage that would prevail nationally would be the language already known to the literate of the whole of Italy and not the spoken tongue of a small geographical area. So though it was Manzoni who initiated discussion of the need for a language through which the whole of the Italian population could communicate, it was left to others, particularly Ascoli, to see the natural implications of this and to predict correctly, in its broad lines at least, what Italy's linguistic future would be.[8]

If with hindsight we can see Ascoli's vision as more far-seeing than Manzoni's and based on a more acute interpretation of history, it seemed far less cut and dried to the intellectuals, politicians and legislators of the last three decades of the nineteenth century. For many, Ascoli's views seemed too much grounded in theory and a recipe for administrative and political inertia. He appeared to be saying (and to a large extent was saying) that history should be allowed to take its course, yet without committing himself as to how long that could be expected to take. Manzoni, on the other hand, could be seen as representing practical action, a way forward, steps to bring about prompt change in a situation that could not be allowed to stand still. Ascoli had argued that you could not impose upon a nation, which was now formally united but had been culturally divided for centuries, a quick linguistic fix, an instrument to iron out those divisions. You could not have 'unity of language' without 'unity of thought'. But enthusiasm for such an ironing-out process, for somehow imposing a new national consciousness through language, was considerable and, even if Manzoni's proposals for linguistic education inevitably ran into the sand, his dictionary of contemporary spoken Florentine continued to be promoted, twenty years after his death, by successive governments until the *Novo vocabolario* was finally completed and published in full.[9]

It had by this time become an irrelevance. The sense of belonging to a national entity which was growing in the better-educated post-unification generation had already begun to express itself linguistically through the medium of a national language which was the traditional literary tongue and definitely not the municipal contemporary Florentine recorded in the *Novo vocabolario*. The language of administration, state education and journalism was the Italian of Dante, as increasingly too was the spoken language of the educated and literate in many parts of Italy, especially in the economically advanced urban areas. And even those who did not readily speak that language were coming to be acquainted with it to the point of understanding it when it was used by others and seeing

an advantage in their children learning and using it. Yet, historically, these were very early days. The vast majority of the
population still expressed themselves on a daily and domestic basis
through the medium of dialect. The dialects still ruled the spoken
domain and would continue to do so for a long time.

A weak linguistic hegemony

In his 'Relazione' of 1868, Manzoni had referred to language as 'a
social and national question' replacing 'a bundle of literary questions', and had called for government action. Yet, against a
background of local and regional cultures and traditions which
stretched back over centuries, post-unification governments could
achieve little by such action. They might vilify the dialects and
minority languages as backward and unpatriotic so that those who
used them would feel humiliated and belittled. But they could not,
by legislation or by any other method, rapidly change the linguistic
practices of centuries. They could not prevent dialect-speakers using
their dialects and they could not force people to use a language,
whether old Tuscan or contemporary Tuscan, which they did not
know or felt uncomfortable in. As Ascoli had predicted, history, not
governments, would shape such matters. A national identity could
not be imposed; it would have to evolve.

Yet even as historically acute a figure as Antonio Gramsci,
writing in the 1930s and looking back to the late nineteenth century,
felt the governments of the period could have had a greater impact
on the language question. His *Quaderni del carcere* argue that,
though in the nineteenth century a unitary culture had spread
together with a 'common unitary language', the slowness of that
spread had been due to the inability of the ruling class fully to
impose its ideological hegemony upon Italian society.[10] The historical development of the nation after unification had, he maintains,
taken place at too slow a pace, because the bourgeoisie and its agents
had not been sufficiently aware of the need to establish the closest
possible identification between its own aspirations and 'the national-
popular mass', the need to reorganize the 'cultural hegemony' of the
newly created nation.[11] The slow progress of the national language
was a guide to the slow rate at which the national bourgeoisie was
promoting national identity among the citizens of a nation whose

past was rooted in a variety of different communities and traditions which needed to be superseded. So while the language used by Gramsci ('The process of formation, diffusion and development of a national language takes place through a whole complex of molecular processes') was decidedly different from Ascoli's, his analysis was quite similar: the historical development of civil society determines the development and shape of language as of other social phenomena.[12] Yet he differs from Ascoli and, perhaps paradoxically, comes closer to Manzoni (whose influence he acknowledges while also recognizing his limitations), in seeing this process as being able to be speeded up by purposeful intervention ('It is useful to be aware of the whole process in its complexity in order to be in a position to intervene actively in it with the maximum result').[13] Gramsci argues elsewhere that Italy has fallen prey to Fascism precisely because its post-unification governments had been backward in creating a solid 'national-popular' identity between the classes, part of which would have been a mastery by all citizens of the country's national language. Whether such a national identity could have been imposed or encouraged by intervention is an unresolvable issue; yet, on the language question at least, hindsight seems to point to Ascoli's view as having been more prescient.

The Fascist linguistic enterprise

Gramsci was clearly right, however, that Fascism fed on and was able to exploit the weak national sense of the Italian masses and their lack of identity with those who governed them. Part of this underdeveloped sense of nation was the still limited use by the masses of the official language of the nation. Fascism would have liked to change this, and its period of power marks a far more determined if, as we shall see, scarcely more successful attempt than the governments of liberal Italy to undermine the dialects and minority languages and to promote Italian as the only language fit to be used. When the Fascist regime came to power, Italian was the normal language of a minority of Italians. When it collapsed in defeat over twenty years later, that situation had not much changed. Nor had the Italian language itself changed significantly in the ways that Fascism's legislative and propaganda manipulations had attempted to direct it.

105

One of the aims of Mussolini's regime was to create a solid nationalism – the kind of cultural hegemony that, according to Gramsci, had been slow in developing – around which Italians could unite. It went about this by creating myths of various kinds associated with Italy's past and present. Some went back as far as the Roman Empire, others not so far back. One of them projected an unbroken linguistic line from Latin to Dante and then from Dante and other fourteenth-century writers to the present day. The modern-day language was thus promoted as the outcome of a glorious past, the natural tongue of the nation, with all other forms of expression being deviations from that ideal norm. In one way, this was no more than a more vigorous continuity of the attitude towards language of previous Italian governments, who, even if they had not been so hot on myth, had been equally prepared to tarnish the dialects and minority languages as an affront to national dignity, and to inflict upon them as profound an inferiority complex as possible.

However, an added dimension of national linguistic purity which Fascism took up, though with different motives, from certain linguistic purists of the eighteenth and early nineteenth century was to discriminate against and, if possible, ban forms from the foreign languages, especially French and English. The phenomenon has been much documented.[14] Suffice it to mention the law aimed at preventing the use of foreign words on shop signs, the official government attempts to exclude the polite third-person singular *lei* form of address in favour of the *voi* form on the grounds that the *lei* had foreign (Spanish) origins, the task given to the Accademia d'Italia of drawing up lists of foreign words to be proscribed and suggesting 'Italian' alternatives, and the debate in academic circles on whether the 'correct' pronunciation of Italian was Florentine or Roman. On this last issue, the two eminent language scholars who were the major proponents of Roman pronunciation, Giulio Bertoni and Francesco Ugolini, quoted Mussolini in support of their case ('The capital in every well ordered state . . . is not a city, but a political institution, a moral organism') and went on to wish for 'the spreading in Italy and beyond of the sweet, warm pronunciation heard in educated Roman conversation'.[15] Piero Monelli, a journalist not a language specialist but one of the regime's best publicists on language matters, wrote, in his *Barbaro dominio* of 1933, of the need to rid the language of foreign forms.[16] In the *Nuova antologia* of 16 August 1926, Fascist Party member Tommaso Tittoni had called upon the Duce to send government representatives around newspaper offices to catch out and sack linguistic offenders, since 'speaking and writing in the correct Italian way is not only a literary question, but one of *national action*'.[17] Even a serious scholar of high repute such as Bruno Migliorini was led to propose a method, usually referred to as *neo-purismo* (neo-purism), to separate the Italian wheat from the foreign chaff.

In historical perspective, such attempts at linguistic manipulation may seem crass or comical, but, most importantly, their failure shows how extraordinarily difficult it is even for a regime with centralized control over most aspects of a nation's life to shift linguistic habits. While it is true that in language, as in many other areas, Fascism's attempts at totalitarian control were patchy and erratic, the fact is that none of its specific linguistic reforms or recommendations, seem to have had a significant impact on the use of language.[18] When the Second World War ended and the new democratic Italy stuttered into being, the elimination of foreign language forms had not taken place and the dialects and minority languages were still the preferred form of communication of the majority of the population. There had been a weakening of dialect and minority-language use, but at no greater a rate than had been taking place before the Fascist period as the cultures expressed by those languages had begun to give way before the onset of twentieth-century development and its centralizing tendencies. Fascism had tried to impose uniformity of thought, but the historically determined lack of uniformity of culture, which Ascoli had pointed to over seventy years before the fall of Fascism, still prevailed and continued to have a powerful influence on Italy's language question.

Language and the democratic constitution

Those who framed the constitution of post-war democratic Italy had lived through the Fascist period and seen the policy of the regime towards the dialects and minority languages. It is perhaps not surprising that the new constitution, made law on 1 January 1948, carried a reference to linguistic equality ('All Italian citizens have equal social dignity and are equal before the law, without distinction of sex, race, language, religion, political opinions, personal or social condition') and a specific commitment to the defence of

107

linguistic minorities ('The Republic will protect linguistic minorities with appropriate measures').[19]

The provision of a clause in the constitution dedicated to the minority (i.e. non-Italian) languages may have been an attempt to head off potential secessionist feeling in certain parts of Italy, but almost certainly it also signalled a genuine desire by Italy's new ruling groups to redress the harsh intolerance to which the linguistic minorities had been subjected not just by Fascism but by all governments which had ruled the Italian state. Fascism had continued a policy towards the minority languages signalled as early as 1861, when a member of the newly formed Italian Parliament, Giovenale Vegezzi-Ruscalla, published a pamphlet on 'Our right and need to exclude French as an official language in certain valleys of the province of Turin', arguing that the newly united nation could not tolerate the use of minority languages if it was to survive as a coherent political and territorial unit.[20] Language, Vegezzi-Ruscalla had written previously, was 'the certificate of origin of nations'.[21]

Compared to the constitutional provision for the minority languages now granted by the constitution, and soon to bring special benefits to some of them, the dialects might be seen to have done rather badly.[22] The dialects were of course covered by the constitution's catch-all reference to linguistic equality (equal before the law, without distinction of . . . language), but it is likely that the framers saw no need to be specific about the dialects since they took the common view that the process of retreat of the dialects, already well under way after nearly ninety years of national unity, would continue apace until the dialects eventually, and perhaps quite quickly, went away. One of the official elementary school curricula published in 1955, stated: 'Care must be taken to make sure that people do not confuse dialectal ways of saying things with the correct forms of the language.'[23] However, though the dialects were generally considered a backward element in the nation's life, they were not seen as a significant danger to national unity. In an age which, it was accepted, would see an increase in the processes already under way of economic development, labour mobility and increased literacy and education, it was taken for granted that people would move increasingly towards the national language and, would above all, make sure that their children knew it in order to be able to make their way in the world and have a say in its development. So, though compared to previous official attitudes the constitution seemed to take an enlightened position on the dialects, viewed from a different angle that position can also be seen as one of benign neglect.

Language and region

The constitution's framers could not of course foresee the specific details of what would happen in Italy in the half-century to come, especially the great rapidity of the changes that would transform the country from a fairly poor, largely agricultural society to one of the world's wealthiest industrial nations. Nor could they foresee the effects this transformation would have on language and national identity. Yet, change in mental processes, which are the essence of language and national identity, always lags behind, sometimes far behind, change in material conditions. There is no doubt that Italians have, under the democratic governments which have ruled since 1948, developed a more cohesive national identity than before. It has been said that, for all its faults and excesses, Fascism laid the ground for this with its ebullient nationalism, transmitting a feeling of pride among Italians, both at home and abroad, and encouraging them to identify with its affairs. This may be true, but what Fascism did not do, and what, despite all the changes that have taken place in Italy over the last fifty years, no government has succeeded in doing, is significantly to break down the strong regional identity most Italians feel. It is often held up as a paradox that, among the economically advanced European nations, the Italians are the most 'regional' yet at the same time the most 'European'. Yet it does not seem too difficult to explain. If, for many centuries, Italy was a socially and politically fragmented territory whose inhabitants owed their allegiance to local or regional centres, less than a century and a half's experience of political unity has not been enough, despite the material change wrought in this period, to prise Italians away from those allegiances. What follows from this still strong identity with region is correspondingly weaker identity with state and nation and the consequent likelihood of Italians viewing the European enterprise through less nationalistic eyes than their fellow Europeans, and seeing it as a development which they can fit into and participate in more readily than neighbours whose countries' national historical experience makes them more attached to an exclusively national identity. So though Italy has, since the Second World War, developed a more cohesive national identity than ever before, its regional roots still show clearly above the ground, and it remains, among its European neighbours, probably the least respectful, and the most suspicious, of calls to national unity or solidarity.

New linguistic conditions

The place of language in this advancing but still lukewarm and incomplete embrace of a national identity is no more neat and tidy than the overall social picture. The picture drawn by Tullio De Mauro in 1963 of the new conditions which led during the first century of unification to a large-scale linguistic Italianizing of the Italian people remains unsurpassed.[24] But most of the factors he pointed to (return emigration, internal migration and urbanization, industrialization, state schooling, national bureaucracy, military service, press, mass entertainment) continued, in the decades to follow, to exercise their influence even more intensively on the Italianizing process. Statistics indicate a considerable change in the linguistic balance between Italian and dialect over the last fifty years. From a minority of people being regular speakers of the national language at the end of the Second World War (no more than 37 per cent),[25] Italian is now spoken by the vast majority – almost 90 per cent, say the most recent figures, though it is hard not to consider this an underestimate based on one's own experience of the country and its people and on the vagaries of polls and surveys.[26] In 1996 Giovanni Nencioni, president of the Accademia della Crusca, saw it in dramatic terms: 'In the last fifty years we have seen a miracle: Italian has gone from being a "virtual national language", that is one written in books, to a "truly national" language, that is a spoken language too.'[27] It goes without saying, moreover, that the sharing by most Italians of a language they did not share before has been a contributory factor in the shaping of a feeling of Italianness among people of diverse cultural origins. The language of newspapers, television, electronic communication, bureaucracy and common (if not necessarily domestic) parlance is virtually the same for everyone and understood by virtually everyone. It also unites Italians by constantly changing and moulding itself to the needs of a living usage which reflects the collective experience of the nation.

110

Yet, it remains at the same time the language of fourteenth-century Florence, the language of Dante, Petrarch and Boccaccio. It is not of course exactly the same language as the Florentine man in the street used six centuries ago. It underwent relatively minor changes in its mainly written use between the fourteenth and nineteenth centuries, but the changes it has undergone since unification have been more considerable. There is more than one view on the extent of this change. In 1987, Claudio Quarantotto, in the introduction to his *Dizionario del nuovo italiano*, wrote: 'Today's Italian is different from yesterday's and is incomprehensible to the reader from not even twenty years ago.'[28] Yet at the very same time Giulio Lepschy, having carried out a detailed comparison between today's language and the Italian of not twenty but a hundred years ago, reported: 'The impression one gets is of great stability and not at all of linguistic upheaval . . . It does not seem that Italian has changed so much.'[29] The difference in perspective here probably derives from the emphasis the two writers have given to different elements of the language. The main differences the twenty-first century reader of Manzoni's novel, *I promessi sposi* (1842), finds compared with today's language are stylistic ones, in addition of course to the absence of terms expressing the new objects and concepts of modern life. If it were possible, however, for literate nineteenth-century observers to come into contact with today's language, they would find a large number of elements they were not familiar with and which might well cause problems of comprehension. Yet these elements would be largely lexical and if such persons were to be presented with a text bereft of much in the way of specific reference to modern life, the amount of difficulty they would experience would certainly be very small indeed. They would have no trouble understanding the language in most of its structures, grammatical form and basic vocabulary. This is the perspective from which Lepschy's findings on linguistic change derive, while Quarantotto, though his claim must be considered something of an exaggeration – perhaps a 'marketing' one – is more concerned with the lexical elements in the language which can give a strong appearance of change and innovation even if the basic structures remain, as they have done, largely constant.

Those mainly lexical elements which the nineteenth-century observer might have difficulty recognizing in today's language would include: (a) the terms from various Italian dialects made current by former dialect-only speakers which have found a place in the national language; (b) the large number of new terms which have been coined to express new concepts, inventions and developments as Italian life and society have continued to transform themselves; (c) the many new, largely unmodified and un-Italian-looking foreign terms, mainly from English, which have come to be an integral part of Italian as the Anglo-Saxon world has exercised its cultural dominance over Italy as elsewhere.[30] If such forms have brought new dimensions to the Italian language, so much so as to lead some commentators to talk about the modern tongue, especially as used by the media and among young people, in terms of 'Italian gone wild', they may also be seen as part of the development of what Tullio De Mauro, as long ago as 1976, saw as a new-found security on the part of the Italian masses in using Italian as a living contemporary language.[31] It is only in given technical or specialist fields, such as information technology, where many of the objects or concepts being dealt with are entirely new, that Italians out of direct contact with the language over a period of years would be likely to find themselves in difficulty. The point has also been made that English, even if it is a ready contributor to contemporary Italian vocabulary, does not, as is often claimed, show signs of flooding the language of everyday spoken or written discourse in Italy.[32] It is true, however, that, in certain specialist scientific fields, it has become difficult to communicate at all in Italian, since the international lingua franca of those fields has become English.[33]

Yet it would be misleading to suggest that the resolution of Italy's language question in terms of the acceptance of living contemporary usage has brought with it no changes to the language which are not purely lexical. Certain of those shifts in syntax and morphology which have asserted themselves gradually over the last 150 years and which might give pause for thought to our nineteenth-century observers were well documented by Francesco Sabatini in 1985 in an article in which he broached the concept, which has found considerable favour since, of an 'italiano dell'uso medio', an everyday Italian language shared by the 'average' person which tends to transcend regional differences and to express the shared culture of an Italy, especially a young person's Italy, which is becoming more and more homogeneous.[34] This is the kind of process which has been called the 'democratization of Italian'.[35] Yet none of the features cited and discussed by Sabatini, which, according to some commentators, form part of the corruption of the contemporary language, 'Italian gone wild', would be likely to present serious obstacles to our visitors' overall comprehension.[36] What would be no real obstacle either, though it might cause puzzlement, would be the regional diversity of accent with which Italian has, over the last 140 years, come to be spoken, as people of different dialect backgrounds have adopted Italian and invested it with phonetic and intonational features from their original tongues.[37]

The dialects: presence, fate and impact

What nineteenth-century visitors would not be surprised at as they travelled round would be to hear languages other than Italian, especially dialects, used more or less everywhere. The phenomenon would, it is true, be less in evidence, both in extent and intensity, than 150 years ago, but the time traveller would still find it very much present. In other words, the dialects are still very much alive.[38] They do not have the universal currency they had in the 1860s, but they are still known by a majority of the Italian population.[39] They can also still be used sometimes, as some of them always have been, for written, especially literary, purposes.[40] They have of course evolved over time, as all languages do under the spoken dynamic, so that, for example, a nineteenth-century speaker of Neapolitan, would undoubtedly have some difficulty with the modern dialect of Naples. One of the main influences on all dialects in recent times has been the dominant national language present all around, so that some commentators have found it possible to talk, not of separate languages – dialect and Italian – being spoken in a given area, but of a continuum from dialect through dialect-influenced Italian to forms of the national language with reciprocal influences operating and the existence of 'code-switching' and 'tactical' use of language.[41] However, as Giulio Lepschy has recently reminded us, despite the Italianizing of dialects, they are still 'mostly unintelligible to speakers of other dialects' – and, it might be added, to monoglot Italian-speakers.[42]

While it is true that the use of dialects now tends to be circumscribed to domestic or other informal contexts, they continue, despite frequent and ongoing forecasts of doom, to play a significant part in the lives of very many Italians.[43] Their continuing use, some

may argue, has been and continues to be an obstacle in the establishment of a firm Italian national identity, since they perpetuate the
primacy and values of alternative local or regional cultures at the
expense of a united national culture. This may be so, but, seeing the
matter from another angle, the disappearance or weakening of many
local dialects that has taken place indicates the prevalence of national
culture over local and regional ones. And T. Gwynfor Griffith is
surely right in stating that 'the dialects can hardly be considered to
be a great threat to the language in the future'.[44] The logic of historical development seems to be that the retreat of the dialects will
continue to its ultimate conclusion. But history can also hold
surprises. Might the truly united Europe which seems to be on at
least a long-term agenda not bring a process of administrative and
cultural decentralization, of regional autonomies within a secure
united framework, which could reverse the national centralizing
trend in language as well as in other areas of life?

Whatever happens to the Italian dialects in the future, they will
have left behind a considerable legacy, for they have, as we have
seen, been part of the shaping of the national language since unification. But apart from their contribution to the lexicon and to the
phonetic diversity of the spoken language, they have also created in
Italian the phenomenon known as 'geo-synonymy', whereby in the
everyday domains of Italian vocabulary a diversity of terms often
exists to express the same concept according to regional usage. Such
terms usually have their origin in the regional forms traditionally
used to express the concepts. So, for example, the concept of a
'kitchen sink' or 'wash-basin' is widely rendered in Italian by
lavandino but can also be expressed by *acquaio*, *lavabo*, *lavello*,
secchiaio or *versatoio*, depending on the locality where the language
is being spoken. And to cite just one more among countless examples, 'coat-hanger' can, according to regional location, apart from
the nationally widespread *attaccapanni*, be *gruccia*, *ometto* or *stam-
pella*. This much-studied phenomenon does of course have parallels
in other European languages, including English, but its very strong
presence in Italy makes it a more significant factor than elsewhere
and probably gives Italian a stronger synonymic dimension than
most other European languages.[45] This regional dimension of Italian
also has a further consequence. Though the views expressed by
observers on the gradual convergence of Italian upon an 'average'
norm seem to have a good deal of validity with an overall favouring

of northern usage (and this applies to pronunciation too, for among the young especially it is becoming increasingly difficult to identify where a person is from by accent), it is still commonly the case that, when non-Italians ask the advice of more than one native Italian-speaker on a linguistic matter, they are likely to get different answers and even contradictory ones. The regional linguistic background of Italians and their associated speech habits still tend to mean that their 'intuition' about what is correct or appropriate linguistically either differs from one speaker to another or is less secure than the 'intuition' of, say, corresponding native English- or French-speakers.

Identity and unity in language: differences of perception

To end this discussion where we began it, we may return to Italy's non-Italian minority languages. If the dialects are still very much alive yet are no longer seen as a significant threat to national identity, what of those other minority tongues whose users are variously put at between 1 and 2 million? They were once, as we have seen, considered an especially large threat to the development of a national consciousness and, for the first eighty or ninety years of the unified state, were regarded as intruders in the national domain and given no official existence. The official admission of existence accorded them by the 1948 constitution led, as we have seen, to an improvement in status for some of them.[46] Francophone speech in north-west Italy and German in the Alto Adige seem in no danger of early extinction, with the bilingual status and administrative set-up in the latter area existing despite, or perhaps because of, the vigorous and often violent secessionist campaign there in the 1960s and early 1970s. But campaigns on behalf of Italy's other minority languages since the 1970s may have come too late to offer them anything but a stay of execution, especially for the weakest of these tongues, Greek and Albanian in the south and Catalan in western Sardinia.[47]

Their position was of course not helped by the shelving of the 1991 legislation. But perhaps the most interesting thing about that episode was the quarter from which most of the opposition to the proposals for linguistic reform came. As we have already seen, it came mainly from cultural and intellectual commentators situated on the political left, the area which in post-war Italy had been loudest in its support of the dialects and minority languages. It was largely due to the attitude and promptings of the left that, from being seen as a backward and unfashionable way of communicating at the beginning of the post-war period, the dialects in particular came to be viewed as a precious part of Italy's cultural heritage, taking on a definite prestige among the middle classes, especially in the cities of northern Italy, and seen as worth cultivating and preserving. In the south, and in rural Italy generally, where the left had less influence, the dialects remained, as is still largely the case today, a symbol of backwardness; people may speak them because they are their normal means of communication, but they will often not be keen for their children to learn or use them. In view of the role played by the left in the revalorization of the dialects, it seems a powerful irony that, when the matter came to a practical head with legislation proposed to promote the use of the minority tongues of the peninsula, including some of the dialects, the very political forces that had voiced support for the cause were at least partly instrumental in shattering it. An added irony was that, in the period preceding this episode, backing for the dialects, at least the northern dialects, had started to be taken up by the right-wing secessionist forces of the Northern League, who saw in the issue a weapon among others to undermine national unity and divide Italy on a geographical basis.[48] In their pronouncements, opponents of the legislation lumped the dialects and minority languages together indiscriminately, portraying any new status for such tongues as a threat to national unity.[49] The insecurity of these forces, when it came to matching actions to words, is perhaps partly explicable in terms of the other perceived threat from the fractionalizing forces of the Northern League, which, though Italy now seems to have ridden out that storm, at the time appeared to many to herald a Balkan-style break-up of the nation. But it also showed that the cultural and political forces which had been the driving force of the Liberation and had been the most progressive and forward-looking area on the Italian scene ever since, were sufficiently insecure about the allegiance of Italians to their nation for many of them not to want to allow some of their fellow citizens to conduct their affairs in a language other than Italian. The words of historian Valerio Castronovo summed up the unease about identity and unity: 'Italy needs to reflect anew on its sense of nation and community. Otherwise municipalism of the worst kind will return and our ongoing loss of a common sense of belonging will continue.'[50]

116

Yet today, almost a decade on, the atmosphere may well have changed. At the end of the twentieth century the shelved minority language bill was dusted down, re-presented to parliament and became law on 15 December 1999.[51] This happened uncontroversially and passed almost without comment in the press and media. The difference from 1991 was startling. The insecurity seems to have disappeared. The opposition in 1991 may have been one of those ideologically unpredictable reactions to matters linguistic among intellectuals which we have referred to earlier. Indeed, if we look at the broad picture of linguistic development in Italy since unification, it seems that the mass of the Italian people have a more secure grip on their identity than many of their intellectual and cultural luminaries give them credit for and they often themselves display. Over the last 140 years the Italian people have, in large numbers, carried on using the tongues of their ancestors, the dialects, while becoming increasingly integrated into the new national state and showing no significant signs of wanting to question its integrity or legitimacy. There is no evidence, furthermore, that the vast majority of those who carry on using their dialect or minority language feel any less identity with, or sense of belonging to, that state than those who use only Italian. Sufficiently confident, in fact, do the majority seem of that identity as to be prepared to accept into the language that expresses it large numbers of terms from a foreign language with alien phonetic forms without such imports having a significant impact on the basic structures of their own language and the way they use it. As national consciousnesses go, Italy's may be relatively weak, but considering that both its state as a rallying focus and its language as a mass phenomenon are recent constructs, it may also be seen as having come a long way in a short time.

Notes

1 The phrase 'perverse effects' was Gian Enrico Rusconi's (see note 50). For accounts and discussions of this episode, see: M. L. Rodotà, 'Dialettomania', *Panorama*, 8 December 1991, 122–5; G. Barbina, *La geografia delle lingue. Lingue, etnie e nazioni nel mondo contemporaneo* (Rome, La Nuova Italia Scientifica, 1993), esp. 144; and T. De Mauro, 'La questione della lingua', in *La cultura italiana del Novecento*, edited by C. Stajano (Bari, Laterza, 1996), 423–44 (440–1).

2 The 2.5 per cent figure was calculated in 1963 by Tullio De Mauro in

117

his ground-breaking study, *Storia linguistica dell'Italia unita*, revised and amplified edition (Bari, Laterza, 1970); under 10 per cent was Arrigo Castellani's estimated figure ('Quanti erano gl'italofoni nel 1861?' *Studi Linguistici Italiani*, 8 (1982), 3–25), while Luca Serianni got it to 12 per cent (*Storia della lingua italiana: Il secondo ottocento* (Bologna, Il Mulino, 1990), 41–67).

3   C. Marazzini, *Da Dante alla lingua selvaggia. Sette secoli di dibattiti sull'italiano* (Rome, Carocci, 1999), 17.

4   This view is first clearly expressed in a letter addressed by Manzoni to the Piedmontese lexicographer, Giacinto Carena, in 1847. This document, known as 'Lettera sulla lingua italiana', is to be found, together with other of Manzoni's writings on language, in A. Manzoni, *Scritti sulla lingua*, edited by T. Mattarese (Padua, Liviana, 1987), 194–212.

5   'Dell'unità della lingua e dei mezzi di diffonderla. Relazione al Ministro della Pubblica Istruzione', in Manzoni, *Scritti sulla lingua*, 216–28.

6   The complete work was first published in four volumes in 1897. It was republished anastatically in 1979 (Florence, Le Lettere) with an introduction by G. Ghinassi.

7   Ascoli's introduction (*Proemio*), together with other writings by Ascoli on language, is to be found in G. I. Ascoli, *Scritti sulla questione della lingua*, edited by C. Grassi (Turin, Einaudi, 1975), 3–45.

8   Much has been written on the Manzoni–Ascoli debate. For a useful digest and evaluation, see A. Castellani, 'Consuntivo della polemica Ascoli–Manzoni', *Studi linguistici italiani*, 12 (1986), 105–29; and L. Serianni, *Storia della lingua italiana*, 41–67.

9   See note 6.

10   A. Gramsci, *Quaderni del carcere*, III, edited by V. Gerratana (Turin, Einaudi, 1975), 2347.

11   Ibid.

12   Ibid., 2346.

13   Ibid.

14   This topic is synthesized by De Mauro, *Storia linguistica*, 362–8, and is thoroughly illustrated and discussed in G. Klein, *La politica linguistica del Fascismo* (Bologna, Il Mulino, 1986).

15   On this debate and these two figures, see Marazzini, *Da Dante alla lingua selvaggia*, 186–8, and C. Marazzini, *La lingua come strumento sociale. Il dibattito linguistico in Italia da Manzoni al neocapitalismo* (Turin, Marietti, 1977), 189.

16   P. Monelli, *Barbaro dominio*, third edition (Milan, Hoepli, 1957).

17   T. Tittoni, 'La difesa della lingua italiana', 377–87.

18   As an example of Fascism's sloppiness in implementing its own linguistic xenophobia, Marazzini (*Da Dante alla lingua selvaggia*, 189) points out that the officially commissioned Italian dictionary of the regime, the

'Vocabolario dell'Accademia d'Italia', in its first and only volume published before the fall of the regime (letters A–C), included many unadapted foreign borrowings (e.g. *golf*, *leader*, *film*).

19 Article 3 and Article 6 respectively of the constitution, which was published as a special edition of the *Gazzetta Ufficiale* (no. 298, 27 December 1947).

20 Quoted and discussed in Marazzini, *Da Dante alla lingua selvaggia*, 177–8 (*Diritto e necessità di abrogare il francese come lingua ufficiale in alcune valli della Provincia di Torino*).

21 Ibid. (*Che cosa è nazione*).

22 Special status-granting statutes for francophone people in the Val d'Aosta and German-speakers in the Alto Adige were passed as early as 1948, and extended in the latter area in 1972, while Slovenian speech received formal recognition in legislation of 1954 and 1975.

23 C. Ciseri Montemagno, *Dai linguaggi alla lingua* (Florence, La Nuova Italia, 1987), 57.

24 *Storia linguistica*, 51–126.

25 Ibid., 126–37. In a more recent study De Mauro states: 'The Italian language . . . did not begin to exist for the majority of the Italian people until the 1960s.' ('Lingua e dialetti', in *Stato dell Italia*, edited by P. Ginsberg (Milan, Il Saggiatore, 1994), 61–6 (61)).

26 For an analysis of recent surveys, see: G. Lepschy, 'How popular is Italian?', in *Culture and Conflict in Post-war Italy*, edited by Z. G. Baranski and R. Lumley (London, Macmillan, 1990), 63–75 (66–7); A. Sobrero, 'Gli italiani che usano il dialetto', *Lettera dall'Italia*, 16 (1989), 49; D. Russo, 'L'ultima rilevazione', *Italiano e oltre*, 8 (1993), 158–63; and T. De Mauro 'Lingua e dialetti'.

27 M. Querci, 'Ma che italiano parliamo?' *Grazia*, 29 December 1995, p. 28 (interview with Nencioni).

28 (Rome, Newton Compton, 1989), vii.

29 See Lepschy, 'How popular is Italian?', 73. See also G. Lepschy and L. Raponi, 'Il movimento della norma nell'italiano contemporaneo', in *Nuovi saggi di linguistica italiana* (Bologna, Il Mulino, 1989), 9–24.

30 Examples of these three categories of lexical elements are: (a) *arrangiarsi, borgata, bustarella, iella, imbranato, malloppo, pignolo, pizza, sberla, scippo, vestaglia*; (b) *economia sommersa, fantascienza, leghismo, lottizzare, pallanuoto, telecomando*; (c) *boom, boss, doping, dribblare, genocidio, jazz, killer, look, management, sponsor, trend, videocassetta*.

31 O. Cecchi, 'Gli italiani cominciano a capirsi', *Il Contemporaneo*, 51–2, 24 December 1976, p. 20 (interview with De Mauro).

32 The literature on foreign (especially English) borrowings in Italian and their impact, real or imagined, is considerable. The formative study is

I. Klajn, *Influssi inglesi nella lingua italiana* (Florence, Olschki, 1972). See also: M. Dardano, 'The influence of English on Italian', in *English in Contact with Other Languages*, edited by W. Viereck and W. D. Bald (Budapest, Kiadò, 1986); G. Nencioni, 'Lessico tecnico e difesa della lingua', *Studi di lessicografia italiana*, 9 (1987), 5–20 (containing the claim that 'we live in a besieged citadel'); A. Castellani, 'Morbus anglicus', *Studi linguistici italiani*, 13 (1987) 137–53; H. Moss, 'Pseudoanglicisms in Italian: concept and usage', *Italian Studies*, 50 (1995), 123–38; and C. Marazzini, 'L'italiano è destinato a creolizzarsi?', *Letture*, 52 (1997), 12–15. Many of the views expressed on the extent of the supposed anglicization of Italian are based on consideration of the numerical presence of unmodified foreign terms to be found in dictionaries and other sources (see Marazzini, *Da Dante alla lingua selvaggia*, 225), while H. Moss, 'The incidence of Anglicism in modern Italian; considerations on its overall effect on the language', *The Italianist*, 12 (1993), 129–36, suggests that a clearer picture is to be gained by an evaluation not of 'presence' of Anglicisms but of 'incidence', and that therefore Italian is very far from becoming 'creolized' with less than 1 per cent of its popular written usage, and far less in the spoken tongue, being made up of unmodified English borrowings.

33 See Marazzini, *Da Dante alla lingua selvaggia*, 226.

34 F. Sabatini, 'L'"italiano dell'uso medio". Una realtà tra le varietà linguistiche italiane', in *Gesprochener Italienisch in Geschichte und Gegenwart*, edited by G. Holtus and E. Rädtke (Tübingen, Narr, 1985), 154–84.

35 See G. Berruto, 'La "democratizzazione" dell'italiano', *Lettera dall'Italia*, 16 (1989), 51–2; and U. Cardinale, 'L'uso ha sempre ragione', in *Dove va la lingua italiana?*, edited by J. Jacobelli (Bari, Laterza, 1987), 44–52.

36 For a discussion of *la lingua selvaggia* (Italian gone wild), see the variety of contributions by many of the best-known scholars and commentators on the Italian language in the issue of *Sigma* (18 (1985)) dedicated to *Italiano lingua selvaggia*. For the reflections of one of the participants in this debate, see Lepschy, 'How popular is Italian?', 67–8, where changes taking place in the language are seen more as an expression of its being used 'in a slightly more informal and uninhibited way' than of its 'going to the dogs'.

37 For critical surveys of variations in modern Italian, see A. L. and G. Lepschy, *The Italian Language Today* (London, Routledge, 1988), 62–86, and M. Maiden, *A Linguistic History of Italian* (London, Longman, 1995), 229–67.

38 The dialects began to be seriously studied in the nineteenth century and their classification was first put on a scientific basis by G. I. Ascoli.

During the last thirty years they have been the subject of intensive research and analysis by many scholars. On dialectology and dialect studies, see: P. Benincà, *Piccola storia ragionata della dialettologia italiana* (Padua, Unipress, 1988); C. Grassi, A. Sobrero and T. Telmon, *Fondamenti di dialettologia italiana* (Bari, Laterza, 1997); and M. Maiden and M. Parry, eds., *The Dialects of Italy* (London, Routledge, 1997).

[39] Recent surveys on Italian speech habits have produced uncertain and sometimes contradictory results. What does seem clear, however, is that at least over half the Italian people have the use of a dialect and perhaps as many as three-quarters (see note 26). T. De Mauro makes the point that 'there is no other country in the North of the globe of a similar size and population with the same and longstanding presence of different dialects and minority languages' ('Lingua e dialetti', 62).

[40] See F. Brevini, 'Ma questo è neodialetto', *Panorama*, 8 December 1991, 124; V. R. Jones, 'Dialect literature and popular literature', *Italian Studies*, 45 (1989), 103–17; and H. Haller, *Other Italy: The Literary Canon in Dialect* (Toronto, University of Toronto Press, 1999). For recent sub-literary uses to which the dialects are being put (e.g. television, pop music), see Rodotà, 'Dialettomania'.

[41] See A. Sobrero, 'Italianization of the dialects', in Maiden and Parry, *The Dialects of Italy*, 412–21; R. Hastings, 'Between Tuscan and Abruzzese; regional Italian in Abruzzo', *Quaderni di ricerca* (Centro di Dialettologia e Linguistica Italiana di Manchester), 1 (1996), 39–61 (40–5); G. Berruto, 'Code-switching and code-mixing', in Maiden and Parry, *The Dialects of Italy*, 394–400; and Russo, 'L'ultima rilevazione', 161–62.

[42] Lepschy, 'How popular is Italian?', 63. Lepschy makes this point after describing how he, a native speaker of Italian, scholar of Italian language and dialects, and familar with a number of other languages, overheard in Venice a conversation between two people which he found entirely unintelligible; when, assuming they were foreign, he inquired what language they were speaking, they replied in ordinary Italian that they were speaking the dialect of their home town in southern Abruzzo.

[43] The calculation of as acute an observer as Manlio Cortelazzo is that dialects will die out over the next five generations. Sobrero ('Gli italiani che usano il dialetto') moots thirty to forty years but concludes by asserting that 'for the time being the show-down has been put off'. The recent decline of the dialects can be seen by comparing the first Doxa survey on the use of dialects (1974) with the fourth and most recent one (1991). Probably the most telling statistic is the fall in the use of dialect in conversations outside the home from 41.5 per cent to 23 per cent. Comparison of these surveys also shows that the areas of Italy where

dialects are most used continue to be the north-east and the south, and that the areas where their decline is least marked are the north-east and the centre. The most up-to-date survey, conducted by the national statistical body, Istat (Instituto Nazionale di Statistica), paints a similar picture: a significant increase in the use of Italian in all contexts and a corresponding fall in the use of dialect, especially outside the home and among the very young (*Mass Media letture e linguaggio. Anno 1995* (Rome, ISTAT, 1997), 74–7 and 359–74). See also: R. Ferguson, 'Il declino dei dialetti in Italia; fenomeno inarrestabile?', *Journal of Association of Teachers of Italian*, 40 (1984), 59–67; and P. Diadori, 'Lingua e dialetto ieri e oggi in Italia. Una sintesi', *Tuttitalia*, 9 (1994), 12–29.

44   B. Migliorini and T. G. Griffith, *The Italian Language* (London, Faber and Faber, 1984), 513.

45   The pioneer in study of regional variations in Italian was R. Rüegg with *Zur Wortgeographie der italienischen Umgangssprache* (Cologne, Kölner romanistische Arbeiten, 1956). G. B. Pellegrini's studies were also seminal: 'Tra lingua e dialetto in Italia', *Studi mediolatini e volgari*, 8 (1960), 137–53; 'L'italiano regionale', *Cultura e scuola*, 5 (1962), 20–9. See also M. A. Cortelazzo and A. Mioni, eds., *L'italiano regionale* (Rome, Bulzoni, 1990); L. Canepari, *Italiano standard e pronunce regionali* (Padua, CLEUP, 1980); and T. Telmon, *Guida allo studio degli italiani regionali* (Alessandria, Edizioni dell'Orso, 1990). Examples of instructive studies of individual regional varieties of Italian are R. Hastings's analysis of Abruzzese Italian (see note 41), and D. Bentley, 'Language and dialect in modern Sicily', *The Italianist*, 17 (1997), 204–30.

46   See note 22.

47   The most influential, and controversial, of the studies to bring to public attention the plight of the minority languages was Sergio Salvi's *Le lingue tagliate* (Milan, Rizzoli, 1975). Greek has an estimated 20,000 speakers, Albanian 80,000 and Catalan 15.000. For comprehensive recent figures, see G. Lepschy, 'How many languages does Europe need?' in *The Changing Voices of Europe*, edited by M. M. Parry, W. V. Davies and R. A. M. Temple (Cardiff, University of Wales Press, 1994), 5–21 (16). See also: *L'Italia plurilingue*, edited by G. Freddi (Bergamo, Minerva Italica, 1983); M. Tessarolo, *Minoranze linguistiche e immagine della lingua* (Milan, Angeli, 1990); the useful if idiosyncratic G. Hull, *Polyglot Italy: Language, Dialects, Peoples* (Victoria, CIS Educational, 1989); A. L. Lepschy, G. Lepschy and M. Voglera, 'Linguistic variety in Italy', in *Italian Regionalism, History, Identity and Politics*, edited by C. Levy (Oxford, Berg, 1996), 69–80, and the two volumes of the journal *Il Veltro* by Mariangela Buogo,

'L'"aura" italiana. Culture e letterature d'oltrefrontiera, frontiera e minoranze', nos 3–4 and 5–6, 39 (1995).

48 Official support for the dialects from the Northern League has turned out to be lukewarm, with its leader Umberto Bossi stating: 'We respect those who speak dialect and we carry it with us. But we know that the improvements we seek do not depend on a few road signs in Lombardy' (Rodotà, 'Dialettomania', 124). See also G. Bonsaver, 'Dialect, culture and politics: the Northern League(s)', *Journal of the Institute of Romance Studies,* Supplement 1 (1996), 97–107 (104–5).

49 See note 1. The distinction between 'dialect' and 'minority language' is a matter of contention, often depending on the agenda of those who discuss the topic. While the proposed 1991 legislation was intended to deal with minority languages, the inclusion among these of Sardinian and the Ladin of Friuli brought to public attention the debate as to whether the definition of a minority language could stretch any wider than tongues of a non-Italian type on Italian soil or whether it could also include tongues of an Italo-Romance kind (e.g. Sardinian and Ladin) on the grounds of their considerable difference from other forms of Italo-Romance, especially if their speakers felt a particularly strong affinity with their separate culture and traditions. For definitions aiming to differentiate *dialetti* and *lingue di minoranze*, see C. Ciseri Montemagno, *Dai linguaggi alla lingua,* 57.

50 *Repubblica*, 22 November 1991, p. 7. Two days later the same newspaper published an equally revealing article by Gian Enrico Rusconi which talked about 'the legitimation of phenomena which disintegrate the cultural fabric ... with general consequences of anti-solidarity. Another hammer blow aimed at the survival of the nation.'

51 This time round the legislation covered twelve languages, excluding the Romany of Italy's gypsy communities from the thirteen languages of the original proposals (see the first paragraph of this study). I am indebted to Professor Mair Parry for drawing my attention to the passing of this legislation in time for me to include mention of it here.

5

Il bel paese: art, beauty and the cult of appearance

STEPHEN GUNDLE

More than any other country, Italy enjoys a reputation as the home of beauty, beautiful things, beautiful places and beautiful people. From the eighteenth century, travellers from northern Europe made pilgrimages to the peninsula to admire its artistic and architectural heritage, enjoy the majesty of its landscapes and benefit from its climate. As the seat of both ancient civilization and the glories of the Renaissance, an Italian experience became a necessary part of the education of a well-rounded person. The idea of Italy's special relationship with the aesthetic, as the *bel paese par excellence*, was informed by a poetic tradition stretching back to Dante and Petrarch, knowledge of the paintings of Cimabue, Giotto and the Renaissance masters and appreciation of its natural phenomena. Foreigners marvelled at ruins, palaces, paintings and sculptures, took pleasure from blue skies and seas, and enjoyed the relaxed lifestyle of the people.

Most Italians took pride in their country's extraordinary heritage. They welcomed visitors and basked in the reputation Italy enjoyed as the birthplace of genius, civilization and the arts. But there was a recurrent dissatisfaction with the idea of Italy purely as a museum, or of it as a civilization that was once great but which had decayed and declined. Even the emphasis on Italy as picturesque irritated through repetition. Moreover, descriptions of the Italian people as comical and theatrical, or alternatively as primitive or threatening, were offensive. In the nineteenth and twentieth centuries all of Italy's governments sought to show due regard for the country's past while also in some way building on the heritage for present purposes. The inferiority complex which Italy exhibited in relation to more advanced industrial powers combined with a sense of the universality of the Italian contribution to western culture to produce the belief that Italy had a right, a duty even, to impress itself more forcefully on the contemporary world. At different moments this aspiration informed imperial, political, economic and cultural ambitions.

The aim of this article is to examine the ways in which Italy's image as the mother of Beauty – to use the definition of Gabriele D'Annunzio, the foremost modern theorist of this notion – informed efforts to give shape to a sense of national purpose and identity in the nineteenth and twentieth centuries. Inevitably, given the wide range of issues involved, the treatment will be selective. First, an attempt will be made to outline the way beauty informed militarism and anti-democratic currents in the early part of the twentieth century. D'Annunzio and Mussolini both stressed the role of art and beauty in their designs for an aggressive, powerful Italy. Second, an anti-modern use of Italy's identification with beauty will be considered. The tradition of feminine beauty was mobilized in the first half of the century to set purportedly national ideas of woman against 'foreign', modernizing ideas. Third, the economically productive idea of Italian fashion as heir to the country's artistic heritage, which informed the strategies of leading designers in the last quarter of the century, will be surveyed.

The sequence of treatments may give the impression that, after being employed for belligerent and anti-feminist purposes with strong political overtones, the cult of beauty found a constructive and peaceable application. In fact it will be shown that the notion of beauty is, perhaps inherently, problematic in so far as it contains within it élitist and potentially anti-democratic values. Thus its place in the Italian national identity always contains an element of ambiguity and instability.

Italian discourses on beauty

For patriots like Mazzini, it was an article of faith that Italy was God's chosen land and that its ambitions were entirely in line with the universal aspirations of human civilization. In the 1840s the great nationalist wrote that 'Italian unification constitutes an indispensable element in the plan of education assigned to humankind'.[1] Unity and independence were not selfish objectives; they were necessary if Italy was to perform the duty that destiny had allotted to it, the mission of 'uniting Europe'. This mission stemmed from the historical and cultural importance of Rome and the Italian contribution to civilisation. The Catholic myth of Italy's supremacy began with Vincenzo Gioberti, who also argued that the Italians had been entrusted by God with a special civilizing mission that it was their duty to fulfil. The fact that the Almighty had chosen Italy as the seat of both civilization and the Church was proof of the special qualities of the Italians; if further confirmation was needed, then this was offered by the achievements of the country's poets, artists and philosophers. Most secular thinkers did not attribute Italy's special primacy to God, but rather to geography and history. Moreover they dated Italian civilization from the birth of the Roman Empire rather than its fall.[2]

Among Italy's cultural and political élite in the mid- to late nineteenth century there was a marked inferiority complex in relation to more developed countries, in particular England and France. Liberals and radical democrats alike shared this outlook, with each finding in the institutions, ideas, cultures and customs of these countries examples that were deemed to be superior to their Italian equivalents. Very often foreign models were seen to provide an illustration of how Italy should develop and evolve. Precisely this feeling was one of the factors which led patriotic idealists to promote the cause of an Italian Risorgimento, but the mere formation of an Italian state, no matter how significant an accomplishment that may have been, was not sufficient to cancel it. On the contrary, in some respects the feeling of inferiority actually grew after 1861 as the gulf between the hopes of the Risorgimento and the reality of post-unification Italy became apparent and led to widespread disenchantment.

In order to counterbalance the inferiority complex which Italians felt towards the great powers, Emilio Gentile has argued,

> a greatness complex developed based on the myth of the universal primacy of the Italian nation . . . The supporters of this primacy appealed, for historical evidence, to the universal civilizations that had sprung up in the peninsula, to Rome and Catholicism, and Humanism and the Renaissance, the two great spiritual movements from which the consciousness of modern man had originated.[3]

In a sense, the discourse on beauty was similarly used to mask uncomfortable realities in that it bolstered and justified an Italian claim to superiority that clearly could not be grounded in any realistic

126

assessment of the country's economy, civic development or military strength.

Italy was not alone in claiming to be the land of beauty. George Mosse has argued that for many Germans in the eighteenth century, including Friedrich Schiller, beauty was the unifying element in society. 'It related to what was common to all members of society, for beauty was considered a timeless absolute that could bring out the capacity for perfection in all men', Mosse argues. 'The beautiful could unite opposites in human nature: strength and passivity, freedom and law. "Beauty", then, was an ideal type arising from that which endures in a man's character and, through this, penetrating his condition in life and ennobling it.'[4] In nineteenth-century Germany, beauty was informed most explicitly by the ideal of ancient Greece. Beauty involved a sense of proportion and balance and the elimination of the chaotic and accidental. It was also a value to be counterposed to modern materialism. In this sense it was a way of introducing a view of life which brought to light an idea of perfection.[5]

In Italy, beauty was not an abstract value; rather it was felt to be an intrinsic national characteristic. Silvio Lanaro cites Angelo Mosso and M. Morasso as two publicists who struggled to reconcile a belief in the special qualities of the Italian people with a conviction that Italy's inferiority could be overcome through economic and social progress, education and good institutions. 'Barbarity and civilization are mixed in Italian blood in the same right quantities that form the characteristics and strength of the American people', argued Mosso, in a statement that sought to make a virtue of Italian backwardness. Intelligence was not the main strength of the Italian people, he asserted, but 'strength of will'.[6] Morasso took the view that the climate and the environment of the Mediterranean, the fertile earth, warm sun and ample seas, combined with the 'virtue of good popular blood' and the 'highly noble supremacy of the chosen and most refined of peoples', constituted ideal conditions for a national resurgence.[7] In contrast to northern peoples whose inhospitable climate drove them to excesses and illness, the Italians could balance modern ways with good health and a harmonious relationship with nature.

These views rested on a more positive assessment of the least modern features of Italy than was normally held in the post-unification period. The new state's mainly northern élite had little interest in or understanding of the south and viewed outbreaks of unrest and banditry as a product not of social or economic difficulties but of the barbarism of the region and its people. Thus the imposition on the whole of the peninsula of the Piedmontese constitution, monarchy, tax regime and system of conscription was not seen as the cause of unease but as the necessary solution. In such a context northern Italians found themselves in a similar position to many foreigners in their view of the frightening yet fascinating inhabitants of primitive Italy. Certainly they identified themselves more with the former than the latter, even to the point of accepting the same picturesque images of the cultures and customs of the backward part of the country. Representations of violence, passion, folklore, popular music and laziness were seen to demarcate the cultural gap that existed with respect to the civilized north. Neapolitan songs, Sicilian puppets and spaghetti were the acceptable face of an internal source of potential instability.

John Dickie has explored some of these meanings. He has suggested that in a magazine like *Illustrazione Italiana*, which served as a sort of house journal of the bourgeoisie, there was a strong tendency to pictorialize those elements of the nation which lay outside the realm of the official and the acceptable, yet which were nonetheless objects of a political discourse.[8] In relation to a dominant aesthetic which valued sentimental effects, the different and the backward could be seen as curious, exotic and amusing. Italy's bourgeoisie could not describe and use as freely as foreigners those elements which it did not accept as representative of the nation as a whole, but it could accept them so long as they were ascribed to the south. Nonetheless, the picturesque was inherently unstable in so far as it depended on stereotypes which were partial. Neapolitan vitality and poverty were acceptable, as was any representation of the beauty of the bay of Naples, but corruption and banditry were not.

Patriotic Italians covered such problems with rhetoric. Thus the formation of the new state was seen as a matter of great world-historical importance. 'With our revolution we have not only reconstituted the organism of a nation', wrote *La Stampa* on the occasion of the fiftieth anniversary of unification. 'We have increased the beauty of the world, we have reconsecrated the nobility of life inasmuch as it is the exercise of duty, the victory of action and the domination of intelligence.'[9] For patriots it was an accepted fact by the early twentieth century that the *patria* was intimately connected with Italy's intellectual, artistic and aesthetic heritage. This extraordinary legacy was not dead, as foreigners seemed to think; rather it was a living patrimony that found a modern extension in the artistic and aesthetic propensities of contemporary Italians.

Beauty and the 'greater Italy'

The term 'beauty' was taken to refer equally to the artistic and cultural heritage, the Italian landscape and the physical beauty of the Italians. Quite commonly, all three were absorbed into a generic, all-purpose portmanteau concept of beauty that served a variety of rhetorical functions. As intrinsic components of Italian patriotism, they could be mobilized for both cultural and imperialist ends. The connection between beauty and belligerence was made by the poet – and, from 1899, the year he was elected to parliament, politician – D'Annunzio. However, in order to understand his political use of the concept, it is necessary briefly to mention Francesco Crispi, the statesman who first launched liberal Italy into an ambitious foreign policy with the aim of acquiring colonies. For Crispi, who presented himself to some extent as the incarnation of the resurgent nation, it was the destiny of the 'greater Italy' to pursue a policy of power and conquest. He responded to those who accused him of megalomania with the counter-accusation that they were enemies of the fatherland because they wanted an Italy that was 'weak and impotent, and therefore the prey of the victorious, as had been the case ever since the fall of the Roman Empire'. He denounced his opponents as preferring an Italy that was 'an artist's study, a museum of antiquities and not a nation'.[10]

D'Annunzio by contrast sought to connect the tradition of beauty to a power policy. John Woodhouse argues that the poet first mixed praise of the privileged land where Leonardo and Michelangelo had produced their masterpieces with strongly nationalistic tones in 1895. In the introduction to a new journal, *Convito*, he referred both to Italy's great artistic past and to the special virtues of 'Latin blood and Latin soil' which justified imperial ambitions.[11] Launched into the political realm, D'Annunzio further developed his blend of aesthetic and politics, harnessing references to beauty to patriotism and anti-materialism. In the twentieth century, he increasingly saw himself as a Nietzschean genius called upon to denounce the mediocrity and materialism of the contemporary world. Italy was the genetrix of beauty, and it was the duty of all, particularly the poets, to revive and perpetuate that great tradition: 'The fortune of Italy is inseparable from the fate of beauty, of which Italy is the mother.'[12]

Unlike Crispi, D'Annunzio was neither a liberal nor a democrat (he regarded his struggle to win support from a plebeian electorate as humiliating). He believed that beauty by definition was élitist. The task of the poet, at bottom, was to save beauty from contagion by the crowd.[13] Yet his actions, grand gestures, public speeches and newspaper articles were increasingly addressed to a wide audience. Several years after the *Mona Lisa* was stolen from the Louvre in 1911, he even implied that he had been involved in the theft. At a time when the theorists of the supremacy of the Germanic race enjoyed a wide audience in Europe, D'Annunzio championed the supremacy of the Latin race. He believed that only Latin genius stood between the world and the onrush of barbarity. In 1914, he described the war not as a simple conflict of interests, but as 'a struggle of races, a confrontation of irreconcilable powers, a trial of blood, which the enemies of the Latin name conduct according to the most ancient iron law'.[14] In contrast to those who saw Rome as the only centre of Italian civilization, in his numerous speeches he conferred qualities of beauty on every Italian city, each of which enjoyed its own special aura.

One city which particularly taxed theorists of Italian beauty was Venice. The lagoon city was at once a triumph of human contrivance at odds with nature, a marvel of artifice, and on the other it was the most supreme example of an image of Italy as a beautiful ruin. For the Futurists, the obsession of foreigners (and complicit Italians) with Italy's past had 'a mummifying influence'.[15] Venice, they believed, should not be preserved to go on dying; on the contrary the canals needed to be filled in, palaces demolished and gondolas burned as a preliminary to the rebirth of Venice as a military and industrial centre from which Italy could dominate the Adriatic.[16] The opening of the first Venice Biennale in 1895 indicated that it was not necessary to go so far to give the city a new role. For all the efforts of the Futurists to invent a new concept of beauty that was anti-traditional and hostile to the picturesque so beloved by foreigners (by 1931 Marinetti was arguing that electricity and radio had abolished old ideas of landscape and replaced them with 'a fast landscape of the machine aesthetic'),[17] the dominant vision of national regeneration required the past to be harnessed to the present. D'Annunzio for example hailed the Biennale and, in the novel *Il fuoco*, enthused about the modern warships along the Riva; yet he also approved the rebuilding of the tower in St Mark's Square in 1912 following its collapse.

Mosse argues that in Germany the Greek ideal of beauty became mixed with the Roman tradition of monumentalism in the combination of aesthetics and nationalism. National grandeur, he observes, had to be symbolized in buildings and rituals.[18] In Italy there was no need for such a detour, as 'Romanity' was one of the well-springs of the cult of beauty. In the 1920s and 1930s, the Fascists merely built on a tradition that D'Annunzio had revived and cultivated. They also took up an idea which found an application in Germany, of beauty as representing a life lived to the fullest, without regard for danger or even reflection. For Mussolini, style, beauty and appearance were central to the Fascist project. As Simonetta Falasca-Zamponi has most recently shown, he considered himself to be an artist-politician, the artificer of a 'beautiful' system and a 'beautiful' doctrine.[19] 'Those who say Fascism say first of all beauty', he said in a speech in Milan in October 1923.[20] More than anything else, this showed that Mussolini's aesthetic conception of politics was founded on an élitist and anti-democratic vision of social relations. In nationalist and right-wing opinion, democracy was incompatible with beauty and style. Thus, 'to give style', 'the aesthetic expression that reflected Mussolini's political aim to transform the populace had as a pragmatic counterpart the expression "to fascistize".'[21]

Feminine beauty and modernity

While in Germany the concept of beauty was often given masculine connotations, Italians boasted a long tradition of feminine beauty. Not only was Italy considered to be a mother, and a city such as Venice a beautiful lady, but there was a poetic tradition which rested on the idealization of women. 'Following the models provided by Petrarch and Boccaccio', Paola Tinagli has written,

> the canon of female beauty became codified by countless descriptions, from Poliziano to Pietro Bembo, from Ariosto to Boiardo. Variations

were constructed around a number of features which were constantly repeated: writers praised the attractions of wavy hair gleaming like gold, of white skin similar to snow, to marble, to alabaster or to milk; they admired cheeks which looked like lilies and roses, and eyes that shone like the sun or the stars. Lips are compared to rubies, teeth to pearls, breasts to snow or to apples.[22]

This poetic tradition informed the representations of women and female portraits that recur in Italian art in the fifteenth and sixteenth centuries. Both idealized representations, such as Botticelli's Venus and Primavera and Titian's Danae, and the portraits of real women, such as Leonardo's unidentified Mona Lisa or Bronzino's paintings of Eleonora di Toledo and Lucrezia Panciatichi, were contributions to an ongoing discourse on beauty.

Feminine beauty formed an important part of the nineteenth-century emphasis on beauty, as the theorists of Italy's cultural supremacy often referred to the poetic and artistic tradition. Frequently there were attempts to harness the tradition to an appreciation of contemporary Italian women. In particular there was a veritable cult of Queen Margherita, who enjoyed special prominence as the consort of King Umberto. Born in 1851, Margherita was only twenty-eight when her husband inherited the throne, and she was the object of a discourse about her beauty virtually from the moment she appeared on the public stage. During a royal visit to Vienna in 1881 a journalist wrote that 'it seemed that she had stepped down from a painting by Titian or Paolo Veronese', while D'Annunzio, catching sight of her at the theatre, called her 'a true triumph of beauty . . . the queen was very beautiful; looking at her yesterday evening I felt as never before the fascination of the eternal regal feminine'.[23] It is well known that Carducci, the country's most famous poet in the late nineteenth century and a one-time republican, was especially responsive to the beauty of the young Margherita. His ode entitled 'Eterno femminino regale' signalled that his conversion to monarchism was not entirely separable from admiration for the queen.[24] A less well known figure, V. De Napoli, author in 1894 of a volume dedicated to *L'eterna bellezza della regina Margherita di Savoja*, described her as 'the perfect woman, who inspires worship like the sight of Titian's Madonna at the Pitti Palace'.[25] Comparing her to Dante's Beatrice and Petrarch's Laura, De Napoli went on to claim that it was 'as though Canova had been resurrected and given life to his works of Venus and Flora, enriched with voices and colours and flowers'.[26]

Margherita was fair-haired, and thus her appearance matched the traditional poetic image of golden beauty. But in a context in which the supremacy of the Italian race was being theorized in opposition to the Teutonic idea,[27] there was an increasing emphasis on the aesthetic appeal of the darker-haired women who constituted the majority in Italy. In particular the development of photography and its use in magazines from the turn of the century, and in cinema, not only introduced a realistic, visual means of comparison, but also permitted the circulation of images from abroad. Between the later nineteenth century and the 1920s and 1930s a new idea of feminine beauty took shape that stressed not naturalness but artifice. Centred first in Paris and then in Hollywood, the new beauty involved fashion, jewellery, perfumes, cosmetics, and above all an emphasis on vanity and self-cultivation. It was modern, urban, fast and highly aestheticized. The birth of the modern woman, who worked, was economically independent and more concerned with pleasure and consumption than family and the domestic sphere, did not have as marked an impact in Italy as elsewhere. But Catholic moralists, nationalists and Fascists nonetheless joined the polemic against the lack of modesty implied by beauty contests (the first Italian pageant took place in 1911), swimming costumes and cosmetics. They also stood out against emancipation, feminism and all other ideas and customs that were associated with the modern city or foreign influences.

Polemicists like Umberto Notari, author of the best-selling pornographic novel *Quelle signore*, argued that the Italian concept of feminine beauty was natural, spontaneous and shaped by the Italian climate and landscape. 'Italian women are the most beautiful women in the world', Notari exclaimed. In the American idea of beauty, by contrast, there was 'something that is "manufactured in series", impersonal and intransitive, all of which subtracts from beauty the air, light and warmth'.[28] 'The most beautiful Americans', he went on, 'are very beautiful roses without perfume'. This sort of reaction was provoked by a concern that the presence of Hollywood films and other such influences was leading to a brusque displacement of Italian traditions. The publication in *Cinema Illustrazione* in 1931 of an old publicity photomontage showing the features of Marlene Dietrich superimposed over those of the *Mona Lisa* – implying that

Hollywood, not Italy, was the modern seat of feminine beauty – had provided the sort of catalyst which mobilized these feelings.[29]

The demographic campaign launched by Mussolini in 1927, together with a general attempt to instil racial pride in the Italians, were the key weapons deployed by the authorities against modernizing influences. But the cultural tradition also played its part. In 1934 the design magazine *Domus* published a handsome large-format collection of Renaissance female portraits under the title *La bella italiana*. In the introduction, art critic Raffaele Calzini asserted:

> This blessed land of ours that is modelled in its landscape of mountains, seas and woods as the most superb matrix of creation, is wrapped in a climate of perennial love and fecundity ... Over the centuries it has produced the most beautiful women in the world. Their true sky, their surest home, their most fruitful alcove, is here ... Still today, in the countryside of the Abruzzo, near Siena or in Romagna, alongside the low-grade cinemas where the brazen American publicity mania pours out photographs of the sterilized and standardized type of Venus born from the froth of Hollywood, beautiful women, authentic Italians, walk upright with jugs and bread-baskets on their heads, or solemnly with a child in their arms, like exiled queens.[30]

Although the fall of Fascism and the return of democracy under Allied auspices softened some of the edges of this polemic, it continued well into the post-war period. The massive return of American films and assorted pin-ups and advertisements provided grist to the mill of conservatives.[31] The hugely popular *La Domenica del Corriere*, a family weekly founded in 1899 as the Sunday supplement of the *Corriere della Sera*, ran a campaign in 1945–6 against the association of beauty with legs, bodies, sex appeal and glamour. 'Italy is full of legs: news-kiosks are covered with them, certain theatres bustle with them, but we don't want to believe that feminine beauty has finished up in the extremities. It shines above all in the face', the magazine asserted in November 1945.[32] Italian beauty was seen as residing in a graceful face whose 'gentle composure of the features' and 'thoughtful tranquillity of expression' did not require 'make-up, swimsuits or ambiguous and studied little smiles accompanied by jazz'.[33] The seductive quality of the Italian female face sprang from the 'sense of intimate goodness' of the woman it belonged to, not from the 'super-modern "perverse glamour"' of the cover girl.[34]

From their different perspectives, Catholics and Communists sought to carry forward the defence of Italian beauty. For the former, the priority was to defend modesty and decency and to resist the display of purely physical assets. The emphasis on the body implied in the beauty contests which became so widespread after the war 'exposed girls to the loss of their virginal reserve' and detracted from a proper emphasis on goodness and virtue.[35] The beatification in 1947 of Maria Goretti, a poor girl from Lazio who had died in the early years of the century defending her purity from a would-be rapist, was designed to restore modesty and spirituality to their proper place. As for the Communists, they also criticized manufactured beauty and the standardized image furnished by Hollywood. They wanted to protect working-class girls not from immorality but from ideological contamination and bourgeois corruption. To this end they launched an annual contest of their own associated with the weekly *Vie Nuove*, that was aimed at finding a new face for Italian cinema. At the final of the Milanese heat of Miss Vie Nuove in 1950, a Communist film critic announced that the aim was to select 'a healthy and robust girl of the people, typically Italian' and not 'an American-style cover girl'.[36]

These concerns also influenced Miss Italia, a commercial contest which from the late 1940s became a national institution. Jurors were instructed to select the ideal fiancée for their sons, respectable and modest girls rather than showy, ambitious women. The first winner in 1946 was a Florentine, Rossana Martini, who won because she corresponded to 'the type of Italian woman that the greatest artists of our country chose as a model and for which they won a world-wide audience through their masterpieces'.[37] The sponsoring magazine, *Tempo*, which described her as having 'brown hair and a virtuous look in her eye', published her photograph surrounded by reproductions of Renaissance portraits. Yet the public present in Stresa noisily championed the claims of the runner-up, Silvana Pampanini, a shapely, confident and 'explosive and exuberant' beauty who in the magazines of the time was termed an 'American beauty' and a 'cinematographic beauty'.[38] Glamorous rather than timid and emotional, Pampanini was preferred by film producers to the virtuous Martini. She made her film debut in 1947 and enjoyed a few years of stardom before being eclipsed by Gina Lollobrigida and Sophia Loren, two other women who were better known for their aggressive sex appeal than their conformity to the Renaissance type. As icons of Italianness, Lollobrigida and Loren were in many ways novel figures, who mixed dark and natural qualities with 'sexy' and 'provocative' mannerisms.[39]

Fashion and art

Through the economic boom of the late 1950s and early 1960s, Italy finally overcame its backwardness with respect to the countries of northern Europe. The country ceased to be mainly agricultural and emerged as a leading industrial power. In the 1980s, this position was consolidated as small and medium-sized businesses spread more widely than ever before, far outside the old industrial triangle of the north-west. In both 'economic miracles' export goods were important, and the aesthetic dimension of Italian products gave them style, kudos and distinctiveness. The Olivetti typewriter, the Vespa and Lambretta scooters and Gaggia coffee machines of the 1950s became desirable, and in certain contexts even status symbols, because they were distinguishable by their rounded forms and sleek, minimalist lines. Between the 1960s and 1980s Italian design acquired great international prestige and a world primacy in interior and furniture design, and in car body design.

Italian fashion was slower to emerge. It did not enjoy the same status in the 1950s and 1960s, although it did acquire export markets in the United States for the first time and won a reputation for simplicity, quality materials and low prices with respect to the unrivalled world fashion centre, Paris. If the clothes were not truly distinctive, the Italian image that was used to market them was. Real aristocratic women were photographed in Renaissance palaces wearing the designs of Capucci, Schuberth, Carosa and the Fontana sisters. Other models were shot out in the open, not amid the rubble and bombed-out cities as was the case with German fashion photography of the time, but among historic Roman ruins and monuments. Foreign purchasers in particular were given the impression that they were buying into a rich and ancient cultural tradition. The cinema of the post-war years was not on the whole stylish or glamorous; the neo-realist movement preferred downbeat settings and protagonists. But American location productions drew on Italian costuming and craftsmanship and helped enhance their reputation. From the later 1950s, films like Fellini's *La dolce vita* and Antonioni's *L'avventura* showcased Italian dress styles in a way that assisted the development of the fashion industry.

In the 1970s and 1980s Italian fashion came into its own. Textile companies like GFT of Turin sponsored ready-to-wear lines that brought fashionable clothes within the reach of a wider section of the population than ever before. Such companies relied on the name-recognition of fashion designers (*stilisti*) who conceived collections in a way that took account of social needs and cultural trends rather than individual clients' requirements. These men and women were not always tailors and dressmakers by origin. Some were architects, others window-dressers or photographers. But they all enjoyed a high media profile and were thus able to shape and guide the trends they sought to interpret. In particular they developed casual classic lines and elegantly functional clothes for a growing category of professional women. By offering clothes that were distinctive, well made and costly, they fuelled a mania for status dressing that relied on the exhibition of labels, logos and price tags. In order to acquire desirability and glamour for their products, designers and their sponsors spent large sums on magazine advertising, eye-catching catwalk shows and celebrity sponsorships. While top-of-the-range dresses and suits were prohibitively expensive, 'diffusion lines', designer jeans, accessories and perfumes brought exclusivity within the grasp of the middle classes.

Italian fashion was immensely successful within Italy, but it also found markets abroad that extended beyond Europe and America to the Far East and the developing world. In the 1980s it became Italy's largest export industry. In this context, designers like Armani, Valentino, Versace and Ferre came to be regarded not just as arbiters of taste and style but as business heroes and authorities on everything, including politics and international affairs. In this context they sought to shake off the reductive definition of tailor or artisan and to take on the mantle of the artist. Most of the major designers aimed to elevate their work from the market-place to the museum and to situate themselves within the Italian artistic tradition.

Versace provides the most interesting case. The most colourful and vibrant of the designers, he deliberately contradicted the understated aesthetic of his rival Armani to offer glitzy, attention-grabbing garments that detractors did not hesitate to define as vulgar. Best known for dressing celebrities like Elizabeth Hurley, Madonna and Elton John, and for his extravagant use of such supermodels as

Claudia Schiffer and Naomi Campbell, Versace was very popular with the brash *nouveaux riches* who came to the fore in the economic boom of the mid-1980s. By his glamour-laden advertisements and opulent lifestyle, he associated himself with modern-day luxury and endowed it with a rock 'n' roll edge.

Versace's influences were many and varied. At various times he claimed to be inspired by the Hollywood movie queens of the 1950s, the splendour of Byzantium, the classicism of ancient Greece and Rome, the magnificence of the Renaissance, the excess of the eighteenth century, the Viennese decorative arts of the late nineteenth century, Pop Art and popular music.[40] The eclectic approach was apparent in the decor of his much-publicized houses in Milan, Como, New York and Miami, the last of which resembled a latter-day Vittoriale in its mixture of styles and juxtapositions of numerous valuable objects. For all his cosmopolitanism, however, the designer liked to stress his roots in the Italian south. He claimed that as a child he was inspired by ancient Greek and Roman ruins and later he filled his houses with classical marble statues. Statuesque nude male models in classical poses featured in a number of Versace advertising campaigns. It has been said that in his work he paid 'cartoonish homage to classical mythology'. By restoring palaces and adopting the Medusa's head insignia, it was also said that he lived like a Renaissance prince.[41]

The designer built up a considerable art collection, designed costumes for ballet and opera and published several books documenting his work. He also collaborated with museums such as the Victoria and Albert in London and the Metropolitan Museum of Art in New York. He systematically donated money to these institutions and pieces from his collections from 1980. Like his designer colleagues, he participated in the Florence Biennale of 1996, which saw the *stilisti* display their creations beside the paintings and sculptures of the Renaissance masters. The purposes of this were to secure kudos and power and to win a place in posterity. It may be said that he achieved this, for shortly after his murder in 1997, the Costume Institute of the Metropolitan Museum staged a Versace retrospective (sponsored by *Vogue*) that hailed his 'encyclopedic knowledge, his virtuoso performance of techniques, the sensibility to experiment, and the equilibrium between history and contemporaneity'.[42] 'In Versace's death his work has been elevated from the plateau of mere fashion to the level of an artistic movement that combines street style and haute couture with a fascination with the iconography of Warhol, the work of the Cubists and elements of the Baroque', noted Colin McDowell. 'The cultural establishment he wooed so elegantly . . . are happy to place his work in a historical context far-removed from the transient world of fashion.'[43]

Conclusion

It has been shown in this chapter that the tradition of beauty informed Italian national identity in a variety of ways. It provided the country with an aesthetic self-awareness and a sense of cultural mission which rested on impeccable, if not always clearly defined, antecedents. It ensured that the country was also always well regarded by foreigners who might have been patronizing about the Italy of the present, but who could not but be in awe of its glorious past and aesthetic appeal. This provided Italy with an extraordinary marketing device that fuelled tourism and a whole range of export goods including clothes, automobiles, craft goods and foodstuffs. But the tradition of beauty was ambiguous. It justified belligerence and imperialism, it could be harnessed to élitism and reaction and it could be mobilized in opposition to the progress of the lower classes. Even today, Italian critics of mass culture justify their stance in relation to concepts such as the sublime and kitsch which barely conceal an aristocratic disdain for the popular.[44] The least anti-democratic use of the tradition discussed here concerns fashion, but even something as innocuous as Italian fashion of the 1980s and 1990s relied for its success on the manipulation of status. Wearers of Armani or Versace flaunted their wealth and taste before the less well-off and drew comfort from the fact that, by so doing, they could resist, temporarily at least, the contagion of the crowd.

The tradition of beauty has gone hand in hand with allegedly typical Italian predilections for the theatrical and the rhetorical, for surface rather than substance. It has not been possible here to investigate the sources of these or the linkages between them, but it has implicitly been suggested that frequently there was something stagey and artificial about the uses of beauty. As a country which struggled to fulfil the grandiose aspirations of its founders, Italy on occasion made pompous and excessive use of its cultural heritage. D'Annunzio, whose dandified persona was theatrical if not caricatural, was, to say the least, an

odd exponent of national resurgence, and Versace too was less a
creative original than a gifted and imaginative synthesizer of images
drawn from the past. The beauty of Italian women continues to be
recognized but here also traditions were perpetuated rather than developed and were occasionally employed to resist change.

Notes

1 Giuseppe Mazzini, *Scritti politici*, edited by Terenzio Grandi and Augusto Comba (Turin, Einaudi, 1972), 554.
2 Emilio Gentile, *La grande Italia. Ascesa e declino del mito della nazione nel ventesimo secolo* (Milan, Mondadori, 1997), 44–6.
3 Ibid., 44.
4 George L. Mosse, *The Nationalization of the Masses* (New York, Fertig, 1975), 22.
5 Ibid., 22–3.
6 Quoted in Silvio Lanaro, *Nazione e lavoro. Saggio sulla cultura borghese in Italia* (Venice, Marsilio, 1979), 59.
7 Ibid., 62.
8 John Dickie, 'Darkest Italy' in *The Nation and Stereotypes of the Mezzogiorno, 1860–1900* (New York, St Martin's, 1999), chapter 3.
9 Gentile, *La grande Italia*, 43–4.
10 Ibid., 52.
11 John Woodhouse, *Gabriele D'Annunzio: Defiant Archangel* (Oxford, Oxford University Press, 1998), 126.
12 Quoted in ibid., p.167. See also Philippe Jullian, *D'Annunzio* (Paris, Fayard, 1971), 264.
13 See Barbara Spackman, *Fascist Virilities* (Minneapolis, University of Minnesota Press, 1996), 94.
14 Quoted in Woodhouse, *D'Annunzio*, 279.
15 John Pemble, *Venice Discovered* (Oxford, Clarendon Press, 1995), 160.
16 Ibid., 159.
17 F. T. Marinetti, *Il paesaggio e l'estetica futurista della macchina* (Florence, Nemi, 1931), 15.
18 Mosse, *The Nationalization of the Masses*, 30–1.
19 Simonetta Falasca-Zamponi, *Fascist Spectacle: The Aesthetics of Power in Mussolini's Italy* (Berkeley, University of California Press, 1997), 16.
20 Ibid., 16.
21 Ibid., 26.
22 Paola Tinagli, *Women in Italian Renaissance Art* (Manchester, Manchester University Press, 1993), 85–6.
23 Both quotations are taken from Carlo Casalegno, *La regina Margherita* (Turin, Einaudi, 1956), 67.

[24] This episode is recounted in detail in Romano Bracalini, *La regina Margherita* (Milan, Rizzoli, 1985), 83–8.

[25] V. De Napoli, *L'eterna bellezza della regina Margherita di Savoja* (Naples, Gargiulo, 1984), 52.

[26] Ibid., 54.

[27] For a systematic rebuttal of the idea of a superior Teutonic race, see Alfredo Niceforo, *I Germani: storia di un'idea e di una 'razza'* (Rome, Editrice Società Periodid, 1917).

[28] Umberto Notari, *Dichiarazioni alle più belle donne del mondo* (Milan, Notari, 1933), 22.

[29] *Cinema Illustrazione*, 26 August 1931, 6.

[30] Raffaele Calzini, ed., *La bella italiana. Da Botticelli a Tiepolo*, supplement to *Domus*, 84 (December 1934), 5.

[31] For a detailed discussion of this controversy, see Stephen Gundle, 'Feminine beauty, national identity and political conflict in postwar Italy, 1945–54', *Contemporary European History*, 8:3 (1999), 359–78.

[32] *La Domenica degli Italiani*, 18 November 1945, p. 3. The *Domenica del Corriere* adopted this alternative title in 1945–6, while the press remained under Allied control.

[33] *La Domenica degli Italiani*, 16 December 1945, p. 6.

[34] *La Domenica degli Italiani*, 23 December 1945, p. 5.

[35] See Raimondo Manzini, 'Le smanie per la Miss', *Famiglia Cristiana*, 15 October 1950, p. 805.

[36] *Vie Nuove*, 2 July 1950, p. 17.

[37] Quoted in Dino Villani, *Come sono nate undici Miss Italia* (Milan, Domus, 1957), 65.

[38] *Tempo*, 4 October 1947, 18.

[39] See Stephen Gundle, 'Sophia Loren, Italian icon', *Historical Journal of Film, Radio and Television*, 15:3 (1995), 367–85.

[40] Hamish Bowles, 'Very Versace', *Vogue* (US edition, November 1997), 342.

[41] Gina Bellafonte, 'La dolce vita', *Time*, 28 July 1997, p. 37.

[42] Richard Martin, 'Introduction' to Martin, ed., *Gianni Versace* (New York, The Metropolitan Museum of Art, 1997), 15.

[43] Colin McDowell, 'The show must go on', *The Times Magazine*, 6 December 1997, p. 39.

[44] See, for example, some of the articles in 'Brutto. Undici atti d'accusa al kitsch italiano', *Parola Chiave*, supplement to *Liberal*, 4 October 1996.

6

The mass media and the question of a national community in Italy

DAVID FORGACS

Introduction

Since the appearance nearly twenty years ago of Benedict Anderson's book on nationalism it has become common to think of national identity as involving a particular type of 'imagined community', one that is closely tied to place.[1] But if nations are place communities which may be made and maintained without direct contact between their members, they are nonetheless reliant, like other communities, on flows of communications among them. It is hard to conceive of a national identity being established or consolidated without continued relays of information among those who share the identity, relays which play back to them their sense of common cultural memory or mutual belonging, for instance by the circulation of symbols and patriotic narratives, a calendar of commemorative events and regular news.

Anderson's book, which took issue with the Eurocentrism of many earlier studies of nationalism, noted that the rise of nationalist movements in Latin America or South Asia did not always coincide with bourgeois revolutions or liberal movements but was always accompanied or preceded, as it had been in Europe, by the rise of 'print capitalism', that is to say printed books and newspapers sold as commodities on non-local markets. The rise of nationalism was also closely related to the emergence of a modern idea of time, what Walter Benjamin called 'homogeneous empty time', as distinct from the time of pre-modern communities, filled and structured by salient memories or millenarian expectations. The newspaper created the preconditions for a national community because it gave its readers the feeling that, though physically separated and scattered, they were connected and synchronized with one another by events happening simultaneously in different parts of the nation, events which changed from day to day. This process, we can add, was subsequently enhanced and extended by the non-print media: newsreels, radio, television. At the other end of the process, from the 1970s onwards, communications media have contributed to a partial erosion of national boundaries, on the one hand as a result of the increasingly transnational flows of telecommunications and television and the globalization of media industries, and on the other because networks of computer-mediated communications (CMCs) – the 'fourth generation' of mass communications technologies after print, cinema and broadcasting – have made possible 'virtual localities' and so-called 'glocalization', in other words the juxtaposition of the local and the global, microcommunities at a global level which bypass national frontiers.

This all suggests that the history of nations has a peculiarly close relationship with the history of the media. It also suggests that the media do not reflect or articulate the identity of a pre-existing national community but are one of the means, maybe even the principal one, by which that community and its identity are brought into being and shaped and later (perhaps) eroded. These points are consistent with a move in social theory away from a conception of identity as static and intrinsic, as something one 'has', already nestling within one's inner self, as it were, towards a view of identity as dynamic and relational, produced and reproduced by communicative interactions, ascriptions and self-definitions. In Habermas's interesting version of this view, which he bases on speech-act theory, the identity and boundaries of the individual ego are marked out by the use of what linguists call deictics or shifters (I/you, here/there, this/that, etc.), demonstratives (him, them, etc.), and performatives (I promise, I do, etc.). These create subject positions and lead to reciprocal suppositions about one's own and others' identity. Thus, 'the basis for the assertion of one's own identity is not really self-identification, but intersubjectively recognized self-identification.'[2] The same applies to collective identities as to individual ones: if an identity is not a state but a process, generated and sustained by outward manifestations and performances (such as physical appearance, way of speaking, participation in collective rituals) and/or by internalized representations (memory, self-image, etc.), then it is crucially dependent on structures and circuits of communication in order to thrive. This holds both for the relatively stable 'social and other-related' forms of identity characteristic of modernity and for the allegedly 'disintegrated' and 'decentred' identities of postmodernity.[3]

However, if the media have helped to bring nations into being and to define their boundaries, it is also important to recognize that nations are not the only communities they have shaped in this way. Newspapers and broadcasting may be local or regional as well as national, and most national newspapers and news channels give information about events in other countries. Moreover, national communities are often also recipients of other nations' media. In other words, the geographical limits of the media and the imagined geographical limits of the nation do not necessarily coincide. So while on the one hand certain media products, such as national news broadcasts, may help maintain and regulate the imagined boundaries of the nation, the flows of other types of product into and out of a nation, for instance film and television fiction, make those boundaries permeable and unstable. Nations are always open at their edges to information flows, and this makes their identity precarious.

All these points may be applied just as much to other countries as to Italy. However, each country tends to develop over time a set of narratives of its own relationship to nationhood, and in Italy what one might call the tragic version of this narrative presents this relationship as a succession of inadequacies and failures: the over-narrow social base of nineteenth-century nationalism; the rhetorical artificiality and social exclusiveness of nationalizing campaigns from above, like that of Fascism; the lack of a popular national consciousness; the failure to establish a solid democratic identity after 1945. If we want to get a new angle on this narrative we should try to recast it as a series of questions about communications and community.

In what follows I shall reconsider five commonly asked questions about national identity in this way. The first is whether the persistence of local and regional affiliations really acted as an obstacle to national identity; second, whether low literacy levels were in fact an insuperable barrier to the spread of national identity; third, how far Gramsci's claims about the lack in Italy of a 'national-popular' culture were valid; fourth, whether the Fascist regime was successful in generating popular consent at a national level; fifth, how far the civil war of 1943–5 and the formation of the Republic successfully refounded national identity. I shall then conclude with two further, more general, questions: whether the mass media in Italy have worked, historically, to impede rather than foster the development of a liberal-democratic public sphere at national level and whether successive communications media have, on balance, done more to reinforce or to undermine national boundaries.

Locality and nationality

There are a number of versions of the argument that the strength of local and regional affiliations in Italy has been the cause of a weak national identity. One is that attachment to one's village or town, or *campanilismo*, and the power of local clientele networks have been more entrenched and persistent than in many other countries and have impeded the formation of national attachments, or at any rate have proved stronger than them. Another is that loyalty to the family as one's primary community, or 'familism', has been more potent than loyalty to secondary communities or to various forms of society, including the nation. A third is that subcultural loyalties (to the Church or a political party) and regional identifications (not necessarily in the form of identification with the political regions constituted after 1861, the majority of which were belatedly given devolved powers only in 1970) are unusually strong, the latter partly because the old pre-unification states persisted in people's minds as imagined communities and partly because of popular disaffection and disillusionment with successive national regimes and governments, which has in some cases been articulated by regionalist and autonomist parties like the Partito d'Azione Sarda, the Südtiroler Volkspartei or the Lega Nord.

These claims all have in common an implicit 'either–or' assumption about identification: one must either identify with the smaller unit (family, locality, subculture, region) or with the larger one (nation). Yet not only is this assumption at odds with the claims themselves (why should loyalty to family be compatible with loyalty to town or region but not with loyalty to nation?); there is also no good reason to assume that different forms of identification may not be co-present and mutually reinforcing rather than mutually exclusive. In fact there are many concrete instances in which the family, party or locality (in the form, say, of a local school or festival) may serve as effective channels for the dissemination and reinforcement of national identifications. Adrian Lyttelton has even suggested that

145

clientelism, as well as having the negative effects rightly imputed to it, was 'a crucial instrument for tying together the threads of Italy's multiple and diverse societies into some kind of knot. It bound local interests to the central state.'[4] A locality or a region may sometimes be set up against a nation, or even as an alternative nation (the 'Padania' created by the Lega Nord), but it does not have to be.

If we recast this question as one about communications we need to ask how far nation and locality have been connected to one another in media relays. The concept of a relay is important because the very idea of a locality presupposes some larger superordinate community in relation to which a designated area comes to be seen as 'local' rather than self-sufficient and all-containing. However, the idea that this superordinate community should be a nation, rather than, say, a province or region or some higher-than-national entity, is by no means automatically given: it needs to be produced.

A good starting-point for this inquiry is the early television quiz show *Campanile sera*, which first went on the air in 1957. The formula of the show was, each week, to have teams from villages in different regions compete to answer questions. Television, with its technological ability to show images live from different localities through link-ups mixed in a central studio, may be said to have produced in this instance a particular version of the locality–nation relay, one in which the lower and higher community were linked to one another in real time. The show also played back a version of Italy's heterogeneity-in-commonality to people in other localities than those participating in the contest. Later examples of this have been the annual televising of the Palio in Siena, a typically local event made into a national media event, and the 1970s game show *Giochi senza frontiera*, a Eurovision production in which local teams from different countries unofficially represented their countries in much the same way as local teams playing in international sports fixtures. In all these cases the interdependence of locality and nation was clinched by the rhetoric of the visible live event, a uniquely tele-visual variant of Anderson's 'horizontal communities' created by the national press.

How far back can this process be traced? If we go backwards from the beginnings of a regular television service (1954) we can find various early post-war examples – from Carlo Levi's *Cristo si è fermato a Eboli* (1945) to the films of neo-realism and the letters column 'Italia domanda' edited by Cesare Zavattini in *Epoca* in 1950

– of documentary investigations of local realities in which there are similar relays (though not, of course, in real time) between localities and the nationwide audience. A symptomatic case is Roberto Rossellini's film *Paisà* (1946), each of whose six episodes is located in a different part of Italy (Sicily, Naples, Rome, Florence, the Apennines in Romagna, the Po delta) but whose structure suggests a unifying journey of the liberating Allied troops from south to north and a shared destiny: the collective struggle of the Italian people against Nazism and Fascism and the hardships of war and occupation. All these examples portray, in different media, locality in a close relationship to nationality even as they dramatize the heterogeneity of Italy's localities. Local needs or problems (poverty, poor health, the effects of occupation, unemployment) are presented as problems of the nation-state, and thus as the state's responsibility, even when the proposed solution, as in Levi's book, is devolution of power and resources away from the central state to local areas.

One might go back even further. Well before the start of a regular television service there were live radio reports of the tour cycle race, the Giro d'Italia, which fulfilled a similar function of presenting the nation to itself as a set of interconnected localities, from large cities on plains to hilltop villages.[5] The immense popularity of cycling in Italy (as in France) as a mass-mediated spectator sport, at its peak in the period 1930–60, no doubt had a variety of explanations, including the idea of its democratic accessibility (the majority of riders were of working-class or peasant origin, suggesting that anyone with enough physical stamina and determination could become a champion), but the particular passion generated by the Giro d'Italia as a regular national appointment, a national race with national stars like those two great rivals of the 1940s and 1950s, Gino Bartali and Fausto Coppi, was clearly dependent on the way it was reported in various media, on the immediacy of news flowing in from the many localities on its route.

Illiteracy

The argument that low literacy levels were historically a barrier to the spread of national identity until the era of mass literacy has also been widely expressed. The logic invoked here is that, since this era came late to Italy – by common consent not till the twentieth century

147

and perhaps, depending on how one defines 'mass' and 'literacy', not till after the Second World War – it must have been difficult, if not impossible, for people in Italy to 'feel' Italian, since Italian identity, as it came to be determined by nationalists in the Risorgimento and the early post-unification period, was largely mediated by a literate, indeed a literary, culture, and information about national events was primarily disseminated in the form of print, at least until the advent of regular cinema newsreels and radio in the 1920s.

However, there are a number of fallacies and potential traps in this argument. For one thing, it takes literary and official expressions of nationalism to be the whole story and neglects those multifarious unofficial expressions which do not require a literary mediation, such as the popular late nineteenth-century cults of Giuseppe Garibaldi and his wife Anita, or that of Queen Margherita, which were expressed in household objects, postcards or songs, or the popular identification with the monarchy manifested, for instance, in the semi-literate letters dictated or written to the king by soldiers fighting in the First World War,[6] or, in the 1930s, the forms of popular support for the Fascist state manifested in mass public events such as the donation of gold wedding rings to help finance the Abyssinian war or the visits to the Decennale (tenth-anniversary) exhibition of the Fascist revolution in Rome in 1932.[7] For another thing, it undervalues the many non-print channels by which national culture could be mediated and disseminated even in the pre-film and pre-radio era, from local intellectuals (priests, mayors, party officials) and the itinerant singers and poets known as *poeti a braccio* or *cantastorie*. Lastly, it undervalues lower-class geographical mobility (internal migration; foreign and return migration; conscription to national service or wars) as a factor in the creation of national or at any rate supra-regional identifications. It is necessary, in all these cases, to recognize the diversity of potential channels of communication other than written or printed texts for the circulation of national identity, even if of an inchoate or 'simple' kind, and for the construction of an imagined national community.

Lack of national-popularity

The notion that Italy historically lacked a 'national-popular' culture derives from Antonio Gramsci, who used this term in his prison notebooks (written 1929–35) to diagnose the failure of Italian intellectuals to create an organic alliance with the mass of the people. Gramsci was building on earlier Italian ways of representing a lack of identification between educated élites and the people as a problem in the formation of the nation-state – Massimo D'Azeglio's injunction to 'make Italians', Francesco De Sanctis's idea of a gap between 'science' and 'life', Stefano Jacini's distinction between *paese legale* and *paese reale* – but he crucially reconceptualized these in terms of a failed class alliance (between the liberal bourgeoisie and the working classes) and the absence of a radical, transformative kind of nation-building. Again, it can be useful to think of this diagnosis as having to do with communities and communications. For Gramsci, the lack of a national-popular culture was attributable on the one hand to the 'cosmopolitan' traditions of Italian intellectuals whose imagined communities, as we might put it, were trans-national (Catholic Christendom, Humanist Latinity, Enlightenment rationalism), and on the other to the influx of non-Italian popular culture: French and English detective fiction, for example.[8] In other words, both the intellectual élites and the masses were involved in a traffic of information and ideas in and out of Italy; they communicated with others but not with each other.

Gramsci's claims about the openness to foreign fiction may be corroborated by various pieces of evidence. Surveys conducted at various intervals from 1905 onwards found that novels in translation were often read in preference to those by Italian authors.[9] Indeed this preference, and the openness to translations of a number of commercial publishers, notably Mondadori (a publisher since 1911) and Bompiani (who founded his firm in 1929), led to protectionist moves towards the end of the Fascist period, but such measures as were taken had no lasting effect. A survey of 1949 carried out by the Istituto Doxa found that thirteen out of the twenty novels read most recently were translations (the most cited author was A. J. Cronin). Moreover, though Gramsci himself said virtually nothing about the non-print mass media, one can make much the same points, *a fortiori*, about cinema and recorded music. Shortly after the First World War, as a combined result of the crisis of Italian film production and the rise of the Hollywood studios and various European film industries, cinema screens in Italy came to show many more imported films than domestic ones. This situation was temporarily reversed between 1939 and 1945 and, for different reasons, in the 1960s, but at all other periods since 1920 consumption of films in Italy has been dominated by imported (and, among these, American) films, despite the revival at various times of a fairly strong national film industry and some popular Italian stars. As for popular music, Italian music has always been popular in Italy, and has been supported by national media, from repertory opera (disseminated from the nineteenth century, to those who could not afford to go to opera houses, by working men's chorales and town bands, and later by gramophone records and radio) to Neapolitan song and the Piedigrotta Festival (which developed in the 1880s and were again given national circulation by records and radio), to the Sanremo Festival (first organized by RAI radio in 1951) and the RAI television song contest *Canzonissima*, first broadcast in 1958. However these same media have also been channels for the transmission of imported music: records and the radio for jazz in the 1940s and early 1950s and for rock 'n' roll and pop from the mid-1950s, and then television, particularly the video music channels.

An attempt to judge the validity of Gramsci's analysis of the non-national popular character of Italian culture must do more, however, than provide evidence for the claim that Italian popular culture has always been primarily an import culture. All nations, and some more than others, import cultural goods as well as producing their own, but it does not follow that those which import more necessarily have a weaker sense of their own cultural identity than those that import less. It is a question, rather, of the meanings of the different cultural goods to domestic audiences and the quality and influence of the national media by comparison with imported media. Did (and do) audiences in Italy perceive imported books, films or music as more interesting, persuasive, seductive, prestigious than their own? Gramsci's own answer, which was that the Italian people, in being drawn to foreign books, underwent the hegemony of foreign intellectuals, now seems over-narrow.[10] It was rooted in his view of culture as part of an educative, alliance-building process, a process involving intellectuals, and it was based largely on nineteenth-century cultural forms: the opera (Verdi was for Gramsci a model of a national-popular artist) and the novel serialized as a *roman-feuilleton* or *romanzo d'appendice* in the newspaper. Indeed it has been argued that Gramsci's way of conceiving the problem of popular culture as a problem of relations between intellectuals and the people carried over nineteenth-century political models too. Franco Venturi and Bianca Maria Luporini both suggested that Gramsci may have coined the term 'nazionale-popolare' on the basis of the term *narodnost*, used by the Russian populists, and Alberto Asor Rosa, in a polemical work of 1965, saw it as strongly influenced by the nationalist populism of Risorgimento writers such as Gioberti.[11]

To put it another way, Gramsci was writing in the era of the growth of modern mass media but he failed to recognize their capacity for national aggregation and identification without the mediation of 'intellectuals'. Even when the left in Italy began to shrug off Gramsci's influence, in the late 1950s and 1960s, and started to get critically to grips with these media, they tended on the whole to see them, through the lenses of the Frankfurt School, as inauthentic, inimical to real culture. Thus the terms of the discussion took a long time to catch up with the reality of the popular influence of non-print media.

Fascism and consent

Gramsci's analysis of the non-national-popular character of Italian culture was part of his wider analysis of a failed national hegemony of Italian intellectuals, and in particular of the political left and the working-class movement. He made this analysis at a time when Fascism had defeated the left and had constructed an alternative, repressive form of hegemony, and indeed at just the time when many historians would claim Mussolini's regime was at the peak of its internal stability, between the consolidation of the single-party state in the mid-1920s and the destabilization produced by economic crises, internal repression, foreign wars and domestic dissent from the late 1930s onwards. Fascism, which Palmiro Togliatti defined in his Moscow lectures of 1935 as a 'mass reactionary regime',[12] was the first form of state after unification to combine a nationalist project with active and concerted mass mobilization: the recruitment of citizens from childhood upwards into mass organizations (Balilla, Piccole Italiane, Avanguardia, Gioventù Italiana del Littorio), the attempt to structure and direct working people's leisure through the Opera Nazionale Dopolavoro, the mass publicity campaigns to enlist popular support for fast population growth, ruralization and self-sufficiency in wheat production, imperialist expansion in East

151

Africa, and the harnessing of the press, newsreels and radio for propaganda purposes.

The question of consent to Fascism, more transparently perhaps than some of the others we are examining, is largely a question about the efficacy of communications apparatuses. For what one is really seeking to establish when one asks how far a political system managed to generate popular consent is how effectively that system managed to produce and control flows of information between itself and the people, and to stem flows of counter-information coming at them either from outside the country (for instance, in the form of anti-Fascist publications and broadcasts) or from clandestine sources within it. Attempts to measure the nature and extent of consent in Fascist Italy which do not take these questions into account, such as Renzo De Felice's attempt to read off and measure 'levels' of consent from the movement of prices and wages or from the absence of open expressions of dissent, are of questionable heuristic value.[13] More valid is the approach of social historians and oral historians, like Luisa Passerini or Maurizio Gribaudi, who have begun to reconstruct, in the case of working-class districts of Turin, how horizontal networks of communication operated within these communities and how these conflicted or intersected and interacted with the vertical communications networks controlled by the regime.[14]

What can be said, in relation to this, is that the Fascist regime, for all its increasing centralization of influence over mass communications from the late 1930s onwards, never controlled the flow of communications to the Italian people absolutely. Indeed it would not have been possible for it, or for any modern state, to have done so, even in the era before transnational flows of television contributed to the undermining, in the 1980s, of the state media monopolies of the Communist regimes in the Soviet Union and eastern Europe. For one thing the Fascist regime never entirely stemmed alternative channels of communication within Italy. Its greatest success probably lay in stopping up the many capillary channels that had been opened up by the left in the liberal era: the newspapers of the Socialist and Communist parties, the left publishers and book clubs, even the drinking places, the *osterie*, *taverne* and *bettole*, which had been associated with political discussions, and which Mussolini proudly declared in 1927 he had partly suppressed.[15] However, this repression was never total, and it is well known that the left press continued to be clandestinely produced, and, together with left books, to have a limited clandestine circulation in Fascist Italy, and, as the reports of police spies noted, the circuits of clandestine discussion never dried up. Moreover, Catholic channels of communication, from publishing houses, newspapers and parish bulletins to film production and distribution companies to Vatican Radio, all thrived during the Fascist period. For another thing, despite the intensification under Fascism of censorship, the enforced reduction in the numbers of translations, the blacklisting after 1938 of books by Jewish authors and after 1940 of American and British authors, the Monopoly Law of 1938 which reduced film imports from the USA, the restrictions on foreign comic strips and on jazz music on the radio and the jamming of foreign radio broadcasts during the war, the fact is that there always remained a relative permeability of national media boundaries, and clandestine and oppositional material had at least a limited circulation. Finally, for all the attempts under Fascism to make over Italian national identity in a new way, or inflect it in new directions, for instance by identifying the true nation with rural Italy, or separating it from 'eastern' influences within and without (Judaism, Bolshevism), or by identifying Italians with 'Aryans' during the period of the racial laws (1938–44), the Fascist reassertion of national identity always appealed to 'tradition' and to history, and this history included a stock repertoire of national types and icons, from Dante to the Renaissance artists and writers to the Risorgimento heroes, which was essentially ecumenical, non-specific to Fascism. In other words, Fascist nationalism ran to a considerable extent within the grooves of pre-Fascist and non-Fascist nationalism.

A contested nation

The next question may be touched on more rapidly, since the question of how far national identity was refounded and remade during and after the crisis and collapse of Fascism is related to the question we have just been examining. If Fascism never wholly succeeded in controlling a national communications space and imposing a new hegemonic national identity in Italy, then the process of remaking that identity was necessarily less total and palingenetic than if the regime had monopolized communications or succeeded in erasing all traces of the national past. What is clear, once again, is how crucial communications and the media were to the process of identity-formation after the crisis of Fascism. The civil war of 1943–5 was conducted, at an ideological level, as a struggle between competing conceptions of the legitimate nation, competing versions of patriotic identification, with both sides – the Resistance and the Fascist die-hards of the Republic of Salò – claiming to represent the true interests of the nation and declaring their willingness to die in order to defend it. In the contest between these conceptions the press (the Fascistized national newspapers of the north and the newspapers of the various parties represented in the Comitato di Liberazione Nazionale), the radio stations (those controlled by the Fascists and those overseen by the Allies and the Psychological Warfare Branch) and film newsreels all played a fundamental role in competing to influence public opinion. The fact that nationalist discourse had an ecumenical and elastic character meant that the same key terms – *nazione, patria, popolo* – circulated on either side, and what was crucial, therefore, was the way that they were combined or, to use Ernesto Laclau's term, 'articulated' with other terms.[16] On the anti-Fascist side, for instance, the articulation linked the terms with 'liberty' or, in some cases, 'socialism', 'communism', 'freedom', in opposition to 'tyranny', 'barbarism'.

The Resistance movement also reappropriated from Fascism the names and symbols of the Risorgimento – the Communist Party partisan divisions in 1943–5 were called 'Brigate Garibaldi', a name which the party had first used in the Spanish Civil War, while the liberal socialists of the Giustizia e Libertà group named the political organization they formed in 1942, in alliance with other anti-Fascist groups, the Partito d'Azione, like Mazzini's party. The anti-Fascist recasting of national identity was thus in large part a process of rearticulation and reinflection of the common stock of shared nationalist terms. In the post-war period, after the formation of the Republic, commemorations of the Resistance, relayed in the media, would play a major part in the reinforcement of this ideological rearticulation as a refounding, with the notion of the 'Republic born out of the Resistance'.

The media and the public sphere: Italian exceptionalism

The media in Italy have often been portrayed as historically lacking two of the essential features they ought to possess in a liberal democracy: independence and impartiality. This view is assembled out of a number of claims about individual media: that the press has never been truly independent, since all newspapers have expressed the interests either of their corporate shareholders or of political factions; that film newsreels and later radio and television likewise failed to develop a proper 'arm's length' autonomy from party and government (radio and film news began and developed under the Fascists; television was born under the hegemony of the Christian Democrats who first turned it into their personal fiefdom, then reluctantly shared it with their Socialist coalition partners; with the rise of commercial television a series of hidden political connections developed alongside the overt ones of state television). Even computer-mediated communications, which have mushroomed in the developed world with astonishing rapidity since the mid-1990s without any political regulation, have been subjected in Italy to state interference.[17] According to this view the media have been genuinely independent, at best, only at the margins or at a local level: in local FM radio, for example, or in certain local periodicals. At national level they have always been tied to some interest or other and journalists are always to some extent, in Giampaolo Pansa's phrase, 'bought and sold'.[18]

These claims are all true up to a point. It would be ingenuous, or disingenuous, to argue that Italy has had or has now a healthy regime of media pluralism and democracy. The political and economic ties which bind the Italian media have been and remain a serious problem. As Mussolini put it, replying in 1932 to Emil Ludwig who had asked him how a former journalist like himself, who had once so ably used the critical role of the press, could now justify press censorship, 'When there is freedom of the press the newspapers publish only what big business and the banks, who pay the newspaper, want them to publish.'[19] What is misleading, however, are the implications that these ties have been an absolute obstacle to the formation of a modern liberal-democratic public sphere or that the media elsewhere are somehow free of similar ties. On the first of these points it is worth insisting that in all phases of the post-unification period, apart from the Fascist regime, there has been enough media pluralism – imperfect, to be sure, but pluralism – to keep open a significant space of public debate. The press, for all its entwinements with industry, corporate finance and the party system, has overall been less compromised by them than national radio and television. One need think only of the role played by the *Corriere della Sera* under the editorship of Luigi Albertini in the first years of the Fascist government, for example its accusations of Fascist complicity in the abduction and murder of Giacomo Matteotti in 1924, or the role played by the party papers of the left or liberal periodicals such as *Il Mondo* or *Belfagor* during the Cold War hegemony of the Christian Democrat right. The role of the journalists' union, the Federazione Nazionale della Stampa Italiana (FNSI), and the reforms of the press which it won after 1970, for instance the increased powers given to the internal editorial committees of journalists, the *comitati di redazione*, and the requirement in journalists' contracts that they report the full facts of a story to the best of their ability, were also significant in limiting the power of major corporate shareholders like Rizzoli or Agnelli.

Television is usually cited as the medium which has been most directly and overtly driven by political and economic interests, and where a genuinely plural arena of public debate has failed to be established. Again, there is some truth in this claim, particularly by comparison with the press, but again it is only relative. The diversity of Italian television schedules, the degree of political debate on television, and the complexity of television's social and cultural role have all tended to be ignored while its alleged intellectual poverty and negative influence on political behaviour have been highlighted. However, as Peppino Ortoleva has recently reminded us, although private ownership and political control of the media undoubtedly increases the influence of the groups which control it and is therefore rightly a source of anxiety in a democracy, 'one cannot find in the last fifty years a single concrete instance where the various political groupings actually admit that public opinion has been swayed or conditioned by this or that means of communication'.[20]

The most controversial case of a politically instrumental control of television has been that of Silvio Berlusconi, particularly when he decided to mobilize the considerable resources of his television empire in support of his newly created party, Forza Italia, in the 1994 general election. When the party emerged victorious with the largest share of the vote and Berlusconi became prime minister there were widespread claims of an emergent 'rule of television' (*videocrazia* or *telecrazia*) in Italy.[21] Personality and style seemed not only to count for more than political content but to have become everything. This diagnosis was applied not just to Forza Italia and

Berlusconi but also to two of his coalition partners, the Lega Nord and Alleanza Nazionale (AN) and their respective leaders, Umberto Bossi and Gianfranco Fini. Bossi's demagogic abilities were already familiar to Italian television viewers. Fini had been less well known on television before the 1994 campaign but proved effective in a quieter way: he managed to give both himself and his 'post-Fascist' party an appearance of calm reasonableness, and this seemed to have been a major factor, together with the legitimation conferred by the alliance with Berlusconi, in AN's electoral success.

One should, however, separate out the different claims that were made about so-called *telecrazia* and examine them in turn. The claim that Berlusconi's political success was helped by his ownership of Fininvest (whose television holdings were separated off in 1996 into a new subsidiary named Mediaset), with its three private networks Canale 5, Retequattro and Italia 1 and its advertising arm Publitalia, is not seriously in dispute. His party did have grassroots organizations – the Forza Italia clubs which sprang up all over the country in the run-up to the March election – but it lacked a real centre or a national structure, and its main channel of communication to the electorate was certainly television. All three Fininvest networks were enlisted in support of its campaign and continued to propagate Forza Italia's message after Berlusconi had been elected. Some subsequent studies of voting behaviour in the election claimed to confirm a direct correlation between exposure to political messages on the Fininvest channels and voter preferences for Forza Italia.[22] On the other hand, few political analysts maintained that television was the *only* factor in Berlusconi's victory. They drew attention also to the desire among many people for a complete renewal of the political system, to Berlusconi's ability to articulate the interests of middle-class voters and play upon their perennial fear of communism, to the electoral geography of the Polo alliances (in which Forza Italia was the national cement between the anti-southern Lega in the north and Alleanza Nazionale in the south) and, not least, to the failure of the left's campaign itself, which had been largely negative, centring on attacks against the existing political class, against corruption and against Berlusconi and his allies, and which had badly misjudged public opinion towards the Mani Pulite magistrates. The latters' alacrity was seen by many voters as excessive and even punitive.

Harder to assess, in the debate over *telecrazia*, were the claims that the 1994 election victory represented a triumph of style over content, of images and advertising slogans over policies. Some observers suggested that politics had now become so intertwined with advertising and the marketing of consumer goods and with performance (*spettacolo*) that many voters could no longer tell the difference between them. Among the examples invoked in support of these claims were the metaphor of Berlusconi's 'entry into the field' (*discesa in campo*), with its mixture of messianic, military and football associations; his pre-election promise to create a million jobs; his well-cut suits and permanent smile.[23] Italian politics, commerce and entertainment, it seemed, had become bonded together, through television, in what Jean Baudrillard called the space of 'hyperreality' or the 'simulacrum', neither real nor imaginary. But by their very nature as descriptions of long-term trends or latent tendencies such claims are hard either to prove or disprove. Even the available facts are open to different interpretations. For instance, the fact that nearly 40 per cent of voters under twenty-five voted Forza Italia was seen by some commentators as confirmation that the generation which had grown up with the private networks was most easily seduced by Berlusconi's appeal and could not separate politics from television. But an alternative explanation is that their choice of Forza Italia was a rational rejection of the established parties and politicians, including the former Communist Party moderates who had formed the PDS (Partito Democratico di Sinistra); this statistic also means, of course, that 60 per cent of young voters chose other parties. As for the claims made at the time that Berlusconi's victory marked the beginning of a primacy of the entrepreneur over the career politician and the economic or financial expert (*tecnico*), a 'dumbing down' of Italian politics or a dangerous slide towards dictatorship, these seem to have been disproved by subsequent events: Berlusconi's own fall from office, the decline of the Lega and AN vote; the successful candidature of the uncharismatic Romano Prodi and the victory of the left in the 1996 campaign; the appointment of PDS leader Massimo D'Alema as prime minister in 1998.[24]

In retrospect, by comparison with the 1996 election campaign, that of 1994 comes to look more of a historical exception and less the beginning of a new trend in Italian political communications that so many observers took it to be at the time. Luca Ricolfi, comparing the two campaigns, wrote of 'the greater "normality"' of that of

1996 and attributed this to the cooling of political passions after the 1994 campaign, dominated as it was by intense feelings about the Tangentopoli bribes scandal and the defects of the old party system, and not least by the novelty of the Forza Italia phenomenon itself, none of which were repeated in 1996. The introduction by the Dini government of stricter regulatory controls on broadcasting clearly made a difference too.[25] In this respect one could say that the 1994 campaign took place in a vacuum into which the old structures of political communication, emanations of party apparatuses which had either collapsed or had been radically delegitimated, had suddenly and violently imploded. This vacuum was filled, massively, by television and a politics of image and personality to an extent that had never been seen before but which has not been repeated since. As Mario Morcellini put it perceptively, just a few months after the 1994 election,

> In the face of a structural and conjunctural decline of the traditional apparatuses of the management of consent, the entire media system became central and privileged compared with all other channels of political 'transmission'. It was able not only to represent the symbolic arena of conflict between the different political groupings but, above all, to dictate the victory of the *politics of the image* over the *concreteness of politics*.[26]

National cohesion or erosion of boundaries?

To conclude with some general reflections, let us consider finally how far, on balance, successive communications media may be said to have helped forge a cohesive national community and how far they have worked in the opposite direction, namely to erode or weaken national boundaries by opening up the country to exchanges and flows of information with communities outside it or by creating new microcommunities within it.

The arguments in favour of the national cohesion view are that the mass media helped unify and standardize the spoken language (even, paradoxically, when what was spoken was frequently dubbed on to the lip movements of foreign actors), produced a series of nationally known cultural products (popular songs, programmes, etc.), stars and regular 'appointments', such as news broadcasts, and at times of national crisis or threatened destabilization, as during the Second World War, the terrorism crisis of the 1970s or the collapse of the

First Republic in the early 1990s when challenges were mounted to the national government by federalist and secessionist tendencies, served to fill a partial political vacuum by ensuring unity and continuity with the past.

The arguments for the opposing view are that at all times there has been a substantial amount of imported material flowing into Italy, that this, as much as domestically generated material, has always played a large role in shaping Italians' identities and has enabled them to make constant comparisons with the world outside, and that the capacity of national élites to regulate and control the boundaries of communications has almost always been severely curtailed. A case in point is the Fascist government's inability to stem the tide of anti-Fascist radio broadcasts and 'clandestine listening' during the war.

Clearly, there is truth on both sides of this argument. The media, historically, have been a factor in national cohesion in Italy, *and* they have also worked the other way, to erode the perceived boundaries of the nation and open up Italy to a wider world. Rather than resign oneself to this as an irresolvable conundrum one should make use of it as a lever with which to get a critical purchase on the relations between media and national community at particular historical moments as well as over the longer term. Thus one might productively inquire what the particular *balance of forces* between cohesion and erosion of the national community was at the end of the Fascist period or during the crisis of the First Republic, or one might ask what the *balance of evidence* is for a disintegration or a remaking of the national community since 1945. What must remain central, in all these enquiries, is the recognition that mass communications are vital to the very notions of national community and identity.

Notes

1   Benedict Anderson, *Imagined Communities: Reflections on the Origin and Spread of Nationalism* (London, Verso, 1983).
2   Jürgen Habermas, 'Historical materialism and the development of normative structures' (1976), in *Communication and the Evolution of Society*, translated by Thomas McCarthy (London, Heinemann, 1979), 107.
3   Douglas Kellner, *Media Culture: Cultural Studies, Identity and Politics between the Modern and the Postmodern* (London and New York, Routledge, 1995), 231, 233.

4   Adrian Lyttelton, 'Shifting identities: nation, region and city', in Carl Levy, ed., *Italian Regionalism: History, Identity and Politics* (Oxford, Berg, 1996), 45.

5   On the reporting of the Giro d'Italia see Franco Cordelli, *L'Italia di mattina* (Milan, Leonardo, 1990) and Daniele Marchesini, *L'Italia del Giro d'Italia* (Bologna, Il Mulino, 1996).

6   See Renato Monteleone, ed., *Lettere al re* (Rome, Riuniti, 1973).

7   On popular reactions to the Decennale, see Jeffrey T. Schnapp, 'Epic demonstrations: Fascist modernity and the 1932 exhibition of the Fascist revolution', in Richard J. Golsan, ed., *Fascism, Aesthetics and Culture* (Hanover, NH, University Press of New England, 1992).

8   Quaderno 21, 'Problemi della cultura nazionale italiana. 1° Letteratura popolare', in Antonio Gramsci, *Quaderni del carcere*, edited by Valentino Gerratana (Turin, Einaudi, 1975), III, 2105-35.

9   See for example *I libri più letti dal popolo italiano. Primi resultati* [sic] *della inchiesta promossa dalla Società Bibliografica Italiana* (Milan, Società Bibliografica Italiana, 1906) and Giambattista Vicari, *Editoria e pubblica opinione* (Rome, Edizioni Cinque Lune, 1957), 44.

10 Gramsci, *Quaderni del carcere*, III, 2117 and 2197.

11 Franco Venturi, *Il populismo russo*, 3 vols (Turin, Einaudi, 1952), I, 35; Bianca Maria Luporini, 'Alle origini del "nazionale-popolare"', unpublished paper read at the conference 'Morale e politica in Gramsci', Rome, 24-6 June 1987; Alberto Asor Rosa, *Scrittori e popolo. Il populismo nella letteratura italiana contemporanea* (1965) (Rome, Samonà e Savelli, fourth edition, 1972), 210-22.

12 Palmiro Togliatti, *Lezioni sul fascismo* (1935) (Rome, Riuniti, 1970), 9-10.

13 Renzo De Felice, *Mussolini il duce*, II: *Gli anni del consenso, 1929-1936* (Turin, Einaudi, 1974).

14 Luisa Passerini, *Torino operaia e fascismo. Una storia orale* (Rome and Bari, Laterza, 1984); Maurizio Gribaudi, *Mondo operaio e mito operaio. Spazi e percorsi sociali a Torino nel primo Novecento* (Turin, Einaudi, 1987).

15 See Benito Mussolini, 'Il discorso dell'Ascensione' in *Opera omnia*, XXII, edited by Edoardo and Duilio Susmel (Florence, La Fenice, 1957), 363, where Mussolini claimed to have already closed 25,000 out of 187,000 *osterie* in Italy and to be proceeding to close more.

16 See Ernesto Laclau, *Politics and Ideology in Marxist Theory: Capitalism - Fascism - Populism* (London, NLB, 1977).

17 See Peter Ludlow, 'Appendix 2: Hardware 1: The Italian hacker crack-down', 'Appendix 3a: Information about electronic frontiers Italy (ALCEI)' and Bruce Sterling, 'Appendix 3b: Why I have joined ALCEI', in Peter Ludlow, ed., *High Noon on the Electronic Frontier:*

Conceptual Issues in Cyberspace (Cambridge, MA, MIT Press, 1996), 487–511.

[18] Giampaolo Pansa, *Comprati e venduti. I giornali e il potere negli anni '70* (Milan, Bompiani, 1977).

[19] Emil Ludwig, *Colloqui con Mussolini* (1932) (Milan, Mondadori, 1965), 69.

[20] Peppino Ortoleva, 'I media. Comunicazione e potere', in *Storia dell'Italia repubblicana*, III: *L'Italia nella crisi mondiale. L'ultimo ventennio*, 2: *Istituzioni, politiche, culture* (Turin, Einaudi, 1997), 866.

[21] See for example Martin Woollacott, 'Italy brainwashed by soft soap and hard sell', *Guardian*, 6 April 1994; Adrian Lyttelton, 'Italy: the triumph of TV', *New York Review of Books*, 41, no. 14, 11 August 1994, 25–9; V. Dreier, 'Forza Italia: Triumpf der Telekratie', *Sozialwissenschaftliche Informationen*, 23 (1994), no. 4, 285–92; Peter Glotz, 'Das Projekt Telekratie', *Die Woche*, 21 July 1994, 20–1.

[22] See Luca Ricolfi, 'Politics and the mass media in Italy', *West European Politics*, 20, 1 (1997), 141–6.

[23] On Berlusconi's language in the election campaign see M. Squarcione, 'Occhetto e Berlusconi: percorsi linguistici e strategie argomentative' in Mario Morcellini, ed., *Elezioni di TV. Televisione e pubblico nella campagna elettorale '94* (Genoa, Costa & Nolan, 1995), 176–83; on his smile see Stephen Gundle, 'Il sorriso di Berlusconi', *Altrochemestre*, 3 (1995), 14–17.

[24] Peppino Ortoleva saw the right's victory in the 1994 election as a symptom of anti-intellectualism, familiar in some other countries, such as the US, but new in Italy, where intellectuals have traditionally been respected. In the 'post-literate society' (*società postalfabeta*) which Italy had now become, where there was mass education and literacy and a diffusion of a general middle-level culture through the media, aggression was being vented, so he argued, against intellectuals who possessed status without effective power. See *Un ventennio a colori. Televisione privata e società in Italia (1975–95)* (Florence, Giunti, 1995), 119.

[25] Ricolfi, 'Politics and the mass media', 146–7.

[26] Mario Morcellini, 'Media e politica alla prova del "nuovo"', in Morcellini, *Elezioni di TV*, 8.

7

Italian national identity and Fascism: aliens, allogenes and assimilation on Italy's north-eastern border

GLENDA SLUGA

There have been few studies of the significance of Italy's boundary regions for analyses of Italian national identity.[1] As spaces of possible threat and potential imperial expansion, enclosure and communication, national definition and national ambiguity, boundary regions mark out the 'internal borders' of national identity, and highlight the problem of difference inside the nation.[2] David Campbell has argued that boundary regions can typify 'the attitudes and expectations at the basis of representations of core national identities'.[3] The post-First World War peace process that awarded Italy territories formerly part of the Austro-Hungarian Empire also introduced new boundary regions into the Italian nations. Italy now shared a border with the new Kingdom of Serbs, Croats and Slovenes (Yugoslavia), and gained new territory from its northern neighbour, Austria. This German-speaking South Tyrol region that became part of the Italian state was renamed 'Alto Adige'. The mainly Slovene- and Croatian-speaking sections of the Habsburg 'Küstenland' region (also known as the Adriatic Littoral) that bordered Yugoslavia were incorporated into Italy as 'Venezia Giulia'. In this article I use the view from Venezia Giulia, Italy's north-eastern boundary region, and particularly its main province and city – both of which were named Trieste – during the Fascist *ventennio*, as a vantage point for the study of conceptions of Italian national identity and nationalizing practices.[4] Under Fascist rule Italy's north-eastern border became a focus for the most vigorous contestation and violent enforcement of an integral Italian national identity. The presence of multi-lingual and non-Italian-speaking minorities in the Venezia Giulia boundary region also brought to the fore the long-standing concerns of Italian nationalists regarding the

Italian nation's (lack of) homogeneity – anxieties about Italy as the 'least of the great powers', and as a place where Italians still had to be made.[5] The strategies adopted in the inter-war period by successive Italian governments to promote and enforce political and cultural uniformity inside Italy's new borders also offers a comparative framework for analysing the contiguities and ruptures between liberal and Fascist conceptions of Italian national identity. Both liberal and Fascist political authorities represented minorities as a 'problem' in nationally defined terrain. In Venezia Giulia, the state, intellectuals and anti-Fascists, tended to endow the 'Slav'-named minority with the status of an alien, anonymous, antagonistic, yet ultimately assimilable Other – as alien or *allogeno,* which meant literally 'of another kind'.[6] These representations of minorities in the boundary region had crucial implications for the modalities of Italian national identity, as well as the everyday lives of Italian citizens singled out as 'alien' or Other. They underline the importance of discursively fashioned cultural representations of identity and difference, and the delineation of borders between Self and Other, in the consolidation of political power and the legitimation of national sovereignty in this period.

The foundations of Fascist nationalism

Denison Rusinow, the author of an expansive study of the inter-war history of the boundary regions inherited by Italy from the Habsburg Empire, has argued that in Venezia Giulia Fascism was 'centralizing, oppressive, and dedicated to the forcible Italianization of the minorities . . . many months before the Fascist regime had destroyed parliament and imposed authoritarianism on Italy'.[7] It could also be argued that even before the Fascist Party had assumed a formidable presence in Venezia Giulia, the spokespersons of liberal and democratic ideals in Italy had characterized minorities as a problem because of their difference, and posited assimilation, or Italianization, as the solution.

The 1920 Treaty of Rapallo which made the Yugoslav government responsible for Italian minority rights in the Dalmatian territory denied to Italy, also awarded Italy the territory of 'Venezia Giulia' without requiring the Italian state to protect the region's 'Slavic' minorities. In some instances, before and after Trieste was officially incorporated into Italy, Italian politicians took it upon themselves to informally address and confirm the linguistic rights of 'Slavs' as a minority.[8] In 1919 the prime minister, Francesco Nitti, instructed the civilian provincial governors 'to pursue a policy of freedom, justice and warm sympathy for the people of another race'. Nitti argued: 'They must have the feeling that Italy does not desire the denationalisation of the Slavs. Italy is a democratic country.'[9] Yet, as Rusinow has shown, regardless of Nitti's instructions, from 1918 to 1922 the treatment of those individuals named as Slavs in each of the provinces of Venezia Giulia was inconsistent, their fate dependent on the discretion of provincial authorities and the 'continued trends established during the period of military government' (from 1918 to 1919).[10] From 1919 until 1922 those provincial authorities headed 'quasi-autonomous regimes'.[11] Known as civil commissioner-generals, they were appointed by the national government in Rome and had the same autonomy as previous governors in the Habsburg political system; the only Italian innovation was the expansion of their autonomy in order to assist the political and economic integration of the new provinces.[12] The civil commissioner-general appointed to Trieste by Nitti was Antonio Mosconi. Mosconi regarded the new minorities as 'aliens' who had to be treated 'with equity and justice', but who were also expected to show 'their loyalty and absolute respect for the state and for our national consciousness'.[13] He usually referred to minorities within Italy as *allogeni*. He assumed that the national and cultural identities of *allogeni* had once been fostered by Austria as a weapon against Italian claims to sovereignty in the boundary region, and that *allogeni* could be subdued by the pacifying and assimilating powers of an ancient and superior Italian *civiltà*.[14] Well aware of events in Russia, Mosconi equated what he referred to explicitly as 'Slav' culture with Bolshevism. In other words, the anonymous category *allogeno* referred to minorities within Italy, while the relatively more specific term 'Slav' was reserved for describing Socialist organizations. Although historians such as Elio Apih have argued that Socialist organizations posed no 'real' threat to the control of the Italian state, Mosconi looked on the local worker organizations and Socialist parties as a combined national and political menace to the already vulnerable authority of the Italian state.[15] For the duration of his tenure, from 1919 to 1922, Mosconi led the assault on Socialists in Trieste by reinforcing the view that they were all 'Slavs'.

Mosconi's view of the synonymity of socialism and 'Slavs' not only echoed pre-war Italian irredentist discourse, but, most importantly, his speeches and actions lent a new national authority and local respectability to representations of 'Slavs' as a restless and dangerous 'mass' eager to 'invade' Trieste.[16] His identification of working-class discontent and agitation as anti-Italian and Slav fuelled representations of the struggle between Italians and 'Slavs' in the boundary region – representations vigorously propounded before and during the war by irredentists such as Scipio Sighele and Virginio Gayda. In the post-war, Gabriele D'Annunzio's military occupation of Fiume – the port town claimed by both Italy and Yugoslavia but designated an international city at the peace talks – and the demands by substantial pockets of Socialists for either the greater autonomy of the new provinces or for their complete independence, only added fuel to the force of this view of a national-cultural struggle.[17] Representations of Slavic-speaking minorities (even those who also spoke Italian) as alien invaders in what was intrinsically Italian territory relegated Slavic culture to the margins of a Bolshevik and Balkan East.[18] By extension, not only were Italians 'indigenous' in the boundary region, but working-class dissent and Socialist agitation could be defined as un-Italian.

Evocations of 'Slavs' as an alien group in Italian terrain also translated into specific anti-Slav policies, including the prohibition of the Slovene language in government institutions and the law courts – contrary to Nitti's promise. More significantly, Mosconi's policies and speeches encouraged and offered ideological protection to burgeoning extremist groups whose main targets were 'Slavs'. In July 1920 Mosconi and the new Giolitti-led liberal government voiced their disapproval of the torching by Fascists of the 'Hotel Balkan' in Trieste (the headquarters of Slovene cultural organizations also known as the Narodni Dom, or National Home).[19] But by this stage Mosconi had already lent explicit support to Fascist attacks on working-class and Slovene organizations. These attacks ranged from physical harassment to grenade and bomb offensives.[20] Two months after the burning of the 'Hotel Balkan', Mosconi turned to the local Fascist Action Squads led by Francesco Giunta for help in countering a general mass strike. After the Treaty of Rapallo legitimated Italy's claims to Trieste and Venezia Giulia in November 1920, Mosconi orchestrated attacks by Fascist squads against Socialists and Slavs, and discouraged arrests of Fascists responsible.[21] The redefinition of ideological antagonisms as 'national' antipathies was reinforced when, during the general election of 1921, Italian Liberal Nationalists in Trieste formed a 'national bloc' with Fascists against the combined forces of the radicalized Slovene, Croatian, and Italian Socialists in the newly created Italian Communist Party (a strategy also adopted at the national level by Giolitti's Liberal Nationalist government).[22] In Venezia Giulia the election resulted in the return of two (out of three) Fascist candidates and the one Liberal National candidate in that coalition, as well as an extremist Communist who later transformed himself into a Fascist. Some historians have attributed the Fascist Party's success to the support of the Triestine bourgeois and commercial class. In the face of the diminishment of Trieste's shipping role and the contraction of markets which had resulted from Trieste's incorporation into the Italian national economy, these commercially orientated groups looked to the Fascist invocation of Italy's imperial destiny east of its new border, in the so-called 'Slav' hinterland, as a means by which lost markets might be recaptured. The Fascist victory can also be accounted for by its members' use of aggression and intimidation among the general population, and the tolerance shown towards Fascists by the provincial authorities, which contributed to the validation of their policies and practices.[23] What is important in terms of Italian national identity is the concomitant, and congealing, designation of antithetical Italian and Slav identities and spaces.

Concern expressed in Trieste and Venezia Giulia by political élites about the political vulnerability of Italy's boundary regions was matched by discussions initiated outside the new provinces by Italian intellectuals about the cultural threat posed to the vitality and reality of Italian national identity by minorities. A series of articles on 'Foreign languages and foreigners in Italy' published in 1922 in the Milan-based reformist review *La Vita Internazionale*, is illustrative of the place of difference, and the concept of assimilation specifically, in formulations of Italian national identity among even the most anti-nationalist of Italian nationalists.[24] *La Vita Internazionale* was a weekly that published articles by Italian Mazzinians, socialists, democrats and feminists concerned with social justice, including support for female suffrage. The author of the series on 'Foreign languages and foreigners in Italy', Antonio Marcello Annoni, speculated on what the results of a national census undertaken in the new Italy might reveal about the assimilation of the 'foreigners' who had long resided in the old Italy: speakers of French, Slovene, Serbian, Albanian, Greek, Catalan, German-Bavarian, and the 'German-Vallese' dialect. Annoni was optimistic about the capacity of these old *'allofone* [of another language] populations in Italy' to live in harmony. He attributed this capacity to their small numbers, their dispersal and Italy's 'great assimilatory *civiltà*'. According to Annoni, the ancient Romans were proof that superior civilizations could absorb inferior ones, and Italy's Roman inheritance made it an equally powerful assimilator.[25] He assumed that Greeks, with their similarly ancient culture and inherent good business sense, and the impressively masculine Albanians, accustomed themselves almost naturally to Italian society. However, despite his general confidence in Italian national identity, Annoni was concerned that, after 1920, the conditions under which *allofoni* had previously assimilated had radically altered: the addition of new provinces had increased the number of Slavic-speakers in Italy tenfold to 300,000 Slovenes, and nearly 200,000 Serbs. Italy's acquisition of Alto Adige had increased the number of German-speakers from less than 10,000 to 300,000. Annoni feared that unlike the existing *allofoni,* the new foreigners (particularly the Germans, whom he regarded as the cultural equals of Italians) might remain close to their co-nationals across their respective borders. The one exception, in Annoni's mind, was 'the new Slav brothers', whose inferior *civiltà* rendered them especially assimilable. Annoni played down incidents of 'resistance' to assimilation among the Slovene cultural circles of Trieste, and emphasized that the Slovenes of the Natisone in the Friuli region adjacent to Venezia Giulia, and annexed by Italy in 1866, had over the course of half a century given up their language for Italian and become invisible. 'The few *allofoni*', Annoni optimistically concluded, 'are easily Italianized.'[26] Ercole Bassi, a regular contributor to *La Vita Internazionale*, stressed that in Italy *allogene* minorities were not a problem because Italy's 'millennium of *civiltà*' had always demonstrated the maximum respect for small groups of *allogeni*.[27] That same *civiltà* ensured that there was no Zionist problem in Italy, just as there was no anti-Semitism or racial hatred.[28] Both Bassi and Annoni argued that one had only to compare Italy with the 'Balkan inferno', where the lack of a dominant nation with the capacity to assimilate minor cultures had led to an endemic minority problem. Their arguments confirmed that the ideal nation was culturally homogeneous by virtue of its ability to absorb and assimilate other cultures, and that the Balkans were the antithesis of this ideal. These representations of the place of difference in the Italian nation, of Slavs as both assimilable and a threat, reflected and reproduced the anxieties and attitudes that were easily exploited by Fascists in Trieste. As I will show in the following section, from 1922 until 1943 Fascist strategies for 'forcibly' rendering invisible political as well as cultural minorities in Italy rehearsed predominant views of the assimilatory power of Italian *civiltà* as definitive of Italian national identity.

The Fascist Italian nation, 1922–1938

In 1922, the Fascist government began the legislative integration of Venezia Giulia into Italy and into a normative vision of Italian national life. Prefects were appointed in the new provinces directly to implement Fascist legislation emanating from Rome. In 1923, toponomy laws reinvented the identities of these provinces, from their 'street names and monuments to contemporary persons'.[29] The process of renaming was a common feature of nation-building in Italy and elsewhere in Europe in the late nineteenth and early twentieth centuries. In this case, the erasure of public traces of an alternative history was compounded by laws which outlawed the public expression of alternative linguistic identities. By 1924, throughout Italy, all 'foreign-language' newspapers were required to publish Italian translations, and schools were prohibited from teaching in 'foreign languages'. The new north and north-eastern boundary regions were depicted as places where a natural Italian identity was artificially muted, and where *italianità* had to be consolidated, against the presence of, respectively, German and Slav minorities. In the first years of Fascism the full brunt of these laws was most ardently felt by the German-speaking population of the new northern province of Alto Adige bordering Austria – possibly because of their status as equal cultural rivals – but their force soon extended to Venezia Giulia.[30] In 1925 when Mussolini announced his intention to 'Fascistize the nation' – to assimilate Italian and Fascist identity – he stated in a 'Letter of the president of the Council of Ministers' that 'the problem of the new provinces was to be resolved in terms of an Italian duty to content herself with having on her very borders subjects who should be obedient, but remain outside the nation'.[31] Between 1924 and 1927 the meaning of the phrase 'outside the nation' was translated in the north-eastern provinces into policies which transformed 500 Slovene and Croatian primary schools into Italian-language schools, deported one thousand 'Slavic' teachers (personified as 'the resistance of a foreign race') to other parts of Italy, and closed around 500 Slav societies and a slightly smaller number of libraries.[32] In addition, by 1926 Slav surnames had to be changed into what were described as more 'aesthetically pleasing' Italian versions.[33] All evidence of non-Italian names, even on old gravestones, was to be erased.

From 1926 the assimilation of Slovenes and other minorities into Fascist Italian life was aggressively enforced by both provincial and national governments. *Carabinieri* and other groups were directed to search houses for evidence of 'foreign-language' literature. 'Alien' cultural and athletic organizations were purged of their non-Italian content. The Italian Ministry for the Interior liquidated Slovene economic associations, including a network of agricultural co-operatives and banks. Land and property were confiscated from Slovene peasant farmers. Slovene residents were deported or relocated, and new Italian settlements were introduced.[34] By the late 1920s these policies supplemented the Fascist government's attempted intervention in other forms of nation-building, particularly the supervision of demography through the control of reproduction, and calls for the integration of the public and private identities of Italian subjects.[35] In the wake of Mussolini's 1927 Ascension Day strategies for the 'defence of the race',[36] Trieste hosted a meeting of the 'Fascist federal secretaries' from the six frontier provinces to co-ordinate an Italianization programme.[37] The meeting produced a memorandum on 'Fascism and the *allogeni*' which stated that *allogeni* did not inevitably pose a problem, but any resistance by *allogeni* to assimilation would be construed as an act of disloyalty against the regime. The connotations of assimilation in this case were both political and cultural. The Fascist federal secretaries described Italy as a nation that by nature treated minorities benevolently and justly, as long as those minorities were loyal. That loyalty was to be openly shown to Fascist Italy. In the sense that this emphasis on assimilation reiterated conventional representations of 'Slavs' as backward and culturally malleable, it could be interpreted as more benevolent than a biological definition of Slav 'otherness'. Considering the German and Slavic-sounding names of leading local Fascists such as Bruno

Coceancig (later Coceani) and Fulvio Suvich, it may have served the personal purposes of newly minted Italian types eager to shed any trace of a culturally hybrid past. But assimilationism also provided Fascists with a convenient rationale for aggressively repressing any culturally focused political opposition.

The idea that Slavs were assimilable was implicit in attempts by provincial and national authorities to transform local minorities into good Fascists as well as good Italians. In 1928 the *Corriere della Sera* emphasized that the Fascist Italian state required

> not trembling obedience, but the true and conscious consent of one who understands that he must be disciplined before he can share in the formation of the new Italian spirit
> ... Those who were but groups of [Slavs] until today are summoned by Italy to be her citizens, with equal rights and equal duties with all the other inhabitants of the peninsula.[38]

In the new provinces, the range of duties to the Italian nation were to some extent traditional (until 1942 men who spoke Slovene and who had once borne Slovene names were conscripted into the military). They were also connected to specifically Fascist political objectives. Fascist youth groups were organized to include the *allogeni*. Special live-in schools were established for Slav boys in order to indoctrinate them in the ways of Fascism and to remove them from the influence of Slav language and culture.[39] As a corollary to nationwide policies on demography, Slav women were targeted as important agents for the assimilation of children as Italians and Fascists.[40] Federico Pagnacco, the editor of the Trieste magazine *Italia* and an advocate of veterans' causes, believed that because Slavs were honest peasants led astray by Austria they were also 'worthy of becoming real Italian citizens, like other Italian rustics'. He even recommended that state creches be established in order to facilitate the earliest introduction of the children of 'mixed' families to Italian, and remove them from the possible influence of surreptitious private expressions of Slav language and culture.[41]

In one of the rare contemporary attempts made to document the Fascist treatment of minorities, Gaetano Salvemini recorded that between February 1927 and July 1932 a special court for crimes against the state, the Tribunale Speciale per la Difesa dello Stato sentenced 106 Slavs to 1,124 years in prison.[42] Salvemini noted that in proportional terms, 'Slav criminals' far outnumbered Italians in the Special Tribunal's sentencing and executions. This situation could be interpreted as evidence of either the existence of widespread resistance among Slovenes, or of the attention that Fascist authorities paid to dissent they identified as Slav. The historian Anna Maria Vinci claims that the effect of Fascist Italianization policies was to disperse the disaffected communities, particularly Slovenes, and to annihilate their memory and their identity.[43] Her own evidence suggests that between 1921 and 1931 there was no decline in the number of individuals in Venezia Giulia identified as Slovene, or judged to be *alloglotte* [of another tongue]. If anything, their number had risen slightly. The more the Fascist government introduced repressive measures to eradicate traces of political and cultural difference, the more resistance intensified, and the more Slovenes were identified as non-Italian and anti-Fascist.[44] Not all resistance was politically motivated, or took the form of terrorism, but measures directed against Slavs and political dissent were effectively creating an 'external' Slav threat.[45] In the 1920s and 1930s (political and/or cultural) anti-Fascists established bases across the border in Yugoslavia (the most notable were two underground terrorist movements known as TIGR and ORJUNA).[46] By the 1930s exiled Triestine Communists were planning the creation of an independent Slovenian workers' and peasants' republic in the boundary region straddling Yugoslavia, Austria and Italy. This republic was to become part of any of those states 'in which a Communist regime might be victorious'.[47] In 1931 a journalist from the *Corriere della Sera* told his readers that the Italian boundary region exuded the 'atmosphere of war'.[48]

The intensification of resistance coincided with renewed efforts by the Fascist government to incorporate the 'problem' of minorities into an Italian national history of political and cultural assimilation and conquest.[49] At the 1932 Rome exhibition of the Fascist Revolution the Slav threat was given national recognition. Arms and ammunitions said to have been found amongst the ruins of the 'Hotel Balkan' destroyed by Fascists in 1920, were displayed as evidence of Fascist vigilance against the Slav enemy.[50] The burning of the 'Hotel Balkan' was transformed into a foundation event in historical narratives celebrating Fascism's fight against Slavs along Italy's border. Publications such as *Il Fascismo nella Venezia Giulia. Dalle origini alla marcia su Roma* claimed that the 'Hotel Balkan' had been a 'foreign fortress in the heart of Trieste', a front for pro-Austrian and pro-Yugoslav activities, the centre of Slav propaganda, and 'a nest of spies and secret agents'.[51] In 1934 the magazine *Trieste* featured the burning of the 'Hotel Balkan' as one of a series of critical moments in the history of Italian irredentism.[52] Just as previous Liberal authorities had portrayed Socialist activities as un-Italian, Fascist authorities consistently characterized anti-Fascism, like the Slavs themselves, as an import, an 'artificial resistance', 'a Balkan manœuvre', 'a foreign activity', and an extension of the history of Habsburg conspiracies against Italy in the past.[53] Yugoslavia (like Austria before) was depicted as a state which fostered this Slav/Balkan enemy. In defending the work of the Tribunale Speciale in Venezia Giulia and its targeting of Slavs, Mussolini argued that 'the centres of criminal infection are created and nourished from the other side of the border'.[54] Bruno Coceani described three young Slovene men executed by the Tribunale in 1930 as Slavs from 'beyond the borders' who had attempted to incite the local population against Italy and to hinder the civilizing work of Italy and Fascism.[55]

Over the period that Fascist laws and policies of enforced assimilation were being implemented in the boundary region, Fascists elaborated theories of Italian national identity, of the diversity of peoples or races in the Italian state, and the unifying and homogenizing spirit of the Italian nation.[56] Historians such as David Horn and Victoria De Grazia have stressed that 'Italy was a nation in which "admixtures" were not feared but were instead imagined to invigorate the stock'.[57] Given official policies and practices in Italy's boundary regions, acknowledgements of Italy's heterogeneity imply the chauvinist tendencies of Italian nationalism, rather than political and cultural inclusiveness or tolerance. Under Fascism, nationalist emphases on a spiritual and racial, vitalist and eugenic conception of the assimilatory capacity of *italianità*, had distinctive political as well as cultural implications for 'different' Italian citizens.[58]

In 1922, Enrico Corradini, the principal theorist of Fascist nationalism, argued that the Italian nation was a racial as well as historical entity. Like France, it comprised a diverse number of regional races or *stirpi* and 'minorities' united by their *anima*. 'It is a common soul', Corradini explained, 'which lies behind so many beings living between the borders assigned in its name.'[59] Luca Dei Sabelli, the author of *Nazione e minoranze etniche*, a 1929 study of minorities within Italian borders sponsored by the legal and historical section of the National Fascist Institute of Culture, situated Italy in the context of a Europe where races had become mixed, and where the mettle of a *stirpe* was proved by that *stirpe*'s ability to expand and to assimilate other cultures. Dei Sabelli argued that Italy had no minority problem because such a problem existed only where assimilation was not effective.[60] Fascist intellectuals distinguished their spiritual version of race from biological racial theories. That they took their racial vocabulary from liberal anti-determinist conceptions of nations did not make their views of Italian nationalism any less useful for legitimating political and cultural uniformity or repression. Horn offers as an example of the Fascist idea of race an interview conducted with Mussolini in 1932 in which the Duce 'explicitly rejected the notion of a "pure" race and observed that "it is often precisely from happy mixtures that a nation derives strength and beauty"'.[61] The political and cultural connotations of this view of 'happy mixtures' were underlined in Mussolini's document 'Doctrine of Fascism' that same year. By evoking Italy's 'single will' and 'single conscience' (terminology fundamental to contemporary liberal conceptions of the nation throughout Europe) Mussolini blurred the borders between the respectability of the theme of *italianità*'s assimilatory capacity and the Fascist preference for political conformity.[62] By 1932, the national Fascist government's homogenizing vision of the nation, described by Ruth Ben-Ghiat as the state 'unmarred by conflicts between capital and labour, centre and periphery', had merged with local and provincial Fascist authorities' repression of different ways of being politically and culturally Italian.[63]

The coincidence of aggressive assimilation practices in the boundary region and the theoretical articulation of the eclectic spiritual bases of Italian national identity, also corresponded to unflagging representations of, on the one hand, minorities within Italy as anonymous *allogeni*, and, on the other hand, of Slavs as inhabitants of a territory *oltre il confine* (beyond the borders) stretching from Serbia in the south to Russia in the north. After denying the existence of a minority problem within Italy, Dei Sabelli concluded that 'it was impossible to conceive of any parity of rights' between Italians and Slavs, because 'the barbarian' was the enemy of 'the civilized world'.[64] Coincident with the intensifying resistance and deterioriating relations between Italy and Yugoslavia, the Trieste press militantly represented Slavs as a biological threat to the Italian body politic. Mussolini's description of anti-Fascists as a 'criminal infection' echoed the language of Triestine exponents of *Fascismo Bonificatore* (literally, the Fascism that had reclaimed the land). Publications such as the *Popolo di Trieste* and *Italia* enjoined the Italian government to 'cut deep into this festering sore and without mercy remove this ulcer',[65] to take steps to 'purify' the region against 'the Slav swamp', and to eliminate 'the residue of Austrian hybridity'.[66] The journalist Livio Ragusin-Righi urged eradication of 'Austrian cancers' to protect Italy from 'infection'.[67] He argued that only Fascism had been able to conduct the necessary 'surgical and hygienic operation' – *un risanamento* (a healing reclamation) – that fended off invasion of the national body.[68] Ragusin-Righi portrayed Fascism's specific contribution to the Italian nation as its ability more effectively to spread 'the breath of a superior *civiltà* among less developed populations than the preceding weak-kneed liberal government'.[69]

In this Fascist period, Slavs were represented as both an external menace and assimilable *allogeni* inside Italian borders, just as they had been during Mosconi's government. In 1930 the local Trieste newspaper *Il Piccolo* described *allogeno* as a denomination that distinguished between Italian citizens.[70] The Italian historians, political scientists, anthropologists and Fascist politicians who referred to minorities within Italy preferred to use these generic terms. In his critique of the Fascist treatment of minorities, Salvemini believed that this preference was meant to accentuate the differences between Italians who naturally belonged and the other (*allo*) 'kind' (*geni*), 'voice' (*foni*) or 'tongue' (*glotte*) minorities.[71] In 1929 Ragusin-Righi implied that these terms were indicative of the insignificance of linguistic minorities in Italy, leaving him to ponder whether even 'to believe or not to believe in the *alloglotte* population'.[72] His own conviction was that 'for Italy *un problema allogeno* does not exist in Venezia Giulia, just as it does not exist elsewhere'.[73] The *allogeni* were 'new Italian citizens who still need to be cultivated/cultured' and who 'with time ... could become truly Italian, even in sentiment'.[74] Slavs specifically were 'a minority which did not exist', the artificial product of Yugoslav nationalism and 'Balkan megalomania'.[75]

Fascist representations of the concomitant invisibility and superficiality of the *allogeni* were bolstered by the argument that Fascism would provide the conditions under which the *allogeni* could recover an original Italian identity. For example, Fascist apologists argued that the Italianization of surnames would restore lost Italian selves.[76] Fascism would help '*allogeni* recover their real being, liberating them from the encrustation of others' ideas', from 'every external influence' and 'every residue of a false past'.[77] A similar supposition was made in respect to the lost Italian identity of the territory. In 1925 Mussolini described the Fascist policy for managing 'the problem of the new provinces' as the restoration to its 'natural' Italian state of Italian territory whose identity had been destroyed under foreign governments.[78] This view validated Fascist planning policies in Venezia Giulia and Trieste, the showpiece of the new provinces. Fascist municipal and national administrators began planning the reinvention of Trieste's urban centre as the modern incarnation of an ancient Roman settlement. The focus of *sventramenti* (literally 'disembowelling') was the area containing Roman temple ruins adjacent to the city's central church of San Giusto, and the *città vecchia*. Much of the old town had to be destroyed in order to uncover the ruins of a Roman amphitheatre. The progress of the amphitheatre's excavation was accompanied by an intensive national and international promotion. The culmination of this promotional activity occurred when the *teatro Romano* was completed in time for the Bimillenario Augusteo (two-thousandth anniversary of Augustus), which featured Trieste and Venezia Giulia and lasted from September 1937 until September 1938.[79]

The excavation of Italy's ancient Roman past conflated the ambitions of late nineteenth-century and early twentieth-century nationalists and inter-war Fascists. Italy's Roman ancestry had been an important aspect of nineteenth-century Mazzinian nationalism, which represented a unified Italy as the 'Third Rome'.[80] Excavations, like the toponomy laws enacted in the 1920s and 1930s, were common features of the late nineteenth-century process of Italian unification and the creation of an Italian identity.[81] Gino Bandelli has shown that plans for digging up Trieste's Roman past had been elaborated in the late 1800s. Under Fascism, however, the recovery of the material traces of Trieste's Italian past also involved the symbolic removal of the layers of a 'foreign' Habsburg history and the German and Slav features of the landscape as well as of its population.[82] The Triestine historian Attilio Tamaro depicted each archaeological discovery as a 'reply to the predatory aspirations of Slavs or a lesson to unconscious Austrian Italophobia'.[83]

The archaeological 'revelation' of the boundary region's Roman imperial past was supplemented by the imposition of new layers of a material culture intended to highlight Trieste's simultaneously Fascist and Italian identity.[84] The city of Trieste was chosen as a national seat of the Littoriali dell'Arte e della Cultura. When Mussolini visited in September 1938, he viewed the *teatro Romano* and laid the foundations for the construction of the Casa del Fascio or Fascist Party headquarters opposite the *teatro*, at the foot of the *zona capitolina*.[85] He also inaugurated the new university which was to be built in monolithic *stile littorio* on an elevated eastern site. The university's mission was to shine 'the light of Italian culture and *civiltà*' 'towards the villages of Trieste's hinterland and to the regions of the East'.[86] In December 1938 Bruno Coceani declared before the Italian parliament that the university would function as 'the spiritual defence of the border and of the cultural expansion of *nostra stirpe*'.[87]

The phrase *nostra stirpe* could be understood as a reference to the spiritual dimensions of Italian national identity, but the prevailing premises of the relative value of different nations and cultures (particularly the lesser status of a group known as Slavs), and the assimilatory and civilizing role of *italianità,* rendered *stirpe* as potentially deterministic as biologically based forms of racial identification. Two months before Mussolini's arrival in Trieste, a group of Italian scientists had published a manifesto attesting to the existence of biological races and to the Aryan origins of the Italian race.[88] By then, spiritual definitions of race and nation had provided adequate validations for state-authorized repression of political and cultural differences.

Race, nation and war, 1938–1943

In the period of Italian nationalism inaugurated by the July Manifesto and by Mussolini's evocation of a nationwide 'Jewish problem' on his visit to Trieste in September 1938, the national status of the boundary region was reaffirmed.[89] During this period, groups of young Fascists had organized attacks on Trieste's synagogue and provoked a climate of 'racial' tension in the region. By

November, a month after the signing of a military agreement between Italy and Germany (the 'Rome–Berlin Axis') the Fascist government had introduced laws aimed at resolving the 'Jewish problem'.[90] These laws prohibited all Jews, regardless of their political loyalty to Fascism, from participating in schools, commerce, professions or politics. Their application in the boundary region transformed Trieste from the most prominent Italian centre of Jewish culture into an 'epicentre' of Fascist anti-Semitism.[91]

During the last five years of the Fascist government (and for most of the Second World War), Jews throughout Italy were the focus of an official campaign to educate the Italian population in a biological understanding of Italian national identity which significantly mirrored the Nazi view of the world. Contributors to new Fascist journals such as *Razza e Civiltà* and *La Difesa della Razza* detailed the biological threat of Jews – and other 'non-Europeans' such as Africans – to the purity of the Italian race.[92] Even though Nazi racial ideology provided a biological grounding for anti-Slavism, in the new Italian racial propaganda there was no biological explication of the alterity of Slavs.[93] Instead Slavs remained an assimilable if threatening Other. There were other continuities between the periods of inter-war assimilationism and wartime racism. Vinci argues that the intolerance cultivated in Trieste against a Slav enemy for nearly two decades had prepared the local population for the politically motivated anti-Semitic campaigns that took place during the Second World War.[94] Four years before the introduction of the racial laws, Salvemini had tried to alert the world to Fascism's treatment of minorities, including Slovenes, Serbs, Greeks, Albanians, Germans and Masons, and had given special emphasis to examples of Fascists singling out Jews as inherent enemies of the state.[95] In 1937, Achille Starace, the national secretary of the Fascist Party, proposed that one enemy of the Fascist revolution – the 'red Slavs' – had been eliminated, but another, 'masonic liberal Jews', remained.[96] Even after the introduction of the racial laws, Fascists continued to describe the Italian 'race' in spiritual terms as *una razza dell'anima e dello spirito* (a race of the soul and of the spirit). Giacomo Acerbo, a key figure in the Fascist Party and national government, wrote in 1940 that 'the great people of Italy' were composed of 'many *stirpi*'. The nation was 'an ethnic mixture', but the 'ethnic complex of the Italian people' had survived generations, just as its 'sentiment for a unified destiny' had not been exhausted.[97] That destiny was guided by the assimilatory spiritual forces of *italianità* and millennial, immortal Roman *civiltà*.[98] The bibliography of Acerbo's study *The Principles of the Fascist Doctrine of Race*, devoted to an impressive array of English-, French-, and Italian-language discussions on nations, integrated his interpretation of Italian national identity into a mainstream western European intellectual tradition.

Further evidence of these continuities was the persistent engagement of municipal, provincial, and national Fascist governments with a Slav–Bolshevik threat from *oltre il confine*. As anti-Fascist and Communist resistance grew more organized and efficient in the region, and as the Fascist government made plans for 'imperial expansion' into territory across Italy's north-eastern border, Slavs (from beyond the borders) were increasingly referred to as the beneficiaries of an Italian civilizing mission.[99] In fulfilment of a promise made to Fascist supporters almost two decades earlier, Trieste was to be transformed into the bulwark of a new Italian Empire. Songs celebrated it as 'the bridgehead of Italy towards the East', the 'centre of the spiritual radiation of *romanità* in the nearby lands beyond its borders'.[100] *Geopolitica* (1939–42), a review based at the Geography Institute of the University of Trieste and dedicated to expressing the 'geographic doctrine of the Empire', described Trieste as the emblem of 'national unity, and . . . of the new shores of expansion and of conquest towards the Balkan Orient'.[101] Published under the auspices of Giuseppe Bottai, editor of *Critica Fascista* and a member of Mussolini's Grand Council, *Geopolitica* involved the participation of academics from the Milan Catholic University, the Political Science Faculty of the University of Pavia, and large numbers of Triestine intellectuals, including the geographer Carlo Schiffrer who, ironically, had cultivated a reputation for writing objective and even anti-Fascist history.[102] Vinci argues that the review was one more scientific instrument for promoting the respectability of Italy's national mandate of cultural and territorial expansionism in the Balkans, and for creating an Italian *spazio vitale* in the Mediterranean and Balkans.[103]

Italian military forces were not sent across the Italo-Yugoslav border to establish Italy's imperial destiny in the Mediterranean and Balkans until 1941, after the Yugoslav state had collapsed under the force of a German offensive.[104] After 1941, Italian forces occupied parts of Yugoslavia and effectively dissolved the relevance of the border. Italian military administrations were established in the

Slovene capital Ljubljana and Dalmatia. Despite the urging of the Triestine Aldo Vidussoni (a secretary of the national Fascist party) that all Slavs in the occupied territory be exterminated, the Fascist authorities awarded their new subjects rights in principle that Slovenes and Croatians living within the inter-war borders did not have. The Italian forces hoped that these rights would gain them popular support and prevent possible challenges to their administration from their German allies who had imperial ambitions of their own in the region.[105] However, James Walston has argued that, in practice, Slavs in occupied Yugoslavia were treated with no more respect than inside Italy's legal borders, where civilian authorities incited pogroms against Jews and Slovenes and any of their remaining businesses.[106]

After 1941 too, Communists from Venezia Giulia who had gone into exile returned to organize mass resistance. As Italian-, Slovene-, and Croatian-based Communist organizations established an anti-Fascist network inside the territory occupied by Italian forces and on both sides of the old Italo-Yugoslav border, the Fascist authorities felt even more under siege from what they perceived or represented as a Slav threat.[107] But now, those authorities labelled anti-Fascist and Communist 'Jewish' as well as Slav and Bolshevik resistance. Between 1941 and the spring of 1943, Fascist death squads operating in Venezia Giulia exacted summary justice against suspected subversives, regardless of whether they were identified as Jewish, Slovene or Italian.[108] From 1942, a Special Italian Inspectorate of Public Security terrorized the city and its peripheries. It was headed by a former specialist in the Italian state's campaign against Sicilian *banditi*. The Italian military erected concentration camps *per scopi repressivi* (for the purposes of repression) in Venezia Giulia, in which they interned 'able-bodied people from ethnic minorities' living inside and outside Italy's pre-1941 borders.[109] In early 1943 an Italian army order called for the internment of individuals from Venezia Giulia identified as *allogeni* 'between the ages of forty-two and fifty-five and non-able-bodied people from nineteen upwards and families of rebel supporters'. The number of so-called *allogeni* internees (including mothers and children) was nearly 70,000 out of a regional Slav population that Italian censuses numbered at 360,000.[110] The most notorious of these camps was at Gonars near Trieste, and on the Adriatic island of Rab. The Rab camp held Slovene and Croatian civilians, many of them originally from Dalmatia.[111] The annual mortality rate in the camps was at least 18 per cent.[112] According to Walston, 'Tens of thousands of internees died of disease and malnutrition.'

With the collapse of the Fascist government in 1943 the history of the Italian military civilian concentration camps and the chauvinism that led to their creation were soon forgotten. As Walston argues, the wartime events 'in the Balkans' 'have not become part of history or general knowledge in Italy'.[113] The attribution of the 1938 Fascist racial laws to Nazi influence, has encouraged historical views of Italians as a characteristically *brava gente*, and racism as an anomalous chapter in Italian history.[114] At the same time, widespread views that Slavs were foreigners on Italian soil, and that assimilation was evidence of the superiority of Italian *civiltà*, have also had an important role in determining what was remembered about the responsibility of the Italian military and political authorities for atrocities, and the meaning attributed to their actions. Historians of Italy and Italian historians, have tended either to describe events in the boundary region during the inter-war period as peripheral to the mainstream of Italian politics and forms of nationalism, or to interpret the war as a struggle between two antagonistic nations rather than between a state and its citizens. This view was given the stamp of authority in 1944 by the liberal historian Benedetto Croce. In a well-publicized speech made at the Roman Eliseo, Croce exalted the creation of a national front against Italy's national enemies: Germans and Slavs.[115] After the Second World War the theme of struggle between Italians and Slavs predominated in the official memorialization of Trieste's Italian history. Since the end of the Cold War, it has been invoked by 'post-Fascists' as a means of validating Fascism itself.[116]

The historian Mario Isnenghi contends that 'the basic political stereotypes that Fascism intended to propagate among the masses were able to take their gestures from the elementary culture and hagiographical Risorgimento historiography of liberal monarchical origin – *patria*, Italia, etc. – activated by early nineteenth-century nationalism'.[117] I have tried to show that included in the storehouse of Fascist stereotypes were conventional images of Italian national identity defined against specific national Others. Fascists were able to exploit stereotypes of the 'Slav' and of antipathy between Italians and Slavs in order to justify political uniformity within Fascist Italy's borders, and to assert Fascist as well as Italian sovereignty in the boundary region, precisely because of the authority that non-Fascist intellectuals, and preceding and subsequent liberal governments, lent those stereotypes and the ideal of naturally homogeneous nationhood. Recent comparative studies of the inter-war period have highlighted the correspondence between nationalist, racist and eugenicist discourses in western and eastern, liberal and totalitarian European states. In a perceptive comparative analysis of nineteenth- and early twentieth-century European population policies, Maria Sophia Quine has claimed that 'many of the features which scholars commonly define as "fascist" were not the exclusive preserve of the Italian and German dictatorships'.[118] Not only did liberal European states share with Fascist Italy eugenicist concerns and demographic policies, but assimilationism was a common state policy measure in liberal states with significant immigration. A comparison between liberal and Fascist conceptions of national identity in Italy, their respective representations of *italianità*, suggests that in the first half of the twentieth century, the difference between their nationalisms was a question of degree and application. Despite the ideological chasm that separated liberals and Fascists, their common national vocabularies and investment in western European cultural hierarchies and the cultural basis of national sovereignty, in both cases shaped the ways in which national communities, borders, and individual identities could be imagined. These forms of national imagining left an indelible impact on the lives of local citizens – rendering those who spoke Slovene or Croatian, as well as Italian, 'Slavs', constituting them as lesser or even illegitimate citizens, and exposing them to the machinations of individuals and state authorities willing to exploit the politics of exclusion and chauvinism for their own purposes. They also influenced the ways in which the history of the region and its diverse populations were written.

In 1932 the Triestine writer Silvio Benco confidently declared that in Trieste the 'anxious preoccupation' with identity on Italy's north-eastern border was over: 'Trieste in the past has been a crucible of peoples; today it is a city which can refer to itself as having one nationality alone.'[119] For Benco, homogeneity was one of the great achievements of a decade of Fascist government in Italy. Propaganda celebrating the effort Italian Fascism put into assimilationism in comparison with the 'failures' of the short-lived liberal Italian national government in the region was hardly inappropriate, but even as Benco wrote, anxiety about Italian national identity remained endemic to the articulation of Italian nationalism. The 1930s saw the intensification of efforts to transform Trieste physically as well as culturally. Fascist and Liberal authorities alike had attempted, and failed, to achieve incontestable political and national sovereignty by iterating the differences between an Italian Self and Slav Other, by employing the anonymous categories of alien and *allogeno,* or by emphasizing the assimilatory capacity of *italianità.* Regardless of the efforts of the inter-war governments, after the armistice in September 1943, when German forces occupied the boundary region, Trieste was once again, as in the period before the First World War, open to identification as 'a hybrid zone, fractured, without an identity'.[120] The borders between Italy and Yugoslavia, between Italy and the Balkans, and between a preferred Italian social order and the various forms of political opposition which placed that order at threat, evaded closure because of the ambiguities of identity immanent not only in the boundary region, but at the core of the nation itself.

Notes
1 The most important exceptions are D. Rusinow, *Italy's Austrian Heritage, 1919–1946* (Oxford, Clarendon Press, 1969), and E. Apih, *Italia, fascismo e anti-fascismo nella Venezia Giulia 1918/1943* (Rome, Laterza, 1966).
2 This description of 'internal borders' is borrowed from E. Balibar, 'Fichte and the internal border: on Addresses to the German Nation' in E. Balibar, *Masses, Classes, Ideas: Studies on Politics and Philosophy before and after Marx,* tr. J. Swenson (New York, Routledge, 1994), 63.
3 D. Campbell, *Writing Security: United States Foreign Policy and the Politics of Identity* (Manchester, Manchester University Press, 1992), 8.
4 Rusinow, *Italy's Austrian Heritage,* 192.
5 C. A. Macartney, *National States and National Minorities* (Oxford, Oxford University Press, 1934), Introduction.
6   Some authors of nationalism have claimed that the self-identity of nations is 'secured partly through the construction of internal Others'; A. M. Alonso, 'The politics of space, time and substance: state formation, nationalism, and ethnicity', *Annual Review of Anthropology,* 23 (1994), 379–405 (390); see also E. Balibar, 'Paradoxes of universality', in D. T. Goldberg, ed., *Anatomy of Racism* (Minneapolis, University of Minnesota Press, 1990), 283–94.
7 Rusinow, *Italy's Austrian Heritage,* 163.

8 See P. Stranj, *The Submerged Community: An A to Z of the Slovenes in Italy* (Trieste, Stampa Triestina, 1992), 75. Apih argues that Di Roreto was sympathetic to Slavs, and was advised by the government to act with moderation and avoid incidents which could harm the Italian cause at the peace conference; Apih, *Italia, fascismo e anti-fascismo,* 45.

9 Rusinow, *Italy's Austrian Heritage,* 97

10 Ibid., 115. Under their rule conditions varied: in Venezia Giulia's southernmost province, Istria, 'attacks on Croat institutions and individual Croats were legion and often conducted with the open co-operation of the authorities.' In the province of Gorizia north of Trieste, Slovene organizations were left relatively unscathed. In Trieste itself, Rusinow explains, the treatment of 'Slavs' was not as bad as in Istria, nor as good as in Gorizia.

11 Rusinow, *Italy's Austrian Heritage,* 84, 111.

12 For an example of Nitti's sensitivity to the problem of assimilation, see Rusinow, *Italy's Austrian Heritage,* 93.

13 Mosconi, cited in ibid., 116.

14 A. Mosconi, *I primi anni di governo italiano nella Venezia Giulia Trieste 1919–1922* (Bologna, Cappelli, 1924), 21, 24.

15 Ibid., 89. Some socialists supported the creation of an Italo-Slav Soviet Republic in Venezia Giulia. The 'Independent Socialist Party of Slovenes and Croats of the Julian Region and Istria' supported a separate Julian Republic, and integrating with the Italian Socialist party.

16 Ibid., 22. Rusinow states that although Mosconi's accounts of his administration were written retrospectively, his views coincide with the tenor of his administration.

17 Ibid., 7.

18 A. Vinci, 'Venezia Giulia e fascismo. Alcune ipotesi storiografiche', *Qualestoria,* 16 (1988), 50.

19 For accounts of the 'Hotel Balkan' episode see Rusinow, *Italy's Austrian Heritage,* 101–3, and M. Pacor, *Italiani in Balcania dal Risorgimento alia Resistenza* (Rome, Feltrinelli, 1968), 64.

20 Apih, *Italia, fascismo e anti-fascismo,* 114. The transformation of Slavs into 'foreigners' and aliens was perpetuated by the national press which defended the Fascists' actions and claimed (with no substantiation) that the 'Balkan' was a repository of Slav arms for use in acts of terrorism against the Italian state; Apih, *Italia, fascismo e anti-fascismo,* 122.

21 Ibid., 127; Rusinow, *Italy's Austrian Heritage,* 95, 96.

22 Rusinow, *Italy's Austrian Heritage,* 108–9.

23 Apih, *Italia, fascismo e anti-fascismo,* chapter 3; A. Vinci, 'Il fascismo nella Venezia Giulia', *Il Territorio,* 6 (1996), 13; Rusinow, *Italy's Austrian Heritage,* 107, 114, 115.

24 In his study of Trieste's history, Elio Apih also emphasizes the assimi-

latory power of Italian culture over *allogeni* (and *alloglotti*) as proof of the robustness of *italianità*. He refers to Slavs as 'strati subalterni allogeni'; E. Apih, *Trieste. Storia della città Italiana* (Rome, Laterza, 1988), 15.

25 A. M. Annoni, 'Le lingue straniere e gli stranieri in Italia', *La Vita Internazionale*, 25 (1922), 310.

26 Ibid., 313.

27 E. Bassi, 'Il problema delle minoranze allogeni', *La Vita Internazionale*, 25 (1922), 165.

28 G. I. Abate di Lungarini, 'Il proletariato ebraico e il problema del mediterraneo', *La Vita Internazionale*, 22 (1919), 217.

29 Decreto: Legge 10, maggio 1923, Numero 1158, Legge 23, giugno 1927, 'Toponomastica stradale e monumenti a personnaggi contemporanei', in O. Ravasini, *Compendio di notizie, toponomastica stradale sulla nomenclatura di località e strade di Trieste* (Trieste, La Editoriale Libreria, 1929).

30 For an account of the implementation and impact of these laws in the Alto Adige see Rusinow, *Italy's Austrian Heritage*, passim; and A. Vinci, 'Il fascismo nella Venezia Giulia', 14.

31 'Letter of the president of the Council of Ministers', 22 June 1925, cited in Macgregor Knox, *Mussolini Unleashed, 1939–1941: Politics and Strategy in Fascist Italy's Last War* (Cambridge, Cambridge University Press, 1982), 357; and Rusinow, *Italy's Austrian Heritage*, 164.

32 *Corriere della Sera*, 7 April 1931, cited in G. Salvemini, *Racial Minorities under Fascism in Italy* (Chicago, The Women's International League for Peace and Freedom, Conference on Minorities, 1934), 14. See also Stranj, *The Submerged Community*, 78.

33 A. Lodolino, *Leggi, ordinamenti e codici del regime fascista. Esposizione e commento ad uso delle scuole e delle persone colte*, Le vie del Duce, Collana di Studi Fascista (Lanciano, Giuseppe Carabba, 1930). These laws were first introduced in the Alto Adige region, and later in Venezia Giulia and Istria.

34 See Lavo Cermelj's *Life and Death Struggle of a National Minority* (Ljubljana, s.n. 1945, second edition) for a survey of Fascist policies in the area and their claimed effects on the local Slovene and Croat population. Cermelj accuses Fascists of genocide.

35 V. De Grazia, *How Fascism Ruled Women: Italy, 1922–1945* (Berkeley, University of California Press, 1992), 275; D. G. Horn, *Social Bodies: Science, Reproduction, and Italian Modernity* (Princeton, Princeton University Press, 1994).

36 B. Mussolini, 'Discorso dell'Ascensione', 26 May 1927, in E. Susmel and D. Susmel, eds., *Mussolini: Opera Omnia* (Milan, La Fenice, 1951–80), XXII, 360. See also L. Salvatorelli and G. Mira, *Storia*

d'Italia nel periodo fascista (Milan, Mondadori, 1972), II, 421–2.

37   Rusinow, *Italy's Austrian Heritage*, 200.

38   *Corriere della Sera*, 29 September 1928, cited in Salvemini, *Racial Minorities*, 16. The reference to Slavs as 'Slaves' was a common conscious *double entendre*.

39   Salvemini remarks that one case in Tolmino was an absolute failure. The boys fled to Yugoslavia; Salvemini, *Racial Minorities*, 21.

40   Apih, *Italia, fascismo e anti-fascismo*, 350.

41   F. Pagnacco 'Minoranze nazionali e lotte di popoli', *Italia*, 7 (1929), 284.

42   'Report of May 7 1931 on the Parliamentary Bill for the Prorogation [*sic*] of the Special Tribunal', cited in Salvemini, *Racial Minorities*, 18.

43   Vinci, 'Il fascismo nella Venezia Giulia', 14.

44   See A. Volk, 'Una realtà multiforme. Omogeneità e disomogeneità nella memoria degli sloveni di Trieste', in M. Verginella, A. Volk and K. Colja, eds., *Storia e memoria degli sloveni del Litorale. Fascismo, guerra e resistenza* (Trieste, Quaderni 7, Istituto Regionale per la Storia del Movimento di Liberazione nel Friuli–Venezia Giulia, 1997), 63. Salvatorelli argues that local Slovene and Italian workers protested against the Tribunal's actions; Salvatorelli and Mira, *Storia d'Italia nel periodo fascista*, 104.

45   For a discussion using oral history of the impact of communism in the inter-war period see M. Verginella, 'I vincitori sconfitti. Testimonianze slovene sul movimento di liberazione a Trieste', in Verginella et al., *Storia e memoria degli sloveni del Litorale*, 12–17.

46   See Salvatorelli and Mira, *Storia d'Italia nel periodo fascista*, 102; Rusinow argues that resistance was nourished from the other side of the border, but also that the 1930 show trials were held for foreign-policy reasons, *Italy's Austrian Heritage*, 207.

47   B. Novak, *Trieste 1941–1954: The Ethnic, Political and Ideological Struggle* (Chicago, University of Chicago Press, 1970), 57.

48   *Corriere della Sera*, 4 April 1931, cited in Salvemini, *Racial Minorities*, 20.

49   Elio Apih describes the Fascist treatment of minorities as exemplary of traditional nationalist ideologies, and the widespread acceptance in Europe of the idea of assimilation; Apih, *Italia, fascismo e anti-fascismo*, 272–3.

50   Apih, *Italia, fascismo e anti-fascismo*, 124.

51   *Il fascismo nella Venezia Giulia. Dalle origini alla marcia su Roma* (Trieste, Edizioni CELVI, 1932), 60.

52   The other two events were 1882, when the Triestine irredentist Gugliemo Oberdan set himself aflame in order to highlight his hatred of Austria;

and 1918, when the Italian navy arrived in Trieste; P. Veronese Sartori and G. Villa Santa, 'La storia, la vita, il domani', *Trieste* (1934).

[53] Apih, *Trieste. Storia della città italiana*, 134.

[54] 'Report of May 7 1931 on the Parliamentary Bill for the Prorogation of the Special Tribunal', cited in Salvemini, *Racial Minorities*, 20.

[55] B. Coceani, *Il Fascismo nel Mondo* (Rocca San Casciano, 1933), 8. See also Apih, *Italia, fascismo e anti-fascismo*, 274.

[56] See for example, G. Gentile, *Che cosa è il fascismo: Discorsi e polemiche* (Florence, Vallecchi, 1925).

[57] Horn, *Social Bodies*, 59; De Grazia, *How Fascism Ruled Women*, 53.

[58] O. Fraddorio, *Il Regime per la razza* (Tumminelle Editore, 1939), 31. David Horn has explained that in the inter-war period new forms of state governance contributed to the views of race and nation; *Social Bodies*, 8.

[59] E. Corradini, *L'unità e la potenza delle nazioni* (1922) (Florence, Vallechi, 1926), 89, 90. Corradini was the founder of the Italian Nationalist Association in 1910.

[60] L. Dei Sabelli, *Nazione e minoranze etniche* (Bologna, Zanichelli, 1929), I, 28.

[61] Horn, *Social Bodies*, 59.

[62] R. De Felice, *Mussolini il duce*, II. *Lo stato totalitario 1936–1940* (Turin, Einaudi, 1981), 297.

[63] R. Ben-Ghiat, 'Language and the construction of national identity in Fascist Italy', *The European Legacy*, 2, 3 (May 1997), 438. Ben-Ghiat argues that Fascism was concerned with independent manifestations of regional cultures as well as *allogene* cultures.

[64] Dei Sabelli, *Nazione e minoranze etniche*, 223. Serbia and Montenegro earned some respect as 'ancient' and 'virile' states; see A. Cronia, *La conoscenza del mondo slavo in Italia* (n.p., 1958), 625.

[65] Cited in Rusinow, *Italy's Austrian Heritage*, 200.

[66] L. Ragusin-Righi, 'Politica di confine', *Italia*, 3 (1929), 98.

[67] Ragusin-Righi's articles in *Italia* were reprinted from a book published that same year. His involvement in the local newspaper *Il piccolo* might explain the articles that appeared in that newspaper in 1925 and 1926 that mentioned similar themes: the non-existence of a nationality problem, and the importance of cleansing 'ripulire, risanamento'; see Apih, *Italia, fascismo e anti-fascismo*, 223, 274.

[68] Ragusin-Righi, 'Politica di confine', 294.

[69] Ibid., 340.

[70] *Il Piccolo*, 18 November 1930, cited in Apih, *Italia, fascismo e anti-fascismo*, 283.

[71] G. Salvemini, 'Il fascismo e le minoranze', in N. Valeri and A. Merola, eds., *Opere, IV: Scritti sul fascismo* (Rome, Feltrinelli, 1966), II, 481.

72 Ragusin-Righi, 'Politica di confine', 499.

73 Ibid., 499.

74 Ibid., 294.

75 Ibid., 244, 394.

76 A. Pizzagalli, *Per l'italianità dei cognomi nella provincia di Trieste* (Florence, Treves-Zanichelli, 1929), 100.

77 Ragusin Righi, 'Politica di confine', 499.

78 Rusinow, *Italy's Austrian Heritage*, 164. For a comparative discussion of urban planning under Fascism see L. D. Nucci, *Fascismo e spazio urbano* (Bologna, Il Mulino, 1992).

79 G. Bandelli, 'Per una storia del mito di Roma al confine orientale. Archeologia e urbanistica nella Trieste del ventennio', in M. Verzar-Bass, ed., *Il teatro Romano di Trieste. Monumento, storia, funzione* (Rome, Istituto Svizzero di Roma, 1991), 260.

80 The depiction of Trieste's Roman past has become standard in histories of the city and region; see, for example, Apih, *Trieste*, and E. Godoli, *La città nella storia d'Italia. Trieste* (Rome, Laterza, 1984). Godoli begins his history of Trieste as Tergeste Romana and ends with a critical commentary on the urban policies of the Fascist period.

81 For a discussion of the importance of the built landscape to the ideals of the Risorgimento in the late nineteenth century, see B. Tobia, *Una patria per gli Italiani. Spazi, monumenti nella Italia unita, 1870–1900* (Rome, Laterza, 1991).

82 Bandelli, 'Per una storia del mito di Roma al confine orientale', 258, 260.

83 *Anon.*, 1933, 14, cited in ibid., 253.

84 Ibid., 261.

85 On the construction of the university see also A. Vinci, 'Bellicismo e culture diffuse', in A. Vinci, ed., *Trieste in guerra. Gli anni 1938–1943* (Trieste, I Quaderni di Qualestoria, 1992), 86.

86 Inauguration speech (1927) by Morpurgo, cited in M. E. Viora, 'L'università degli studi di Trieste', *Umana. Le istituzioni di cultura della Trieste moderna*, VII, 1–8 (1958), 13–27 (20).

87 B. Coceani, *Trieste e la sua università. Discorso pronunciato alla Camera dei Deputati. Nella 2 tornata del 2 dicembre 1938–XVII* (Rome, Tipografia della Camera dei Deputati, 1938), 10.

88 Salvatorelli and Mira, *Storia d'Italia nel periodo fascista, II*, 411.

89 S. Bon Gherardi, *La persecuzione antiebraica a Trieste (1938–1945)* (Udine, Del Bianco, 1972), 49.

90 E. Ginzburg Migliorino, 'L'applicazione delle leggi antiebraiche a Trieste. Aspetti e problemi', *Qualestoria*, 1 (1989).

91 E. Collotti, 'Prefazione', in S. Bon Gherardi, *La persecuzione antiebraica a Trieste*, 12.

[92] See for example the first isue of *La Difesa della Razza. Scienza, Documentazione Polemica*, 1 (1938).

[93] B. Skerlj, 'Rapporti di razza fra Jugoslavia e Italia', *La Difesa della Razza*, 18 (1940), 48, 49. *La Difesa* occasionally printed correspondence from Yugoslavia; one case concerned the success of Yugoslav attempts to deal with Jews: 'Il problema judaico in Jugoslavia', *La Difesa della Razza*, 19 (1940), 44. In her study of *Difesa della Razza*, Sandra Puccini has noted the influence of the racially based ethnographies of Yugoslavia and the Adriatic region published by Francesco Musoni and Francesco Pullè; S. Puccini, 'Tra razzismo e scienza. L'antropologia fascista e i popoli balcanici', *Limes*, 1 (1994), 283–94.

[94] Vinci, *Trieste in guerra*, 77.

[95] Salvemini, *Racial Minorities*, 30, 31.

[96] Cited in Apih, *Italia, fascismo e anti-fascismo*, 338-9.

[97] G. Acerbo, *I fondamenti della dottrina fascista della razza* (n.p., 1940), 11, 27, 28.

[98] Ibid., 28.

[99] G. Gaeta, *Trieste ed il colonialismo italiano. Appunti storici giornalistici* (Trieste, Edizioni Delfino, 1943).

[100] Vinci, *Trieste in guerra*, 75.

[101] Ibid.

[102] Marco Antonsich has argued that *Geopolitica* reflected the 'particular reality of the border', and was only of remote interest to Bottai; M. Antonsich, 'La rivista "Geopolitica" e la sua influenza sulla politica fascista', *Limes*, 4 (1994), 269–78. See also A. Vinci, '*Geopolitica* e Balcani. L'esperienza di un gruppo di intellettuali in un Ateneo di confine', *Storia e società*, 47 (1990), 87–127.

[103] Vinci, *Trieste in guerra*, 75.

[104] Macgregor Knox has argued that Mussolini's geopolitical objectives in expanding east were framed in the early and mid-1920s; M. Knox, 'The Fascist regime, its foreign policy and its wars: An "anti-anti-Fascist" orthodoxy?' *Contemporary European History*, 4, 3 (1995), 357 and 365.

[105] Apih, *Italia, fascismo e anti-fascismo*, 219.

[106] J. Walston, 'History and memory of the Italian concentration camps', *Historical Journal*, 40 (1997), 169–183; S. Bon Gherardi, 'La politica antisemitica a Trieste negli anni 1940–43', *Qualestoria*, 1 (1989), 91–98.

[107] Novak, *Trieste 1941–1954*, 57, 58.

[108] Vinci, 'Il fascismo nella Venezia Giulia e l'opera di snazionalizzazione delle minoranze', *Il Territorio*, 6 (1996), 15.

[109] Walston, 'History and memory of the Italian concentration camps', 175, emphasis in original. Giacomo Scotti refers to 200 of these internment

camps in Yugoslavia and Italy; G. Scotti, *Bono Taliano: gli Italiani in Jugoslavia 1941–1943* (Milan, La Pietra, 1977), 89.

[110] Walston claims that these figures are comparable with those in the records kept by the Italian army, as is the civilian make-up of the camp populations. Yugoslav sources however claim the figures were twice as high; Walston, 'History and memory of the Italian concentration camps',175.

[111] Ibid., 177.

[112] Ibid.

[113] Ibid., 170. During the war and after, any criticism of the role of the Italian state and of the military in the war was vulnerable to being dismissed as *filo-slavo*, even by Italian Liberal-Democrats and Socialists.

[114] For a useful discussion of the historiography of the impact of German Nazism on Fascism, see N. Zapponi, 'Fascism in Italian historiography, 1986-1993: a fading national identity', *Journal of Contemporary History*, 29 (1994), 551.

[115] D. Ward, *Anti-Fascisms: Cultural Politics in Italy, 1943–46, Benedetto Croce and the Liberals, Carlo Levi and the Actionists* (Madison, Associated University Presses, 1996), 175.

[116] For further discussion of this point, see G. Sluga, 'Fascism, anti-Fascism, and *italianità*: contesting memories and identities', in R. Bosworth and P. Dogliani, eds., *Italian Fascism: Memory, History and Representation* (London, Macmillan, 1998).

[117] M. Isnenghi, *Intellettuali militanti e intellettuali funzionari* (Turin, Einaudi, 1979), 40 and 61.

[118] M. S. Quine, P*opulation Politics in Twentieth Century Europe: Fascist Dictatorships and Liberal Democracies* (London, Routledge, 1996), 132.

[119] S. Benco, *Trieste* (Florence, Casa Editrice Nemi, 1932), 8, 11.

[120] Bandelli, 'Per una storia del mito di Roma al confine orientale', 262.

8

Making better Italians: issues of national identity in the Italian Social Republic and the Resistance

JONATHAN DUNNAGE

Current debate among Italian historians, journalists and politicians on the Italian Social Republic and the Resistance reflects both a desire to shake off a highly politicized and rhetorical interpretation of the period concerned and the need to end fifty years of bitter ideological division originating in the civil conflict taking place during the final eighteen months of the Second World War. The end of the Cold War in 1989, together with the threat of national disintegration posed by the separatist politics of the Northern League, encouraged such debate,[1] much of which has focused on questioning the extent to which the two main ideological contenders (republican Fascist[2] and anti-Fascist) in the civil war were able to create a sense of national unity among the Italians in the wake of the fall of the Mussolinian regime in July 1943 and the ideological and territorial division of Italy following the Armistice of 8 September 1943. As a result of such debate, which, moreover, has been strongly influenced by the controversial claims of revisionist historians,[3] greater emphasis has been placed on the alleged 'patriotic' (over and above 'Fascist') qualities of the Italian Social Republic, as a key to understanding the motives behind the choice of many of those who supported it,[4] while the traditional claim of the anti-Fascist parties to be a 'nationalizing' force has been challenged.[5]

Effectively, the political forces of both the Italian Social Republic and the Resistance, though ideologically opposed to one another, claimed to be founded on national ideals. Without wishing to enter directly into the above debate, this chapter will consider the role played by the idea of nationhood and national issues in both the individual support given to the two sides, and the propaganda used to encourage such support. Based mainly on an analysis of journalistic sources and personal writings representing a wide range of positions within each ideological camp, I examine how the civil war was related to matters of the Italian state, culture and race. I focus particularly on interpretations of 'Italianness' and the manner in which the battle for supremacy on either side was seen as an opportunity not only to continue a historical process of nation-building, but also to create better Italians.

Such analysis requires a vigilant approach, given the types of sources consulted. There is an obvious possibility of memory distortion, rhetoric or apology in personal testimonies. It is also necessary to take into account constraints on the freedom of the press, whether in the form of central party directives or censorship, given its use in both camps for propaganda purposes. In practice, however, political control of the press was not total, while much of what this article addresses was presented in the form of debate rather than pure propaganda. Indeed, a number of dilemmas over questions of nationhood, faced by both the anti-Fascists and the republican Fascists, are easily discernible in the press and private writings. Both sides claimed to be the heirs of Italy's spiritual and cultural wealth. Yet, they also had to deal with apparent weaknesses in 'Italian-ness', which recent historical events had demonstrated. For the Resistance forces there was the question of whether or not the rise to power of Mussolini and the survival of his regime for over twenty years could be blamed on the Italian people and weaknesses inherent in the Italian character. Similarly, there was controversy between moderate and intransigent republican Fascists over the question of how much the fall of Mussolini in July 1943, the surrender to the Anglo-American forces in September 1943, and the limited mass support of the Social Republic was an indication of the spiritual inferiority of the Italian people. Another problem facing each side lay in the need to claim representation of the great majority of Italians in the struggle against a minority of individuals, who were considered 'anti-Italian', within the context of a civil war in which the enemy in fact represented a significant number of Italians.

The Italian Social Republic and the theme of national reconciliation

Among supporters of the Social Republic there was a clear belief in the Fascist concept of national identity based on the idea of Italy becoming a world power, being respected and feared, and on the need to remove the reputation Italians had for being cowards. In an article in *Corriere della Sera* dated 1 November 1943, the one-time Futurist and *Vociano*, Ardengo Soffici, argued that as a result of the excessive power of other nations and the treachery of Liberal governments, Italians had suffered grave injustices, a situation which Fascism had corrected. Fascist wars had aimed to affirm the equality, if not superiority, of the Italian people in relation to other nations, while the surrender to the Anglo-American forces had been plotted by those wishing Italy to be a servant of the world powers.[6] Even in their awareness that they did not have national support there was still the desire among many republican Fascists to show the world that not all Italians were 'slaves'.[7]

The above conviction was closely linked to the idea that, following a series of humiliating military defeats during the Second World War, and above all the shameful betrayal of her German ally by monarchic forces through the signing of the Armistice of 8 September 1943, Italy's national honour could only be restored through continuation of the war on the side of Germany, which represented a moral and spiritual cleansing of the nation.[8] There was little sense of having committed an act of treason on the part of those who chose to support the Social Republic in view of the treachery of King Victor Emmanuel III which, they argued, had freed Italian subjects from any obligations towards the constitutional order that had replaced the Fascist regime after 25 July 1943. Many younger Fascists automatically supported the Social Republic as a result of the oath they had sworn to Mussolini.[9]

The basis of propaganda for raising support for the Social Republic, as evident in the moderate press,[10] was the idea of reconciliation between Italians in the name of the fatherland and independently of political affiliation in a new spirit of freedom of thought and open criticism that did not threaten national interests. However, as demonstrated below, this increasingly clashed with the propaganda of the more radical exponents of the Social Republic, who argued that to be a good patriot one had to be a good Fascist.[11]

Service to the fatherland became the overriding *raison d'être* of human existence, without which man was condemned to slavery.[12] Belief in the fatherland and self-sacrifice in its name was seen as the only means of dealing with the huge spiritual void that had been opened up in the wake of the Armistice.[13] The newly formed Italian Social Republic was portrayed as representing the miracle of national resurrection and sacrificial purification.[14] In material terms its policies of socialization became the basis for the re-creation of national unity.[15]

Both moderate and radical republican Fascists claimed that the Social Republic was the heir to the great cultural and political traditions of Italy. They urged Italians to follow the example of writers and poets (Dante, Foscolo, Manzoni, Carducci and Alfieri, for example) whose artistic creativity had been inspired in far-off yet equally tragic times.[16] An article in the Catholic *Avvenire d'Italia* of 28 October 1943 claimed that the Italian people, who had brought great spiritual wealth into the world, would not be vanquished. It urged Italians to find the strength and faith necessary to bring light back into the world, just as their ancestors had brought light into the Dark Ages.[17] According to an article in the Bolognese *Resto del Carlino* of 24 March 1944, the traditions of ancient Rome and the Renaissance were hailed as proof, contrary to Anglo-American propaganda, that Italians were neither slaves to the foreigner nor second-class warriors,[18] while those defending Florence against the Anglo-American invasion in August 1944 were described as representing the 'rebellious spirit of Alfieri, the political mind of Machiavelli, the creative geniuses of Dante, Michelangelo, Galileo and Rossini, and the poetry of Foscolo'.[19]

The Social Republic claimed to be the natural heir to the Risorgimento, of which the 'Fascist' war was the continuation.[20] This process had been taken off its course by the monarchy. Mazzini and Garibaldi had renounced their aspirations for the founding of an Italian republic in order to prevent a civil war, leading to the betrayal of Risorgimento ideals by the monarchy. Mussolini had been betrayed by the monarchy, in spite of his efforts to reconcile republican and monarchic ideals through Fascism.[21] In its propaganda the Social Republic modelled itself on the Roman Republic of 1849. In the wake of the Anglo-American capture of the capital in June 1944, for example, it was argued that Rome would be retaken just as it had been regained after the Roman Republic of 1849 had fallen.[22]

The value of similar Resistance claims on the Risorgimento process was clearly denied in the republican Fascist press. It was argued that while Garibaldi had fought to free the Italian people, the Communist partisan brigades carrying his name would lead the Italian people to slavery; while Garibaldi had opposed foreign domination of the Italian people, the 'Garibaldini' accepted foreign rule; while Garibaldi had wished to be honoured less as a warrior and more as a farmer, the 'Garibaldini' exploited the toils of others; while Garibaldi had admired and respected the chastity of Italian girls, the 'Garibaldini' were deflowering them in preparation for mass rapes that would be committed by the savages belonging to the multiracial Anglo-American armies.[23]

As such rhetoric demonstrates, much of the propaganda urged the defence of Italian civilization against the barbarism of the invading enemy. Emblematic in this sense was a poster displayed in a number of cities showing a Negro in American military uniform carrying off a statue, which implied both the plundering of Italian cultural wealth and the rape of Italian women.[24] The Anglo-American invasion was seen as culturally devastating for Italy. Hence, an article in *Il Resto del Carlino* of February 1944 invoked the spirit of Alfieri, Foscolo, Guerrazzi, D'Azeglio, Manzoni, Carducci, Pascoli and D'Annunzio against the baseness and aridity of American culture, which risked perverting the minds of Italians.[25] This was partly contradicted, however, by an ongoing debate about whether the lack of support of the Social Republic by the intelligentsia was a result of too many foreign influences from the past in Italian culture.[26]

The enormous responsibility that patriotic Italians had for preventing the destruction of Italian civilization was reinforced by the presentation of Italy as the centre and origin of European civilization and Christianity. An article in the paper of the Bolognese Republican Fascist Federation, *L'Assalto*, of 29 February 1944 urged, for example, the defence of ancient Roman civilization, which the Mussolinian revolution had once again brought to the rest of the continent.[27] Closely connected to this was the concept of a Christian civilization, of which Italy formed the epicentre. Continuation of the war on the side of Germany was justified as a European Christian crusade.[28] It was argued that the Catholic Church had to put the needs of the fatherland before universalist considerations, especially since God had chosen Italy as the seat of Catholicism, which was under attack by the atheist forces of America and the anti-Catholic forces of Britain.[29]

The above arguments were clearly linked to defence of the Italian race, suggesting that the Social Republic did not merely formally imitate Nazi racial and anti-Semitic policies or try to oppose them, as has often been claimed. Cadets of the officer training school of the Republican National Guard (Guardia Nazionale Repubblicana) argued in their course assignments that the Italian race had been 'bastardized' by Jewish and American culture. In harking back to the racial purity of ancient Rome, they claimed that Fascism had not addressed race questions sufficiently and that this was to blame for the disaster of 1943.[30] Yet, such statements were not restricted to the political élite. Giorgio Pini, moderate republican Fascist and director of *Il Resto del Carlino*, who would later be isolated for his open criticism of the Republican Fascist Party, portrayed Mussolini as a victim of Jewish conspiracy, comparing him with Christ betrayed by Judas.[31] It needs to be emphasized that racism and anti-Semitism were an integral part of the patriotism of the Social Republic. This brings into question the validity of the separation by several ex-republican Fascists of love of the fatherland, which they claimed was the overriding motive for their actions, from the more controversial aspects of the Social Republic, including the deportation of Jews, which they denied having been involved in.[32]

The effectiveness of the propaganda of national reconciliation is questionable in view of a number of factors. For many of those who joined the armed forces of the Social Republic there was disillusionment at the bitter reality of being employed above all in the repression of partisan activities, rather than in fighting the Anglo-American enemy at the war front, and this was partly a motive for the high rate of desertion from the armed and police forces. Carlo Mazzantini, a member of the Tagliamento Brigade, claimed that when military formations were unexpectedly used for anti-partisan action, many of his comrades deserted in order to join units destined for the front.[33] The success of patriotic propaganda was above all hindered by the fact that in reality the Social Republic had lost most of its autonomy to the Nazis, who, moreover, exploited Italian economic and human resources to such an extent that socialization policies could not be put into practice.

As a result of the limited autonomy of the Social Republic from Germany, there was a growing divide between the moderate and intransigent forces. The position of the former is epitomized in the words of the Hegelian philosopher, Giovanni Gentile, who at the end of 1943 urged the Social Republic to be sparing in its vendetta against the traitors of 8 September and to place the values of the fatherland before the ideological requirements of the party.[34] From the columns of *Il Resto del Carlino*, Giorgio Pini argued that the Republican Fascist Party should become a democratic organization in view of the future decisional role of the Italian people. He asserted the need for apostles for the Republic outside the party and insisted that persuasion rather than force should be used to gain the support of the Italian people.[35] The armed forces of the Social Republic, whose commander-in-chief, Rodolfo Graziani, had from the start advocated the creation of an apolitical national army to oppose the Anglo-American advance,[36] also belonged to the moderate faction. They were aware of Italy's diminishing sovereignty over her own territory and resented their increasing assimilation into the German military forces. In this sense, the refusal of a high percentage of members of the air force of the Social Republic to be incorporated into the Luftwaffe is seen as representing a stand against the Germans and emblematic of the overriding patriotic credentials of many of those who supported the Social Republic.[37]

It has been argued that several moderate republican Fascists lent their support to the idea of creating links between anti-Fascists and republican Fascists on the principle of defending Italian territory from both the German and Anglo-American occupiers. This has been particularly attributed to journalists and newspaper directors, including Giorgio Pini of *Il Resto del Carlino* and Concetto Pettinato of *La Stampa*.[38] It is noticeable that while the radical republican Fascist press made frequent references to the merits of the Nazi occupation, Pini's paper merely referred to the military movements of the Germans at the war front, while remaining silent on the question of German occupation of Italian territory. In two articles of September 1944, there is a clear reference to the desire to make alliances with partisans opposed to 'any form of foreign dominance'.[39]

A similar position was adopted by other small groups. They included the Movimento dei Giovani Italiani Repubblicani, composed mostly of university students who had been brought up as Fascists and, who, according to the newspaper of the Pisa organization, were highly critical not only of the conservative faction of supporters of the previous regime, but of the Fascist leaders themselves, whom they saw as having taken advantage of the blind obedience of Fascist youth for their own corrupt purposes. In the light of the disaster of 8 September, they were prepared to fight for their country, but not for the Fascist leadership or German occupiers. They were openly critical of the intransigence of the Republican Fascist Party, which they saw as unjustly blaming the war catastrophe on the weaknesses of the Italian people, and they appealed to all patriotic Italians (whether Fascist or anti-Fascist) to help them fight for the creation of a social republic of Mazzinian inspiration and the end of foreign domination.[40] We have to bear in mind, however, that the above initiatives were those of a minority. They were swiftly repressed by the Republican Fascist Party and Nazi occupiers, and found very limited mass support. As the defeat of the republican Fascists became imminent, it is likely that such initiatives were motivated by a desire for self-preservation, and as such they were rejected in the anti-Fascist camp.[41]

While the moderate factions of the Social Republic gave priority to patriotism over pure ideological concerns and moved away from support of the German ally, the more radical republican Fascists refused a politically neutral and democratic approach to support-gathering in the belief that one could not be a true Italian without being a Fascist.[42] In view of this, and the reality of limited mass support for the Republic, their attitude towards the Italian people became increasingly coercive and vindictive. Represented by the party leader, Alessandro Pavolini, and the commander of the Republican National Guard, Renato Ricci, this faction advocated the creation of a strongly politicized militia, as opposed to an apolitical mass army, as partly achieved with the founding of the Black Brigades (Brigate Nere), directly controlled by the party, in the summer of 1944.[43] The atrocities of the Black Brigades and similar organizations only further isolated the republican Fascists from the rest of society.

In its support for the German occupiers, the propaganda of the intransigent republican Fascists, by emphasizing the military, racial and cultural superiority of their ally, contradicted the message of national reconciliation of more moderate propaganda. Articles of October 1943 in the Cremona-based *Regime Fascista*, directed by Roberto Farinacci, suggested, for example, that it was thanks to Germany that Italy was being defended from the threat of British colonization and international Bolshevism. In spite of the betrayal of the previous month, Hitler, out of loyalty to Mussolini, was prepared to give the Italians another opportunity to take up the struggle once again to save future generations from catastrophe.[44] Visual images were particularly effective in getting an anti-Italian message across. These included a sketch in *L'Assalto* of a group of men engaged in lively discussion at a table with a German soldier in the foreground. The caption read: 'Italy won't be saved through discussion.'[45] Their newspapers lamented the spiritual insufficiency and lack of national consciousness of the Italians. Comparison was made between the present conflict and that of the Risorgimento. It was argued that 'then' and 'now' the majority of Italians remained indifferent and passive towards the struggles of a minority.[46]

In an attempt to generate support for the Italo-German alliance, it was argued that historically Austria, not Germany, had been Italy's traditional enemy. Both countries had shared common intentions to free themselves from Austrian dominance. The German and Italian national insurrections of 1821, 1830, 1832 and 1848 represented a struggle against Austrian militarism, while Germany had militarily assisted the Italian Risorgimento.[47] This line was supported by publications emphasizing that Europe was a creation of Roman and Germanic elements fused together, and claiming that Austrians and Germans were racially separate, the former being Slavs.[48] For some intransigent republican Fascists Germanization was the only means of removing Italian weaknesses. This was the reason behind the creation of an Italian SS, according to whose newspaper, *Avanguardia Europea*, it was necessary to remove weak Mediterranean characteristics from Italian soldiers and replace them with 'Germanic ruthlessness'.[49] However, such propaganda clashed with the reality of treatment of the Italian SS as second-class soldiers within a general context of Nazi contempt for all Italians on account of the betrayal of September 1943 (though Schreiber argues that such betrayal served as a pretext for the expression of a longer-standing Nazi belief in the racial inferiority of Italians).[50]

Issues of national identity in the partisan Resistance

One of the main dilemmas for the Resistance movement lay in the need to emphasize the national character of the partisan war of liberation, minimizing the reality of a civil war. This was seen as necessary in order to avoid creating the impression that the war had been fought by two factions that were equally represented and well-grounded. Officially the Germans were seen as the main enemy, while the republican Fascists represented a minority of individuals, who were not to be considered 'real' Italians. This line was contradicted by the fact that in reality a significant number of Italians supported the Social Republic, and many of them were prepared to commit atrocities against other Italians. This in practice resulted in greater hatred of the republican Fascists, as is evident in the most direct and spontaneous documents of the Resistance. The Communists in particular feared that the national aspect of the struggle risked being eclipsed because of this. Party directives clearly betrayed the feeling that Fascism was not a minor residue and that a civil war was being fought. Yet, the leader, Palmiro Togliatti, who was particularly concerned to present the party as a national party, attempted to remove the idea that 'the Fascists, in spite of everything, were Italians, too'.[51]

The above dilemma is evident in the Resistance press. Following the torching by the Fascists of the village of Funo in the province of Bologna as a reprisal for partisan destruction of their headquarters in Argelato, an article in the paper of the local Communist partisans, *Il Combattente*, argued that the republican Fascists responsible were not Italians, even if they had seen their heyday in 'our Italy which they have martyred and sold to the barbaric invader'. They were 'bastards, ignoble slaves, who for money had sold themselves to the Hitlerian master, becoming his instrument of terror and oppression'.[52] Yet this type of language was in contradiction to words of warning frequently directed against those Italians supporting or collaborating with the Social Republic and German occupiers, words that made it clear that a significant number of Italians belonged to the enemy camp.[53]

The Resistance forces also had to deal with the problem of Italy's Fascist past. To what extent could Fascism be blamed on negative characteristics of 'Italianness'? In some cases the answer given tended towards an absolution of the Italian people, though this line contained many ambiguities. A number of Liberal writings, including those of the philosopher-historian, Benedetto Croce, lay stress, for example, on the idea that the Italians were victims of Fascism. They, particularly the youngest, had been naively led on by it. They were certainly guilty of having passively accepted Fascism, but Fascism was the product of one man alone.[54] This was linked to the idea of Fascism being a mere 'parenthesis' with no relation to the course of Italian history set by the Risorgimento.[55]

Others took the debate a step further by arguing that there clearly were defects within the Italian character if Fascism was born and had survived for so many years in Italy. The younger generation of political Catholics argued, for example, that the problem lay in the intellectual immaturity of the Italians.[56] The Socialists claimed that the experience of Fascism had revealed the spiritual inadequacies of the Italian people.[57] From as early as January 1943 the clandestine paper of the Action Party (Partito d'Azione), *L'Italia Libera*, had urged the Italians to overcome their passiveness, 'which threatens to poison the national spirit for ever', in order to end a state of servitude towards Germany,[58] while in an article entitled 'Responsibility' of 11 November 1943 it was argued that Fascism was a product of the opportunistic character of the Italians.[59]

In many cases judgements of this nature were conditioned by pragmatic considerations. Within Catholic circles it was feared that an intransigent position would lead to criticism of the relationship between the Church and the Fascist regime. The Communist and Socialist parties agreed to minimize the responsibility of the Italian people for Fascism, in order to safeguard their reputation abroad. The Communist leadership was particularly intolerant of public statements to the contrary by its members, and attempted to impose the adoption of an image of the Italian people united behind the political avant-garde in the struggle against Fascism, arguing that if the Italian people had failed in the past, this was to be blamed on the evident failure of the avant-garde to lead them.[60]

An examination of individual motives for joining the partisan Resistance reveals a rejection of the Fascist concept of fatherland (based on blind obedience to Mussolini and aggressive imperialism), and the rediscovery of a fatherland founded on personal responsibility for one's actions, humanitarian ideals and a more conscious involvement of the Italian masses in national development. Pavone notes a sense of liberation felt by partisans in their refusal both to enrol in the armies of the Social Republic and to recognize the authority of the royal government in Allied-occupied territory, on account of its abandonment of northern and central Italy to the Nazi occupiers after the Armistice. Moreover, the betrayal of both the king and Mussolini was seen as freeing Italians from obligations to either of them resulting from oaths previously sworn.[61] Croce spoke of a more general attitude of disobedience and betrayal among Italians, which he traced back to the Italian entry to the Second World War in 1940: the Italians had ended their obedience to Fascism and had desired the military defeat of Italy as a means of saving her from enslavement to Germany and restoring her independence and liberty.[62] Similarly, Romolo Iacopini, a Communist partisan, stated in a letter that he had been forced to act against the 'fatherland which the Fascists had falsified' for love of the true fatherland, for which he had fought during the First World War.[63]

According to the edition of 15 February 1945 of *Patrioti*, the Bologna-based newspaper of the First 'Justice and Liberty' Brigade, the new Italy was to be constructed without the false myths, political speculation or rhetoric of the Fascists.[64] For most partisans and anti-Fascists, the monarchy would be excluded from it. The Communist partisan paper, *Il Partigiano*, claimed that the monarchy was just as responsible as Fascism for its exploitation of Italians under the guise of patriotism, while an article of *Patrioti* argued that the House of Savoy, through its treachery of 8 September 1943, had destroyed its own myth for which hundreds of thousands of Italians had died in war.[65] The Republican Party press claimed that the monarchy had knocked the democratic Risorgimento off course and had called on Fascism for help in order to maintain its dynastic powers. It had consequently lost all rights to lead the Italians in the struggle for the new Italy, as had those political forces closest to it.[66]

Participation in the Resistance struggle was seen as allowing a future role in national life for those groups and social classes that had previously been excluded. Particularly important in this sense were the new rights gained by the lower social classes and by women, so ending centuries of servitude and humiliation. An article in the Communist Party paper, *L'Unità*, of March 1945 claimed, for example, that the Bolognese peasantry through their contribution to the Resistance had earned a place in the new Italy,[67] while a representative of the partisan Women's Defence Groups (Gruppi di Difesa della Donna) stated: 'By contributing to the liberation of Italy we women are earning the right to participate in the rebuilding of the fatherland tomorrow. By fighting for the independence of Italy, we are also fighting for our freedom as women and as workers.'[68]

For many the struggle and sacrifice which the war against the republican Fascists and German occupiers entailed was seen as a form of self-punishment for previous responsibility for Fascism and the crimes it had committed.[69] Only through sacrifice would the Italian people gain rights in the future. An article in *L'Unità* of 12 October 1943 claimed, for example, that through the Resistance struggle the Italian people would gain the right to independence, democracy and the help of the other free nations in the post-war reconstruction of Italy.[70] This was linked to the need for Italians to improve their qualities as a people or rediscover old virtues that Fascism had eclipsed. In this sense the Rome-based clandestine students' newspaper, *Nostra Lotta*, urged the young to rise against a general attitude of fatalism and resignation in Italian society in order to defeat the Social Republic in the north and a pro-Fascist reaction in the liberated south.[71]

More optimistically, an article in *La Voce Repubblicana* claimed that though the Italian people had been judged incapable of a free existence by those who had wanted to rule them with violence, the manner in which they had managed the difficult situation created by the Armistice was proof of their 'native virtues of wisdom and dignity'.[72] Similarly, the refusal of members of the Italian armed forces interned by the Germans to continue fighting the war on the side of the Axis forces was often experienced as a form of national rebellion against a previous state of Italian submission to Germany during the war and the need to restore a sense of national dignity.[73] Yet, privately, less optimism was often expressed. Emblematic in this sense is the letter in which the intellectual partisan, Giaime Pintor, described the Italian people as 'feeble, profoundly corrupted by their recent history and always on the point of surrendering to cowardice or weakness'.[74]

Like the republican Fascists, the Resistance claimed to be fighting a second Risorgimento. While Croce described a perfect process of unification which had brought prosperity and civilization to Italy before being destroyed by Fascism,[75] those forces opposed to the monarchy officially modelled themselves on the Mazzinian democratic concepts of Risorgimento, in the belief that the only way forward for uniting the Italians once again was the creation of a republic. Hence, the Action Party writing in *L'Italia Libera* played on Crispi's warning to Mazzini that 'The Republic divides us, the monarchy unites us', with the idea that the Republic would unite the Italians, while the monarchy would divide it.[76] Yet, Pavone argues, the names of partisan groups or newspapers were not widely inspired by the Risorgimento, suggesting that on a purely ideological basis identification with it was difficult.[77] Moreover, some partisans feared that adoption of the idea of a second Risorgimento would lead to a second disappointment.[78] In Catholic circles there was fear of the creation of a second anti-Catholic Risorgimento and, subsequently, a strong desire not to be excluded from playing a role in it.[79] Debate concerning this was clearly the cause of some controversy and recriminations between Catholic and lay groups concerning the value of the first Risorgimento.[80]

Concepts of nationhood were conditioned by the fact that the Resistance struggle was seen within the context of a European (if not universal) civil war. Among the Communist partisans this was seen in terms of a class conflict, though the party leadership attempted to discourage this view.[81] In this sense an article of January 1944 in *Il Partigiano* hailed a future Italian workers' republic within a European federation of republics.[82] It was, indeed, the underlying class basis of the Communist partisan struggle, together with the party's subordination to the Soviet Union, that brought Communist national credentials into question among other partisan brigades. Hence, an article in the 'Freedom and Justice' paper, *Patrioti*, of February 1945 accused the Communists of exploiting the myth of the fatherland, as the Fascists had, but in order to wage a bloody war against the bourgeoisie.[83] Yet, there is little doubt that many Communists saw themselves as primarily engaged in a patriotic struggle, even though this involved some form of social revolution. An analysis of letters written by Communist partisans reveals, for example, frequent references to the 'rebirth of the fatherland', the creation of a 'free Italy', the 'freeing of Italy from foreign dominion' and 'having done one's duty as an Italian', alongside references to communism and socialism.[84]

From the columns of *Bologna Liberata*, the Christian Democrats of Emilia-Romagna hailed the liberation as defeating those ideologies that had attempted to destroy European Christian civilization founded on fraternity between her peoples.[85] For the Action Party the European democratic revolution being fought was linked to the need to create a future federation of nations that would prevent further war and oppression.[86] As one of the main contributors to the cultural and political paper of the party, *La Nuova Europa*, the distinguished anti-Fascist historian Luigi Salvatorelli spoke of a future association of European states, as envisaged by Mazzini.

While Salvatorelli argued that Europe had an important task of bringing civilization to the rest of the world, this was intended in terms of democracy, culture and religion, rather than imperialism. Indeed, because in the past the absolute sovereignty of nations had prevented international organizations from halting the advance of Fascism, the threat of nationalist imperialism could only be removed through the creation of international organs with the legal right to keep individual nations in check.[87]

In spite of Resistance concepts of nationhood based on respect for other peoples there is evidence of a transfer of nationalistic values in the transition from Fascism to anti-Fascism that would emerge clearly when the post-war anti-Fascist coalition government discussed the fate of Italy's frontiers, colonies and armed forces. Though this attitude was most prominent at government and party levels, it was not lacking in the partisan environment.[88] This is manifested in varying forms in Resistance writings. As Giovanni Falaschi points out, the language used in partisan documents and papers often showed the linguistic influence of Fascist or nationalistic rhetoric, particularly among the older generation of anti-Fascists.[89] But, more seriously, Resistance writings also betrayed the influences of Fascist concepts. Interesting in this sense are references made to race. Women Socialists of Emilia-Romagna in their newspaper, *Compagna*, claimed, for example, to support the institution of marriage as a fundamental condition 'for the health of the Italian race',[90] while in their paper, *Rivoluzione Socialista*, an organization of young socialists, formed by ex-Fascist university students, described themselves as the 'flower of the Italian race'.[91]

The extent to which the Resistance struggle eradicated previous nationalistic concepts of nationhood, particularly among the more conservative partisans, is also questionable. This is evident in the words of Franco Balbis, an army officer condemned to death by the republican Fascists, who saw the African war campaigns and Resistance as equally valid in patriotic terms.[92] In this sense, Resistance writings betrayed traces of long-standing national frustrations that had been at the root of Fascism. These particularly hinged around traditional Italian superiority and inferiority complexes towards the world's leading nations. They were a result of the contradiction between the desire implicit in the Resistance struggle for Italy to be internationally recognized once again and the reality of her subordination to the Allied occupying powers. Articles of January 1944 in the Communist partisan newspaper, *Il Partigiano*, argued, for example, that the war of liberation was an opportunity for the Italian people to regenerate themselves, rather than be regenerated by external forces, and attacked the monarchy in southern Italy for 'preventing free Italians ... from liberating Italy from a position of inferiority in which the armies of the United Nations were concerned to maintain her'.[93] Similarly, from the columns of *La Nuova Europa*, Luigi Salvatorelli accused the liberal-democratic countries of having initially supported Fascism as a means of preventing 'inferior peoples' from falling to Bolshevism.[94] At the same time pretensions of cultural and spiritual superiority, another important factor behind the rise of Fascism,[95] were evident as a means of justifying the international rehabilitation of Italy. Croce, in his appeal for fair treatment of Italy by the Allies, argued, for example, that the Italians were valued for their generosity, intelligence, humanity and artistic and intellectual qualities and that 'Europe cannot do without the spiritual force of Italy'.[96]

Conclusion

In this chapter I have attempted to demonstrate in the limited space available that both the forces of the Resistance and the republican Fascists were in their struggle concerned with aspects of Italian national identity. This manifested itself at two levels. Firstly, in order to gather support, both sides claimed to represent the interests of Italy and to be founded on patriotic ideals – while denying this quality to the enemy. This was particularly evident, therefore, in press publications and other forms of propaganda. Secondly, there was a genuine preoccupation with questions concerning the cultural, racial and spiritual qualities of the Italians. This was often in contrast with propaganda in that it revealed a certain pessimism about such qualities in view of recent events, which could be seen as demonstrating serious weaknesses in the Italian character. While this was manifested privately or within the confines of political groups, the propaganda itself often betrayed similar doubts and dilemmas. Each side claimed, however, that the current struggle was an opportunity to overcome national weaknesses, so permitting the resurgence of the nation.

The difficulties which the above ambiguities created for both sides also illustrate the multiplicity of ways in which nationhood was conceived. In the case of the Italian Social Republic, a call for support on the basis of national reconciliation was difficult to put into practice. As the defeat of the Axis forces became increasingly certain and the Republic's subordination to the German occupiers prevented the achievement of policies aimed at the greater well-being of the Italian people, there was a growing contrast between the moderate faction of republican Fascists, who believed that national unity could only be achieved through tactful persuasion and avoidance of ideological extremism, and the intransigent faction, for which Fascism and patriotism were inseparable, but which, in its support of the Nazis, emphasized Italian inferiority.

The virtue of the vision of nationhood proposed by the forces of the Resistance lay in its embodiment of humanitarian and anti-imperialist ideals and in its attempt to involve Italians more directly in the process of national development, thus giving them a greater sense of individual responsibility. Yet, if the Resistance was able to achieve greater national support, it is important to bear in mind that the task was, without doubt, made easier by the increasingly imminent victory of the Anglo-American forces. Moreover, behind the rhetoric of national unity, there were a number of de-unifying factors that would come to the fore after the conflict. There was an underlying pessimism among many individual partisans regarding the ability of the Italians to overcome their spiritual weaknesses through the Resistance struggle. There were also ideological divisions among and within the invididual political groups. These partly centred on recriminations over the extent to which each could claim to represent national interests, and over previous political responsibilities for Fascism. Finally, the extent to which the Resistance, particularly on a mass level, fully embodied new visions of nationhood remains questionable, suggesting that there was often a subconscious transfer of Fascist or nationalist values involved in the conversion to its cause.

Notes
1 'Meglio Salò oggi che Bossi domani', *L'Espresso*, 27 June 1996.
2 Translated from the term *fascista repubblicana* used to indicate the Fascists of the Italian Social Republic.
3 The most distinguished revisionist historian was Renzo De Felice who analysed the period 1943–5 in *Rosso e nero*, edited by Pasquale Chessa

(Milan, Baldini and Castoldi, 1995), then in a posthumously published work, *Mussolini l'alleato 1940–1945, II: La guerra civile 1943–45* (Turin, Einaudi, 1997). For an analysis of revisionist interpretations of the period 1943–1945, see R. J. B. Bosworth, *The Italian Dictatorship: Problems and Perspectives in the Interpretation of Mussolini and Fascism* (London, Arnold, 1998), chapter 8.

4   See, for example, the interview with Piero Vivarelli, veteran of the Decima Flottiglia Mas (Tenth Torpedo-Boat Squadron) in 'Erano marò, mica fascisti', *L'Espresso*, 13 June 1996.

5   For the most outspoken revisionist criticism of the anti-Fascist parties in this sense, see Ernesto Galli della Loggia, *La morte della patria* (Rome–Bari, Laterza,1996).

6   'Risaliremo l'abisso', *Corriere della Sera*, 1 November 1943.

7   Claudio Pavone, *Una guerra civile. Saggio storico sulla moralità nella Resistenza* (Turin, Bollati Boringhieri, 1991), 60–1.

8   This was the overriding motive for the decision of the commander-in-chief of the Tenth Torpedo-Boat Squadron, Valerio Borghese, to continue the war on the side of Germany, according to Giampaolo Pansa, *Il gladio e l'alloro* (Milan, Mondadori, 1991), 181–5. See also Bruno Guarino, *La guerra continua* (Acireale, Baranno Editore, 1989) 29; Benito Bollati, *Un ragazzo di Salò, 1943–1946* (Milan, Mursia, 1998), 40–1; Carlo Mazzantini, *I balilla andarono a Salò* (Venice, Marsilio, 1995), 34–5, 68. In his account Mazzantini emphasizes the sense of shame that many felt at being Italian in the wake of the Armistice. Mazzantini's personal experience of the civil war on the side of the republican Fascists is also the subject of his novel, *A cercar la bella morte* (Milan, Mondadori, 1986).

9   Pavone, *Una guerra civile*, 52, 58–9.

10 By *moderate* press I am referring particularly to mainstream newspapers, such as *Il Corriere della Sera*, *Il Resto del Carlino*, *La Stampa*, etc. (rather than papers run directly by the Republican Fascist Party or the most intransigent republican Fascists), which were nonetheless subject to political control through censorship and the appointment of republican Fascist directors.

11 See, for example, 'Carità di patria', *Corriere della Sera*, 2 October 1943.

12 'Ritrovarsi', *Corriere della Sera*, 6 October 1943.

13 'Servire la patria', *La Stampa*, 18 September 1943; 'Attendere', *Corriere della Sera*, 29 September 1943.

14 'Risaliremo l'abisso', *Corriere della Sera*, 1 November 1943.

15 'Il nuovo stato', *Corriere della Sera*, 7 October 1943. In fulfilment of the ideals of the corporate state and social justice, which the previous Fascist regime had betrayed as a result of conservative influences,

socialization policies envisaged the participation of workers and employees in the running of companies.

16   'La grande voce', *Corriere della Sera*, 10 October 1943.
17   'Il posto dell'Italia', *L'Avvenire d'Italia*, 28 October 1943.
18   'Il popolo italiano sa riprendersi', *Resto del Carlino*, 24 March 1944.
19   'L'esempio fiorentino', *Il Resto del Carlino*, 19 August 1944.
20   'Chiarimenti', *Italia e Civiltà*, 29 January 1944.
21   'Repubblica italiana', *L'Assalto*, 28 October 1943.
22   'Garibaldi', *Resto del Carlino*, 3 June 1944.
23   'Garibaldi e la Brigata Garibaldi', *Valanga Repubblicana* (Modena), 15 December 1944, reproduced in Ermanno Gorrieri, *La Repubblica di Montefiorino. Per una storia della Resistenza in Emilia* (Bologna, Il Mulino, 1966), 210–11.
24   Published in *Il Resto del Carlino*, 13 January 1944.
25   'Torniamo ai padri antichi', *Resto del Carlino*, 16 February 1944.
26   See, for example, 'Declino dell'"intelligenza"', *Resto del Carlino*, 16 March 1944.
27   'Europa Romana', *L'Assalto*, 29 February 1944.
28   'Civiltà che redime', *L'Avvenire d'Italia*, 17 October 1943.
29   'Dovere dei cattolici di servire la Patria', *Resto del Carlino*, 13 January 1944; 'Gli anglosassoni nemici del cattolicesimo', *Resto del Carlino*, 29 January 1944; 'Lupi, gregge e pastori', *Il Resto del Carlino*, 5 February 1944.
30   Paolo Ferrari and Mimmo Franzinelli, eds., 'A scuola di razzismo. Il corso allievi ufficiali della Gnr di Fontanellato', *Italia contemporanea*, 211 (1998), 417–44. For other examples of racist language, see 'Degli ebrei', *Italia e Civiltà*, 13 May 1944; 'Questi sono i liberatori', *L'Assalto*, 16 January 1944; 'Gli ebrei del mondo', *L'Assalto*, 23 March 1944.
31   'Oltre il calvario', *Resto del Carlino*, 9 April 1944.
32   Interesting in this sense is Piero Vivarelli's denial that the Tenth Torpedo-Boat Squadron had anti-Semitic tendencies in 'Erano marò, mica fascisti', *L'Espresso*, 13 June 1996.
33   Mazzantini, *I balilla andarono a Salò*, 140.
34   'Ricostruire', *Corriere della Sera*, 28 December 1943.
35   'Scongelare – rapporto a Pavolini', *Resto del Carlino*, 2 April 1944; 'Idee repubblicane', *Resto del Carlino*, 28 April 1944; 'Indirizzi', *Resto del Carlino*, 28 May 1944.
36   Mirco Dondi, *La Resistenza italiana* (Milan, Fenice 2000, 1995), 51.
37   Gregory Alegi, 'La legione che non fu mai. L'Aeronautica Nazionale Repubblicana e la crisi dell'estate 1944', *Storia contemporanea*, 23, 6 (1992), 1047–85.
38   Felice Bellotti, *La Repubblica di Mussolini* (Milan, Zagara, 1947),

148-51.

[39] 'Niente capitolazione', *Resto del Carlino*, 8 September 1944; 'Fuori l'intelligenza', *Resto del Carlino*, 23 September 1944.

[40] Paolo Nello, *Autobiografia politica del fascismo universitario pisano (1926-1944)* (Pisa, Nistri-Lischi, 1983), 335-46. See also Renzo De Felice, *Mussolini l'alleato,* II, 504-10.

[41] See, for example, *L'Unità*'s rejection of Concetto Pettinato's invitation in *La Stampa* that Italians 'hold out their arms to each other over foreign bayonets' ('I piani criminali del nazifascismo', 1 March 1945) and of Edmondo Cione's Ragruppamento Repubblicano Socialista, which aimed to create a 'bridge' between Fascists and anti-Fascists of socialist and republican leanings (3 April 1945).

[42] See, for example, 'Essere brutali', *Il Regime Fascista*, 2 November 1943; 'L'apoliticità', *Il Regime Fascista*, 5 August 1944.

[43] Dondi, *La Resistenza Italiana*, 51-2.

[44] 'Verrà giorno', *Il Regime Fascista*, 13 October 1943; 'Parliamoci chiaro', *Il Regime Fascista*, 14 October 1943; 'Per l'onore d'Italia, a fianco della Germania', *Il Regime Fascista*, 15 October 1943.

[45] 'L'Italia non si salva con discussioni' (drawing), *L'Assalto*, 19 December 1943. The caption under a drawing in the edition of 15 April 1944 read: 'The English strike; the French play; the Italians argue; the Germans work.'

[46] 'Mazzini aveva ragione', *L'Assalto*, 7 April 1944. See also 'Questi italiani' in the Catholic republican Fascist weekly, *Crociata Italica*, 24 July 1944 and 'Verità sul popolo', *Il Regime Fascista*, 20 August 1944, in which it was argued that the Italian people did not deserve Mussolini on account of their limited national consciousness. Such discussions were not absent from the more moderate press, though the language used did not betray so vividly a sense of disillusionment regarding the Italian people. See, for example, 'Del complesso di inferiorità', *Italia e Civiltà*, 15 April 1944; 'La fede vince', *Resto del Carlino*, 28 January 1944. In spite of the different positions in the press, privately there was a general condemnation of the Italian people: 'Mussolini's most serious error was to have overestimated his people, a people that does not want to suffer in order to become great, rich and powerful', were the words written in the diary of a twenty-two-year-old republican Fascist before his execution by the partisans (Pavone, *Una guerra civile*, 228).

[47] 'Peggio di una portinaia', *Il Regime Fascista*, 17 October 1943.

[48] Luigi Cajani and Brunello Mantelli, *Una certa Europa. Il collaborazionismo con le potenze dell'Asse, 1939-1945. Le fonti* (Brescia, Annali della Fondazione Luigi Micheletti, 1994), 193-6.

[49] Ricciotti Lazzero, *Le SS Italiane. Storia dei 20.000 che giurarono fedeltà a Hitler* (Milan, Rizzoli, 1982), 186.

50 Ibid., 259; Gerhard Schreiber, *I militari italiani internati nei campi di concentramento del Terzo Reich, 1943-1945* (Rome, Ufficio Storico SME, 1992), 457-62. Schreiber notes (531-8) that Italian soldiers training in Germany and Italian workers were treated as racially inferior. They were not allowed to marry German women for racial motives and sexual relations with German women were discouraged.

51 Pavone, *Una guerra civile*, 221-4, 268-9.

52 'I "caini", i nostrani', *Il Combattente*, 1 September 1944.

53 See, for example, 'Contegno dei funzionari', *Avanti!* (Milan), 18 October 1943.

54 Pavone, *Una guerra civile*, 563-4; Benedetto Croce, 'I diritti dell'Italia . . .', *Risorgimento Liberale*, 22 September 1944; Benedetto Croce, 'La gioventù Italiana' (originally published in *Libertà* (Naples) 11 March 1944), in *Scritti e discorsi politici (1943-1947)* (1963) (Bari, Laterza, 1973), 39-42.

55 Thus, according to Croce, Fascism was of foreign rather than Italian origin (Benedetto Croce, 'L'Italia e l'avversione suscitata contro di lei in Europa dal fascismo', speech given at first congress of the Liberal Party, 2 June 1944, reproduced in *Scritti e discorsi politici*, 77-81).

56 Pavone, *Una guerra civile*, 564-5.

57 'Scherziamo?', *Avanti!* (Milan edition), 8 November 1943.

58 'Italiani!', *L'Italia Libera*, first edition dated January 1943.

59 'Responsabilità', *L'Italia Libera*, 11 November 1943.

60 Pavone, *Una guerra civile*, 565-7.

61 Ibid., 23, 28, 49.

62 Benedetto Croce, 'La libertà italiana e la libertà del mondo' (speech given at CLN congress, Bari, January 1944), reproduced in *Scritti e discorsi politici*, 51; 'I diritti degli italiani . . .', *Risorgimento Liberale*, 22 September 1944.

63 Piero Malvezzi and Giovanni Pirelli, eds., *Lettere di condannati a morte della Resistenza italiana* (1952) (Turin, Einaudi, 1994), 154-5.

64 'La generazione infelice' and 'Ai giovani', *Patrioti*, 15 February 1945.

65 'Compagni!', *Il Partigiano* (Rome), 23 January 1944; 'Lettera al luogotenente', 15 February 1945.

66 'Ricominciare dal popolo' and 'La nostra Repubblica e la nuova Italia', *La Voce Repubblicana*, 15 January 1944; 'Il Partito Repubblicano al Congresso di Bari', *La Voce Repubblicana*, February 1944.

67 'La lotta dei contadini', *L'Unità* (Emilia-Romagna edition), 8 March 1945.

68 'A fianco dei combattenti per la libertà e l'indipendenza nazionale', *Noi Donne* (May 1944).

69 Pavone, *Una guerra civile*, 30.

70 'In Corsica . . .', *L'Unità* (northern Italian edition), 12 October 1943.

71 'Impegno', *Nostra Lotta*, 26 March 1944.

72 'Attività del Partito', *La Voce Repubblicana*, 1 January 1944.

73 Giuseppe Caforio and Marina Nuciari, *'No!' I soldati italiani internati in Germania. Analisi di un rifiuto* (Milan, FrancoAngeli, 1994), 46, 59. Cases of refusal by Italian soldiers to surrender to the Germans after the Armistice were interpreted in a similar way. This is dealt with in Alfonso Bartolini, *Per la patria e la libertà. I soldati italiani nella Resistenza dopo l'8 settembre* (Milan, Mursia, 1986).

74 Pavone, *Una guerra civile*, 563.

75 Croce, 'La gioventù Italiana', in *Scritti e discorsi politici*, 39–42.

76 'La sola via', *L'Italia Libera*, 1 November 1943.

77 Pavone, *Una guerra civile*, 184–6.

78 Ibid., 181.

79 Gorrieri, *La Repubblica di Montefiorino*, 254–5.

80 Interesting is the controversy (voiced in 'Due risorgimenti', *La Nuova Europa*, 4 February 1945) caused by the assertion in an article of *L'Osservatore Romano* of 27 January 1945 that the anticlerical character of the post-1848 Risorgimento had led to the Fascist dictatorship.

81 Pavone, *Una guerra civile*, 306–7.

82 'Precisiamo', *Il Partigiano*, 23 January 1944.

83 'Richiamo alla coscienza', *Patrioti*, 15 February 1945.

84 Malvezzi and Pirelli, eds., *Lettere di condannati a morte della Resistenza italiana*, 8, 27, 89, 111, 169, 176, 223, 306.

85 'Risorgere', *Bologna Liberata*, 22 April 1945.

86 Pavone, *Una guerra civile*, 305–6; 'Verso il cittadino d'Europa', *La Nuova Europa*, 4 February 1945.

87 'Presente e avvenire d'Europa' and 'Internazionale degli Stati e le internazionali dei popoli', *La Nuova Europa*, 24 December 1944.

88 Pavone, *Una guerra civile*, 201.

89 Giovanni Falaschi, *La Resistenza armata nella narrativa italiana* (Turin, Einaudi, 1976), 15–16. Falaschi also argues (pp. 9–15) that Resistance writings were influenced in their prevalent use of standard Italian rather than dialect or regional language by the desire to overcome problems of regional linguistic divisions and autonomist attitudes among partisan bands.

90 'Femminismo socialista', *Compagna*, 1 March 1945.

91 'Perché combattiamo', *Rivoluzione Socialista*, 15 December 1944.

92 Malvezzi and Pirelli, eds., *Lettere di condannati a morte della Resistenza italiana*, 17.

93 'Valore della lotta partigiana' and 'Precisiamo', *Il Partigiano*, 23 January 1944.

94 'Presente e avvenire d'Europa', *La Nuova Europa*, 10 December 1944.

95 Writing in exile in 1938, the anti-Fascist intellectual G. A. Borgese saw

Italian claims to cultural superiority as one of the main causes of Fascism. This had been combined with another Italian complex: that of being cowards in a world of heroes. Italians resented a reputation for gentleness, and Fascism was a result of the idea that if they were able to become intrepid killers like the Gauls, Teutons and Britons and combine this with their cultural genius, they would be able to conquer the world; G. A. Borgese, *Goliath: The March of Fascism* (London, Victor Gollancz, 1938), 484–5.

[96] Croce, 'L'Italia e l'avversione suscitata contro di lei', in *Scritti e discorsi politici*, 77–81.

9

The Christian Democrats and national identity

GINO BEDANI

The Church in Italian history

In his short volume on Italian national identity, Ernesto Galli della Loggia observes that 'the Christian faith in its Catholic confessional form has, for many centuries, represented the only trait really common to all Italians, and therefore we could well say the only unifying factor on the peninsula, the only really "Italian" characteristic'.[1] There is, however, an additional feature which gives this characteristic, on the peninsula, a unique significance: what we could call, for want of a better term, the historical 'pride of place' accorded to Italy in the thinking of the official Church. The theocratic doctrine that the pope as bishop of Rome had inherited not simply the apostolic succession from St Peter as head of the universal Church, but also supremacy over all monarchs, was first announced by Pope Gregory VII in 1075 (*Dictatus papae*). But this doctrinal issue embroiled the peninsula in a special way. Just over a century later, Innocent III, in reasserting the power of the Papacy over the Empire in his encyclical *Sicut universitatis conditor*, added:

> Both these powers or guides have had their centres in Italy, so that this country has acquired pre-eminence over all others by divine disposition. Thus, while we must extend our loving care to all provinces we must do so with a special and paternal solicitude in the case of Italy.[2]

Subsequently the idea that Rome, and by extension Italy, had been entrusted with a providential mission was reinforced by the fact that every pope from 1523 until the election of the Polish pope, John Paul II, in 1978, for more than four and a half centuries, was an Italian.

Thus while on the one hand the Church provided the peninsula with a strong element of continuity in its historical identity, Italians also had to pay the price 'of finding the road to the creation of a nation-state barred to them, and of being the only European country without a national Church to help them'.[3] In order to protect its own independent status as a universal authority, the Church could not allow its temporal powers to be subsumed within a larger domain encompassing the peninsula. It thus engaged in the kind of geopolitical divisive intrigue, as John Thomson puts it, which meant that the sense of national identity was less advanced in Italy than elsewhere in Europe.[4] Given the historical absence of a 'national' Church, this impressed upon Italian Catholicism a particularly strong universalist perspective, which in the longer term would eventually have a bearing on how Italians conceived of themselves as a nation.

While the observations about the Church's historical antagonism to a united peninsula are certainly true at one level, national identities are complex constructions, highly culture-specific, and follow no pre-established institutional or historical patterns. Coming closer to our own period, it is for this reason that despite the force of the comments by John Thomson, Agostino Giovagnoli is nevertheless able to refer to the DC (Christian Democrat) party in the post-war period as 'the national party' with some persuasive arguments, because, as he claims, the DC's 'roots are to be found in the all-pervading presence of the Church in Italian history: Christian Democrat culture is built on the historical interplay, over the centuries, between Church and state.'[5]

Italian unification

Although Catholics did not govern the country as an organized force until after the Second World War, there were a number of developments leading up to this which gave their entry into the political arena special significance. The Christian Democrat victory at the polls in April 1948, for instance, had the emotional charge of an act of salvation of civilization itself. Galli della Loggia attributes the weight and importance given to political ideologies in Italy to the exclusion of Catholics from the ideological foundations of the Italian state, because 'excluded from the state and from its legitimization, the religious element flowed in force into politics, and found on this terrain the place where it could forge its indestructible link with the people's fears and hopes'.[6] It is not by chance, he argues, that in the West Italy is the country where the two most powerful 'secular religions' of the twentieth century (Fascism and Communism) have been the most successful. Without wishing to follow della Loggia into all the negative conclusions he draws from his insights, one must agree with two points he makes: on the importance of the Church as a common historical point of reference for all the inhabitants of the peninsula, and on his assertion that ideologies, and the political parties promoting them, have had a more all-pervasive role at all levels of Italian life than has been the case in most other western nations.

Fascism and the development of political Catholicism

The experience of Fascism influenced the manner in which political Catholicism was reshaped, after the demise of Luigi Sturzo's PPI (Partito Popolare Italiano), founded in 1919, shortly before Mussolini came to power. Under Sturzo's leadership, the PPI was too anti-Fascist, too pluralist and too detached from the Church to survive the need for the fostering of good relations between Mussolini and the pope which were necessary for the signing of the Concordat in 1929. The next generation of Catholics developed their political perspectives in a completely changed environment and with little knowledge of the PPI, which folded in 1926, following the ban on opposition parties. Thus while Fascism was itself busy trying to 'nationalize' the masses into new forms of *italianità*, its need to gain ecclesiastical approval by granting the Church and its lay organizations a measure of manœuvrability, inevitably created opportunities for politically orientated Catholics to develop their own ideas.

A number of important developments within Italian political Catholicism resulted from the newly acquired status of the Church in Italian society, as Catholics began turning their attention to issues of national identity, a question brought to the fore under Fascism. The regime's drive for ideological hegemony provoked an almost competitive search for an alternative among those young Catholic intellectuals who derived their values primarily from their faith. It is at this point that for the first time, on the peninsula, Catholicism began to be linked to the question of nation-building on a significant scale.

216

From the latter part of the nineteenth century the Vatican had been in search of strategies which would enable the Church to regain positions of influence in society which it had largely lost with the demise of the European Catholic monarchies. With this collapse had vanished that component of the Thomist 'natural law' tradition which had defined the 'natural order' of society in terms of rigidly defined feudal social hierarchies. The Church needed to renew its doctrinal and institutional framework. The Concordat of 1929 offered it the possibility of experimenting with a number of strategic alternatives in seeking a Catholic restoration in a world threatened by a flood of secularization. In place of the defunct schema based on the Catholic monarchies, it promoted Catholic Action, under whose umbrella the various professional and social organizations of the laity could introduce Catholic values into all walks of life. This was a better model for influencing society in the modern world, more suited to the greater influence being exercised by a wider range of social groups. In 1931 Catholic Action was brought more firmly under the strategic and doctrinal control of the ecclesiastical hierarchy, to ensure that the laity would not stray off course.

The consequence of this was that the new generation of Catholic intellectuals and future political leaders were more 'ecclesiastical' in orientation than the PPI generation of *popolari*.[7] The idea began to take root that in place of the ideals being propagated by the regime, Catholics in public life ought to 'make Catholicism the religious and social soul of the nation'.[8] Alcide De Gasperi, who had become leader of the PPI shortly before its banishment, and would later be the first leader of the DC after the war, could see the way things were changing. But his colleagues in exile still linked the promotion of liberty at the institutional level to the emancipation of Catholic thinking from ecclesiastical authority. As Giovagnoli has pointed out, this was akin to mobilizing a few 'heretical' Catholics for the struggle for liberty, instead of involving the Catholic masses for promoting democracy.[9] De Gasperi, supported by Monsignor Giovanni Battista Montini (later to become Pope Paul VI), saw that the immediate need was to prepare Catholics to become future leaders of the nation, a role from which they had been excluded at unification.

But while on the one hand the Church was exerting greater control over the thinking of Catholic lay activists, with Pius XI (the pope who signed the Concordat) these future leaders were, on the other hand, released from the anti-state Catholicism which earlier generations had inherited from the *Non expedit*, the papal decree which had refused to recognise the legitimacy of the Italian state at unification. The Papal encyclical *Quadragesimo anno* (1931), sympathetic to the corporate state, stressed, for example, the need for the state to intervene in such matters as defining 'accurately what is licit and what is illicit for property owners in the use of their possessions'.[10] In this way the ground was being prepared for what in the post-war period would become a collateralist network of influential Catholic organizations, including a political party not afraid to wield state power.

In the encyclical *Divini Redemptoris* (1937), where Pius XI made a frontal attack on Communism, there was a section which was remarkable for the detailed manner in which it discussed how Catholic Action should be mobilized, with Catholic groups of 'workers, farmers, engineers, doctors, employers, scholars ... to form guilds and similar professional bodies ... seeking solutions to the questions of the day in the light of Catholic teaching, and in that of action, participating loyally and willingly in the new institutions'.[11] While the regime was pleased with the pope's attack on its enemy number one, it could not fail to be alarmed at the potential challenge to its own hegemony, which is why the terms of the Concordat of 1929 had excluded politics from Catholic Action's spheres of activity.[12] But such a veto had in many ways been counter-productive: it drew attention to the organization's potential to create a specifically Catholic response to national issues. The pope's message generated the idea of creating a new type of *civiltà cristiana*, which inspired the generation of young Catholic intellectuals who would join the post-war DC.

What added to the impetus of this new development was the recall to the providential role of Italy, and Rome in particular, with 'the "sacred city" being taken up by the Catholic press as a symbol of "Christian civilization"'.[13] Yet this never developed into a narrow Catholic nationalism. Given its history, Italy had never developed a 'national' Church, so that Italians looked for guidance directly to the Vatican, whose perspectives were by nature predominantly universalist. The spiritual power which historically had kept the peninsula politically and institutionally divided, and had opposed unification, was now encouraging the widespread civic and public engagement of Catholics in the nation's future development.

The position of the Church, now strong in Italy, was further strengthened during the Second World War. Diplomatic relations, kept open between the USA and the Vatican as an independent sovereign state, became particularly important, with the pope becoming Roosevelt's main interlocutor regarding the future of Italy after the war. These relations also helped to check the Vatican's anti-Communism, since the USSR was important in securing victory, and Italy could not afford to adopt a hostile posture towards one of the major victorious powers.

The Church in the immediate post-war period

Shortly before the end of the war, in January 1945, in a speech to the Roman nobility, the pope observed that the work of reconstruction which would follow would be greater and more demanding than ever before. It would require not simply the rebuilding of individual nations, because 'the whole world, we could say, must be rebuilt; the universal order is to be re-established. Material, intellectual, moral, social and international orders are all to be rebuilt . . .'.[14] This task would only be fully realized within the context of a *civiltà cristiana*, in the construction of which the Eternal City of Rome, and by extension Italy, had a special mission. A few weeks after the Liberation, in June 1945, Pius XII made this point in a speech to Catholic Action:

Rome is a unique city . . . unique above all because of its supernatural mission, which places it outside the temporal flux and above national divisions. Rome is the mother country of all Catholics scattered over the surface of the globe. We can thus understand why divine Providence has so miraculously protected her in the storm. But all this imposes on all of you the duty to preserve the Christian character of the Eternal City and, for this very reason, of your Italian fatherland.[15]

In January of the following year the Pope reminded the university section of Italian Catholic Action of the importance of working for the establishment of a *civiltà cristiana*.[16]

It is clear that the presence of Rome in the Italian state, the position of the Vatican as the centre of world Catholicism, with international diplomatic status, and its peculiar international perspective, were simply the latest of a set of historically determining factors having a profound influence on the way in which Italians could conceive of their national identity. We have seen that, given the special interest of the Vatican in the role of Italy, Italians were being encouraged to take a greater part in the construction of their nation, but with an eye to the *universal* application or significance of what they achieved.

It is for these reasons that the arguments of some commentators, that the universalist perspective of the Church was inherently in conflict with the creation of a sense of national identity, are flawed. What we see instead is Italy's population being encouraged to construct a national identity precisely around universalist values. For this reason, Remo Bodei is right when he argues that in the immediate post-war period, in Italy, 'relations of loyalty and of complete dedication to a cause no longer tend to be associated with the ideas of "nation" and "fatherland" as such'.[17] Emerging from twenty years of Fascism, this was not surprising. It was inevitable from this perspective, looked at through the optic of the kind of nationalism the regime had tried to impose, that there would be a strong appeal, especially among the new generation of politically active Italian Catholics, for a 'weak' form of national identity, an outward-looking rather than 'exclusive' one.

One of the paradoxes of Italian history emerged at this point. We have already noted the historical absence in the country of a 'national' Church. But it was precisely the emphasis on its universality which prevented the Church of Rome being too closely associated with Fascism and its nationalistic objectives. It did not have to suffer anything like de Gaulle's calls for the French Church's 'defascistization', nor did it suffer the loss of personnel and property as did the Church in Poland, where its national vocation had also been strong. The tensions between the pope and Mussolini which lasted throughout the 1930s, the role of the clergy in protecting sectors of the population from the ravages of the last two years of the war, the preservation of its organizational structure intact, and the Vatican's diplomatic standing with the USA and the other victorious powers, gave the Church the appearance of a rock of stability in a sea of uncertainty, and seemed to wipe out all memories of its less palatable early relations with Fascism. After the war it pressed hard the message of reconciliation, and national prelates, such as Cardinal Schuster of Milan, opposed the adoption of anti-

Fascism as the cornerstone of reconstruction and identity for the new Italy: 'We are too few and too poor to continue to tear each other to pieces at a time when civil harmony is more urgent than ever. What we need is national unity in the form of a single faith and with a single Italian flag.'[18]

The Christian Democrats and the Church

The return of the political parties with the CLN (Committees of National Liberation) was a major new phase in the country's development. Bodei observes:

> Given the intrinsic weakness of democratic traditions in Italy, and the fact that in this country the mass party developed under the aegis of Fascism (the National Fascist Party was the only 'modern' party which was directly experienced), in this new phase political parties represented the main support for collective identity.[19]

Although we may differ from Bodei in explaining its causes, there is no doubting the point he makes about Italians shaping their collective identities around the mass parties. But the existence of a single mass party for Catholics was not a foregone conclusion.

As De Gasperi was meeting old *popolari* and representatives of the new generation of Catholic activists in 1943 to give birth to the new Catholic party, there were a number of views in religious circles about the position the Church should take *vis-à-vis* a Catholic party. The Church's relationship with the PPI had not been harmonious, but the situation had changed considerably since then. Although they would not be its immediate leaders, the generation of Catholic activists entering the new party were mostly doing so as part of their Catholic apostolate, either directly or indirectly through links with Catholic Action. Aldo Moro, for example, was encouraged by his local bishop to enter politics. In this sense, the new party could be seen as an organic part of a collateral network of Catholic organizations committed to promoting the teachings of the Church.

Yet there were reservations in the Vatican about the prospect of a single party for Catholics. The secretary for Extraordinary Ecclesiastical Affairs at the Vatican, Domenico Tardini, favoured the laity joining many parties as a way of maximizing Catholic influence.

Roberto Ronca preferred the idea of a Catholic party of the right, with the Church as an explicit point of reference. Giovanni Battista Montini, however, convinced of the need for Catholics to mobilize around a single party of the centre, gave his support to De Gasperi's DC. Despite De Gasperi being from the generation of *popolari*, the new party he would lead had closer links than its predecessor with the Church, and was imbued with a greater sense of Catholic apostolate. When, therefore, the Church did decide in favour of throwing its support behind the DC, this effectively guaranteed it mass support for generations.

The PPI had never enjoyed such privileged support. As a mass party, the DC had its roots in the parish and in the collateral network of Catholic associations. By comparison with the old PPI, the DC had been 'confessionalized', but this, in the words of Giovagnoli, was simply 'a contingent form of a deeper and more long-standing compenetration between Church and society, ecclesiastical institutions and national identity'.[20]

The other advantage to be reaped from the support of the Church was in extending its appeal to a wide range of social groups, above all the urban middle class which had found Fascism reassuring. The Church had a moderating effect on the more militant tendencies of the party's left wing, and at the same time prevented the development of right-wing tendencies into a strong political force to rival the DC. The 'interclass' character of the DC was intended to make it a mass party appealing to all sectors of society, able to realize the objectives of Montini to place a Catholic leadership at the head of the country, and De Gasperi's objective of enabling Catholics, for the first time since unification, to participate in the political life of the country through a mass party.

De Gasperi's conception of a 'national' party

When De Gasperi attended the London peace negotiations in September 1945 as foreign minister in Parri's coalition government, he made what to historians and political commentators of the right seems a weak defence of national interests in connection with territories on Italy's eastern borders. Admittedly, in Catholic thinking national boundaries do not correspond to any particular set of absolute values. But the status of Italy at these talks also required

De Gasperi to employ a sense of realism. Despite the armistice of September 1943, many of the ministers attending the talks considered Italy a defeated nation. By contrast with the boundaries issue, he took a firm line on the question of self-government in relation to what had been imposed by the armistice. De Gasperi commented on the support received on this issue from the Socialists, and above all Togliatti and the Communists,[21] who were also considered to have been weak on the border issue, given their 'internationalist' perspective, the left's equivalent of Catholic 'universalism'. In terms of national self-determination, De Gasperi displayed considerable dignity in the face of the evident contempt of his interlocutors.

De Gasperi clearly did not see it as necessary to adopt a pugnacious international posture in order to promote national interests. From his own background in the Austrian Parliament before the First World War he had acquired a strong commitment to the principle of tolerance, in a pluriconfessional state, which in the Habsburg Empire had also had a multinational character. What De Gasperi wished to create, therefore, was a party with a strong European orientation, with Christian rather than narrowly Catholic roots, as a protection against any form of religious or nationalist bigotry. Although himself a devout Catholic wishing to promote his religious values in Italian society, he wished at the same time to break down the historical divide between the 'lay' and Catholic cultures which had been the source of such deep divisions in the country.

Once, therefore, it became clear that the DC had become the major party in the country with the Church's support, along with that of the USA, and of Italian commerce and industry, De Gasperi conceived of the party's role as that of remaining at the centre of the political system, but with the smaller 'lay' centre parties (Liberals, Social Democrats and Republicans) in coalition, even if this was not strictly necessary electorally. In this way, the country would have Catholics leading it, but in an open and tolerant manner. De Gasperi led the party until 1953, and succeeded in his aim of bringing Catholics back into political and public life on a mass scale. But in many ways, even from the very beginning of his leadership, the future role of the DC had already begun to be shaped by the 'second generation'.

The 'second generation' of the DC and Catholic collateralism

It was the 'second generation' of leaders who brought to fruition De Gasperi's ambition to make the DC the centre of gravity of Italian politics, but not in the way he imagined. They were helped by the closeness of prelates such as Montini and others in the Vatican to their cause. Montini wanted the Catholic laity to 'come out of the sacristy, to which it had been confined by the Fascists',[22] and take up the political leadership of the country. But it was, of course, the period spent in the sacristy which had changed Italian Catholicism. Montini could now see the prospects of a governing class, close to the institutional Church, but at the same time having popular roots and able to act as a unifying national force in a way that neither the Liberals nor the Fascists had been able to achieve.

The first high point of Catholic mobilization occurred after the elections to the Constituent Assembly in June 1946, in preparation for the drafting of the new republican constitution. Although the leadership of the party was in the hands of De Gasperi, his group, the ex-*popolari*, had little influence in shaping the objectives of organized Catholicism at the Constituent Assembly. Catholic input, at least on the first drafting subcommittee, which dealt with the principles on which the Republic was to be founded, was dominated by a small group of young Catholic intellectuals, including Aldo Moro and Giorgio La Pira, led by Giuseppe Dossetti. Amintore Fanfani, also a member of this group, served on the third subcommittee, which dealt with socio-economic matters. Although the *dossettiani,* as this group came to be known, were on the left of the DC, they had risen through the ranks of the Catholic associations, and could be trusted to put the Catholic case reliably. One great advantage they enjoyed was that their 'progressive' political views put them in a strong position to collaborate with and draw concessions from the Communists and Socialists.

The contribution of the *dossettiani* to the shaping of the Constitution should not, though, be seen as the virtuoso performances of a theologically literate Catholic élite. They should instead be placed within the context of the setting up of Catholic Action committees, such as Il Fronte della Famiglia and La Commissione per la Scuola, to give guidance to Catholic members of the

Constituent Assembly on such questions as the family, divorce, Catholic education in schools, the role of women in society, Church–state relations and freedom of religious expression.[23]

Two points should be made in connection with these developments. The first is that the enormous mobilization of Catholic associations at this point, together with the organized support of the Catholic press, was the first experience of civic engagement of Catholics attempting to shape the nation. The other point, which relates closely to this, was the frequent use of the argument by Catholics on the drafting subcommittees, that concessions had to be made on the issues mentioned earlier on the grounds that the vast majority of Italians were Catholics. This was an argument to which the Communists, in particular, were attentive, given their leader Togliatti's anxiety not to alienate the Catholic masses. But Togliatti had also understood that Catholicism had penetrated the fabric of Italian society well beyond the contingent question of whether particular individuals were practising their faith or not. From this flowed numerous Communist concessions in the debates, particularly the decision to vote in favour of including the 1929 Concordat, which had granted widespread privileges to the Church, as an article in the republican constitution.[24] As Togliatti was busy 'nationalizing' his own party, he was tacitly recognizing that Catholicism was an important component of the identity Italians would create for themselves in the future.

In the political arena Catholic collateralism was of enormous electoral advantage to the DC. In preparation for the 1948 elections, at a private audience with the pope, Luigi Gedda was given the task of mobilizing the Catholic world in support of the party.[25] Gedda used all the organizational and propaganda resources of Catholic Action to create 'civic committees' all over the country and construct an electoral machine far outstripping the mobilizing capacity of the DC itself. This activity was added to that of the ACLI (Catholic workers' association), the Coldiretti (peasant-owners' organization), FUCI (federation of Catholic university students), and other Catholic associations, all of which 'brought closer to politics . . . millions of women, above all in the south and the north-east of the country'.[26] By the early 1950s well over 3 million Italians could be counted in the ranks of this Catholic network of organizations. When we add fellow travellers, sympathizers and DC voters to these, we can see that the world of Catholic collateralism, with the DC as its point of reference, united millions of Italians across the country for the first time in history in the task of shaping the nation.

The notion of the 'organic' party

The second generation of DC leaders fitted into the Catholic collateralist world more easily than did the *popolari*, the elder statesmen of political Catholicism, whose influence had all but disappeared by the early 1950s. But there were important respects in which the new generation of Catholic leaders differed from De Gasperi and his generation.

We have already indicated the shift in Catholic thinking on the state which followed after the publication of Pius XI's encyclical *Quadragesimo anno* (1931). The *dossettiani* brought the new 'statism' with them into the debates at the Constituent Assembly. It was, in the words of Giovagnoli, 'a peculiar "statism", characterized by a strong social content, and singularly lacking in attention to the institutional framework'.[27] Fanfani used his influence in the third drafting subcommittee to ensure that the constitution provided for state intervention in the economy. The significance of this point becomes even more important when it is seen in connection with the *dossettiani*'s view of the role of political parties, which had much in common with that of the Communists and Socialists at the time.

On the first drafting subcommittee, the Socialist Lelio Basso argued that the role of political parties should be understood in the context of 'a clear process of transformation of our democratic institutions, in which *parliamentary democracy, which no longer responds to the current situation, has been replaced by the party democracy* already in being'.[28] In the view of Socialists and Communists, the old liberal parliamentary democracy was characterized by the representative function of élitist parties having no mass base, and thus incapable of securing any genuinely popular input into the polity. The *dossettiani* shared this view about the importance of mass parties. Basso's conception was given explicit support by the Catholic Giorgio La Pira, who argued that 'it corresponds to an organic view of the state and is also a conception belonging to Catholic doctrine'.[29]

But the younger generation of DC leaders tended to see the party more in terms of its collateralist links with the Catholic world, with a strong emphasis on its 'social' vocation, than had the *popolari*. From this perspective it derived its potential for spreading its influence into vast sectors of Italian society. It was an instrument for the creation of a *civiltà cristiana*, but also had available to it a state which was by no means conceived of as 'neutral' or 'secular'. At the Constituent Assembly, in arguing for the intrinsically religious nature of all human experience, and rejecting the very concept of a 'secular' state, La Pira argued that it was the task of Italians to 'construct a state which respected this intrinsically religious orientation of the individual and the community, and also made all its juridical and social structures conform to it'.[30] It was clear that Catholics were intended to have a major role in shaping the Republic, and that Catholic collateralist organizations were seen as supporting the process.

DC penetration of Italian society

It would be misleading to suggest that the perspective of the *dossettiani* amounted to a well-defined strategy for the 'Catholicization' of Italian society, although this existed among a small minority. Overall, the religious motivations of DC members and supporters were often combined with broader political aspirations and fears, particularly during the period of the Cold War, when supporting one side or the other of the ideological divide amounted to a strong statement of identity. For most DC supporters, whatever else it meant, the party was the only bulwark against the ever-present Communist threat to the western way of life.

What, from the mid-1950s onwards, became a visible omnipresence of the DC in Italian society had its roots in the second generation's conception of political parties. Broadly speaking, with the demise of De Gasperi, and the new leadership of Amintore Fanfani from 1954, the notion of DC 'centrality' to *the system of government* was shifted to one of DC 'centrality' to *Italian society*. Fanfani set about reorganizing the party to compete with the Communists, so that it should have branches and flanking organizations in as many areas as possible of Italian life. To many Catholics, the DC was a form of Catholic Action. And given the DC's position of permanence in government, and an ideology of state intervention without the constraints of a liberal culture of institutional correctness, the penetration of the state and of vast areas of civil society by the party was inevitable. It was the product of the 'party democracy' discussed at the Constituent Assembly, which subsequently developed into the *partitocrazia* of political analysts.

It is common to condemn the *partitocrazia*, to point to how it drew other parties into a system of spoils in which the DC was always the senior partner, in the end leading to further malfunctions, deformities and outright corruption which brought the political system to collapse. Whilst the Catholic party must indeed bear a great deal of responsibility for much of this, it would be a peculiarly Manichaean view of reality to identify this development with only the negative features of Italian post-war history. One important way in which DC developments can be seen to have entailed both benefits and disadvantages for the country was in its dealings with the south.

After the revolt of the peasants and land workers in the cycle of protest between 1944 and 1947, and a renewed wave of disturbances between 1949 and 1950 which spread from Sicily and Calabria to other parts of the Mezzogiorno, with Communists heavily involved in both, the government response in this area was amplified by a broader social response of the DC itself. A first step had already been taken by the DC with the creation of Coldiretti (a confederation of small farmers and peasant owners) in October 1944, a brilliant move which outflanked the Communists by gaining the support of the peasantry with the promise of cheap credit and various forms of assistance. This organization was to become almost a party within the DC, with a membership of 5 million by the early 1950s. It integrated itself into the southern public administration, and gained priceless electoral support for the party. Alongside the creation of Coldiretti, the government responded to the protests of 1949–50 with a series of legislative measures. The Sila Law was passed in May 1950 setting up a body which would control the expropriation and distribution of land in the region, and was followed in October by another law (*legge stralcio*) extending this provision to other parts of the south. The Cassa per il Mezzogiorno, a fund for creating an infrastructure in the south and extending industrial development, was created in August of the same year.

Although the reforms proved limited and inadequate, they brought about irreversible changes in the south. The centuries-old agrarian power bloc had been dismantled. A new system of social alliances was created, built around the DC and its control of the incipient network of private and public agencies. Apart from disgruntled elements of the old establishment who turned to the extreme right, most of southern society rushed to integrate itself into the new structures. The ownership of land was no longer the focal point of power. It was now the control of state resources. For most southerners, therefore, the DC was more than merely a political party. It was an agency for advancement, and provided a network of support for aid when in difficulty. The DC thus managed to establish ruling strata mediating between the state and society in all parts of the country. It gave its masses of members and supporters, stretching from the extreme north to the deepest south, a sense of belonging to a vast ideological and/or socio-political family group. While the Communists had also managed to achieve a good measure of national representation, they were not in control of national resources, nor did they have the foreign recognition which helped the DC make itself into what Giovagnoli has called 'the party of Italian society'.[31]

DC 'centrality' to the system

From the early 1960s the man who more than any other shaped the strategic thinking of the DC was Aldo Moro. He shared with Fanfani and other 'second-generation' leaders the conviction that the Catholic party was essential for the country. But he was more flexible and less integralist than Fanfani, who never ceased to believe that the DC could govern alone. Another quality Moro possessed was an ability to fashion a principled approach to DC 'centrality', while the party itself was becoming increasingly factionalized and focused on the retention of power for its own sake. These negative developments within the DC have often led its critics to attribute to Moro little more than a subtle capacity to meander through the increasingly murky dealings of a degenerating power machine. Frequently opposed within his own party, however, he would continue his ultimately forlorn attempt to theorize the strategic role of the DC in Italian society and attempt to guide its transformation until, with his death in 1978, it sank into its final stages of degeneration and decay.

Moro first emerged as a major strategist in the party with the beginning of the centre-left governments in the early 1960s. He stressed the importance of the political parties in Italian society, arguing that social forces could not, on their own, bring about reforms and achieve the necessary consensus for these to succeed. It was his conviction that, given its mission to give programmatic shape to a corpus of Catholic social teaching which was open to the historical process, the only party able to guarantee development with stability and harmony in Italian society was the DC.

The idea of DC 'centrality' was deep-rooted in the thinking of most members of the party. At the DC National Assembly in October–November 1965, the introductory document to the debates refers to the need to examine the party's capacity 'to be present in the country', and its manner of being present 'in its institutional fabric and in the state'.[32] The document goes on to stress that in a society in constant transformation the DC must ensure that its organization is such as to correspond to 'the new centres of social life which have arisen out of the present tendency to reshape the social fabric (the factory, urban conurbations, socio-economic districts, regions, etc..)',[33] and counteract tendencies towards 'forms of individualistic atomism and the resulting danger of an ever-diminishing presence of parties in Italian society'.[34]

But the 'party democracy' required the DC as its main component. In his concluding speech to the assembly, the party secretary, Mariano Rumor, reminded the delegates that the DC's *raison d'être* 'finds in our national character, in our capacity to represent and mobilize a vast variety of different social groups, its natural and essential fulfilment'.[35] As far back as 1919, even the Communist leader Antonio Gramsci had observed that the creation of the Catholic PPI was a major event in modern Italian history. He had seen the importance of bringing the Catholic masses into national life. Alluding to Gramsci's observation, Rumor gave it a twist of his own, adding that a weakened DC would spell not only political failure for Italian Catholics, but more importantly 'the end of both the experience and the regime itself of democracy in our country'.[36]

Such observations were not without a strong basis in the social and political reality of the country. As the historian Piero Craveri has observed, by this time the DC had become a party 'the social composition of which was, to a greater or lesser degree, representative of almost all the collective interests of Italian society, which it had learned to mediate through its enduring occupation of state power'.[37] Historians and political analysts may well point to the negative effects of such mediation, yet the fact remains that for many years the DC was the major national unifying force, the automatic point of reference not only for Italians but also for its foreign partners. Italy without the DC was inconceivable.

Attempting to retain 'centrality'

The very processes which had both spawned and fed on DC 'centrality', however, had sown the seeds of its eventual demise. Even as the party's embeddedness continued to grow, from the mid-1960s the development of the protest movements, the rapid secularization of Italian society, and the gradual loss of faith in the DC's ability and fitness to govern had slowly begun to undermine it. The DC continued to govern because of the practical impossibility of a Communist alternative, but this could not conceal the growing doubts of its supporters, or stop an increasing numbers of Catholics looking elsewhere, including to the PCI (Communists), for leadership.

The last phase of Moro's strategic thinking was connected with the period of 'national solidarity', when from 1976 the electoral strength of the Communists required their abstention in Parliament for the DC to be able to govern, and eventually their inclusion in the 'parliamentary majority' in 1978. At a speech to the party congress in June 1973 Moro reminded the party that it still had the task of 'producing within itself that dialectic which will be practised in the country' if it aspires to 'lead the masses to be a powerful yet orderly part of the life of the state'.[38] After the Catholic defeat at the divorce referendum in 1974, and following the Communists' leap forward at the regional elections in 1975, Moro observed that his party had not been as responsive to the needs and protests of the young, of women and of workers as had the left, the Communists in particular. He added that the future was no longer in the hands of the DC alone, and that if the party wished to survive as a major force in society, and not simply as a power machine, it had to face up to dialogue with the Communists. If the DC was to be renewed, he continued, 'I hope it does so liberated from the arrogance of power', since nobody in the party could now believe that the DC could avoid dialogue 'with the main force of opposition in relation to the political programme'.[39]

In his last speech to the party, in February 1978, shortly before his capture by the Red Brigades and subsequent assassination, Moro reiterated the need 'to preserve the soul, the shape, the ideological patrimony of Christian Democracy. What is important in this phase is to preserve at all costs the unity of Christian Democrats.'[40] At this point he was appealing to the party to accept his proposal to bring the Communists into the 'parliamentary majority' because 'up to now our flexibility has preserved more than our retention of power, it has saved Italian democracy'.[41] Even the inclusion of the Communists in the 'parliamentary majority' was intended to enable the DC to remain at the helm and lead the country's social forces to become 'an orderly part of the life of the state'.

The assassination of Moro, and the decision of the PCI the following year to bring an end to the government of 'national solidarity', amounted to the closing of an epoch. In hindsight it is easier to see that both Moro and the Communist leader Berlinguer shared the illusion that the political parties could continue to guide Italy's great ideological families indefinitely. The results of the referenda on divorce and abortion in 1974 and 1981 respectively, and the electoral results from June 1979 onwards, showed that the ideological blocs had been considerably eroded, were taking new, more flexible forms, and in some cases being challenged by new loyalties. The connection between the Italian Catholic hierarchy and the Catholic collateralist world had itself been loosened by the effects of the Second Vatican Council from the mid-1960s, so that the very notion of a political party for all Catholics came increasingly into question.

The end of the DC

For a few years after the election in 1978 of the Polish pope, John Paul II, the Vatican seemed to take a less active interest in Italian politics. Perhaps this was a signal to the Italian Church that it should cease to give explicit support to the DC. At a convention of the standing Conference of Italian Bishops (CEI) in Loreto in April 1985, this was the view put by two cardinals, the president of the conference, Anastasio Ballestrero of Turin, and Carlo Maria Martini of Milan. Their message that the Church should return with greater vigour to its evangelical role and that Catholics should make politically autonomous choices was echoed by the president of Catholic

Action, Alberto Monticone. Unexpectedly, the pope attended the convention and put an end to speculation, asserting that the political unity of all Italian Catholics had to be maintained at all costs.[42] In July, the pope replaced Ballestrero as president of the conference with his own man, Ugo Poletti, who was in turn replaced in 1991 by the energetic Cardinal Camillo Ruini, determined to revitalize an increasingly moribund DC as it approached its end.

The efforts of Ruini were in vain. They demonstrated, in effect, how out of touch the greater part of the Italian hierarchy was with developments in the country. The DC's mediating role between the state and Italian society which had, for decades, unified the country and given the party's supporters, and even those who opposed it, a sense of belonging to the same nation, had been transformed into something negative in the popular imagination. By the 1980s there was a widespread feeling among the population that the institutional fabric of the country had been grotesquely distorted by the parties of government, and that the long-overdue reform of the public administration was a forlorn hope. Judicial investigations had revealed that high-ranking members of the DC, along with politicians from other parties of government, were deeply implicated in the sinister workings of Licio Gelli's masonic lodge P2. Party members had been linked to corrupt financial deals, Mafia activity, intimidation of journalists and judges, to a point where the very career of politics had been brought to a high level of disrepute.

Members of the DC, such as Leoluca Orlando and Mario Segni, despairing, in their different ways, of their party's ability to change, started their own political movements which responded to new civic aspirations arising among Catholics and others. Segni campaigned, against the DC, for electoral reform, while Orlando created an anti-Mafia political movement, giving courage to the Sicilian population, at great personal risk to himself and in open hostility to members of his former party.

Further factors contributed to the end of the need for a party for all Catholics. In the first place, the collapse of the Berlin Wall and the dissolution of the Soviet world liberated Italians definitively from an ideological divide which was in any case becoming progressively weaker. The Catholic party was no longer needed to ward off a Communist threat. Catholics were by now as secure in their identity as Italians as they needed to be, and neither a strong ideology nor lifelong allegiance to a party cause seemed so important. From the mid-1980s, for example, many former DC supporters had been giving their votes to the Northern Leagues. It was no longer possible to recognize the DC as 'the Italian party'.

The 1992 Clean Hands trials, which shocked even the inured Italian public at the depth of corruption and collusion between politicians and the world of business and finance, eventually brought the DC to its knees, and despite the efforts of Ruini behind the scenes,[43] in January 1994 it ceased to exist, and a new party, taking the name of its predecessor, the PPI, arose out of its ashes, with smaller parties being formed to the left and to the right. The event was in effect the seal of approval for a Catholic diaspora which was already in train. The DC had served its purpose, and if Catholics wished to bring their religious perspectives to bear on their political and civic commitments, they were now free to do so in a greater spirit of pluralism than ever before.

Conclusion

Galli della Loggia has convincingly argued that for centuries Italian intellectuals, by contrast with intellectuals elsewhere, where national Churches were established, tended to create an élite culture in opposition to the Church, and out of touch with the religious sentiments of the populace.[44] This deficit, as we saw earlier, accounts for the appeal of the strong political ideologies on Italian soil since unification – Socialism, Fascism, political Catholicism and Communism – as a kind of sublimation of the popular religious spirit allowed to function at a national collective level elsewhere. Whatever the explanatory power of this part of his argument, Galli della Loggia is right to claim that

> the greater part of the production of political ideologies on the peninsula for the past century, along with the efforts and mobilization they have inspired, have been undertaken with the desire ... finally to bring the populace (*popolo*) into the life of the state, thereby wiping out the original blemish with which the latter came into being.[45]

What is more questionable is Galli della Loggia's negative characterization of the 'weak' national identity Italians have inherited from these ideologies.[46] His argument is not without merit if we take account of the deficit in both political Catholicism and Communism in terms of a culture of institutional correctness, a theme with which the sense of national identity is intimately linked in his writings. Although this is not the place to develop the argument, one can make the counter-observation in passing that the overwhelming concentration in post-war historiography on the country's institutional malfunctions has obscured the considerable achievements of the political movements inspired by the two major political cultures. To their credit, neither the DC nor the PCI used their considerable strengths in different parts of the country to exacerbate existing divisions at times when Italian democracy could have been threatened. On the contrary, both parties used their strong links with localities to further their own national vocations. As Remo Bodei has observed, the perspectives of the two parties differed considerably, yet ideological confrontation led 'millions of citizens (and this is the novelty) to accept political democracy as the territory where they can exchange, in a reasoned manner, deeply held and conflicting views'.[47]

To return, finally, to the universalist perspective of political Catholicism, we have seen that it is doubtful whether this has played the totally negative role which Galli della Loggia and others attribute to it. In the first place, despite the continued existence of a neo-Fascist party, the DC has had, in post-war Italy, an undervalued role in liberating the greater part of the Catholic population from the pressures of its previous twenty-year dose of chauvinistic nationalism.[48]

In foreign affairs, Italy has on the whole been a loyal and valued member of the western alliance. Galli della Loggia rightly sees DC universalism as influential in this domain, where Italy has occasionally displayed a tendency to break ranks with its allies, which, at least for most of the Republic's history, has almost uniformly been presented in a negative light. Italian conduct has been berated under various guises: as the result of an absence of foreign policy; as disloyalty to its allies; as self-seeking; as insufficiently intransigent towards its internal enemy; and as a pacifist-infected irresoluteness in the face of international aggressors. DC-dominated governments have certainly been presented as less coherent in their behaviour than other nations in the western alliance. But the value of coherence must be set against the particularities of the questions at issue. Whether or not further historical reflection will produce a different evaluation of Italy's occasional habit of dealing with powers outside its immediate cluster of allies in a manner disapproved of by the latter, remains to be seen. What is clear, however, is that Catholic universalism, over the centuries, has made deep inroads into the mentalities of the peninsula. Some may judge the ensuing 'weak' sense of national identity as a disadvantage. But it is also possible to view it in a more positive light, as a greater openness to, and flexibility towards, the international community. The possession of a 'strong' sense of national identity, where this is inward-looking, may not be the ideal prerequisite for coping with the phenomenon of globalization in course.

Note

1 E. Galli della Loggia, *L'identità italiana* (Bologna, Il Mulino, 1998), 44.
2 C. Falconi, *Storia dei Papi e del papato*, 4 vols. (Rome–Milan, CEI, 1967–72), III, 659.
3 Galli della Loggia, *L'identità italiana*, 123.
4 See J. A. F. Thomson, *Popes and Princes 1417–1517* (London, George Allen & Unwin, 1980), 48.
5 A. Giovagnoli, *La cultura democristiana. Tra Chiesa Cattolica e identità italiana 1918–1948* (Rome–Bari, Laterza, 1991), ix.
6 Galli della Loggia, *L'identità italiana*, 157.
7 See F. Traniello, *Da Gioberti a Moro. Percorsi di una cultura politica* (Milan, Angeli, 1990), 229ff.
8 Giovagnoli, *La cultura democristiana*, x.
9 See A. Giovagnoli, *Il partito italiano. La democrazia cristiana dal 1942 al 1994* (Rome–Bari, Laterza,1996), 36ff.
10 *The Christian Faith in the Doctrinal Documents of the Catholic Church*, edited by Jacques Dupuis, SJ (Bangalore, Theological Publications in India, 1996), 836.
11 *Atheistic Communism*. Encyclical letter of Pope Pius XI *Divini Redemptoris* (London, Catholic Truth Society, n.d.), paras. 72–3. See the whole section, paras. 64–86.
12 See Article 43, 'Patti Lateranensi', in F. Salvo, *Dalla Magna Charta alla costituzione italiana* (Palermo, Palumbo, 1968), 302–12 (311).
13 Giovagnoli, *La cultura democristiana*, 134.
14 *Discorsi e radiomessaggi di Sua Santità Pio XII,* 22 vols. (Vatican City, Tipografia Poliglotta Vaticana, 1955–69), VI, 273.
15 Ibid., VII, 87.
16 Ibid., VII, 333.
17 R. Bodei, *Il noi diviso. Ethos e idee dell'Italia repubblicana* (Turin, Einaudi, 1998), 20.

18 Cited in Giovagnoli, *La cultura democristiana*, 223.

19 Bodei, *Il noi diviso*, 21.

20 Giovagnoli, *La cultura democristiana*, xii.

21 See A. De Gasperi, *Il ritorno all pace. Discorsi 1944–1947 di politica estera*, edited by E. Scotto Lavino (Rome, Cinque Lune, 1977), 71.

22 Giovagnoli, *Il partito italiano*, 39.

23 For more detail on this see G. Bedani, 'The *dossettiani* and the concept of the secular state in the constitutional debates: 1946–7', *Modern Italy*, 1, 2 (Autumn 1996), 3–22.

24 For further discussion, see G. Bedani, 'Pluralism, integralism, and the framing of the republican constitution in Italy: the role of the Catholic left', in G. Bedani, Z. Barañski, A. L. Lepschy and B. Richardson, eds., *Sguardi sull'Italia. Miscellanea dedicata a Francesco Villari* (Leeds, Society for Italian Studies, 1997), 158–70.

25 See Gedda's own account of his meeting with the pope: L. Gedda, *18 aprile 1948. Memorie inedite dell'artefice della sconfitta del Fronte Popolare* (Milan, Mondadori, 1998), 115–29.

26 Bodei, *Il noi diviso*, 45.

27 Giovagnoli, *La cultura democristiana*, 208.

28 *La costituzione della Repubblica nei lavori preparatori della Assemblea Costituente*, 8 vols. (Rome, Camera dei Deputati, 1970–1), VI, 709. My italics.

29 Ibid.

30 Ibid., I, 323.

31 Giovagnoli, *La cultura democristiana*, xvii.

32 A. Damilano, *Atti e documenti della Democrazia Cristiana 1947–1967*, 2 vols. (Rome, Cinque Lune, 1968), II, 1984.

33 Ibid., 1987.

34 Ibid., 1991.

35 Ibid., 2012.

36 Ibid., 2012–13.

37 P. Craveri, *La Repubblica dal 1958 al 1992* (Turin, UTET, 1995), 109.

38 A. Moro, *Scritti e discorsi*, ed. G. Rossini, 6 vols. (Rome, Cinque Lune, 1982–90), V, 3088.

39 Ibid., VI, 3342 and 3362.

40 Ibid., 3781.

41 Ibid., 3790.

42 See S. Magister, 'La Chiesa e la fine del partito cattolico', in M. Caciagli and D. I. Kertzer, eds., *Politica in Italia. I fatti dell'anno e le interpretazioni. Edizione 96* (Bologna, Il Mulino 1996), 237–56 (239–40).

43 See ibid., 242ff.

44 See, in particular, Galli della Loggia, *L'identità italiana*, 121, 124 and 128.

[45] Ibid., 156.
[46] This argument is bolstered by Galli della Loggia's identification of these ideologies, particularly the Catholic and Communist, with their universalist and internationalist perspectives, and the low civic culture he sees as having been generated by both. See also his *La morte della patria* (Rome–Bari, Laterza, 1996).
[47] Bodei, *Il noi diviso,* 22.
[48] See, for example, excerpts from Moro's speeches on Fascism and anti-Fascism in the anthology edited by A. Ambrogetti: A. Moro, *La democrazia incompiuta* (Rome, Riuniti, 1999), 170–7.

10

The Italian Communists and Italian national identity: the question of difference

PATRICK McCARTHY

Introduction

The *Shorter Oxford Dictionary* defines identity as 'absolute sameness'. According to this definition national identity becomes what is shared by every Italian or by every Welshman and by no one else. This is, however, an example of the games that 'definitions' can play with words. A 'definition' is a linguistic characterization that is separate from the word it supposedly explains. In its attempt to embrace the word, a 'definition' can create fresh differences stemming from the explanation, but it can also be in conflict with the way in which the word is actually used. Indeed perfect 'Italianness' is not implied in the everyday use of 'Italian' within language. Identity is partial, leaving room for difference; indeed identity is frequently defined by using the notion of difference. When Seamus Heaney writes as an Irish poet in the tradition of Yeats, he tends towards lyrical monologues. His work is more dialogical when he is defining himself as a certain kind of Northern Irish poet.[1] What is quintessentially Welsh belongs in the category of which the young Wittgenstein said: 'Whereof one cannot speak, thereof one must be silent.'

There are many kinds of identity: cultural, political, geographical and psychological. Each category has several subcategories and also overlaps with other categories. Most categories, and hence identities, are invented. This does not in itself matter, but difficulties arise if the invention is designed to mask a troublesome reality, or if it is challenged by a different identity. When Mussolini came to power, he decided that the people in Süd Tirol-Alto Adige, the province Italy had taken from Austria at the end of the First World War, were

239

all Italians and descendants of the ancient Romans, whereas by language and custom they were German, and politically they wanted to remain Austrian. That their identity was invented by a non-democratic ruler rather than by their community was the defect rather than the invention itself.

A national identity is usually something of which one is proud, but this is not always the case, especially not with Italy. Interviewers discover that people are proud of Italy's past culture but ashamed of its present political system. They recognize themselves in this and it constitutes a negative form of national identity.

A person may, in the geographical or political domain (not that the two are the same), display an identity with her or his city, region, country and continent. Meanwhile Marx spoke of *Gattungswesen* or identification with the human species. This is an extreme version of the 'we-feeling' which is part of identities. There must also be a 'them-feeling' which should not, however, be allowed to become hostile, although that is its natural tendency.

A middle-class observer may be inclined to think that working-class people are miserable without strong, simple identities. But a south Wales steelworker may think of himself simultaneously as Welsh, Celtic and British. In the 'Welsh' category he may accentuate his southernness, feeling less in common with a north Walian. Conversely he may feel that a north Walian is more likely to be truly Welsh than he is. Such geographical-political identities may overlap with linguistic categories if he identifies with English-speakers or with Welsh-speakers or with the bilingual. So multiple identities are common and in most identities there is an element of choice.

Some identities will grow weaker and others stronger as lives and history change. National identity alters, as the nation and the world around it develop: until the 1960s Ireland saw itself as Celtic, Catholic, traditional and the only legitimate political community on its island; nearly three decades after entering the EC–EU Ireland sees itself as an economically advanced nation, it looks outward rather than inward and it is more tolerant of the North.

The relative importance of identities is complex. It is assumed that political are usually stronger than sporting identities. But the PCI (Communists) had many members in the province of Romagna who balanced their allegiance to the party against their identities as hunters and fishermen. It has been argued that in Italy the sporting nation has outlived the nation as it was traditionally defined: the victory in the 1982 World Cup unleashed an outburst of patriotism that was otherwise almost unknown in the decade.[2]

Communism posed problems of identity that were, and in the present post-communist period still are, special. An important part of national identity is political. To reverse this statement, one might affirm that, in order to participate in the national political system, a party must display an identity that does not contradict the national political culture. Normally a party makes choices: it emphasizes certain traits of that heritage and it neglects others, which may be taken up by the remaining parties. Communist parties, however, do not accept a vital part of the national and western culture; the national may be considered as a subcategory of the invented half-world or the West as the sum of certain, carefully selected nations. Either way there are elements of imagination and choice. The multi-party state and the alternation of parties in power are pieces of bourgeois artifice. Logically, communist parties should have been unable to gain support or to legitimize themselves: they were too different from the national political culture.

And so it has proved in Italy as elsewhere: the PCI was never able to come to power. Yet it was able to attract 34 per cent of the vote, to rule major cities and regions, such as Bologna and Emilia-Romagna, and to draw nearly 2 million members. How was it able to overcome the contradiction between its identity and the national identity? What does this teach us about Italian political identity which the PCI helped shape by its participation in the system? Clearly one must confront the theme of difference, which is not, here again, a vital obstacle to national identity.

Nationalizing Lenin

Firstly one realizes that scepticism about the value of ordinary democracy formed part of the Italian heritage. Segments of the weaker social groups believed or could be brought to believe that the multi-party state was an illusion which dominant social groups used to maintain themselves in power. Thus one trait of Italian identity was the belief that a fundamental part of this identity was false.

The PCI's birth shows the existence of the doubt that hung over the democratic political system. The dominant maximalist wing of

241

the Italian Socialist Party had welcomed the Bolshevik Revolution. The difference between those who left to found the PCI at the Livorno congress of 1921 and those who stayed is that the first group believed that the revolution was possible and even imminent, while the second had more doubts. But the two groups agreed on the shortcomings of the existing system, while Filippo Turati, who believed he could work within that system, was in a minority.[3]

After the Second World War, when the PCI had become a strong, influential party, it decided that the key figure in its early history had been Antonio Gramsci. While it is true that in the 1921-6 period the party opted for Gramsci and the Lyons congress line against its first leader the intransigent Amadeo Bordiga, from November 1926 on Gramsci was in prison where he was increasingly isolated from the party. Banned by Mussolini, the PCI regrouped at its foreign centre in Paris, but it was led from Moscow by Palmiro Togliatti who had to take account of Stalin's every ideological whim. Not merely was Gramsci isolated, but his views took no account of Stalin. He was a heretic who protested against the way Trotsky was treated and who ignored the class-against-class thesis that Stalin imposed, roughly from 1928 until 1932, according to which the Socialists were the prime enemy.[4]

Gramsci became a vital influence on the PCI because the party chose to make him one. Togliatti, who published Gramsci's writings, omitted or downplayed certain things: he did not publish some of Gramsci's letters to his family because they depicted quarrels, and Togliatti felt it was unbecoming for a Communist leader to quarrel with his father. The *Quaderni del carcere* (Prison Notebooks) were given greater importance than the simpler, more radical *Ordine nuovo* articles. Togliatti's softening of Gramsci is symptomatic, although readers must decide for themselves which is the 'real' Gramsci. But the prime question is why Togliatti chose to accord such importance to Gramsci.

The reasons lie in Gramsci's 'Italianness': he allowed Togliatti to give his party a national identity which it had not possessed before the Second World War and which was necessary if it was to participate in the political system of the new republic. This 'Italianness' took various forms. At the simplest level Gramsci was an Italian who had had the courage to oppose Fascism and who had paid for his opposition with a long prison sentence. There were foreign Communist heroes and martyrs, who ranged from Lenin to Rosa

Luxemburg; now there was to be an Italian too. The second reason was that Gramsci's writings took special account of Italy: he understood that the rural, Catholic regions posed for a revolutionary party problems that were not to be solved with orthodox clichés about the opium of the masses. Still more important: Gramsci was recognizably influenced by the neo-Hegelian, idealistic current of Italian thought. This appealed to young, lay Italian intellectuals, a group that Togliatti wished to attract because it was able to legitimize the PCI as the inheritor of Benedetto Croce. Togliatti wished to praise but also to bury Croce, and to set Gramsci in his place. Finally Gramsci was explicit about the need for an Italian brand of socialism in the stress he placed on the concept of the 'national-popular'.

In these various ways Gramsci was to strengthen the Italian identity of the PCI even as Togliatti simultaneously insisted on its 'Russian' identity. This meant not only adopting the notion of the one-party state but also the model of the October Revolution, the cult of Stalin and the whole myth of the Soviet Union. As already argued, various segments of this story were not un-Italian but the identification with the leading nation defined by the Cold War as the enemy brought calls for the PCI to be banned and made it impossible for the party to come to power.

Gramsci's role was to counterbalance the 'Russianness' by nationalizing Lenin and mapping out an Italian road to socialism. Hence the importance attributed to the *Prison Notebooks*, which provided a subtle analysis of the specifically Italian malady of Fascism. The two components, national and international, were complementary. The more the PCI insisted on the cult of Stalin to attract the social groups that had been left outside the Risorgimento (unification) state, the more it insisted on Gramsci as an Italian leader to appeal to social groups that had not been left out and to the far larger groups that the PCI was bringing into the republican system.

The contrast between Gramsci and Lenin, if contrast there be, was not officially acknowledged, and Gramsci was perceived as having adapted Marxism-Leninism to a western country. His theme that civil society was stronger in Italy than in the USSR and hence that there could be no Italian storming of the Winter Palace until the struggle for hegemony was completed was, however, allowed to stand as the Italian road to socialism. Implicitly there was a contrast and Gramsci offered a way to nationalize Lenin.

So the PCI acquired a strong Italian identity and set off on a thirty-year period of growth. Other communist parties throughout the West tried to root themselves in the soil of the country they were in. Why was the Italian party so successful when the north European and even the French parties were not? One answer has already been given: the strength of the doubt about parliamentary democracy in the country at large. The British Communist Party had to compete with a Labour Party that had established a strong presence in Parliament and would come to power with a huge majority after the Second World War. To discard the gains offered by the parliamentary system and gamble on a revolution because there had been one in remote Russia seemed absurd. But this argument may be extended: the notion of a British Gramsci was equally absurd. Britain produced hard-headed trade unionists like Ernie Bevin, most of whom were anti-communist. It was more difficult for the British Communist Party to nationalize itself.

The French Communist Party (Parti Communiste Français, PCF) resorted to the creation of the counter-community. In its strongholds like the Paris red belt, the ring of working-class suburbs around Paris which grew in the inter-war period and where the PCF was dominant after 1945, the party set up a state for the stateless, a community (a *Gemeinschaft*, not a *Gesellschaft*) for those left out by the national community.[5] The party organization filled the vacuum left by the civil service, found jobs for unemployed youths, organized social gatherings, including Saturday night dances where Communists could feel sure that their teenage children would meet, and hence marry, only the children of other Communists, and sent out patrols of militants on a Sunday morning to sell *L'Humanité*, often the party member's only trusted source of information.

It seemed a foreign world where Marxism was taught in evening schools, Stalin was venerated as no French non-communist leader was and the party, centralized but omnipresent, was the source of all legitimacy. If one looked closely, however, this community was an exaggerated form of the French national community. The centralization reflected the Jacobin heritage, the simplified version of Marxism replaced the Catholic catechism or the ultra-logical version of Descartes taught in the state elementary schools, while Stalin, father of the workers, answered the need for authority which permeates French society. The counter-community was a kind of super-France and the Communists were the best Frenchmen. The numbers of them who were killed in the anti-Nazi Resistance was another proof of that.

The counter-community too may be seen as an attempt to nation-alize Lenin, but it was vulnerable. Once television invaded working-class homes *L'Humanité* lost its monopoly on information. Increasing prosperity made the workers more like other French citi-zens. But the PCF, content with its compromise, remained, to borrow the much-used phrase, *un parti qui n'est pas comme les autres* or, as de Gaulle used to call it, *le parti de l'étranger*. By contrast the PCI distrusted the notion of the counter-community, which had allowed the PCF to remain too 'Russian', and it sought to enter the mainstream of Italian life.

Nor did the French Communists inherit as strong a doubt about the democratic structures of government as their Italian comrades. When they allowed themselves to be isolated from French parlia-mentary culture, as when they broke up the Union of the Left in 1977, they were severely punished by the voters. In 1981 they lost 25 per cent of their electorate and in 1984 they lost a further 25 per cent.

The argument about doubt may be extended further. How much do Italians believe in the discourse of a wholly different system? In the 1990s Fausto Bertinotti, the head of Rifondazione Comunista (RC, Communist Refoundation), which was founded in 1991 by the PCI minority that wished to remain a communist party, maintains that his party's role is to incarnate this possibility, which has always existed within the Italian left. Do the voters believe him? RC has fared well since it broke away from the PCI majority. In the 1992 elections, three years after the collapse of world communism, RC gained 5.6 per cent of the vote, while in 1996 it rose to 8.6 per cent.

Yet few Italians believe in some future proletarian revolution. One can only conclude that they vote for Bertinotti's band as a protest. While they may have specific grievances, they are also protesting, as Bertinotti affirms, against what is. In the 1999 congress of RC, Bertinotti quoted from Che Guevara in Kurdish (a tribute to Ocalan), and the delegates sang the 'International' with clenched fists. A huge poster on the wall called for 'an alternative society' and several dele-gates expressed their satisfaction at no longer being in the government. 'We are back where we belong', said one enthusiast; 'the word revolution is no longer taboo.'[6] Of course, it was easier to believe in the proletarian revolution in the 1940s than it is in the 1990s. But we are suggesting that for much of the time many Italians considered that the PCI's discourse of a wholly different society was only true in that it considered what was to be unacceptable.

Togliatti's decision to soften Gramsci's thought takes on fresh significance. By stressing the Crocean elements in Gramsci, Togliatti was implying, without of course stating, that the PCI's Italianness made it less of a revolutionary party. He was inviting the electorate to consider the party's performance in Parliament and in local or regional government. Not that the PCI was a 'reformist' party, if one may use that term of Third International contempt. The construction of Emilia-Romagna entailed a mixture of Communist idealism and social-democratic practice.[7] But although it was designed to demonstrate that what existed at national level need not exist, it also showed the PCI leading a daily struggle against poverty that meant collaborating with other parties and other social groups far removed from the industrial working class.

So the PCI renationalized itself as a part of Italian reality. It reflected and fostered a strand in national culture that was deeply pessimistic about the unification and the state it had produced, but believed in the capacity of the family, the local community and 'the people' to work together. Gramsci's populism was in the mainstream of Italian thought.

The PCI established itself in Italy because it meshed with important elements of the national identity: with the willingness, born of scepticism, to believe in revolutionary movements and with the faith in the capacity of the people for work. Both traits may be contradicted by other strands in national identity: populism's foe is the pessimistic current in Italian Catholicism that believes in sin but not in redemption. Conversely these traits are entwined with others: the scepticism about the state is one aspect of the universal, disintegrating suspicion depicted by Lampedusa in *Il Gattopardo* (The Leopard). Shaped by key strands in Italian identity, the PCI then developed and reinforced them.

To demonstrate the influence of the Communists on national identity, one might glance at three historical moments: the early post-war years when Togliatti set the policy of the 'new' party; the historic compromise of Enrico Berlinguer; and the post-communism of the 1990s, including the D'Alema government. At each period the PCI and its successor parties have displayed variations on the same themes.

Togliatti's duplicity

When Togliatti returned from the USSR in 1944, he decided that the PCI should remain a 'Russian' party, an integral part of the Soviet-led world communist movement, and that it should also become a mass party that could compete in the democratic Italian political system. The verb 'decided' is, of course, too simple: Togliatti had to take account of the revolutionary aspirations of many northern farm and factory workers who were the PCI's natural constituency. The PCI did not invent the cult of Stalin: the first communist orga-nizers to arrive in northern Italy in 1943 found that the cult was already alive, born of the battle of Stalingrad and of popular scepti-cism about Mussolini's war propaganda. It was an Italian myth, just as the 'Russian' party was an Italian anti-system party.

Similarly it was part of Soviet foreign policy that the PCI should respect the Yalta agreement and, since it was located in the western zone, should not launch a revolutionary insurrection. Togliatti's Salerno speech (1944) announcing the new mass communist party had nothing heretical about it.

But Soviet foreign policy changed at the outbreak of the Cold War and, while Stalin never pushed the PCI towards insurrection, he would have liked the party to be tougher in its opposition to Marshall Aid and the integration of Italy in what the USSR had come to consider an aggressive, capitalist bloc. 'Tougher' meant strikes, demonstrations and blurring the line between legality and illegality. But Togliatti opposed this, fearing that his party might be banned, or that it would be unable to follow the constitutional path he had mapped out for it.[8]

The contradiction between what one might with misleading simplicity call the 'Russian' and the 'Italian' identities of the party was apparent, and it gave rise to the concept of *doppiezza*. This is best understood not as a moral or psychological term, a condemna-tion of Togliatti's duplicity, but as a way of describing the PCI's two identities. Togliatti had not heeded his own collaborators, who had led the partisans in northern and central Italy and who wanted to bring to Rome the 'northern wind', the new social thinking of the Resistance, which consisted of measures like the *consigli di fabbrica* or works councils, that gave the workers some say in management decisions. Togliatti attached a secondary importance to reforms. He declined to press for a currency exchange which would have made it possible to tax war profits. He backed a generous amnesty that allowed Fascists who had committed serious crimes to go unpunished.

Most of all, Togliatti wanted to prevent the partisans from turning the national struggle against the Nazis into a revolutionary insurrection. Many of them sorely wanted to do this, and they convinced themselves, as many anti-communists did, that Togliatti's duplicity lay in following a parliamentary line to lull his opponents into a false security. Then, at some mythical zero hour the buried guns would be brought out again, the parliamentary strategy would be revealed as a subterfuge and the PCI would become once more a revolutionary party.

The reverse, however, was true. The new PCI intended to work within the guidelines laid down by the new constitution, even as it masqueraded as a revolutionary party. Therein lay the true relationship between its two identities. Why then was Togliatti so uninterested in reforms? Is not a non-revolutionary left-wing party doomed to reformism? The matter was not so simple. The role of the new PCI was to defend the immediate interests of the working class, while waiting for the zero hour to arrive.

This had two effects on Italian political culture and hence on national identity. Firstly it reinforced the belief that reforms were rare and difficult and thus contributed to the lack of reformist parties. Secondly it taught the lesson that things were not what they seemed, that reality was difficult to grasp and that powerful forces lurked behind seemingly ordinary phenomena. The science of uncovering such forces was called *dietrologia*.

The PCI did not invent either of these beliefs. The lack of reformism in Italy, represented in the post-war period by the dismal failure of the PSDI (Partito Social Democratico Italiano), was counterpoint to the doubt about democracy. In pre-Fascist Italy it was symbolized by the failed co-operation between Filippo Turati and the perennial prime minister, Giovani Giolitti. This inability to shape Italian society triggered the second belief that reality resisted the best efforts of ordinary mortals but could be manipulated by more or less mysterious beings like the CIA or unidentified *Grandi Vecchi* or Grand Old Men (whose gender and age also tell us much about Italy).

The PCI contributed, then, to convincing Italians that they lived in a world that they could not control. This view has implications for foreign policy since other, more powerful nations can control the world and it is important to be on good terms with them. The USA is the supreme example but 'Europe' is another and hence the threat of exclusion from the EU's monetary union was a grave matter. Some countries react to their perceived weakness with defiance – this was historically true of Ireland – but Italy reacts with (calculated?) displays of good will. Until 1991 the USSR was another country that could control its and others' destinies and, as the Soviet representative in Italy, the PCI shared in its mysterious power. To most Italians this power was evil; hence the image of the double-dealing Togliatti, who overcame ordinary politicians by intrigue and deception, was an integral part of anti-communist propaganda.

In fact the reverse was true. Togliatti's achievement was considerable: he created the most powerful communist party in the western world and he also brought large segments of the peasantry and the factory workers into the democratic republic. But, despite the sound and the fury of the 1948 elections, the PCI never really challenged the Catholic domination of post-war politics.[9] Moreover Togliatti's policy of co-operating with the Catholics was a failure. In 1947 the PCI voted in favour of incorporating into the new constitution the Lateran Pacts. The Vatican noted the action, offered no thanks and, since it no longer needed the Communists, backed their expulsion from the government shortly afterwards.

The Vatican was a formidable foe. Pius XII knew exactly what he wanted: an Italy where the Church wielded via 'its' DC more power than ever before and where Communist influence was reduced to a minimum. The Church had gained prestige as the only organization to remain independent of Fascism. It possessed via its parishes a grassroots organization that the PCI might have envied, and it had competent spokesmen like Cardinal Montini, the future Pope Paul VI, and the underrated Cardinal Tardini. To very many Italians the Church was, after Mussolini's overthrow, the only source of legitimacy that remained. The Church's strength goes a long way towards explaining its very considerable role in shaping post-war Italy. But Togliatti contributed by sacrificing reforms for fear of alienating the Catholics.

Why did he give priority to working with them? The reason lies in the PCI's role as a maximalist party in the Italian tradition. Since it declared itself to be opposed to the political system, and since it simultaneously wanted to be inside the system, the PCI was in perennial need of legitimacy. Only the Catholics could offer this legitimacy. Put the other way around, only the Catholics could enable the PCI to remain an atheistic, Soviet-style party and to stay within the system.

In his pursuit of legitimacy, Togliatti rendered the Catholics great services. The PCI could not oust the DC from power, but it could and did prevent any other party from doing so. Similarities between the PCI and the Church abound: a hierarchical structure of organization, a 'total' world-view, a tenacious dislike of consumer capitalism; and the list is much longer. Communism cohabits with Catholicism better than with Protestantism. Small wonder that it should flourish in the homeland of the Vatican. One might argue that the two have collaborated to fix certain traits of Italian identity: both argue that reality is difficult to comprehend, whether because man's judgement is clouded with sin or because reality is shaped by the well-hidden force of class conflict. It is true that reality becomes intelligible when grace and revolution come into play, but Italians are less ready to accept this, perhaps believing that sin is unforgivable and class conflict impossible to resolve. In the meantime, however, both may be mitigated by human tolerance and willingness to live and work together.

But this kinship does not mean that Catholics were likely to embrace Togliatti's PCI. The subtle rivalries matter less than the open clash between religion and atheism, or than the persecution of Catholics undertaken by the Red Army. The Catholic Church was indeed capable of helping the PCI to nationalize Lenin, but it was not likely do so. The PCI reinforced the existing balance of power in Italy. At least in this context it was not a force for change.

Enrico Berlinguer and the end of the PCI

Berlinguer's name is associated with the project of the historic compromise and with the governments of national solidarity in 1976–9 which were its imperfect manifestation. In the context of this article, however, Berlinguer's project may be seen as another effort to nationalize Lenin by using the Catholic Church to legitimize a 'Russian' party. It was a more complete attempt than Togliatti's because it addressed the central problem of Italian politics, namely the historic weakness of the state. When Berlinguer's project failed, he drew one of the correct conclusions and cut the umbilical tie with the USSR. Yet he did not give up the notion that the PCI was a party which operated outside the existing system. When Berlinguer died in 1984, the PCI's existence reached its end, although it lingered, ghostlike, until 1989.

When he launched the historic compromise, Berlinguer invoked the fate of the Allende government to demonstrate that the left could not rule with a bare majority of 51 per cent of the electorate. But Chile was politically as well as geographically distant from Italy, and while Allende provided a dramatic example of a failed left-wing experiment, Berlinguer's thinking was thoroughly Italian. Like Gramsci a Sardinian, Berlinguer was precisely the kind of lay, upper-class young man whom Togliatti recruited into his party at the Liberation. When he became the leader of the PCI in 1972, Berlinguer's thinking was permeated by Togliatti's. Indeed this provides an example of that concern for continuity, which is a feature of communist culture.

It is also typical of Italian political, although not economic, culture and a case where the PCI did not invent but reinforced a trait that is of dubious value. In one important respect, however, Berlinguer was very different from Togliatti: he could not convincingly be accused of duplicity. Rather he was the model of a political leader who acted out his beliefs, and he was contrasted not only with Togliatti but with the endlessly compromising DC leaders. In part Berlinguer was the exception who proved the rule (obvious to Italians) that princes and politicians are secretive, unreliable and devoid of any solid core of character, except for the desire to do harm to their subjects. If one strays outside the political realm, this judgement is considered by Italians valid for all men of power.

In another sense not merely Berlinguer but many PCI members were exceptions. Its exclusion from the spoils of power, its record in local government and the asceticism that supposedly characterized the Communist militant set the PCI apart from the other parties. This ethic, which was and is summed up in the phrase *il rigore del vecchio PCI*, belonged to what we call the discourse of the Italian people rather than of the Italian state. It was particularly strong in the red regions of central Italy like Emilia-Romagna and its capital, Bologna (where it has now been replaced by the discourse of decline). It was well, although not perfectly, suited to the 1970s: the decade of the oil crisis, of labour unrest and of social movements.

Under Berlinguer's leadership the PCI spoke of women's right to divorce and abortion, of the need to govern Italy's big cities honestly and efficiently, and to fight inflation with austerity rather than with cuts in employment. This was reformism by another name and it worked. The PCI entered on a period of startling, and dangerous, success. In 1974 a referendum was held on the issue of whether to scrap the 1970 divorce law: rather to Berlinguer's surprise as many as 59 per cent of the electorate voted, as the PCI had advocated, to keep the divorce law. The next year the PCI won every major Italian city in the local elections.[10]

It was obvious from the nature of the consultations that people were not voting for or against socialism. Were they voting for the historic compromise? In the absence of polling data, one can do no more than hazard a guess. Since Berlinguer's project received vast publicity, the electorate could hardly have ignored it. Yet voters wanted to punish the DC for its corruption, which was less tolerable at a time of economic crisis. One might conclude that they wanted to place restraints on the maximalist culture of the PCI and that joint PCI–DC rule was one, unwelcome way to achieve that. A more welcome way would have been for the PCI to become a reformist party, and Berlinguer seemed to understand that the central issue was the need to reform the Italian state, which would remove the reason for the existence of maximalist parties and for the immobile, mediating DC. Italian political culture and with it national identity would be relaunched.

Two dangers threatened the state: economic chaos and left-wing terrorism, perhaps manipulated by segments of the state and/or foreign secret services. To meet the first Berlinguer won the help of the Confederazione Generale Italiana del Lavoro (Italian General Confederation of Labour, CGIL). In 1978 its Communist leader, Luciano Lama, agreed to a programme of wage restraint in exchange for investment that would limit unemployment. In the second case Berlinguer hurled the PCI's grassroots organization into a campaign to isolate the Brigate Rosse (Red Brigades, BR) in the factories and in the big cities. Both initiatives had some success, for which the PCI received scant credit. Jobless young Italians could see no value in economic austerity which did not produce enough or the right kind of investment to help them. The Movement of 1977 took to the streets in Rome and in Bologna chanting anti-PCI slogans. Meanwhile the Communist base could not understand how one could combat terrorism without combating the DC, which had created conditions where terrorism could flourish.

The Church and the DC acted as they had done when Togliatti supported the proposal to write the Lateran Pacts into the post-war constitution. They deigned to accept PCI aid, waited for the Communists to make themselves unpopular and then allowed the governments of national solidarity to break up in 1979. Why had Berlinguer been willing to pay such a high price for Catholic support or tolerance? The answer is that, like Togliatti, he wanted the PCI to remain a maximalist party. Had he been willing to turn the PCI into a social-democratic party, he could have dispensed with legitimization by the Catholics. On this second occasion, however, more was at stake. Togliatti was the leader of a new kind of communist party that needed time to grow; Berlinguer's party was mature, its Fordist underpinnings were growing rusty, and it needed to come to power. For the PCI this was an opportunity to change itself and Italy.

Berlinguer did not, however, want a reformist, social-democratic PCI. Never closely identified with the Soviets, he had taken his distance from them in the run-up to, and during, the national solidarity years.[11] But he clung to the notion of an alternative to capitalism. To him austerity was not a device to preserve employment, or a chip to be bargained away in return for the legitimization of the PCI. It was an ethical and economic alternative to consumer capitalism and the starting-point of a different kind of society that was less egotistic and more caring. The hard core of Italian Communism was an ethical choice to sacrifice one's own self-interest in order to promote such a society. Berlinguer incarnated this belief, and the PCI base rewarded him with an affection that has proved embarrassing to his successors, up to and including D'Alema.

This was the aspect of Berlinguer that also attracted to his funeral in 1984 large numbers of people who had never voted for his party but who wished he had found a better political form for his ethical vision.[12] His failure to do so had profound effects on his party and on Italy. For Italy it meant there would be no great renewal of national identity, born out of the battle with OPEC. Although the need for a more positive identity remained, the possibility vanished with the (self?)-isolation of the PCI after 1979 and with the emergence of Bettino Craxi's PSI (Partito Socialista Italiano, Italian Socialist Party) as a reinforcement for DC mediation and immobility. One can hardly imagine a figure more precisely opposed to Berlinguer than the egotistical, power-hungry, wheeler-dealing Craxi. We argued at the outset that national identity is not fixed eternally but involves flexibility and choice. This was an occasion when a different choice might have been made.

Berlinguer's break with the USSR over the imposition of military rule in Poland put an end to the 'Russian' version of maximalism, but not to maximalism itself. His critique of consumer capitalism provides another overlap with Catholicism. Both Berlinguer and Pope John Paul II were waging a losing battle, but the Church remained stronger than the party.

Massimo D'Alema and the normalization of the ex-PCI

The luckless Alessandro Natta took over from Berlinguer and led the party to defeats in the 1984–5 battle over wage indexation and in the 1987 elections, where the Communists' share of the vote went down to 26.6 per cent. He was replaced as secretary by the younger Achille Occhetto, who had a promising first year but then ran, figuratively, into the Berlin Wall. Occhetto had already been thinking of giving up the PCI's communist identity and autumn 1989 provided new reasons. The task proved, however, to be herculean and it was not until the Rimini congress of 1991 that the Partito Democratico della Sinistra, PDS, emerged alongside Rifondazione Comunista (Communist Refoundation).

There were four directions the PDS might have taken, some of which overlapped. It could have collapsed as the French Communists did. The follow-up question would have been what the limit was below which it could not be pushed: in France it seems to be around 8–10 per cent. But the PCI was too deeply rooted in Italian soil to wither away. The second option for the PDS was to follow its vocation as an anti-system party and become a force of permanent opposition, which was the choice made by RC, with which the PDS would have to compete. It would mean opposing Fiat, the US and the Church, and championing the environment, immigrants and the Third World. There was a tendency to play this role during Occhetto's leadership, although, like Togliatti and Berlinguer, he had his own Catholic–Communist collaborators: the PCI's habit of trying to work with the Catholics died hard. The third and seemingly the most plausible choice was to become a social-democratic party. But having spent decades resisting the near-truth that it was already a social-democratic party, the PCI felt that this was an inglorious reward for a long, painful transition. The party right, led by Giorgio Napolitano, was happy to become social-democrat but the rest of the Communists were not.

The fourth option, which overlapped with the second, was to accept the PCI past and become an ex-communist party. This could not be avoided or avowed. The influence of the 'no' group during the transition demonstrated that the mourning for the death of the PCI was greater than the collapse of world communism might lead us to believe. The PCI had, for better or worse, succeeded in Italianizing itself: it was convinced the world was full of plots and enemies, it was slow-moving, it executed reforms but was not a reformist party, it was subservient to the Church and it was very local. Even the maximalism, which constituted the difference between the ex-Communists and other political groups turned out to be important. Pietro Ingrao, the well-liked champion of the PCI left, called for a communist horizon, situated in the alternative society, which would provide a viewpoint from which to judge the existing society.

Occhetto tried to do away with the notion of totality: 'there is no final moment in history when conflict ceases for ever because the left comes to power.' He insisted on the need for limits and on seeing oneself as a part of a greater process rather than as the process itself. Yet Occhetto also claimed that the PDS would attempt to offer 'a unified vision of human liberation'.[13]

The need to mourn the PCI was, however, a minority need, as the PDS's poor election result in 1992 demonstrated: 16.1 per cent, 10.5 per cent fewer than the moribund PCI won in 1987. Italy was entering on another potential period of change: the Clean Hands investigation had begun to expose the corruption of DC–PSI rule, the state's dealings with the Mafia took a new and violent turn as the militaristic Corleonesi killed two magistrates who were investigating them, and Italy's European policy received a harsh blow when the lira was forced out of the EMS. In 1992 a period of uncertainty and reforms began and the chance to create a new political system and new rules for the economy, thus changing the national identity, was clear. The DC and the PSI were swept aside, whereas the PCI–PDS, which had only marginally been a part of the spoils

255

system and which could flaunt the name of Enrico Berlinguer, was the only major party to come through the Clean Hands investigation virtually unscathed. Here was its chance to reshape itself and the nation. The task, however, would not be easy: it would entail a radical break with the PCI's past.

Alas, the PDS initially failed to become an instrument of change. Italy needed a party with some sense of the national past and a robust vision of the national future. The PDS failed the second part of the test.[14]

Between 1992 and 1994 Occhetto tried to make up for the time lost and the errors made. In 1993 there were a series of mayoral elections (direct election of mayors was an innovation and a part of the process of change) where the PDS and its allies won Naples, Rome, Trieste, Genoa, Turin and other cities. But this triggered the entry into politics of Silvio Berlusconi, whose Forza Italia ('Let's Go Italy', which is the chant of support for the national soccer team), allied with the ex-Fascists of Alleanza Nazionale (National Alliance) and, implausibly, with the separatist Northern League, easily defeated the left-wing coalition formed around the PDS in the 1994 elections.

Berlusconi offered the electorate a brilliant version of that familiar Italian figure, the entrepreneur: he would be their guide to the future. The PDS-led coalition had an implausibility of its own: the party did not clarify what its relations with the non-PDS mayors and with its coalition partners were. It was not even clear who would have become prime minister if it had won the elections. Occhetto had to resign as party secretary, and in the race to succeed him Walter Veltroni, the candidate most open to the world outside the PDS, was defeated by Massimo D'Alema who had the backing of the party organization.

The difficulty of finding a new identity revealed yet again the success the PCI had had in nationalizing Lenin, but that was scant consolation for the trouble of finding one's way around a post-Cold War world where there was no longer a Lenin.[15] The PDS played a minor role in bringing down the Berlusconi government and then allowed the initiative to slip into the hands of Romano Prodi, who became prime minister in 1996. A Catholic and a university professor, Prodi reassured the electorate while offering Europe and entry to the EU's monetary union as Italy's future. The price was a tough, deflationary programme but in Italy the prestige of Europe is high and people have been willing, throughout the post-war period, to make, in the name of Europe, sacrifices they would not make in the name of Italy.

The PDS supported Prodi's government, exacting as its price a pension law that was too generous. When Prodi slipped on a confidence vote in autumn 1998, D'Alema became prime minister. He had and continued to demonstrate a sense of what Italy needed to do in order to take its place as a leading European nation: a state that intervened less but with greater efficiency, constitutional reform to produce stronger governments capable, among other things, of a more autonomous foreign policy, and less state interference in the economy but a clear set of rules to govern the private sector.

But D'Alema was also steeped in the bad habits of the PCI. He accepted the Italian party system as a given, seeing little reason to experiment with other forms of organization. He inherited from Togliatti the belief that the PDS (which he rebaptized DS, Democratici di Sinistra or Democrats of the Left) needed to be legitimized. To achieve this, he was willing to offer the Catholics state funding for Church schools. He formed the alliance Togliatti sought in vain with the (Catholic) *popolari* and had paid the price of not pursuing electoral reform. He offered scant support to the organizers of the 18 April referendum which, had it obtained a quorum, would have scrapped the 25 per cent of House seats awarded by proportional representation. This did not win him *popolari* support and by late May 1999 his government looked weak. He stood solidly behind the US position in Kosovo while allowing members of his coalition to dissent publicly, thus weakening Italy's international position.

In short D'Alema behaved exactly as one would expect the heir to Togliatti and Berlinguer to behave (although he had no trace of that special Berlinguerian blend of self-criticism and charisma). He and the DS ruling group were the living proof that the PCI's difference was real but also that such difference can form part of a national identity. The heirs to the PCI have played a useful secondary role. Paradoxically they have, however, become too Italian to offer a lead to Italy.

Notes

1   No attempt can be made here to define the concept of national identity. I emphasize the notion of 'difference' because it is central to my topic of the Italian Communists. My thinking on national identity was stimulated by a lecture given by Thomas Risse at JHU Bologna on 17 May 1999.

2   Aurelio Lepre, *Storia della prima repubblica* (Bologna, Il Mulino, 1993), 306.

3   Paolo Spriano, *Storia del partito comunista italiano* (Turin, Einaudi, 1965), I, 109.

4   Paolo Spriano, *Gramsci in carcere e il partito* (Rome, Riuniti, 1977).

5   Ronald Tiersky, *The French Communist Party 1920–1972* (New York, Columbia University Press, 1974). See chapter 9 for the counter-community.

6   *La Repubblica* 19 March 1999.

7   Fausto Anderlini, *Terra rossa, comunismo ideale, socialdemocrazia reale* (Bologna, Istituto Gramsci, 1991).

8   On duplicity see Pietro di Loreto, *Togliatti e la 'doppiezza'* (Bologna, Il Mulino, 1991), 169. On Togliatti's leadership see Donald Sassoon, *Togliatti e la via italiana al socialismo* (Turin, Einaudi, 1980). For a brilliant, often cutting, depiction of the PCI leadership see Serio Bertelli, *Il gruppo* (Milan, Rizzoli, 1980).

9   Gianni Baget Bozzo, *Il partito cristiano al potere* (Florence, Vallecchi, 1974), 110.

10 The best biography of Berlinguer is Giuseppe Fiori, *Vita di Enrico Berlinguer* (Bari, Laterza, 1984). On the historic compromise see Stephen Hellmann, *Italian Communism in Transition: the Rise and Fall of the Historic Compromise in Turin* (Oxford, Oxford University Press, 1989). Also Gianfranco Pasquino, 'Il PCI nel sistema politico degli anni settanta', in *La giraffa e il licorno* edited by S. Belligni (Milan, Franco Angeli, 1983), 45.

11 Joan Barth Urban, *Moscow and the Italian Communist Party* (London, Tauris, 1986), 304.

12 Stephen Gundle, 'Popular culture in post-war Italy' in *Italy since 1945*, edited by Patrick McCarthy (following Oxford University Press).

13 'La relazione di Occhetto al 19 congresso', *L'Unità*, 8 March 1990.

14 Patrick McCarthy, 'The Communists divide and do not conquer', in G. Pasquino and P. McCarthy, eds., *The End of Post-war Politics in Italy: The Landmark 1992 Elections* (Boulder, Westview Press, 1992), 31–50.

15 Martin J. Bull, 'The great failure: the Democratic Party of the Left in Italy's transition', in *The New Italian Republic*, edited by Stephen Gundle and Simon Parker (London, Routledge, 1996), 143–58.

11

Challenging the nation-state: the Northern League between localism and globalism

ANNA CENTO BULL

Introduction

This article argues that the Northern League represents primarily an expression of regional identity, or, to be more precise, an expression of the politicization of regional identity in one part of Italy today. As such its political project should be seen in connection with the process of economic globalization, which seems to be requiring a loosening of the central structures of nation-states and the acquisition of greater administrative and political autonomy on the part of regional societies and economies. However, as is well known, the Northern League is a political party which advocates the secession of northern Italy from the rest of the country and the creation of a new independent state, that of Padania. There may therefore be a prima facie case for arguing that the Lega is primarily a nationalist movement.

What is Padania? Section 2.1 of the provisional constitution for the new Federal Republic of Padania, of 15 September 1996, entitled 'Territory', specified: 'The Federal Republic of Padania comprises the following regions: Emilia, Friuli, Liguria, Lombardy, the Marche, Piedmont, Romagna, Südtirol-Alto Adige, Tuscany, Trentino, Umbria, Valle d'Aosta, Veneto and Venezia Giulia.' The Declaration of Independence and Sovereignty of Padania, bearing the same date, runs as follows:

> We belong to a historic area, Padania, which is strongly integrated socially and economically . . . We therefore constitute a natural, cultural, social and economic community founded on shared values, culture, history, and on harmonious social, moral, and economic conditions . . .

We are conscious that a free and independent Padania will become a political and institutional focal point for the construction of a Europe of the Regions and of the Peoples.[1]

With the invention of Padania, the Northern League seeks the kind of status and official recognition that accrues to the so-called 'minority nationalisms' of historic nations such as Scotland, Wales, Catalonia, Quebec, the Basque country, etc.[2] As is well known, all nations have been defined as 'imagined communities', i.e. intellectually constructed communities which have come into being largely through a process of cultural and bureaucratic homogenization of pre-existing ethnic groups or 'ethnies'.[3] Such a process often took place from the top down, as was the case with the creation of the Italian 'nation-state' out of distinct territorial entities and identities in the late nineteenth and early twentieth centuries. Today, in Europe, we witness a 'current revival of *ethnies* below the level of the national state . . . This revival, which is summed up in the slogan of "L'Europe des *ethnies*", appears to threaten the integrity and question the legitimacy of the national state.'[4] Such a revival has often been presented as the rebirth of dormant nations.[5]

Since minority nations are also to a large extent 'imagined communities', whose rebirth is largely due to the construction and popularization of a common identity by intellectuals and professionals, it could be argued that Padania can indeed be considered on a par with Catalonia or Scotland. By embracing an ethno-regionalist, indeed nationalist, project, the Northern League has put Padania on the map of Europe, as one of the oppressed historic nations striving to achieve rebirth. However, according to Smith, most 'minority nationalisms' are also based on clearly recognizable ethnic communities, such as the Slovene, Czech, Scottish and Catalan peoples.[6] They may possess a common language, religion or educational and legal system, or they may have constituted an independent polity in the past. Yet it is clear, from the list of Italian regions which are supposed to comprise the nation of Padania, that they never formed a single polity or have ever shared a common language apart from Italian. Individually or in pairs they may perhaps be deemed to constitute 'dormant nations' (e.g. the Lombards, Venetians, Tuscans, etc.) but together they do not have much in common. Bossi himself made it clear that he was not advocating the autonomy of Padania on the basis that it formed an *ethnie*, but on the basis of its social, cultural and economic homogeneity.[7] As I have argued elsewhere, socio-economic homogeneity does constitute a reality for some northern Italian areas, but these do not coincide with Padania either.[8]

It is not surprising, therefore, that in many of the regions supposed to constitute Padania, the Northern League has consistently performed badly at both administrative and political elections, whereas in others it has successfully established itself as the (or at least a) dominant party. It is these latter regions, specifically eastern Lombardy, Veneto, Friuli-Venezia Giulia, and Trentino, all located in the north-east of Italy, which appear to express the aspirations of a regional political class in pursuit of a regional (national?) political project. Indeed a recent survey by Diakron found that, while only 8.6 per cent of Italians were in favour of secession, the figure rose to 15.6 per cent in the northern regions and to 20.6 per cent in the north-east.[9] Thus, while Padania enjoys some publicity and recognition outside Italy, not least as a folkloristic and entertaining phenomenon, it is in fact the north-east which has acquired a strong sub-national identity within the country, and which is being treated increasingly seriously.

Political regionalism in Italy's north-east was recently defined as 'fundamentalist' and 'integralist', with reference to its growing intransigence and radicalism. In the same article, the author addressed the question, What do these regions expect politics to do for them? He answered it, in the words of the sociologist Ilvo Diamanti, as follows: 'They want politics to continue to play a subordinate role *vis-à-vis* economic development.'[10] Here, in a nutshell, is the key to an understanding of the Northern League's success in the north-eastern regions, its imagery and symbolism, as well as its ethno-regionalist project. The process of economic globalization and its effects on different levels of governance and individual nation-states provide, in my view, an important and so far somewhat neglected angle from which to approach the relationship between the League and its territorially based electoral constituency. In this chapter I will assess these effects and then proceed to analyse in their light the regionalist project of the Northern League and its north-eastern constituency. I will also address the issue of a possible recent decoupling of the League from its regional constituency, due partly to the Padanian project itself. First, I want briefly to address the regionalization of politics in the north-eastern regions of Italy.

An emerging identity: Italy's north-east

Economically and socially, Italy's north-eastern regions form part, together with the central regions, of what Bagnasco identified, back in 1977, as the 'Third Italy', with reference to the prevailing model of small-scale industrialization, low social polarization, and the persistence of strong kinship and social networks. This model differed substantially from both the large-scale industry typical of the north-west and the underdevelopment of the south. Politically, the north-eastern regions were traditionally Catholic ('white') areas which voted regularly for the Christian Democratic Party from 1946 until the late 1980s. In this they differed from the central regions, which were traditionally socialist and communist ('red') areas, where the Communist Party obtained a majority of votes throughout the post-war period. These two political traditions are generally known to Italian scholars as political subcultures, because of the shared ideology and moral values of each, a high degree of identification with a political party, strong community values, and the identification of a common 'enemy', which took the form of both liberalism and socialism in the 'white' areas, and liberalism and Catholicism in the 'red' ones. It can therefore be said that both the north-east and the centre presented specific socio-economic and political characteristics which could have formed the basis, in the post-war period, for the emergence of strong regional identities and even regionalist movements. Yet this did not happen, owing primarily to two main factors. The first was ideological, and refers to the fact that both communism and Catholicism held universalistic, as opposed to localistic, values, based on class for the former, on religion for the latter. The second factor relates to the relationship between centre and periphery. Both Christian Democracy and the Communist Party provided political linkages between the central state and their regional strongholds, and contributed to channelling funds and benefits from the one to the others, particularly in support of small business development. The Communist Party, despite being in opposition, was able to take part in the decision-making process, largely through participation in parliamentary standing committees, which in Italy had the power to approve legislation. Within the Christian Democratic Party, the MP Antonio Bisaglia represented for many years the main political referent of the Veneto in Rome, skilfully mediating between the centre and the north-eastern periphery. When Bisaglia died prematurely, this marked the beginning of a growing decoupling of his party from the needs and demands of the local economy and society.

Since the collapse of Italy's First Republic in the early 1990s, election results have shown that the socialist subculture remains fairly resilient, whereas the Catholic subculture has experienced great changes. In particular, the main heir to the old Communist Party continues to represent the dominant political force in Emilia-Romagna and other central regions, whereas in the late 1980s Christian Democracy started to lose support and votes, after a century of 'symbiosis' between political Catholicism and this area, particularly the Veneto. The north-east became a 'political orphan', and turned increasingly to the Liga Veneta and later the Lega Nord. Here the Lega established itself as the new subcultural party, commanding the loyalty of voters at successive political and administrative elections.[11] The success of the Lega is an important indication that the north-eastern regions have now constructed a strong regional boundary around them which has led to 'the politicization of regional identity and the emergence of the region as a framework for political action'.[12] In 1992, assessing the reasons for this change, I wrote:

> The Lombard League's political success in the early 1990s can be explained partly by the fact that it has taken on the representation of the local model of economic development at a time when this is perceived to be in difficulty and in need of support, at least in terms of efficient public services, widespread services to industry, access to finance, and better infrastructure.[13]

I believe that this analysis is still largely valid, but it has now become clear that the north-eastern economic model is above all in search of a new (regional) level of governance and of a loosening up of the Italian nation-state within the context of Europe.

It is important at this stage to understand the very rapid process of industrialization and economic growth the north-east (particularly the Veneto and Trentino-Alto Adige) experienced during the last two decades of the twentieth century. Between 1970 and 1993 both regions doubled their gross domestic product, whereas Italy as a whole experienced a growth of 75 per cent.[14] Indeed, in the 1980s the Veneto had the highest rate of growth in Italy. While in 1970 the north-eastern regions were only slightly above the national average in terms of GDP per head, in 1993 they were considerably ahead, and only just behind the wealthiest regions of Lombardy and Emilia-Romagna.[15] The area is also favourably placed within the European Union, and can be compared, in terms of wealth, to Rhône-Alpes, Baden-Württemberg or south-east England. An important indicator of the type of economy characteristic of this area relates to the quota of production that is exported, which for the Veneto is now roughly 30 per cent, as opposed to 10.5 per cent in 1972. Whereas in the 1960s the Veneto contributed only 5 per cent to the country's exports, this reached 14 per cent in 1994.[16]

The period of rapid growth was thus accompanied by the loss of political stability, unlike the Communist-dominated central regions of Italy. In terms of centre–periphery relations, the situation is now made worse by the fact that the heir to the Italian Communist Party is in government, whereas the Lega is in opposition. Therefore the central regions are now fully represented at the level of the central state, but the north-eastern regions are not. This situation reinforces regional identity. What needs to be addressed is the question of why the politicization of territory has taken place in this particular area of Italy following a period of rapid economic growth. To this end we need to examine the effects of the process of globalization.

Globalization

The process of economic globalization refers primarily to the growing internationalization of trade, finance and production. This process is partly due to the presence of multinational companies whose turnover exceeds that of individual countries, but also, increasingly, to the emergence of a few world cities which have replaced states as 'the collective decision-making of global finance',[17] as well as to the transition from a Fordist to a post-Fordist production system. The latter is based on a

> core–periphery structure of production, with a relatively small core of rela-
> tively permanent employees handling finance, research and development,
> technological organization, and innovation, and a periphery consisting of
> dependent components of the production process. While the core is inte-
> grated with capital, the fragmented components of the periphery are much

more loosely linked to the overall production process. They can be located partly within the core plant, e.g. as maintenance services, and partly spread among different geographical sites linked to the overall production process.[18]

Economic globalization is, in the view of many commentators, closely linked to the reduction in scope and sphere of influence experienced by the nation-state. According to Cox, the state has been converted into 'a transmission belt from the global to the national economy, where heretofore it had acted as the bulwark defending domestic welfare from external disturbances'.[19] Held also has stressed that 'it is much harder for individual governments to intervene and manage their economies faced with a global division of labour, the absence of capital controls and the operation of the world financial markets'.[20] Indeed, for Underhill, 'the transnationalization of economic structures has reduced the economic space controlled by the state and intensified the competition its domestic economic constituency has to bear. That is the crux of the management problems of the contemporary international political economy.'[21]

There are two main political consequences related to the process of economic globalization. One is the emergence of what is known as 'multi-level governance', while the other is a shift of political power from certain domestic agencies to others. The first term refers to the emergence of supranational entities, or 'macro-regions', such as the European Community, which have acquired some of the powers previously reserved for nation-states because they are better placed to develop co-ordinated and collective policies to deal with the internationalization of trade, production and finance. It also refers to the parallel emergence of sub-national constituencies, or 'micro-regions', partly as a result of increasing regional disparities due to the free movement of capital and labour and to the weakening of the national state's regulatory powers. As Held remarked, strategies of regulation of economic activity will inevitably take place at local, as opposed to national, level.[22] Multi-level governance has been accompanied by a reshaping of cultural and political identities 'leading many local and regional groups, movements and nationalisms to question the nation-state as a representative and accountable power system'.[23] As for the shift of political power from certain domestic constituencies to others, this process refers to the different positioning of power centres and agencies within the nation-state *vis-à-vis* globalization. While competitive and export-orientated industrial and service sectors realize the need to adjust quickly to the process of globalization and seek to promote change, nationalized and uncompetitive industries and some social groups mobilize to resist and slow down change.[24]

The overall scenario evoked by the process of globalization resembles, for some commentators, the political order of the Middle Ages. Held, following Bull, argued in particular that the new order coincides with 'a modern and secular counterpart to the kind of political organization that existed in Christian Europe in the Middle Ages, the essential characteristics of which were overlapping authority and divided loyalty'.[25] Cox also argued that 'the whole picture resembles the multilevel order of medieval Europe more than the Westphalian model of a system of sovereign states that has heretofore been the paradigm of international relations'.[26] For anyone who is familiar with the symbols and images portrayed by the Northern League this scenario immediately rings a bell, for the party uses as its main symbol a medieval warrior and constantly refers to the medieval north Italian city-states as its 'ideal-type' for economic and political institutions. I will now analyse this uncanny parallel between the scenario raised by globalization and the political project actively pursued by the League, and link both to the north-eastern society and economy.

Regional identity and autonomy in a global era

I argued some years ago that the Northern League was the political voice of the north-eastern industrial districts, or areas of small-scale production. Various studies have confirmed this hypothesis, and a few have started to address the issue of why these districts have raised their voice and even threatened exit from the Italian nation-state. Wild argued that the political programme of the League, and in particular its insistence on regional autonomy, must be considered a response to the constraints of scale faced by industrial districts, which need increasingly to develop new forms of regional co-operation, interaction and governance.[27] Wild pointed out that regional governance was much more advanced in some central regions, particularly Tuscany and Emilia-Romagna, and argued that this was an important factor in accounting for the non-politicization of regional identity in the communist subculture. Anastasia and Corà also stressed the increasing importance of the regional milieu for the future development of Italy's north-east, and presented various possible future scenarios for the area, all of which contemplated the strengthening of the regional dimension in one form or another. They suggested that a regional strategy of development was the inevitable consequence of the process of economic globalization. Various scholars have also shown how industrial districts in the north-east have started to decentralize part of the production process to eastern European countries such as the Czech Republic, while also becoming subcontractors to west European, predominantly German, firms. Some larger firms, such as Luxottica, have entered the capital markets via the London and New York stock markets, in preference to the Milan bourse. According to Lago, the north-east has already started to think of itself in terms of a distinct macro-region, conscious of the fact that it is surrounded by strong and highly autonomous regions such as Bavaria: 'the institutional unification of the north-east is . . . an obligatory perspective along the road of achieving greater efficiency.'[28]

Seen in this light, it is not surprising perhaps that some scholars have accused the new regionalism of selfishness and greediness. Torpey defined the secessionism of the Northern League, as well as that of Slovenia and Croatia, as the 'secessionism of the affluent'.[29] The Italian historian Bevilacqua lamented the fact that 'today, in Northern Italy, there are huge parts of the small and medium-sized business sector which would gladly dismember Italy if their firms could derive some advantage from it'.[30] There is some truth in what they say, and this goes back to what I referred to in the Introduction, namely Diamanti's view that the north-eastern regions want politics to remain subordinated to economic development. The process of globalization has accelerated regional disparities, as we saw, creating both winners and losers. The process of European integration, on the other hand, has reduced the price regions have to pay if they want to acquire political autonomy, thanks to the abolition of internal customs barriers and the European single currency. In this context, the 'winning' regions are tempted to go it alone and leave the losers to their fate. This is an illusion, of course, since the issue of how to achieve a redistribution of resources and reduce regional disparities will almost certainly not go away; rather, it will simply reappear at a European, as opposed to a national, level.

What has been said so far makes it easier to understand the parallels between the medieval symbols and imagery used by the Lega and the future scenario of a neo-medieval Europe raised by globalization. The starting-point is a consideration of the nature of the Italian city-states in relation to both capitalism and territory. According to Arrighi, Italy's city-states in medieval Europe constituted

> a quintessentially capitalist system of war- and state-making. The most powerful and leading state in the subsystem (Venice) is the true prototype of the capitalist state, in the double sense of 'perfect example' and 'model for future instances' of such a state. A merchant capitalist oligarchy firmly held state power in its grip. Territorial acquisitions were subjected to careful cost-benefit analysis and, as a rule, were undertaken only as mere means to the end of enhancing the profitability of the traffics of the capitalist oligarchy that exercised state power.[31]

He went on to say that if there has ever been a state whose executive met the 'Communist Manifesto' standards of the capitalist state ('but a committee for managing the common affairs of the whole bourgeoisie'), it was fifteenth-century Venice.

If we replace the definition 'representatives of the interests of small-scale industry' for 'capitalist oligarchy', we have a fairly accurate picture of how both politics and territory are conceived *vis-à-vis* economics in some parts of Italy today. Indeed some commentators have described politics in the north-east as being characterized by increasing pragmatism, rather than intransigence. Thus various leading industrialists of the north-east's wealthiest provinces recently expressed support not just for federalism but even for a more drastic divorce from the rest of Italy.[32] This suggests that territorial questions are subjected to the type of cost-benefit analysis which was typical of the city-states. It is no coincidence perhaps that the city-states operated in what was, for the times, a global economy and 'had revenues that compared very favourably with the revenues of the most successful dynastic states of Western and North-western Europe.'[33] The same can be said of today's industrial districts, which, as we saw, have become nodes of global networks.

We live in times when the primacy of economics over politics is being asserted increasingly forcefully. As Ohmae openly advocated in his latest book, a new economic rationality is destined to prevail around the world, against which political and social interests and pressures will be of no avail. As for nation-states,

> the current paralysis of nation-states now shows them to have been a tran-
> sitional mode of organization for managing economic affairs ... Given
> suitable autonomy, region states – by virtue of their unique ability to put
> global logic first – can provide precisely the kind of change agent the
> times require: effective engines of prosperity and improved quality of life
> for the people of the global economy.[34]

It is not the purpose of this chapter to prove or disprove the validity of theories such as Ohmae's. I would only point out that the
experience of the Italian city-states provides a fitting reminder of the
risks involved in pursuing the ideal of 'pure capitalism' devoid of
political, social and territorial constraints. As all history textbooks
will explain, the wealth and trading superiority of the city-states did
not save them from the loss of political independence, followed by
economic decline. Indeed, Padania itself, particularly if limited to
the north-eastern regions, would probably become a political and
economic satellite of Germany, rather than a fully independent entity
within the context of a Europe of the Regions. It is also notable that
the political project of the Northern League, even though it makes
sense in the context of economic globalization and the advocacy of
the supreme rationality of the new world order, relies heavily on
emotional ties, a charismatic leader and a populist style.

Secessionism, however, has been only one – albeit admittedly the
most dramatic – of different ways in which regional identity has
found political expression in the north-east. We should start from the
premise that the process of globalization has created anxiety in all
regions, both winners and losers, as they are all having to adjust and
respond to growing international competition. Indeed the League
itself has in recent times shifted its emphasis from an aggressively
independentist and neo-liberal stance to a defensive and protectionist position, no longer arguing for Padania to 'go it alone' but to find
its place within a wider Mitteleuropean entity. More importantly, the
League has recently adopted a strong anti-American and anti-global-
ization rhetoric, moving closer to populist and radical right-wing
parties, such as the French Front National and the Austrian Freedom
Party than to the Scottish National Party, the Catalan Convergència
i Unió or the Canadian Parti Quebecois.[35] It is perhaps not a

coincidence that the adoption of a defensive stance on the part of the Lega Nord has coincided with a general slowdown in economic growth in the regions which form the party's stronghold.[36]

There is no doubt that in the north-east itself there are strong feelings that the regional model of small-business development is at a crossroads, but this does not translate into a request for protectionism. By politicizing territory the north-east is reminding the nation-state that it is one of the engines of economic growth in the country today, and that its capacity for wealth creation must be enhanced rather than hindered. In this sense it is not advocating the primacy of economics; rather, it is asking politics to perform a new role and to provide an innovative regulatory framework for dealing with and responding to economic globalization.

The response of the nation-state

After a period in which the 'selfish' interpretation of regional identity and the rise of the Northern League seemed to dominate the intellectual debate in Italy, leading to various attempts to demonize and stigmatize both phenomena, a growing body of scholars and politicians have produced less emotional diagnoses and put forward more rational political solutions. Massimo Cacciari, mayor of Venice and a leading exponent of the left, was one of the first to realize the significance of the emergence of a 'North-Eastern Question'; Cacciari also became an ardent and vocal supporter of a Catalan-style solution for Italy's north-east, stressing the urgency of the creation of a federalist state. Cacciari is aware that the best response to the secessionism of the League is to give frustrated regions such as the Veneto a high degree of autonomy within the nation-state. He is also aware that the process of globalization requires institutional change: 'A centralized and bureaucratic administration cannot cope with the challenge of globalization nor with the new need felt by people all over Europe for stronger links to their local territory.'[37]

Indeed federalism has now become the new buzzword in the Italian political world, enjoying a veritable renaissance in public discourse. Federalism, however, means different things to different people. For some it means decentralization not just to the regions, but also to the provinces and communes. For others, it means a new

version of Italy's current administrative structure, with the important novelty of the granting of tax-raising powers to the regions. Still
others reject the idea that the current regional structure can provide
a sound basis for a federal state, and stress the need to create new
macro- or meso-regions to replace the existing ones, which are
considered too small to be viable. One suggestion is the division of
the country into five meso-regions, each considered homogeneous
from an economic point of view: north-west, north-east, centre,
Adriatic south, other south.

In 1997, a proposed new bill for constitutional change contained
elements of a federal state, but it was severely criticized by various
sources for failing to address adequately the problem of the relationship between the different tiers of government. Vassallo, in
particular, pointed out that the bill attributed to the central state the
task of defining the functions of local government and to Parliament
the power to regulate relations between communes, provinces and
regions. In this way the role of the regions was restricted and federalism was flawed: the bill 'risks making relations between the central
state, the regions and local government even more confusing and
conflict-ridden'.[38] Cacciari was critical, too, mainly because of the
excessive powers attributed to the state in the proposed Bill.

It is clear that the relationship between the different tiers of
government constitutes the main point of contention and the main
obstacle to a restructuring of the Italian state. This is not surprising,
since in Italy strong municipal identities have long preceded the
emergence of regional ones. Italy's large cities, in particular, have
their own identities and do not generally form part of their own
region's model of development or socio-cultural configuration. As
Lago remarked, Venice does not belong to the 'modello veneto',
since it possesses a different socio-economic structure and cultural
environment.[39] Milan has very little in common with eastern
Lombardy, which, in turn, is undoubtedly part of the 'modello
veneto'. Indeed Bagnasco pointed out, quite perceptively, that the
regional capitals of northern Italy have not been capable of interpreting and representing the interests of their regions, precisely
because they have little in common with the socio-economic systems
which characterize the wider regional territory.[40]

It is in this context that we can appreciate the novelty of the emergence of a strong regional identity and regional party in the
north-east of Italy. To be able to overcome long-standing local and

municipal rivalries, as well as the dispersion of a myriad of industrial districts across the area by constructing a collective regional identity and putting forward a regional political project, testifies to a significant effort on the part of a multitude of social, economic and political actors to provide an effective response to the process of globalization.[41] It is an effort which requires an adequate and corresponding ability to think innovatively and creatively on the part of the nation-state. This is especially crucial now that the electorate of the Northern League seems to have become disillusioned with the whole Padanian project itself, as indicated by the poor results registered by the Lega Nord at the 1999 European and administrative elections. In particular, the League's defensive and protectionist vision of a Mitteleuropean Padania as a bastion against globalization and Americanization did not appeal to a society and economy long used to operate successfully in a global environment.[42] There are signs, therefore, that the Northern League may have become a prisoner of its own invention, believing its own myths and privileging virtual reality at the expense of social reality.[43] The party, in other words, has stopped producing credible political proposals, and is wasting precious time in staging complex pageantry, celebratory rites and quasi-religious ceremonies in the name of Padania. Yet 'what is irrefutable is that the problems which generated the League have not been solved'.[44]

Conclusions

In a recent article, Curi remarked that the Lega Nord has embarked on a road of no return: either secession or self-dissolution.[45] This constitutes both an opportunity and a threat for the opponents of the Lega. In terms of opportunity, it is clear that a federalist solution to the problems created by globalization and uneven regional development has been discarded by the League, providing a clear demarcation between this and the other parties, which can now occupy the political space vacated by the League and regain the initiative. However, a half-baked and half-hearted commitment to a federal structure on the part of the government, as was the case with the proposed (later discarded) bill for constitutional change, may have the effect of hardening attitudes and increasing the attractiveness of the secessionist solution. We have already seen how secession commands the support of a fifth of residents in the north-eastern regions.

The League is offering exit from the Italian state, while the politicization of regional identity in the north-east can be interpreted primarily as an expression of voice.[46] There are now some indications that the League is losing momentum and may even become a spent force, unless it can elaborate serious political proposals to deal with the 'Northern Question'. Even if this were to happen, the other parties would be making a serious mistake if they were to conclude that the issues raised by the League in the 1980s and 1990s were no longer relevant. It is precisely the modernity of political regionalism in these global times which accounted in great part for the political success of the Northern League. What many often found puzzling and mystifying about this party, its being a mixture of the parochial and the neo-liberal, the folkloristic and the managerial, was in fact a direct function of the modern relevance of sub-national regionalism, not just in Italy but in Europe. Padania may remain an unrealized dream, a virtual nation invented entirely from scratch, but the knot of problems vexing nation-states in the age of economic globalization will almost certainly require as much political imagination and innovative thinking as the Padanian project itself.

Notes

1. *Gazzetta Ufficiale della Padania*, 'Dichiarazione di indipendenza e sovranità della Padania', 15 September 1996, pp. 1–2.

2. The League appears to have succeeded in gaining this kind of status in the media outside Italy. In its analysis of the referendum on devolution in Scotland, no less a paper than *The Observer* titled one of its sections 'Scotland inspires other stateless nations'. I was surprised to find that Padania had its place alongside Catalonia, Brittany and Bavaria. The newspaper reported that the Northern League 'which has proclaimed its intention of creating a breakaway state of Padania, free of control of Rome, found inspiration in the referendum', adding that Umberto Bossi, the leader of the party, had declared, 'Today begins the great march towards liberty'. See *The Observer*, 14 September 1997, p. 28.

3. A. D. Smith, *Nations and Nationalism in a Global Era* (Cambridge, Polity Press, 1995), 85–97. The first to coin the term 'imagined communities' was B. Anderson, *Imagined Communities: Reflections on the Origin and Spread of Nationalism* (London, Verso, 1983).

4. Smith, *Nations and Nationalism in a Global Era*, 102–3.

5. The caption on the front page of the *Guardian* after the Scottish

referendum on devolution read: 'The rebirth of a nation – or still a United Kingdom?' Inside, one article stated: 'Labour may have made a fundamental mistake by playing on Scottish patriotism . . . The Scottish lion has been let out and Labour might not find it that easy to prod him into a cage again.' See E. MacAskill, 'SNP cheers statute for liberty', *Guardian*, 13 September 1997, p. 4.

6 Smith, *Nations and Nationalism in a Global Era*, chapter 3.

7 U. Bossi and D. Vimercati, *La rivoluzione. La Lega: storia e idee* (Milan, Sperling & Kupfer, 1993), 100–1. One chapter of this book is entitled 'Il Veneto e altre nazioni' and explicitly recognizes that only individual Italian regions can aspire to the status of historic nations.

8 A. Cento Bull, 'Ethnicity, racism and the Northern League', in C. Levy, ed., *Italian Regionalism: History, Identity and Politics* (Oxford, Berg, 1996), 177–83.

9 Diakron, *Italian People and Secession* (Milan, 6 September 1996), p. 2.

10 A. Statera, 'Dalla Laguna ai Pirenei', *La Repubblica. Affari e Finanza*, 30 June 1997, p. 2.

11 R. Biorcio, 'La Lega come attore politico. Dal federalismo al populismo regionalista', in R. Mannheimer, ed., *La Lega Lombarda* (Milan, Feltrinelli, 1991); A. Cento Bull, 'The Lega Lombarda: a new political subculture for Lombardy's industrial districts', *Italianist*, 12 (1992), 179–83; A. Cento Bull, 'The politics of industrial districts in Lombardy: replacing Christian Democracy with the Northern League', *Italianist*, 13 (1993), 209–29.

12 M. Keating, *State and Regional Nationalism: Territorial Politics and the European State* (New York, London, Toronto, Sydney and Tokyo, Harvester Wheatsheaf, 1988), 17.

13 Cento Bull, 'The Lega Lombarda', 181.

14 B. Anastasia and G. Corò, *Evoluzione di un'economia regionale. Il Nord-Est dopo il successo* (Portogruaro, Ediciclo, 1996), 36–7.

15 Ibid., 44.

16 Ibid., 40–1.

17 R. W. Cox, 'Global restructuring: making sense of the changing international political economy', in R. Stubbs and G. R. D. Underhill, eds., *Political Economy and the Changing Global Order* (Basingstoke and London, Macmillan, 1984), 48.

18 Ibid., 47.

19 Ibid., 49.

20 D. Held, *Democracy and the Global Order: From the Modern State to Cosmopolitan Governance* (Cambridge, Polity Press, 1995), 131.

21 G. R. D. Underhill, 'Conceptualizing the changing global order', in R. Stubbs and G. R. D. Underhill, eds., *Political Economy and the Changing Global Order* (Basingstoke and London, Macmillan, 1994), 36.

22 Held, *Democracy and the Global Order*, 133.

23 Ibid., 136.

24 Cox, 'Global restructuring', 49. See also H. Kitschelt (with A. J. McGann), *The Radical Right in Western Europe: A Comparative Analysis* (Ann Arbor, University of Michigan Press, 1997), 5.

25 Held, *Democracy and the Global Order*, 137.

26 Cox, 'Global Restructuring', 53.

27 S. Wild, 'The Italian Northern League: the self representation of industrial districts' (University of Bath, unpublished Ph.D. thesis, 1998).

28 G. Lago, *Nordest chiama Italia. Cosa vuole l'area del benessere e della protesta. Intervista di Gianni Montagni* (Vicenza, Neri Pozza, 1996), 112.

29 J. Torpey, 'Affluent secessionist: Italy's Northern League', *Dissent*, 41, 3 (Summer 1994), 36–40.

30 P. Bevilacqua, 'New and old in the Southern Question', *Modern Italy*, 1, 2 (1996), 81–92.

31 G. Arrighi, 'The three hegemonies of historical capitalism', in J. Iivonen, ed., *The Future of the Nation-State in Europe* (Aldershot, Edward Elgar, 1993), 55–7.

32 See 'Tra federalismo e secessione. Timori e speranze degli imprenditori', *Mondo Economico*, 20 May 1996, pp. 18–23. See also G. Lago, 'Il vento del Nord-Est: imprese a caccia di politica', *La Repubblica. Affari e Finanza*, 17 February 1997, pp. 1–5.

33 Arrighi, 'The three hegemonies of historical capitalism', 59.

34 K. Ohmae, *The End of the Nation-State: The Rise of Regional Economies* (London, HarperCollins, 1996), 149.

35 This new position emerged very clearly from an analysis of *La Padania*, the newspaper of the Northern League, in the second half of 1998 and the first half of 1999. Giulio Tremonti, MP for Forza Italia, recently referred to a 'fundamentalist' path followed by the League, whose characteristics were a Le Pen-style ethnic stance, a romantic vision of the 'small fatherland', a reaction against the Americanization of society, and ideological and democratic 'regression'. See an interview by V. Postiglione with G. Tremonti in *Corriere della Sera*, 28 July 1999.

36 See, for instance, S. Livadiotti, 'Allarme, si è rotto il Nordest', *L'Espresso*, 20 February 1997.

37 J. L. Graff, 'Building Europe from the bottom up', *Time* (Winter 1998–9), 43.

38 S. Vassallo, 'Il federalismo sedicente', *Il Mulino*, 46, 372 (April 1997), 694–707 (694).

39 Lago, *Nordest chiama Italia. Cosa vuole l'area del benessere e della protesta*.

[40] A. Bagnasco, 'Bossi trenta in sociologia ma bocciato come leader', *La Repubblica. Affari e Finanza*, 29 April 1996, p. 1.

[41] In its early days, the economic and political programme of the Northern League constituted a fairly coherent attempt to develop a realistic strategy to deal with the challenge of globalization. See Cento Bull, 'The politics of industrial districts in Lombardy'. In his already mentioned interview with V. Postiglione, Giulio Tremonti, MP for Forza Italia, stated that the Northern League risked losing everything by embracing a 'Le Penist' type of programme, whereas its great merit consisted in having initiated a modern phase for politics, based on the 'glocal', i.e., on achieving a balance between international openness and local needs. See *Corriere della Sera*, 28 July 1999.

[42] Following the recent loss of votes in the 1999 European and administrative elections, numerous mayors and local administrators of the League voiced the opinion that their electorates were not interested in the issue of (anti-)globalization, but wanted their party to focus on questions of autonomy, federalism (especially fiscal federalism) and administrative efficiency. See F. Cavalera, 'La fronda dei "nordisti" contro Bossi', *Corriere della Sera*, 23 July 1999.

[43] According to Cavalera, the party's current problems are 'due to the fact that in the last few years it has . . . constructed the myth of Padania and other symbolisms, but it has forgotten the North'. See F. Cavalera, 'La fronda dei "nordisti" contro Bossi'. Lago also referred to the League's 'great escape from the reality of its own north' and to its taking refuge into 'the rhetoric of the north'. See G. Lago, 'Gli slogan integralisti che nascondono la paura', *La Repubblica*, 26 July 1999, p. 8.

[44] Lago, 'Gli slogan integralisti che nascondono la paura', 8.

[45] U. Curi, 'La Lega e l'eversione', *Micromega* (April 1997), 41–53 (49).

[46] According to Albert Hirschman's well-known terminology, citizens can express their dissatisfaction with a firm, an organization or a state either through exit or by raising their voice, i.e. protesting and acting to bring about change. See A. O. Hirschman, *Exit, Voice and Loyalty: Responses to Decline in Firms, Organizations, and States* (Cambridge, MA, and London, Harvard University Press, 1970).

12

Concluding reflections: Italy, Europe and multiform identities

BRUCE HADDOCK AND GINO BEDANI

In this book we have sought to explore the developing character of Italian national identity from a number of disciplinary perspectives. What finally emerges from our pages is certainly much more complex than the nationalist theorists of the nineteenth century had ever imagined. That it makes some *sense* to talk of a shared national culture in Italy is beyond question. But this cannot be reduced to a core of attitudes, values, character traits or feelings that are evident in each of the guises that 'Italian' culture has assumed in the modern period. Essentialist or primordialist theories of national cultures can no longer be seriously defended, though the havoc such views can wreak in political life is all too evident in east central Europe and beyond. Instead we are faced with the complex task of interpreting shifting currents in cultural, economic and political life which have enabled groups to present themselves in particular ways and to secure effective institutional contexts for their pursuits. Abstract theoretical discussion of the process of constructing hegemonic positions or defending minority interests can barely scratch the surface of the phenomenon. Our approach has been different. We have tried to focus on specific issues which highlight the varied and problematic nature of Italian culture and identity as it has emerged in response to different crises and circumstances.

Generalization is thus especially hazardous. It is nevertheless clear that the contested nature of national identity has been reflected in the ambivalent conceptions Italians have often formed of the state. From the earliest national stirrings of the Risorgimento, through the liberal regime, Fascism and, finally, the post-war Republic, there has never been a settled view of the character of the state or the role it should play in relation to culture, economy and society. The initial conception of the existence of a coherent national movement demanding political expression is the least plausible of the popular misconceptions to have survived the Risorgimento. In so far as a consensus emerged in 1860, it was based on the views of the dominant Piedmontese élite that had managed to channel the national movement to suit its ends. The fragility of the consensus was exposed as the liberal regime sought to consolidate itself. The integration of the south involved a virtual civil war between 1861 and 1865. Effective peace necessitated the subtle accommodation of local élites through the distribution of patronage and influence from the centre. Everyday administration and government has since continued to rely on the absorption of opponents through the grant of office or favours (*trasformismo*) in one form or another, despite the very clear ideological divisions between the liberal, Fascist and republican regimes. It is almost as if stability in Italy has depended upon practices that could not be ideologically avowed. This has made it relatively easy for marginalized regions or groups to expose official politics as a sham, with the unspoken assumption that the Italian people deserve better. But precisely who the relevant people are has remained an open question. Advocates of religious and secular identities for Italy have never been theoretically reconciled, though they have had to learn to live with one another. The north and south have enjoyed the same kind of uneasy relationship, surfacing in recent years in claims that the centralized state should have its powers radically devolved along federal lines. Beneath these broad divisions are the more fundamental attachments that people have formed to local urban centres. Cattaneo had identified this as a distinguishing feature of Italian culture at the height of the Risorgimento; and it has continued to be dominant in people's perceptions of who they are, despite the best efforts of government-sponsored propaganda, civic education of various kinds and the mass media.

This book has concentrated on developments within Italy. But it should not be assumed that Italian identities have been formed in isolation. Since the ancient Roman period, political order in Italy has been inextricably·linked to the wider institutional configuration of Europe. Indeed two of the foremost institutions in shaping European identity, Roman law and the Catholic Church, have Italian roots. And Renaissance Italy has good claims to be the home of double-entry bookkeeping and the modern banking system. Max Weber may have chosen to link the spirit of capitalism with Protestantism; but very many of the institutional preconditions of European capitalism can be traced back to the Italian medieval city- states and republics. The point, of course, is not to stress Italian primacy in these matters in the manner of Gioberti; rather to be aware that innovations in specific states are linked to historical, cultural and structural factors that affect the continent as a whole in different ways.

In the modern period, the fortune of Italy has always been tied to the balance of political and economic power in Europe. The Italian state was initially formed as a consequence of fundamental political adjustment in Europe, accommodating the retreat of the Austrian Empire and the emergence of new states. Subsequent Italian regimes have also been sensitive to the prevailing European climate. The increasing authoritarianism of the liberal state in the 1880s reflected a shift that occurred throughout continental Europe, with states openly endorsing the Prussian model as the best means of securing national interests in hostile circumstances. The First World War can be seen as a European crisis which effectively undermined the liberal state in Italy, as indeed the economic crisis of 1929 would make life difficult for parliamentary democracies throughout Europe. Key dates have a European resonance: 1789, 1815, 1848, 1914, 1917, 1929, 1945, 1956, 1968, 1989. To be sure, national cultures would respond in a variety of ways to these crises. What we see is cultural capital being deployed and extended. Outcomes in crises are always uncertain. In difficult times, however, a capacity for constructive reinvention is vital for political and cultural flourishing. The cultural history of modern Italy has not always been happy; but it shows a remarkable flair for renewal, even in the face of folly and inefficiency in politics.

The inter-war period is especially instructive. The liberal state had clearly been unable to adapt to the demands of an emerging mass culture. It was outflanked by nationalism, socialism, Fascism and the emergence of political Catholicism. This is not the place to explore in any detail the cultural shortcomings of the liberal paradigm, at least as matters stood in 1920. At the very least, however, some of the problems of the liberal state can be attributed to a failure of cultural imagination. Despite the awareness of a Liberal leader like Giolitti that the new mass forces which had emerged in Italian society could not be disenfranchised, the narrowly self-conscious élite by which he was surrounded proved unable or unwilling to embrace the vulgarity of mass politics. The projection of political imagery to a politically illiterate audience could not be achieved in

Italy within the terms of conventional Liberal theory. When it was attempted at all, it was largely by exploiting the language of nationalism. Principled nationalists were thus given a clear boost as the old élite legitimized their language and rhetoric. But the masters of Liberal politics were always ill at ease beyond the confines of smoke-filled rooms. As advocates of a mass-based Italian political culture, they looked remote and sounded tired, and were easily marginalized.

The Fascist experiment in Italy served as a model for much of continental Europe in more than a narrowly political sense. Avant-garde culture was decidedly more vibrant on the right than the left. For a while both liberalism and socialism began to look like relics from the nineteenth century. The traumas of authoritarian government and military defeat, however, led to a decisive shift in popular opinion. The Fascist achievement was exposed as bogus. The gulf between theory and practice was so vast that the regime was barely intelligible in the end to even reasonably well-informed citizens. Confusion was complete in 1945. Italians had a future to create for themselves, yet in political terms they only had experience of two failed experiments to guide them. In the circumstances, the creation of a stable and prosperous republic is a remarkable achievement.

The principal casualty of the Fascist period was the lofty conception of the state. The idea that Italian culture could not flourish unless Italians could identify with a strong state was rejected. In the early years of the Republic, and in the period of the Cold War which followed, the mass movements, Catholic and Communist, involved in negotiating post-war reconstruction were led by individuals who were able sufficiently to subordinate their ideological differences to the need for a broader social solidarity. Despite the bitter struggles which were experienced, they knew when to draw back. Given the potential for unleashing conflict with disastrous political and historical consequences this was no mean achievement. Both movements were collectivist but not statist in orientation. The Communists, for example, remained profoundly perplexing to their west European counterparts as they proceeded to administer the region with the most successful model of small and medium capitalist enterprise in the country, with considerable facilitating input of their own, and support from their followers. Indeed the state was justified in the view of both Catholics and Communists only as a means of bolstering more fundamental social bonds. Despite their original cultural and historical hostility to liberal doctrine, in the long term they both contributed to the creation of a liberal polity in which the distinction between state and civil society was central. Their flexibility allowed secularizing and pluralizing trends at work in Italian society to emerge and in the end transform their own movements.

The wider process of European reconstruction was crucial for the restoration of stability in Italy. The point to stress here is that the diversity and resilience of civil society made the choice of 'low' politics both apt and appealing. Italy, like Germany, had a tainted political tradition; yet focus on the artificial foreign nature of Fascist culture and institutions enabled Italians to treat Fascism as an aberration. No doubt this involved a good deal of wishful thinking. Without the resources of her cultural tradition, however, the case could not have been made at all. Family, region, class or religion could be treated as alternative and richer sources of personal allegiance. Within these terms of reference, celebration of an Italian way of life need not involve, and in many ways actively discouraged, excessive preoccupation with nation or state. Indeed in the 1950s the language of nationalism, even in its benign forms, was conspicuously absent from public discourse. The country was aided in this by the residual 'internationalism' of the Communists, and the peculiar 'universalism' of Italian Catholicism, where the influence and perspectives of the Vatican had historically supplanted those of a national Church. In whatever way the sense of nationhood was evolving, it was doing so with a peculiarly outward-looking focus.

It was thus relatively straightforward for Italy to take full advantage of moves towards European integration. Neither politicians nor citizens worried too much about giving up the sovereign prerogatives of the state. Article 11 of the republican constitution expressly sanctions 'limitations on sovereignty which are necessary for a system guaranteeing peace and justice among nations; it [Italy] supports and favours international organizations having this purpose'. Instead of treating the state as an abstract entity that enjoyed rights, it became natural (or more reasonable) to focus on public measures as means of facilitating the many and various interests of citizens. A Neapolitan Catholic working in an automobile factory in Turin would have a host of tangible interests to defend. None had anything directly to do with the sovereignty of the state. The initial establishment of the European Coal and Steel Community in 1951 presented no problems of principle for Italy. Stress on a common market in the Treaty of Rome (1957) likewise suited the Italian desire to avoid political symbolism at all costs. Indeed whenever the Italian state has felt threatened in the post-war period, usually because of the fragility of public finances, the favoured response has always been towards closer European integration. The huge efforts made by governments in the 1990s to meet the criteria for membership of Economic and Monetary Union are an illustration of the priority the political élite have accorded to the presentation of Italy in European terms.

The final decade of the twentieth century has been especially turbulent for Italy. The patronage politics that had done so much to give Italy stability in the 1950s and 1960s eventually became a financial liability that could not be sustained in a world of open financial markets. The political crisis broke in 1992 as the scale of irregular financing of parties, of illicit release of contracts, and the exchange of financial and political favours hit national headlines. The oddity is not that there should have been an explosion of popular anger, rather that tolerance of systemic corruption should have lasted as long as it did. The detailed story of these developments cannot be told here. What occurred between 1992 and 1995 was essentially a crisis of legitimacy on a massive scale. It was quite different from the standard governmental crises that had bedevilled Italian politics since 1948, where arguments about the distribution of patronage would be cloaked in the language of policy. In one sense, the crisis may be seen as a belated attempt to make Italian democracy more transparent. Popular criticism was not ideologically motivated. The concern was not to show that representative democracy was a delusion (as had been the case with the terrorist groups of the 1970s) but rather that democracy Italian-style failed to meet even lax standards of honesty and efficiency. A great deal of empirical work will be required before we can explain satisfactorily how and why the political parties lost control of the system. Attention to the question of the *de facto* distribution of power, however, should be conducted in the context of the profound normative changes that have swept through Italy and Europe in the 1990s.

The collapse of the Soviet bloc affected Italy more directly than most west European states because of its large Communist Party. Parties on the left had to endure a painful period of self-examination and reinvention. Paradoxically, however, the Christian Democrat Party found itself most dangerously exposed. Its claim to constitute the only reliable bulwark against creeping communism could no longer be plausibly deployed, even as a rhetorical device. It was left, along with the Socialist Party, as a naked power broker in a game of political patronage that got out of control. Political patronage had been used throughout the history of the Republic to reinforce a state that had initially been regarded as vulnerable.

Yet despite the widespread habit of DC-bashing, it must be granted that the Christian Democrats were remarkably successful in giving a solid foundation to the Republic. The isolation of the political élite in the liberal era was overcome by a systematic deployment of resources, giving millions of people a vested interest in the status quo. In the end, however, adapting the practice of *trasformismo* to the demands of a mass society turned out to be prohibitively expensive. The scale of transfer payment, both licit and illicit, far exceeded the productive capacity of the Italian economy. In a difficult economic climate, public patience was finally exhausted. The political class seemed to have lost touch with the wider society, effectively severing the link between patronage and legitimacy. But this should not lead us to underestimate the very real contribution made by the country's political leaders in fostering, among the public, a sense of belonging to the Republic, for better or worse.

In the European context, the further integration of the European economy has made political options available which would otherwise have been dismissed as too costly or disruptive. Italy's initial commitment to European integration, it must be remembered, was part of a sustained effort to legitimize the fledgling Republic. The policy has proved to be strikingly successful. Italy's access to the growing European market in the 1950s was guaranteed, enabling the economy to enjoy a period of export-led growth which doubled GDP in little more than a decade. The emergence of a European Community was not necessarily the decisive factor in this development. But it became associated in the public mind with unprecedented well-being. Successive Eurobarometer soundings consistently show a level of support for European integration significantly above the European average. Even politicians whose domestic political vision has been notoriously short-sighted (such as Andreotti) have seen deepening European integration not simply as a means of furthering Italian interests but also as a possible strategy for radical structural reform of the Italian state. The public, incipiently aware by the late 1970s of a creeping malaise at the heart of the political system, harboured a more receptive view of centralized European intervention than most of their European counterparts, despite the national administration's lamentable record in implementing European regulations.

Commitment to Europe provided a solid foundation where the nation's political culture was shaky and fragmented. After 1992 the European dimension became even more significant as the fragility of the national consensus became increasingly evident. A vote for radical or separatist parties, for example, need not be regarded as a threat to the Italian economy, provided political innovation in Italy was seen to be compatible with a wider commitment to the European Union. Shifting circumstances have thus opened up political possibilities that had previously been foreclosed. Radical devolution, for example, which had generally been dismissed as dangerously disruptive by some, and feared by others as moving towards breaking up the nation, is now regarded as both possible and desirable by a wide spectrum of opinion.

Yet change is never without a cost. Pressures for closer economic and monetary union have exposed public finances to international scrutiny. The crisis of the early 1990s, which began as a reaction against political corruption, must be set in the context of the global integration of economies. 'Globalization' has affected all states in a myriad of ways. It does not follow, however, that effective response presupposes the adoption of any specific cultural model. The idea that advanced economies and cultures were destined to converge is one of the myths of high modernism. Integration at the level of international financial markets has been coupled with a diminution of cultural and economic control at the level of the nation-state. It is no accident that the principal countries of western Europe have all pursued devolutionary policies in the last twenty years. The bewildering development of information technology, too, has made the pretence that states can control the exposure of their citizens to knowledge, opinions and forms of expression wholly ineffective. In these circumstances, regional cultures have necessarily to assume a wider range of responsibilities. They have not all flourished. Competitive pressures have left some regional cultures stranded like relics of a bygone age. With the slackening of central control, however, space has been created for a proliferation of cultural responses.

Prospects for Italy in this environment are mixed. Regions that have depended upon the redistribution of resources from central government will clearly be disadvantaged. Urban centres with strong identities, by contrast, are already accustomed to thinking and working on a European scale, pursuing a variety of styles of funding for initiatives. The path pioneered by Bologna in the 1970s is now more appropriate than ever. Modern economies are essentially cross-cutting networks. Local administration can facilitate endeavour where it cannot direct. Proven success, even in the face of inefficient central government, suggests that the Italian civic model may be well placed to negotiate an open future.

Italy's principal asset remains the diversity and flexibility of her cultures. Paradoxically, for example, Bologna was the capital of Italian communism. With Massimo D'Alema, the nation was led into the twenty-first century by a member of the only west European Communist Party to undertake a successful transformation into social democracy and remain a force in national life. Italy has a gift for producing the unexpected. Till now it has helped the nation to survive. In the nineteenth century economic development was hampered by lack of natural resources for heavy industry. In the twenty-first century, such resources have a negligible role to play. Economies are knowledge-based; and knowledge is a cultural artefact. Flexibility and creativity are essential attributes in a world that is destined to change ever more rapidly. It is ironic that the persistent weakness of central government and administration has effectively furnished Italy with an invaluable resource to confront the complex interdependence of modern polities and cultures – a civil society with a capacity for devising alternative routes towards unpredicted outcomes and unlikely destinations.

Index

Abba, Giuseppe Cesare 94
Abyssinian war 148
Accademia della Crusca 110
Accademia d'Italia 106
Acerbo, Giacomo 178-9
ACLI 225
Adelfi 20, 30
Adriatic Littoral *see* Venezia Giulia
Aglianò, Sebastiano 87
Agnelli, Giovanni 156
Agrigento 88, 90
Albanian 98, 115, 168
Albertini, Luigi 156
Alfieri, Vittorio 194, 195
Allende, Salvador 251
Alto Adige *see* Süd-Tirol-Alto Adige,
    Trentino-Alto Adige
Amari, Michele 78, 91
Ambrosini, Luigi 58
Anastasia, B. 267
ancien régime 12, 13, 14, 16, 20, 40
Andalusia 91
Anderson, Benedict 76, 86, 142, 146
Angeloni, Luigi 26-7
Annali universali di statistica 27
Annoni, Antonio Marcello 167-9
anti-Fascism 164, 191, 192, 198, 205,
    216, 221
anti-Semitism 177-8, 180, 196
Antologia 2, 28-9
Antonioni, Michelangelo 136
*Aperçus sur les causes qui ont dégradé
    l'esprit public en Italie ...* 19
Apih, Elio 165
April's Wound 92
Archivo glottologico italiano 102
Argelato 200
Armani, Giorgio 137, 139
Arrighi, G. 268

Arthur, King 77
Ascoli, Graziadio Isaia 102-3, 104,
    105, 107
Assalto, L' 195, 199
Austria 12, 20-21, 22, 23, 24, 27-8,
    29, 33, 37, 38, 39, 42, 43, 80,
    163, 165, 169, 171, 172, 173,
    175, 177, 199, 223, 239-40, 269
Austro-Hungarian Empire *see* Habsburg
    Empire
Avanguardia Europea 199
Avanti! 65
Avvenire d'Italia 194
Avventura, L' 136

Baden-Württemberg 264
Bagnasco, A. 262
Balbis, Franco 205
Balbo, Cesare 11, 36-7
Ballestrero, Anastasio 232, 232
Bandelli, Gino 176
Baratta, Mario 50-1
Barbaro dominio 106
Barcelona 86
Barozzi, Luisa Pirani 63-4
Bartali, Gino 147
Barzini, Luigi 52, 58, 59
Basque country 260
Bassi, Ercole 168-9
Basso, Lelio 226
Baudrillard, Jean 158
Bavaria 267
Belfagor 156
bella italiana, La 134
Bellini, Jacopo 90
Bellonci, Goffredo 58, 68
Benco, Silvio 182
Ben-Ghiat, Ruth 174
Benjamin, Walter 142

Index

Berlin, Isaiah 76
Berlinguer, Enrico 232, 246, 250–4, 256, 257
Berlusconi, Silvio 156–7, 158, 256
Berti, Antonio 60
Bertinotti, Fausto 245
Bertoni, Giulio 106
Bevilacqua, Piero 53, 267
Bevin, Ernest 244
Biblioteca Italiana 23
Bisaglia, Antonio 262–3
Bissolati, Leonida 58
Bocca, Giorgio 82
Boccaccio, Giovanni 99, 111, 131
Bodei, Remo 220, 221, 235
Bologna 83, 194, 200, 202, 241, 251, 252, 285
Bologna Liberata 204
Bolognese Republican Fascist Federation 195
Bolshevik Revolution 242, 243
Bonaparte, Joseph 13
Bonfadini report 81
Bonn 87
Bordiga, Amadeo 242
Borgese, Giuseppe Antonio 87–8
Borsellino, Pietro 83
Borsieri, Pietro 24
Bossi, Umberto 82, 157, 260–1
Bottai, Giuseppe 179
Botticelli, Sandro 132
Bourbons 3, 16–17, 37, 38, 60
Brancati, Vitaliano 89–90, 91–2
Brigate Garibaldi 154, 195
Brigate Nere (Black Brigades) 198
Brigate Rosse (Red Brigades) 232, 252
Britain 21, 42, 196, 197, 244
Bronzino, Agnolo 132
Brydone, Patrick 80, 93
Bufalino, Gesualdo 85–6, 88–9, 91
Buonarroti, Filippo 17–18, 20, 30
Burke, Edmund 15
Byzantium 138

Cacciari, Massimo 270
Calabria 57, 60, 61, 93, 228
Calzine, Raffaele 134
Camilleri, Andrea 91
Campanile sera 146
Campbell, David 163
Campbell, Naomi 138
Canada 269
Candido 92

Canosa, Principe di 21
Canova, Antonio 132–3
Canzonissima 150
Capponi, Gino 29
Capuana, Luigi 72, 83, 85, 87
Capucci, Roberto 136
Carbonari 20, 30, 34
Carducci, Giosuè 132, 194, 195
Carlo Alberto of Piedmont 39
Carosa, Vittorio 136
Cassa per il Mezzogiorno 82, 228
Castelvetrano 90
Castronovo, Valerio 115
Catalan 98, 115, 168
Catalonia 76, 91, 260, 269, 270
Catania 90
Catholic Action 217, 218, 219, 221, 224–5, 227, 232–3
Catholic Church 3, 7, 37, 51, 126, 133, 135, 145, 149, 194, 195–6, 204, 214–36, 253, 254, 255, 262, 278, 280–1
  and Fascism 153, 201, 216–19
  Papacy 26, 29, 36, 38, 43, 99, 214, 216, 217–18, 219–20, 221–2, 224, 232, 233, 249, 250, 254, 281
  and politics 5, 25–6, 41, 44, 78, 201, 215–36, 249–50, 253, 254, 255, 279
Cattaneo, Carlo 2, 11, 25, 27, 28, 35, 39, 40, 278
Cavour, Count 32, 41–3, 44, 93
Cena, Giovanni 65
Chile 251
China 52
Ciaculli 83
Cimabue, Giovanni 124
Cinema Illustrazione 133
Cipolla, Arnaldo 65
Clean Hands investigation 234, 255, 256
Coceani (Coceancig), Bruno 171, 173, 177
Colajanni, Napoleone 62, 81, 82
Cold War 181, 191, 227, 243, 247, 256, 280
Coldiretti 225, 228
Combattente, Il 200
Comitato di Liberazione Nazionale 154
Comitato Provinciale Bergamasco pro Calabria e Sicilia 67
Commissione per la Scuola, La 224–5

Committees of National Liberation (CLN) 221
communism 6, 135, 152, 154, 172, 179, 180, 200, 202, 204, 206, 216, 218, 222, 224, 225, 226, 227, 228, 229, 233, 234, 235, 241–57, 262, 264, 280–1, 283, 285
Communist Party of Great Britain 244
Como 138
Compagna 205
Conciliatore, Il 2, 22–4, 27, 28
Concordat (1929) 216, 217, 218, 225
Condizioni sociali e amministrative della Sicilia 81
Confalonieri, Federico 22
Confederazione Generale Italiana del Lavoro (CGIL) 252
Conference of Italian Bishops (CEI) 232
Consolo, Vincenzo 4, 85, 89, 90–1, 92
Conspiracy of Equals 18
Constant, Benjamin 28
Constituent Assembly 224, 225, 227, 228
Convergència i Unió (Catalonia) 269
Convito 129
Coppi, Fausto 147
Corà, G. 267
Corleonesi 255
Corradini, Enrico 173
Corriere della Sera 51, 52, 54, 63, 64, 65, 67, 134, 156, 171, 172, 193
Courier, Paul-Louis 93–4
Cox, R. W. 265, 266
Craveri, Piero 230
Craxi, Bettino 253–4
Cremona 198
Crispi, Francesco 129, 130, 203
Cristo si è fermato a Eboli 146
Critica 73
Critica Fascista 179
Croatia 267
Croatian 98, 163, 170, 182
Croce, Benedetto 73, 181, 200, 201–2, 203, 206, 243, 246
Cronin, A. J. 149
Cuoco, Vincenzo 14–17, 20, 31
Curi, U. 272
Czech Republic 267

D'Alema, Massimo 158, 246, 253, 256, 257, 285
Dalla Chiesa, Nando 84

Dalmatia 180, 181
D'Annunzio, Gabriele 125, 129–30, 131, 132, 139–40, 166, 195
Dante Alighieri 99, 103, 106, 111, 124, 132, 153, 194
D'Arrigo, Stefano 4
D'Azeglio, Massimo 3, 11, 36–7, 41, 45, 149, 195
De Felice, Renzo 90, 152
de Filippo, Eduardo 86
De Gasperi, Alcide 217, 221, 222–3, 224, 226, 227
de Gaulle, Charles 220, 225
De Grazia, Victoria 173
de Maistre, Joseph 15, 21
De Martino, Ernesto 57
De Mauro, Tullio 110, 112
De Napoli, V. 132
De Roberto, Federico 72, 87
De Sanctis, Francesco 2, 4, 17, 149
Dei Sabelli, Luca 173–4
Del primato morale e civile degli italiani 26, 36
Delianova 61
Delinquenza della Sicilia e le sue cause, La 81
Descartes, René 244
Di Giovanni, Vincenzo 78–9
Di Grado, Antonio 86
di Lampedusa, Tomasi 89, 92, 246
Di Marzo, Gioacchino 72
Diamanti, Ilvo 261, 267
Dickie, John 128
Dictatus papae 214
Dietrich, Marlene 133
Difesa della Razza, La 178
Dilthey, Wilhelm 87
Dini, Lamberto 159
Divini Redemptoris 218
Dizionario del nuovo italiano 111
'Doctrine of Fascism' 174
dolce vita, La 136
Dombroski, Robert 80
Domenica del Corriere, La 63, 134
Domus 134
Dossetti, Giuseppe 224
dossettiani 224, 226, 227
Dumas, Alexandre 80

Edinburgh 86
Elena, Queen 4, 51, 59–64, 65, 67–8
Emilia 259
   see also Emilia-Romagna

Emilia-Romagna 204, 205, 241, 246, 251, 263, 264, 266
England 23, 75, 93, 126, 149, 264
English 106, 112, 115, 179
Enlightenment, the 13, 87, 93, 149
Epoca 146
Estonia 76
eterna bellezza della regina Margherita di Savoja, L' 132
'Eterno femminino regale' 132
European Community (EC) 240, 265, 281, 283-4
European Union (EU) 240, 249, 256-7, 264, 265, 284

Falasca-Zamponi, Simonetta 131
Falaschi, Giovanni 205
Falcone, Giovanni 83
Fanfani, Amintore 224, 226, 227, 229
Fanon, Frantz 89
Farinacci, Roberto 198
Fascism 5-6, 7, 43, 72, 105-7, 108, 109, 131, 133, 134, 143, 147, 148, 149, 151-4, 155, 156, 160, 163, 164, 166-7, 169-83, 193, 194, 196, 197-8, 200-1, 202-3, 204, 205, 206, 207, 216-19, 220, 221, 222, 224, 234, 242, 243, 248, 249, 277, 279, 280, 281
  republican Fascists 191, 192, 193, 194, 195, 196, 197, 198, 199, 200, 202, 203, 205, 206, 207
Fascismo Bonificatore 175
Fascismo nella Venezia Giulia, Il 172-3
federalism 2, 11-12, 18, 19, 26-7, 29, 35, 39, 270-1
Federazione Nazionale della Stampa Italiana (FNSI) 156
federazione repubblicana, La 40
Fellini, Federico 136
Ferrari, Giuseppe 35-6, 39-40
Ferre, Gianfranco 137
Fiat company 254
Filadelfi 30
Filosofia della rivoluzione 39-40
Fini, Gianfranco 157
Fininvest 157
Finland 76, 91
First World War 52, 148, 149, 163, 202, 223, 239, 279
Fiume 166
Flanders 72
Florence 24, 28, 83, 99, 106, 138, 147

Florentine 99, 100, 101-2, 103, 104, 106, 111
Fontana sisters 136
'Foreign languages and foreigners in Italy' 167
Forti, Francesco 29
Forty-Eight, The 92
Foscolo, Ugo 26, 28, 194, 195
Foster, Roy 76
France 2, 12, 13-14, 15, 17, 18, 19, 20, 21, 23, 25, 28, 35, 36, 37, 40, 42, 126, 147, 149, 173, 244-5, 269
Franchetti, Leopoldo 81-2, 83, 85
Franco-Provençal 98
Franco-Prussian War 43
Frankfurt School 151
Freedom Party (Austria) 269
French 98, 100, 106, 115, 168, 179
French Revolution 1-2, 15, 16, 25, 26, 29, 31, 36, 40, 93
Friulan 98
Friuli 168, 259
  see also Friuli-Venezia Giulia
Friuli-Venezia Giulia 261
Front National (France) 269
Fronte della Famiglia, Il 224-5
FUCI 225
Funo 200
fuoco, Il 131
Futurists 130

Gadda, Carlo Emilio 90
Gaelic League 76
Gaeta, Francesco 66
Galileo Galilei 194
Galli della Loggia, Ernesto 214, 215-16, 234-5
Garibaldi, Anita 148
Garibaldi, Giuseppe 42-3, 73, 79, 83, 92, 94, 148, 195
gattopardo, Il 89, 246
Gayda, Virginio 166
Gedda, Luigi 225
Gelli, Licio 233
Genoa 37, 256
Gentile, Emilio 126
Gentile, Giovanni 17, 72-5, 78-9, 80, 81, 84, 87, 90, 91, 92, 197
Geopolitica 179
German 98, 115, 168, 169, 170, 240
Germany 23, 26, 35, 127, 131, 178, 193, 195, 196, 197, 198, 199, 200, 201, 202, 203, 207, 269

GFT 137
Giner, Salvador 85
Gioberti, Vincenzo 2, 11, 26, 29, 36, 126, 151, 279
Giochi senza frontiera 146
Gioia, Melchiorre 19, 20
Giolitti, Giovanni 52, 53, 54, 56, 60, 62, 166, 167, 248, 279
Giordano, Tullio 62, 63
Giornale Italiano 16
Giorno, Il 83
Giotto, Bondone 124
Giovagnoli, Agostino 215, 217, 222, 226, 229
Giovine Italia, La 34
Giro d'Italia 147
Giuliani, Salvatore 79, 80
Giunta, Francesco 166
Goethe, Johann Wolfgang von 93, 94
Gonars 180
Goretti, Maria 135
Gorizia 72
Grammatica del dialetto e delle parlate siciliane 77
Gramsci, Antonio 5, 44, 74, 104–5, 106, 143, 148–51, 230, 242–3, 244, 246, 251
Grassi, Silvana 4
Graziani, Roberto 197
Greece 76, 127, 138
Greek 98, 115, 168
Gregory VII 26, 214
Gribaudi, Maurizio 152
Griffith, T. Gwynfor 114
Guerrazzi, Vincenzo 195
Guevara, Che 245
Guttuso, Renato 87

Habermas, Jürgen 143
Habsburg Empire 35, 163, 164, 165, 173, 176, 223, 279
Heaney, Seamus 239
Held, D. 265, 266
Helsinki 86
Hemingway, Ernest 92
Herder, Johann Gottfried von 76, 77
Hitler, Adolf 6, 198–9, 200
Hobsbawm, Eric 76
Hollywood 81, 94, 133, 134, 135, 138, 149
Horn, David 173, 174
'Hotel Balkan' *see* Narodni Dom
Humanité, L' 244, 245

Hume, David 87
Hurley, Elizabeth 137

Iacopini, Romolo 202
Illustrazione Italiana 128
Illustrazione Popolare 63
Imagined Communities 86
Ingrao, Pietro 255
Innocent III 214
insurrezione di Milano nel 1848, L' 39
Ireland 76, 91, 240, 249
Ischia 60
Isnenghi, Mario 181
isola di carta, L' 86
Istituto Doxa 149
Italia 171, 175
Italia Libera, L' 201, 203
Italian Geographical Society 50–1
Italian Journey 94
Italian language 2, 4–5, 8, 32, 35, 91, 98–123, 170, 171, 179
  dialects 4–5, 78, 99, 100, 101, 104, 105, 107, 108–9, 110, 111–12, 113–15, 116, 117
  fascist policy regarding 43, 105–7
Italian National Society 42
Italy's 'Southern Question': Orientalism in One Country 85

Jacini, Stefano 149
Jacobinism 14–15, 18–19, 20, 22, 26
Jameson, Frederick 86
John, Elton 137
John Paul II 214, 232, 233, 254
Joyce, James 90
July Manifesto 177
Justice and Liberty (Giustizia e Libertà) Brigade 154, 202

Kalevala 76
Karelia 77
Kosovo 257
Küstenland region *see* Venezia Giulia

La Farina, Giuseppe 42
La Pira, Giorgio 224, 226, 227
Laclau, Ernesto 154
Ladin 98
Lago, G. 267, 271
Lama, Luciano 252
Lampedusa *see* di Lampedusa

Lanaro, Silvio 127
Lateran Pacts 249, 253
Latin 106
Lauretta, Enzo 92
Lawrence, D. H. 92
Lazio 135
leghismo 84
Lenin, V. I. 243, 245, 250, 256
Leonardo da Vinci 129, 132
Leopard, The, see gattopardo, Il
Leopardi, Giacomo 28
Lepschy, Giulio 111, 113
'Letter to the president of the Council
    of Ministers, A' 169–70
Lettere meridionali 81
Levi, Carlo 146, 147
liberalism 5–6, 18, 31, 32, 41, 42, 44,
    126, 164, 173, 193, 200, 224,
    262, 279, 280, 281
Liguria 259
Littoriali dell'Arte e della Cultura 177
Livorno congress 242
Ljubljana 180
Lollobrigida, Gina 135–6
Lombardy 13, 21, 22, 27, 35, 84, 259,
    261, 264, 271
Lombroso, Cesare 81
London 138, 222, 267
Lonnrot, Elias 76, 77
Lorca, Federico García 91
Loren, Sophia 135–6
Ludwig, Emil 155
lunga vita di Marianna Ucria, La 87
Luporini, Bianca Maria 151
Luxemburg, Rosa 242–3
Luxottica 267
Lyons congress 242
Lyttleton, Adrian 145–6

Maastricht, Treaty of 84
McDowell, Colin 139
Machiavelli, Niccolò 15, 16, 57, 194
Madonna 137
mafiusi di la Vicaria, I 81
Malavoglia, I 78
Man without Qualities 80
Mani Pulite magistrates 157
Manin, Daniele 42
Manzoni, Alessandro 2, 25–6, 101–3,
    105, 111, 194, 195
Maraini, Dacia 87
Marche, the 259
Margherita, Queen 132–3, 148

Marinetti, F. T. 130–1
Marino, Santo 87
Marsala 75
Marseilles 34
Marshall Aid 247
Martini, Carlo Maria 232
Martini, Rossana 135
Martoglio, Nino 90
Marx, Karl 89, 240
Marxism-Leninism 243, 244
Matteotti, Giacomo 156
Mazza, Lieutenant General 59–60
Mazzanati, Carlo 196
Mazzini, Giuseppe 2, 28, 33–5, 36,
    39–40, 125–6, 154, 198, 203,
    204
Mazzinians 37, 39, 41
Melzi, Francesco 13, 20
Mercalli, Giuseppe 50
meridionalismo 78, 81–2, 84
Messina 50, 52, 57–8, 59, 60, 64, 65,
    84, 93
Messina-Reggio Calabria earthquake 4,
    50–71
Metropolitan Museum of Art 138
Metternich, Klemens 30
Mezzogiorno *see* South, the
Miami 138
Michelangelo Buonarroti 129, 194
Migliorini, Bruno 107
Milan 17, 20, 22, 27, 28, 37, 38, 39,
    51, 67, 83, 101, 131, 135, 138,
    167, 179, 220, 232, 267, 271
Minghetti, Marco 44
minorities 164, 165, 168, 170, 171–2,
    174, 178, 180
  Croat 180–1, 182
  German 169
  Slav 164–7, 168, 169, 170, 171,
    172–3, 174, 175, 177, 178, 180,
    181, 182, 183
  Slovene 170, 171, 172, 173, 178,
    180–1, 182
minority languages 98, 104, 105,
    107–8, 115–17, 163, 164–5, 167,
    168, 169, 182
Mirabello, Carlo 62, 64
Miss Italia 135
Modena 21, 27, 37
Mondo, Il 156
Monelli, Piero 106
Monopoly Law 153
Monticone, Alberto 233

Montini, Giovanni Battista (Pope Paul VI) 217, 222, 224, 249
Morasso, M. 127
Morcellini, Mario 159
Morgari, Oddino 65
Moro, Aldo 221, 224, 229–30, 231–2
Mosconi, Antonio 165–6, 175
Moscow 242
Mosse, George 127, 131
Mosso, Angelo 127
Movimento dei Giovani Italiani Repubblicani 197
Mukden 52
municipalism 25, 33
Murat, Joachim 13, 17, 20
Musil, Robert 80
Mussolini, Benito 6, 106–7, 125, 131, 134, 151, 152, 155, 169, 170, 173, 174, 176, 177, 179, 191, 192, 193, 194, 195, 196, 198, 201, 216, 220, 242, 247, 249

Napione, Galeani 19
Naples 13, 14, 16–17, 20, 21, 27, 37, 38, 59, 60, 93, 113, 128, 147, 256
    Neapolitan 113
Napoleon 12, 13, 16, 17, 19, 20, 21, 29, 30, 31, 34
Napolitano, Giorgio 255
Narodni Dom 166, 172–3
National Fascist Institute of Culture 174
nationalism 37–8, 39, 40–3, 44, 55–6, 57, 79, 173–4, 177, 260
Natta, Alessandro 254
Nazione e minoranze etniche 173–4
Nazism 147, 178, 181, 196, 197, 199, 201, 207, 248
Negri, Ada 67
Nel regno della mafia 81
Nencioni, Giovanni 110
neo-Guelph movement 25
New York 138, 267
Newman, John Henry 94
Nitti, Francesco 165, 166
Non expedit 218
Nostra Lotta 203
Notarbartolo, Emanuele 78, 82–3
Notari, Umberto 133
Note autobiografiche 34
Noterelle 94
Novo vocabolario della lingua italiana secondo l'uso di Firenze 102, 103
Nuova antologia 106–7

Nuova Europa, La 204, 206

Ocalan, Abdullah 245
Occitan 98
Ochetto, Achille 254, 255, 256
Ohmae, K. 268–9
Old and the Young, The 86, 92
OPEC 253
Ordine nuovo 242
organized crime: 80–1, 233, 234, 255
    Mafia, the 3, 78, 79, 80, 81, 82–4, 85, 88, 233, 255
Oriani, Alfredo 83
ORJUNA 172
Orlando, Leoluca 233
Orlando, Vittorio Emanuele 58, 59, 62–3, 64
Ortoleva, Peppino 156
Osservazioni sulla morale cattolica 25
'Our right and need to exclude French …' 108

Pachino 89
Padania 8, 146, 259–61, 269, 272, 273
Pagnacco, Federico 171
Paisà 147
Palermo 32, 37, 38, 72, 73, 77, 82, 87, 88
Palizzolo, Raffaele 78, 83
Pallavicino, Giorgio 42
Pampanini, Silvana 135
Pansa, Giampaolo 155
Paris 32, 133, 136, 242, 244
Parma 37
Parri, Ferruccio 222
Parti Communiste Français (PCF) 244–5, 254
Parti Quebecois 269
Partigiano, Il 202, 204, 206
Pascoli, Giovanni 195
Pasquale Bruno 80
Passerini, Luisa 152
Patrioti 202, 204
Pavia 179
Pavolini, Alessandro 198
Pavone, Claudio 201, 203–4
Pellaro 50
Pestalozzi, Johann Heinrich 16
Petrarch, Francesco 99, 111, 124, 131, 132
Piazza, Giuseppe 58, 66
Piccolo, Il 175
Piedigrotta Festival 150

Index

Piedmont 14, 21, 30, 36, 37, 38, 39, 40-3, 44, 75, 93, 128, 259, 278
Pettinato, Concetto 197
Pini, Giorgio 196
Pintor, Giaime 202
Pirandello, Luigi 72, 74, 85, 86, 87, 90, 92
Pisa 197
Pitrè, Giuseppe 72, 73, 74, 75, 76-8, 81, 83, 85
Pius IX 44
Pius XI 217-18, 226
Pius XII 219, 249
Pizzuto, Antonio 80
Placanica, Augusto 53
Platone in Italia 16
Poland 220, 254
Poletti, Ugo 233
Politecnico, Il 27, 35
political parties
    Alleanza Nazionale (AN) 6, 157, 158, 256
    Democratici di Sinistra (DS) 257
    Democrazia Christiana (DC – Christian Democrats) 6, 7, 155, 156, 204, 215-16, 217, 218, 221-36, 249, 250, 251, 252, 253-4, 255, 262, 263, 282-3
    Fascist Party 106, 164, 167, 178, 180, 221
    Forza Italia 156-7, 158, 159, 256
    Lega Lombarda (Lombard League) 82, 263
    Lega Nord (Northern League) 4, 7-8, 116, 145, 146, 157, 158, 191, 256, 259-64, 266-73
    Liberal National Party 167
    Liberal Party (PLI) 200, 224
    Liga Veneta 263
    Partito Comunista Italiano (PCI) 7, 158, 167, 200, 201, 202, 223, 224, 225, 231, 232, 235, 240, 241-4, 245-57, 262, 263, 264, 282, 285
    Partito d'Azione (Action Party) 154, 201, 203, 204
    Partito d'Azione Sarda 145
    Partito Democratica della Sinistra (PDS) 158, 254, 255-7
    Partito Popolare Italiano (PPI) 78, 216, 217, 221, 222, 224, 227, 230, 257
        second PPI 234

Partito Social Democratico Italiano (PSDI) 223, 248
Partito Socialista Italiano (PSI) 165, 166, 201, 223, 224, 241-2, 253, 255, 283
Republican Fascist Party 196, 197, 198
Republican Party (PRI) 202, 223
Rifondazione Comunista (RC) 245, 254
Südtiroler Volkspartei 145
Popolo di Trieste 175
Porro-Lambertenghi, Luigi 22
Prague 86
Principles of the Fascist Doctrine of Race, The 179
Prison Notebooks, see Quaderni del carcere
Prodi, Romano 158, 256-7
promessi sposi, I 2, 111
Pro Sicilia committee 78
Prospetto generale della storia politica dell'Europa nel Medio Evo 24
Proudhon, Pierre Joseph 35
Prussia 43, 279
publishing houses:
    Bompiani 149
    Mondadori 149
    Rizzoli 156
Putnam, R. D. 2
Puzo, Mario 81

Quaderni del carcere 104-5, 242
Quadragesimo anno 218, 226
Quale dei governi liberi meglio convenga all'Italia 19
Quarantotto, Claudio 111
Quebec 260
Quelle signore 133
Quine, Maria Sophia 182

Rab 180-1
Ragusin-Righi, Livio 175
RAI 150
Rapallo, Treaty of (1920) 164, 166
Rapisardi, Mario 90
Razza e Civiltà 178
Reggio Calabria 50, 59, 64, 65
Regime Fascista 198
'Relazione' 104
Renaissance, the 35, 124, 126, 134, 135, 138, 153, 194, 278
Renda, Francesco 93

Republican National Guard 196, 198
Resistance, the 154, 191, 192, 195,
 199–206, 207
Resto del Carlino, Il 194, 196
Retablo 90
Rhône-Alpes 264
Ricasoli, Bettino 44
Ricci, Renato 198
Ricolfi, Luca 158–9
*Riflessi sul governo federativo applicato
 all'Italia* 18
Rimini congress 254
Risorgimento, the 2–3, 11–45, 75, 77,
 78, 81, 84, 87, 92, 93, 126, 148,
 151, 153, 154, 181, 194, 195, 199,
 201, 202, 203–4, 243, 277, 278
Rivoluzione Socialista 205
Rizzotto, Giuseppe 81
Robespierre, Maximilien 18
Romagna 147, 240, 259
 see also Emilia-Romagna
Romagnosi, Gian Domenico 28
Roman Empire 106, 126, 129, 176, 177
Romania 76
Romano, S. F. 84
Romano, Sergio 75–6
Romany 98
Rome 25, 27, 29, 36, 38, 42, 43, 51,
 63, 64, 79, 99, 100, 106, 126,
 130, 138, 147, 165, 169, 172,
 176, 194, 203, 214, 218, 219,
 247, 253, 256, 262
Rome, Treaty of 282
Ronca, Roberto 222
Roosevelt, F. D. 219
Rosa, Alberto Asor 151
Rossellini, Roberto 147
Rossini, Gioacchino 194
Ruffo, Cardinal 15
Ruini, Camillo 233, 234
Rumor, Mariano 230
Rusinow, Denison 164, 165
Russia 21, 165, 174
 see also Soviet Union
Russo-Japanese War (1904–5) 52

Sabatini, Francesco 112–13
*Saggio storico sulla rivoluzione
 napoletana del 1799* 15–16
Said, Edward 84–5
Saint-Just, Louis Antoine 18
Sales, Isaia 78
Salfi, Francesco 26, 27

Salò, Republic of 6, 154
Salomone-Marino, Salvatore 72
Salvatorelli, Luigi 204–5, 206
Salvemini, Gaetano 171–2, 175, 178
San Giuliano, Marchese di 90
Sanfedisti 15
Sanremo Festival 150
Santa Caterina 65
Sardinia 115
Sardinian 98
Savoy, House of 60, 202
Scaglione, Pietro 83
Scarfoglio, Antonio 68
Scarfoglio, Paolo 58
Schiffer, Claudia 138
Schiffrer, Carlo 179
Schiller, Friedrich 127
Schneider, Jane 85
Schreiber, Gerhard 199
Schuberth, Emilio 136
Schuster, Cardinal 220–1
Sciascia, Leonardo 74, 75, 79–80, 85,
 86, 89, 90, 91–2, 93
Scotland 75, 260
Scott, Walter 75
Scottish National Party 269
Second Vatican Council 232
Second World War 82, 103, 107, 110,
 148, 159, 178, 191, 202, 215,
 219, 242, 244
Segni, Mario 233
Serbia 174
Serbo-Croat 98, 168
Serbs, Croats and Slovenes, Kingdom
 of *see* Yugoslavia
Sgroi, Salvatore 86
Shorter Oxford Dictionary 239
Siccardi Laws 41
Sicilia e il brigantaggio, La 83
Sicilian 78–9, 90–1
Sicilian, The 81
Sicilian Vacation 92
Sicily 4, 42, 51, 72–94, 147, 228, 233
Sicut universitatis conditor 214
Siena 146
Sighele, Scipio 166
Signorina Rosina 80
Sila Law 228
Simmel, Georg 87
Sismondi, J. C. L. Simonde de 24,
 25–6
Slovene 98, 163, 166, 168, 170, 171,
 182

Slovenia 267
Smile of the Unknown Mariner, The 92
Smith, A. D. 260
Smith, Denis Mack 93
socialism 5, 42, 51, 56, 152, 154,
    165-6, 167, 173, 201, 205, 223,
    224, 226, 234, 242, 252, 279, 280
Soffici, Ardengo 193
Sonnino, Sidney 81-2, 83, 85
South, the 8, 14-15, 20, 55, 81-5, 93,
    115, 116, 128, 138, 228
Soviet Union 204, 219, 243, 247, 249,
    250-1, 253, 254, 257, 282
Spain 91
Spanish 100, 106
Special Italian Inspectorate of Public
    Safety 180
Stalin, Joseph 242, 243, 244, 247
Stalingrad, battle of 247
Stampa, La 52, 128, 197
Starace, Achille 178
Storia dei Musulmanni di Sicilia 91
Storia della letteratura italiana 2, 4
*Storia delle repubbliche italiane del
    Medio Evo* 24, 25-6
Stresa 135
Sturzo, Don Luigi 78, 83, 216
Sublimi Maestri Perfetti 30
Süd Tirol-Alto Adige 115, 163, 168,
    169, 239-40, 259
    see also Trentino-Alto Adige
Suvich, Fulvio 171
Switzerland 39

Tamaro, Attilio 176-7
Tangentopoli scandals 98, 159
Tardini, Domenico 221, 249
Tempo 135
Thomson, John 215
TIGR 172
Tinagli, Paola 131-2
Titian (Tiziano Vecellio) 132
Tittoni, Tommaso 106-7
Todorov, Tzvetan 79
Togliatti, Palmiro 151, 200, 223, 225,
    242-3, 246-50, 251, 253, 254,
    257
Torpey, J. 267
tramonto della cultura siciliana, Il 72
Trapani 88
Trentino 259, 261
    see also Trentino-Alto Adige
Trentino-Alto Adige 263

Treves, Claudio 56-7, 58, 63
Tribuna, La 62, 66
Tribunale Speciale per la Difesa dello
    Stato 171-2, 173
Trieste 6, 163, 164-5, 166, 167, 168,
    169, 170, 171, 172, 173, 175,
    176, 177, 178, 179, 181, 182,
    183, 256
Trieste 173
Trotsky, Leon 242
Turati, Filippo 56-7, 242, 248
Turin 27, 30, 34, 37, 38, 137, 152,
    232, 256
Tuscan *see* Florentine
Tuscany 21, 28, 29, 100, 102, 259,
    266
Tuzet, Hélène 93

Ugolino, Francesco 106
Umberto, King 60, 132
Umbria 259
Umorismo 90
Underhill, G. R. D. 265
Unione Femminile 67
Unità, L' 202, 203
United States of America 27, 136, 153,
    195, 196, 197, 219, 220, 223,
    249, 254
uomo delinquente, L' 81
*Usi e costumi, credenze e pregiudizi del
    popolo siciliano* 77

Val Demone 90
Val di Mazara 90
Valentino (Valentino Garavani) 137
Valle d'Aosta 259
Vassallo, S. 271
Vatican Radio 153
Vegezzi-Ruscalla, Giovenale 108
Veltroni, Walter 256
Venetia 21, 27
Veneto 259, 261, 262, 263-4, 270
Venezia Giulia 163-5, 166, 167, 168,
    169, 172, 173, 175, 176, 180, 259
    see also Friuli-Venezia Giulia
Venice 22, 24, 38, 43, 130, 131, 268,
    270, 271
Venturi, Franco 151
Verdi, Giuseppe 150
Verga, Giovanni 72, 78, 85, 87, 90, 92
Veronese, Paolo 132
Versace, Gianni 137-9, 140
Viceroys, The 92

Vico, Giambattista 15, 16
Victor Emmanuel II 41, 42, 43, 51,
    59–60
Victor Emmanuel III 193
Vidussoni, Aldo 180
Vie Nuove 135
Vienna 132
Vieusseux, Gian Pietro 28, 29
Villari, Pasquale 81
Villari, Rosario 82
Vinci, Anna Maria 172, 178, 179
Vita Internazionale, La 167, 168
Vittorio Amadeo III of Savoy 19
Voce Repubblicana, La 203
Vogue 138

Wales 240, 260

Walston, James 180, 181
Warhol, Andy 139
Weber, Max 278
Wild, S. 266–7
Wittgenstein, Ludwig 239
Women's Defence Groups (Gruppi di
    Difesa della Donna) 202
Woodhouse, John 129
World Cup (1982) 241

Yalta, agreement of 247
Yeats, W. B. 239
Yugoslavia 163, 164, 166, 172, 173,
    175, 179–80, 183

Zavattini, Cesare 146